THE RO

D0865761

San Francisco
Restaurants

2003 EDITION

There are more than two hundred Rough Guide
travel, phrasebook and music titles, covering
destinations from Amsterdam to Zimbabwe,
languages from Czech to Vietnamese, and musics
from World to Opera and Jazz

Rough Guides on the Internet

www.roughguides.com

Rough Guide Credits

Text editor: James McConnachie **Series editor**: Mark Ellingham
Production: Katie Pringle, Julia Bovis
Cartography: Katie Lloyd-Jones
Photography: Erica Katz

Publishing Information

This first edition published October 2002 by
Rough Guides Ltd, 80 Strand, London WC2R 0RL.

Distributed by the Penguin Group

Penguin Books Ltd, 80 Strand, London WC2R 0RL.
Penguin Putnam, Inc., 375 Hudson Street, New York 10014, USA
Penguin Books Australia Ltd, 487 Maroondah Highway,
PO Box 257, Ringwood, Victoria 3134, Australia
Penguin Books Canada Ltd, 10 Alcorn Avenue,
Toronto, Ontario, Canada M4V 1E4
Penguin Books (NZ) Ltd, 182–190 Wairau Road,
Auckland 10, New Zealand

Typeset in Bembo and Helvetica to an original design by Henry Iles.
Printed in Spain by Graphy Cems.

THE ROUGH GUIDE TO

San Francisco Restaurants

2003 EDITION

Written by
Elgy Gillespie

About the Author

Elgy Gillespie is from London and Dublin, where she worked for many years on the Irish Times. Since defecting to San Francisco, just before the last major earthquake, she has nurtured her deep appreciation of the city's many local and ethnic cuisines. She lives in an old farmhouse in the heart of the Mission which she shares with lodgers and cats, and where she loves to cook, entertain and talk.

Acknowledgements

Elgy Gillespie would like to thank: Isadora Alman, Catherine Barry, Larry Beresford, Doreen Bermudez, Caroline Bouguereau, Zeenat Burns, Chuong Chung, Garrett Culhane, Tara Duggan, Lynn Ferrin, Conor Fleming, Renée Gibbons, Lois Glanting, Michael John Gorman, Travis Grant, Eileen Hirst, Arja Kajermo, Jeanne Kearsley, Mike Learned, Rose Mark, Hermanto Notodihadjo, Mary O'Donoghue, Nicole Okamu, Carl Parkes, Richard Piellisch, Charlie Quaid, Joe Quirk, Francesca Reinhardt, Kevin Roth, Andrew Santosusso, Richard Sterling, Malaika Susulu, Patricia Unterman, Kim Wainio, GraceAnn Walden, Patrick and Hannah Ward, Kurt Wolff, and of course the ever-hungry Robert Shepard!

Help Us Update

We've tried to ensure that this first edition of The Rough Guide to San Francisco Restaurants is as up-to-date and accurate as possible. However, San Francisco's restaurant scene is in constant flux: chefs change jobs; restaurants are bought and sold; prices and menus change. There will probably be a few references in this guide that are out of date even as this book is printed—and standards, of course, go up and down. If you feel there are places we've underrated or overpraised, or others we've unjustly omitted, please let us know—we'll send a copy of the next edition (or any other Rough Guide if you prefer) for the best letters. Please address letters to Elgy Gillespie at:

Rough Guides, 80 Strand, London WC2R 0RL or
Rough Guides, 4th Floor, 375 Hudson St, New York, NY 10014

Or send email to: mail@roughguides.co.uk

Contents

Introduction	viii
Bests...	x
San Francisco map	xvi
Bay Area map	xviii

Downtown

Union Square & the Financial District	3
The Tenderloin	41
Chinatown	57
North Beach	71
Fisherman's Wharf & the Waterfront	95
Nob Hill & Russian Hill	111

North & Central

The Marina, Cow Hollow & Pacific Heights	128
Japantown, Fillmore & the Western Addition	153
The Richmond	171
The Civic Center & Hayes Valley	199
The Haight Ashbury District & Cole Valley	219

South

SoMa & South Beach	233
Potrero Hill & Bernal Heights	255
The Mission	275
The Castro & Noe Valley	309
The Sunset & West Portal	335

The Bay Area & Outlying Districts

East Bay	357
North Bay & Marin	381
South Bay & the Peninsula	397

Indexes

Index of restaurants by name	415
Index of restaurants by cuisine	431

Introduction

San Francisco smells like food.

Jack Kerouac

Welcome to the first edition of the **Rough Guide to San Francisco Restaurants**. When it comes to food, San Francisco is spoiled. The vineyards of Northern California are enjoying a golden age, the Bay Area is bountiful in fish, and quality produce—much of it organic—is championed everywhere. Where dining out is concerned, San Francisco's old nickname of "The City that Knows How"—bestowed by a former president after an especially liquid banquet—is wholly deserved. There's something to the theory that this town is where all crazes begin, and in the food world that means anything from tandoori pizzas to duck quesadillas or a dash of sea salt in your grapefruit sorbet.

Never has there been a better time to eat at the frontier of new food. Nearly 5,000 restaurants jostle to serve an ethnically diverse and remarkably food-conscious population, and Asian and Latino cuisines are strongly represented, as well as East-West "fusion" food. The energy of this colorful community seemed at risk after the boom in the Bay Area's dotcom explosion gave way to bust, but many former tech-heads took the opportunity to open their own restaurants, and the result was hot competition and terrific value. Tourism faltered after September 11, 2001, but even this tragedy had a wake-up effect on the industry that could be seen (in a grim light) as salutary. Restaurants have added hours, introduced prix fixe menus, slashed prices—the $30 entree has faded away—and tuned up service.

The 350-plus San Francisco restaurants reviewed here are organized into sixteen sections reflecting the city's village-like neighborhoods, with three final chapters on notable restaurants in the East Bay (notably Oakland and Berkeley), Marin County (destination spots across the Golden Gate Bridge), and the Peninsula, to the south of the city. The reviews reflect the huge diversity of atmospheres, ethnic cuisines, and price ranges found in San Francisco—the possibilities range from prix fixe lunches in America's finest dining rooms to complete dinners for $5 at tiny hole-in-the-wall joints. We've included only places we liked and which offer good value, with one further rule: you have to be able to eat for under $50.

Tipping

American diners tip 15 percent because the waiters and kitchen staff depend upon the tips for their livelihood and daily income. Indeed, it's considered rude not to tip in San Francisco unless you truly and sincerely hated your service. Good service deserves—and gets—more like 20 percent.

Prices and credit cards

Every review in this book includes a spread of prices (eg $25–50). The first figure relates to what you could get away with—this is the minimum amount per person you are likely to spend on a meal here (assuming you are not a non-tipping, non-drinking skinflint). The second relates to what it would cost if you don't hold back. Wild diners with a taste for fine wines will leave our top estimates far behind, but the figures are there as a guide. For most people, the cost of a meal will lie somewhere within the spread.

For a more detailed picture, each review sets out the prices of various dishes. At some time in the guide's life these specific

Introduction

prices (and indeed the overall price spreads) will become out of date, but they were all accurate when the book left for the printer. And even in the giddy world of restaurants, when prices rise or prices fall, everyone tends to move together. If this book shows one restaurant as being twice as expensive as another, that situation is likely to remain.

Opening hours and days are given in every review, as are the credit cards accepted. Where reviews specify that restaurants accept "all major credit cards", that means at least AmEx, Diners, MasterCard and Visa, but if you're relying on one card it's always best to check when you book.

Bests...

Every restaurant reviewed in this book is wholeheartedly recommended, but it would be a very strange person who did not have favorites, so here are some "six of the bests".

Best Bang For Your Buck (high end)

Ana Mandara, Fisherman's Wharf & the Waterfront	98
Kokkari Estiatorio, Union Square & the Financial District	26
Boulevard, SoMa & South Beach	241
Gary Danko, Fisherman's Wharf & the Waterfront	106
Zuni Cafe, The Civic Center & Hayes Valley	217
Jardinière, The Civic Center & Hayes Valley	210

Best for Brunch

Dottie's True Blue Cafe, The Tenderloin	44
Chloe's Cafe, The Castro & Noe Valley	315
Fattoush, The Castro & Noe Valley	318
Town's End Restaurant and Bakery, SoMa & South Beach	253
Just For You, Potrero Hill & Bernal Heights	267
Miss Millie's, The Castro & Noe Valley	328

Best Chinese

Harbor Village Restaurant, Union Square & the Financial District   21
Tommy Toy's Cuisine Chinoise, Chinatown   68
Koi Palace, South Bay & the Peninsula   408
R&G Lounge, Chinatown   66
Ton Kiang, The Richmond   194
Fook Yuen, South Bay & the Peninsula   407

Best for Diners In Love

Jardinière, The Civic Center & Hayes Valley   210
Perlot, Japantown, Fillmore & the Western Addition   165
Le Colonial, The Tenderloin   43
Cafe Tiramisu, Union Square & the Financial District   13
Woodward's Gardens, The Mission   307
Cafe Jacqueline, North Beach   77

Best Eccentric Vibe

Citizen Cake, The Civic Center & Hayes Valley   207
AsiaSF, SoMa & South Beach   236
Foreign Cinema, The Mission   285
Forbes Island, Fisherman's Wharf & the Waterfront   104
Bistro e Europe, Potrero Hill & Bernal Heights   260
Lefty O'Doul's, Union Square & the Financial District   28

Best Gay Haunts

Chow, The Castro & Noe Valley   316
Anchor Oyster Bar and Seafood Market, The Castro & Noe Valley   313
Mecca, The Castro & Noe Valley   326
2223 Market Street, The Castro & Noe Valley   311
Firewood Cafe, The Castro & Noe Valley   320
Destino, The Civic Center & Hayes Valley   208

Introduction

Best Italian

Delfina, The Mission   283
Buca Giovanni, North Beach   76
Albona Ristorante Istriano, North Beach   73
L'Osteria del Forno, North Beach   86
Scala's Bistro, Union Square & the Financial District   36
Oliveto Cafe, East Bay   373

Best Japanese/Sushi

Takara Sushi and Seafood, Japantown, Fillmore
  & the Western Addition   169
Sanraku Four Seasons, Union Square & the Financial District   35
Kabuto Sushi, The Richmond   183
Ebisu, The Sunset & West Portal   339
Okina Sushi, The Richmond   187
Yoshi-San's Monkichi, The Richmond   197

Best for Kids

MacArthur Park, Union Square & the Financial District   29
McCormick & Kuleto's, Fisherman's Wharf & the Waterfront   107
E&O Trading Company, Union Square & the Financial District   16
Pizza Inferno, Japantown, Fillmore & the Western Addition   166
Hahn's Hibachi, East Bay   366
Benihana, Japantown, Fillmore & the Western Addition   156

Best Mexican

Las Camelias Cocina Mexicana, North Bay & Marin   385
Restaurant Doña Tomas, East Bay   376
Maya, SoMa & South Beach   247
Guaymas, North Bay & Marin   387
Pancho Villa Taqueria, The Mission   294
Mom Is Cooking, Potrero Hill & Bernal Heights   271

Best New Californian

Cosmopolitan Cafe, SoMa & South Beach	242
Redwood Park Upstairs, Union Square & the Financial District	32
Bacar, SoMa & South Beach	238
Boulevard, SoMa & South Beach	241
Chez Panisse Cafe, East Bay	363
Bay Wolf Restaurant, East Bay	361

Best Oldtime San Francisco Joints

Tadich Grill, Union Square & the Financial District	38
Swan Oyster Depot, Nob Hill & Russian Hill	123
Schroeder's, Union Square & the Financial District	37
Original Old Clam House, Potrero Hill & Bernal Heights	272
Tommaso's Ristorante Italiano, North Beach	91
Sam's Grill and Seafood Restaurant, Union Square & the Financial District	34

Best for Outdoor/Sidewalk Dining

Enrico's Sidewalk Cafe, North Beach	82
Rose's Cafe, The Marina, Cow Hollow & Pacific Heights	151
Hung Yen Restaurant, The Mission	287
Ti Couz, The Mission	300
Cafe Bastille, Union Square & the Financial District	9
Bay Wolf Restaurant, East Bay	361

Best Rock-Bottom Budget Meal

Hung Yen Restaurant, The Mission	287
King of Thai Noodle House, The Richmond	186
Pancho Villa Taqueria, The Mission	294
Soups, The Tenderloin	50
Naan 'n' Curry, The Tenderloin	47
House of Nanking, Chinatown	63

Introduction

Best for Seafood

Aqua, Union Square & the Financial District   6
Farallon, Union Square & the Financial District   17
Alamo Square Bar & Grill,
   Japantown, Fillmore & the Western Addition   155
Swan Oyster Depot, Nob Hill & Russian Hill   123
Thanh Long, The Sunset & West Portal   352
Great Eastern Restaurant, Chinatown   61

Best Southeast Asian

Thep Phanom Thai Cuisine,
   The Haight Ashbury District & Cole Valley   230
Khan Toke, The Richmond   185
Basil Thai, SoMa & South Beach   239
Saigon Saigon, The Mission   299
La Vie, The Richmond   196
Angkor Borei, Potrero Hill & Bernal Heights   258

Best for Vegetarian Dishes

Golden Era Vegetarian Restaurant, The Tenderloin   45
Greens, The Marina, Cow Hollow & Pacific Heights   143
Millennium, The Civic Center & Hayes Valley   213
Lucky Creation, Chinatown   64
La Méditerranée, Japantown, Fillmore & the Western Addition   163
Axum Cafe, The Haight Ashbury District & Cole Valley   221

Best Views

Guaymas, North Bay & Marin   387
Waterfront Restaurant, Union Square & the Financial District   39
Pier 23 Cafe, Fisherman's Wharf & the Waterfront   109
Greens, The Marina, Cow Hollow & Pacific Heights   143
The Cliff House, The Richmond   179
Ondine, North Bay & Marin   390

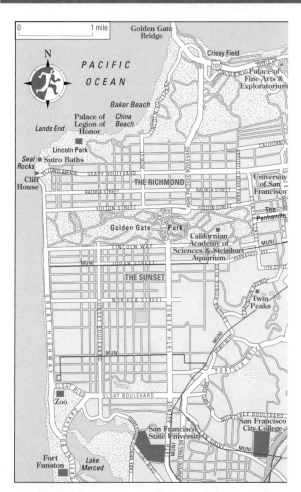

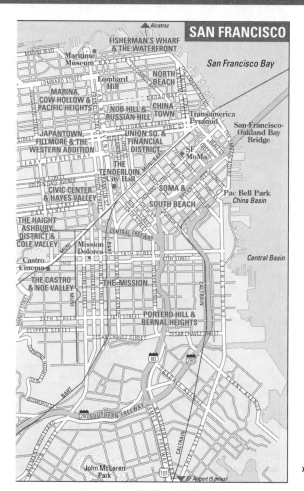

Alcatraz

SAN FRANCISCO

San Francisco Bay

FISHERMAN'S WHARF & THE WATERFRONT

MARINE BLVD

Maritime Museum

LOMBARD STREET

Lombard Hill

BAY STREET

NORTH BEACH

MARINA, COW HOLLOW & PACIFIC HEIGHTS

BROADWAY

NOB HILL & RUSSIAN HILL

CHINA TOWN

CALIFORNIA STREET

Transamerica Pyramid

San-Francisco-Oakland Bay Bridge

JAPANTOWN, FILLMORE & THE WESTERN ADDITION

PINE ST

UNION SQ. & FINANCIAL DISTRICT

GEARY EXPRESSWAY

MUNI/BART

SF MoMa

THE TENDERLOIN City Hall

PARK STREET

GOLDEN GATE AVENUE

CIVIC CENTER & HAYES VALLEY

SOMA & SOUTH BEACH

Pac Bell Park
China Basin

OAK STREET

THE HAIGHT ASHBURY DISTRICT & COLE VALLEY

CENTRAL FREEWAY

MUNI

BART

Mission Dolores

16TH STREET

17TH STREET

Central Basin

Castro Cinema

MARKET STREET

THE CASTRO & NOE VALLEY

MUNI

THE MISSION

MISSION AVE

CALTRAIN

24TH STREET

24TH STREET

PORTERO HILL & BERNAL HEIGHTS

CLIPPER STREET

CESAR CHAVEZ STREET

CESAR CHAVEZ STREET

80

280

BART

SOUTHERN FREEWAY

280

AMERICANO FREEWAY

CALTRAIN

VAN NESS AVE

John McLaren Park

101

SF Airport (5 miles)

xvii

Bay Area & Outlying Districts

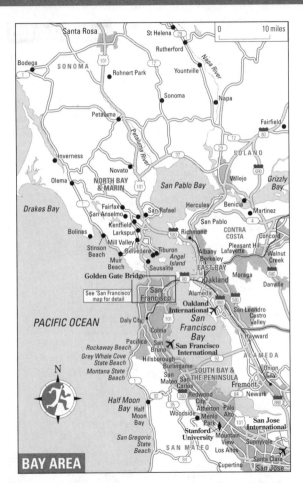

Downtown

Union Square & the Financial District

p.3

The Tenderloin

p.41

Chinatown

p.57

North Beach

p.71

Fisherman's Wharf & the Waterfront

p.95

Nob Hill & Russian Hill

p.111

Union Square & the Financial District

UNION SQUARE & THE FINANCIAL DISTRICT

Pier 1

Waterfront Restaurant (Pier 7)

Ferry Building

JUSTIN HERMAN PLAZA

Harbor Village Restaurant

Schroeder's

Embarcadero (MUNI/BART)

Tadich Grill

Federal Reserve Bank

MacArthur Park

Kokkari Estiatorio

Embarcadero Center

EMBARCADERO

SPEAR STREET

STEWART ST

BEALE STREET

MONTGOMERY STREET

B44 Catalan

Café Claude

Tiramisu

Plouf!

Sam's Grill

Seafood Restaurant

Café Bastille

CALIFORNIA STREET

KEARNY ST

PINE STREET

BUSH STREET

ST MARY'S SQUARE

QUINCY ST

Chinatown Gateway The Food Center

Globe

Bix

Henry Chung's Hunan

Caffè Macaroni

JACKSON SQUARE

COLUMBUS AVE

Columbus Tower

GOLD ST

JACKSON STREET

WASHINGTON STREET

MERCHANT ST

Trans America Pyramid

Redwood Park Upstairs

CHINATOWN

GRANT AVE

CLAY ST

WAVERLY PL

COMMERCIAL STREET

SACRAMENTO STREET

Aqua

Jeanty's at Jack's

FINANCIAL DISTRICT

California St

See inset

CALIFORNIA STREET

MONTGOMERY STREET

BUSH STREET

PINE STREET

SANSOME STREET

BATTERY STREET

FRONT STREET

DAVIS STREET

DRUMM ST

Museum of Modern Art

Montgomery St (MUNI/BART)

MARKET STREET

Palace Hotel

NEW MONTGOMERY STREET

Yerba Buena Center

Café de la Presse

Café Claude

Chinatown Gateway

E & O Trading Company

Anjou

Circle Gallery

Campton Place

Kuleto's

UNION SQUARE

STOCKTON STREET

GRANT AVENUE

MAIDEN LN

POWELL STREET

MASON STREET

TAYLOR STREET

NOB HILL

Grace Cathedral

Cable Car Barn

Huntington Park

Rue Lepic

Café Mozart

Sanraku Four Seasons

Jeanne d'Arc

Scala's Bistro

Harry Denton's Starlight Room

Farallon

Postrio

Lefty O'Doul's

First Crush

THEATER DISTRICT

COSMO PLACE

SHANNON STREET

CYRIL MAGNIN STREET

O'FARRELL STREET

GEARY STREET

POST STREET

SUTTER STREET

BUSH STREET

PINE STREET

SACRAMENTO STREET

CLAY STREET

WASHINGTON STREET

JACKSON STREET

CALIFORNIA STREET

TAYLOR STREET

JONES STREET

LEAVENWORTH STREET

HYDE STREET

LARKIN STREET

POLK STREET

VAN NESS AVENUE

ELLIS STREET

Powell St Cable Car Line

Cable Car Line

Cable Car Line

BROADWAY

PACIFIC AVENUE

KEARNY STREET

POLK STREET

0   200 yds

Anjou

Ladies who lunch swear by this bijou alleyway bistro, claiming that it's a bit of chic Gallic heaven that fell to earth one day, and that its prix fixe lunch makes it a bargain-priced charmer. That means Anjou is always full to the brim with chirpy shoppers dropping their bags, and sticking well-bred pumps beneath its sunshine-colored awnings. Space is limited, to put it mildly: your elbows will be thoroughly jostled here as you grab a glass of Vouvray to go with chef Pierre Morin's trademark pear in Sabayon. Making reservations is a must—no walking in off the street here unless it's off-peak. It's a little less crowded earlier in the week, as well as at lunch or pre-theater, and Anjou never sticks a couple of extra dollars onto their dishes the moment "lunchtime" turns into the cocktail hour.

Cost $15–45
Address 44 Campton Place
☎ 415/392-5373
Open Tues–Sat 11.30am–2.30pm & 6–10pm
Transportation Powell St cable car, BART Powell St
Accepts All major credit cards except AmEx

Does the food live up to the popularity here? Morin's choices change with the seasons and his prix fixe menu is as French as can be, with the kind of daily specials you'd expect to read scrawled on a blackboard in Angers. It almost always contains a steak and pommes frites ($19), an unusual seafood version of cassoulet with loup de mer and lobster ($19), a duck confit ($15.50), and any number of variations on local fish. Chef Morin is from the Loire Valley—as you may have guessed from the name of his restaurant—so inevitably his food is regional in its touches. Fish of the day ($18) is executed with tender concern and served with copious cress or endive salad. Another Anjou signature is seafood quiche ($12), alternating according to season between lobster in béchamel, and Dungeness crab in a tartelette with tartar sauce and romaine hearts.

It's desirable to leave a spot for Morin's best-known dish: the celebrated Anjou poires au Sabayon ($7), a creamy Cointreau-infused custard lapping the cheeks of a rosy, fresh pear. The problem is going to be getting a seat to try it: consider coming later in the evening, or reserving a weekend table ahead. And the less shopping you lug into the restaurant the more comfortable you'll be.

Aqua

With the kind of razzmatazz and cachet more often found in high-end New York restaurants, Aqua lives up to its stratospheric reputation on more than one level. Visitors may hurl themselves upon the good-natured maitre d' at the door on the off chance that someone didn't make it and that they'll pick up that magical place on the list, but cancellations are rare. Putting the hype aside, however, it's the serious and imaginative seafood that makes Michael Mina's Aqua so unattainably booked out. So is the buzz justified?

Cost $25–75
Address 252 California St at Battery
☎ 415/956-9662
Open Mon–Thurs 11.30am–2.15pm & 5.30–10.30pm, Sat 5.30–11pm
Transportation Market St lines, California St cable car, BART Embarcadero
Accepts All major credit cards except Diners

Just gazing around its pearly seashell-pink interior wafts you away to the giant nautilus of Jules Verne's imagination, convincing you this is the ideal spot for mouthfuls of marine bliss. Massive bouquets stand strategically beneath a few spotlights, but after that the focus is all on fish. Wherever you look, the beautiful people breathlessly await their monkfish, ahi tuna, abalone, scallops, or lobsters. At night entrees soar to almost $40, and are elaborate in construction, with clever combinations; lunch is more affordable. Dishes change daily with the catch, but certain items are always on the menu. Mina's celebrated mussel soufflé ($10) is one, and since this was one of the first places to pull off the ubiquitous seafood tartare, you will likely find an ahi tuna version ($15), served with a bisque of lobster or crab. Mina is also famous for his potato "encrusted" fish ($28), his tuna and foie gras napoleon ($38), his roasted foie gras ($42), and his lobster pot pie ($18). To finish, exquisite ices and delectable tartlets cry out for attention (from $5.50).

The waiters are at pains to help with the wine list, perhaps because it is so very long. Yes, Aqua is a sensory experience that lingers. Two caveats, then: you'll have to book ahead and, if you want to get out again, you'll have to study the menu with care and pick accordingly. Lately, however, they've been trying harder to meet a curious and star-struck public who want to sample Champagne dining on a Chardonnay budget.

B44 Catalan Bistro

Among the downtown canyons and in the shadow of the skyscrapers, there's a little corner of Barcelona at the end of Belden Place's "Little Europe" where you can grab a glass of Rioja and pretend you're sitting off the Ramblas over tapas. B44 is certainly Catalan: the menu is in the Catalan language, and it carries a picture of those Catalan "castells" of men balancing on each other's shoulders—in the toilet there's even a tiny continual movie of them going up and falling down. The empty interior resembles an art gallery, but unless

Cost	$8–25

Address 44 Belden Place
☎ 415/986-6287
Open Mon–Thurs
11.30am–2.30pm &
5.30–11pm, Fri
11.30am–2.30pm &
5.30pm–midnight, Sat
5.30pm–midnight
Transportation BART
Montgomery St
Accepts All major credit cards
except Diners

there's sleet or hail, everyone prefers wobbly tables outside. Even in foggiest August, there's a mob scene in the closed-off street.

Daniel Olivella's menu is mainly rustic Catalan, though ceviche and a traditional cod brandade are pan-Iberian staples. The ceviche ($8), or marinated seafood salad, contains everything from scallops or squid to Alaskan crab (if available) in chile and lime aioli, all stuffed inside a sundae cup and accompanied by chewy, sweet baguette chunks. Esqueixada de bacalla ($8.50) is the Catalan version of salt cod, mashed with potato and fried. Calamari ($8) is battered squid tossed into a pan and crisped up with plenty of garlic, cilantro, and squirts of lemon, plus aioli on the side. Fried sardines, scallops, anchovies, mussels, or clams fill out the appetizer choices; count on anything caught earlier that day for around $8. Olivella also does a plate of the humble Catalan blood sausage, or boudin, with fava beans ($8). If there's any room for more substantial fare, his dinner deals include dishes such as Catalan-style rabbit ($18), jointed and crisped. Paella Barceloneta ($20), a dish of monkfish, squid, shrimp, mussels, clams, peas, and beans bursting from a skillet full of rice, is plenty for two.

The wine list is rich in Riojas with the best labels costing from $30 or so; they're not cheap but usually worth it. This is not ruinously expensive for downtown dining. While portions are hardly lavish, the food is simple and honest. It's festive enough for a celebratory outing and, if it's raining, there's always indoors.

Bix

There's a vintage cocktail-lounge glamour about Bix, redolent of a 1920s nightclub or Prohibition-era hideaway. Owner Doug Beiderbeck is a jazz fan who stole his near-namesake's nickname for his supper club. Hidden down an obscure alley, it's tricked out with New York-ish "moderne" chrome trimmings and romantic gloom. You half expect a Broadway legend to stride by and order a Tanqueray martini straight up—and ah, those martinis! Carefully assembled by white-tuxedoed waiters and given a maraca-style shake in antique silver mixers, they are poured off with a suggestive, graceful flourish. Alternatively, try a Negroni, Caipirinha, or Herb's Vitamin V—a stiff vodka martini on the rocks with a squirt of orange.

Cost $20–50
Address 56 Gold St at Sansome
☎ 415/433-6300
Open Mon–Thurs 11.30am–11pm, Fri 11.30am–midnight, Sat 5.30pm–midnight, Sun 6–10pm
Transportation Market St lines, BART Montgomery St
Accepts All major credit cards

Bix's food manages to be trendy yet make reference to the 1920s, too, with "early American" dishes that deliberately evoke a more fun-loving and easy-going era. An old-fashioned classic Cobb Salad with butterball lettuce, eggs and ham opens the special three-course lunch menu ($20.01); follow it with "Harry's Bar" steak sandwich—juicy sirloin on a baguette—and finish with dessert. Wouldn't they have eaten that lunch back then? Yes, for a tenth of the cost, but it wouldn't have tasted this good. On the dinner menu, the steak tartare ($10) or generous smoked salmon blini with caviar ($14) are ample starters, almost enough on their own. The Waldorf salad ($9) is the real thing, chock full of apples and walnuts and blue cheese. Entrees change frequently, but you can almost always get rib-eye steak, filet mignon, roast chicken, pork, or lamb chops, and braised lamb shanks, all of which start at around the $20 mark. Desserts are something of an afterthought here, but there's a respectable and quivery crème caramel ($7).

If you had Woody Allen in tow, you'd probably bring him here. Bix's decor and cocktails do threaten a hefty price tag, in line with a kind of "if you have to ask the price…" shrug. But the restaurant has successfully hedged its bets with a comfortably priced prix fixe menu (you've got to love that extra penny), the possibility of late-night jazz over cocktails, and a stylish ambiance that makes even pricey dishes seem worth it.

Cafe Bastille

On Bastille Day, Belden Place is full to bursting with French-for-a-day revolutionaries, singing French songs to the stars and generally behaving as though this were the West Coast's Rive Gauche. But when it first opened back in the early 1990s, the owners had to lobby hard to pedestrianize this alleyway under the heel of the office blocks. *Et voilà!* San Franciscans got a taste of open-air dining and rapidly took to it, fog or no fog. Now a row of mini-restaurants—it runs to Italian, Provençal, Greek and Catalan, as well as French, with different accents on the staff—it truly earns the nickname "Little Europe." It's a choice lunch-hour spot for downtown workers, and the scene of an ongoing block party by night, with live music.

Cost $7–30

Address 22 Belden Place
☎ 415/986-5673
Open Mon–Sat
11.30am–10pm
Transportation Market St
lines, BART Montgomery St
Accepts All major credit cards
except Diners

FRENCH

The Bastille boasts the first tables, as befits the earliest bistro on the block. Their lunch menu starts with an onion soup ($4.50) and Croque Monsieur ($7.95), and continues with ratatouille and mushroom crêpes ($8), brie or prosciutto baguettes ($7.25), and salade Niçoise ($9). Nothing fancy, and a safe bet. At night the menu gets a bit more Californian and ambitious; sharing a clutch of bistro-style appetizers is a good choice here. The spinach salad ($10) has polenta and brie, and the moules marinières ($12) comes with a creamy wine sauce. They are staples on the nightly roster, along with the baked goat cheese on eggplant ($5.50), the Mexican cheese tortilla sandwiches known as quesadillas ($7), and steak frites ($15.50). Hashis parmentier ($12) is France's answer to corned beef hash. Crêpe Suzette is the dessert of choice ($5).

This is carnival central and it helps that the bright young French staff are so *sympathique*, since the food seems secondary and the atmosphere here is more about contagious charm than first-rate food. Critics point out that Bastille gets away with erratic performance and small portions on sheer Gallic shrugs and a few posters of the Tour Eiffel. But sometimes a lively bistro is just what's needed on a foggy San Francisco evening, and their long, bright basement is a blessed haven for large parties who want to crack open a bottle over a few shared plates.

Union Square & the Financial District

Cafe Claude

If this cafe feels like an authentic cobblestone torn from the Boul' Mich, it's probably because it used to be Le Barbizon, an actual Paris cafe bought by local boy Steve Decker. Brick by brick, Gitanes ashtray, Nouvelle Vague posters, zinc bar and all, Decker reinstalled it down this dark and dreary lane a block away from the other French bistros and now it's a regular Parisian oasis. By bringing umbrellas and tables outside, Decker—like his fellow restaurateurs in nearby Belden Place—helped to pioneer outdoor eating and did downtown a favor. As an added draw, live jazz heats up the joint at weekends when office regulars are gone.

Cost $7–30
Address 7 Claude Lane at Bush ☎ 415/392-3505 **Open** Mon–Sat noon–midnight **Transportation** Market St lines, BART Montgomery St **Accepts** MasterCard, Visa

For lunch, grab a handsome Croque Monsieur ($7.75), chewy Camembert baguette ($6.50) or croissant sandwich ($6.50), all filling. At cocktail time, the long and sinuous zinc bar is fully stocked with anything from pastis or pruneau to calvados, making it an after-work spot to linger. Later, Chef Jeffrey Lebon's deft way with dinner classics gets more formal. He offers a straightforwardly French menu from soupe à l'oignon ($5) to convincing cassoulet ($13.95), fragrant moules marinières ($11.95), roast duck au poivre ($13.25), a rich coq au vin ($13.25), or roast salmon with beet nage and thymed potatoes ($14). The execution is faultless, portions adequate, and everything on the seasonal menu is available at reasonable prices ($11–14). Wines are French, and start at $6 per glass. This is decent, genuine French food. It's true that sensitive customers who feel unstroked have made tart comments about the hoity-toity manner of the staff, but I suspect the waiters lay it on just a teensy bit to amuse, and for the same reasons that Italian waiters flirt. In any case, Claude regulars feel carpings are a backhanded compliment and this is the way a fine Paris cafe should be; it will not deter those who seek a civilized meal.

Decker has also given unreformed smokers a reprieve—outside, if not inside. Here, beneath an umbrella, smokers can puff away to their hearts content over a *très* continental Kir or a Stella Artois.

Cafe de la Presse

(🍴) A stone's throw from Chinatown's oriental gateway, yet still firmly in the world of nearby Union Square, Cafe de la Presse is a hive of international activity by day. It serves a cappuccino with the kick of a mule, and a bargain tartine (or some other casse-croûte) to have alongside it. Small round tables beckon inside and outside, and it boasts a wall of continental newspapers and magazines

Cost $20–40	
Address 352 Grant Ave at Bush	
☎ 415/249-0900	
Open Daily 7am–11pm	
Transportation 15, 30, BART Montgomery St	
Accepts All major credit cards	

FRENCH

for riffling—always good for a *Guardian* or *Le Monde*. A Basque who trained at the École Hôtelière de Toulouse, chef-owner Pierre Palomes once owned the Hotel de France on Broadway, and rarely misses a trick. Popular as the cafe is with visitors, few know of its dining annex, where a well-stocked bar-restaurant remains underused, despite seasonal prix fixe deals.

Palomes' dining room is to the back of the busy cafe, offset from the hurly-burly. A central mahogany bar offsets floor-to-ceiling windows, and prints of *Paris-Match* and *Der Spiegel* covers that flaunt nostalgic headlines. The menu tries hard with a homemade foie gras plate ($14.50), confit de canard ($13), a scrumptious bouchée à la reine seafood vol-au-vent ($12.50), and mainstream choices like veal Marengo ($15.50) and coq au vin ($16). Straightforward daily specials of fish and meat include steak au poivre ($22.50) and filet mignon with potatoes and peas, and bordelaise, peppercorn, or Roquefort sauce ($22.50), as well as creations like butter-flied Cornish hen ($19.50). Palomes even makes a quick-fix hamburger ($9.50), a superior half-pounder upon a sesame bun, also available in the cafe. Profiteroles ($6.50) fill any remaining space.

You can also eat on a linen napkin at the bar counter, where Palomes' splendid array of Pernod, Ricard and countless other bottles of pastis make you feel you're cruising the Croisette. They rival the list of over a hundred French wines, which is a splendor in itself. But while the cafe carries much of the menu for less money by day, the restaurant tab leaps up at night—one reason, perhaps, why they recently adopted a promotional $19.50 three-course lunch here, and a similar $29.50 dinner menu (excluding drink, tips and tax). But it's still a mystery why more evening diners don't find this useful pocket of calm.

Cafe Mozart

(YI) Perhaps it's Cafe Mozart's appeal to a slightly older, more gracious crowd that keeps it looking its frou-frou romantic best. The cafe's charm comes from the Mozart operas playing in the background, the beveled picture windows, the carved fireplace with blazing logs, the tasseled velvet curtains, and so many decorative touches that you wonder if customers raid the auction houses to keep it in china. Whatever the reason, it's charming and sweet, and will stay that way—Freddy Fahrni has run the place for a quarter of a century.

Cost $30–50
Address 708 Bush St at Powell
☎ 415/391-8480
Open Tues–Sun 5.30–10.30pm
Transportation Powell St cable car, BART Powell St
Accepts All major credit cards except Diners

Chef Jason Neekor's food is perhaps better described as continental than French, though the crêpes, pâtés, and soufflés are all enough to delight your godmother. And while Cafe Mozart isn't a bargain, from time to time they offer a prix fixe or tasting menu that is better value. Start with home-cured gravlax on a giant blini ($7.20), served with sour cream and a whisker of caviar. It's a common appetizer but they do it generously. Or try Magic Flute appetizer crêpes filled with duck, spinach, and leeks in ginger plum sauce ($8.25). The filet mignon Salieri in a Béarnaise sauce ($24.75, ouch) or special rib-eye steak Mozart with porcini and wild mushrooms in a sherried cream sauce ($25.50) are deliciously retro. Fettucine al pesto ($13.75) comes in shrimp, chicken, or vegetarian versions. For dessert, the ginger crème brûlée ($6) is just the thing. More than sixty French and California wines are offered, a dozen or so by the glass ($6–7).

At times things are so kiss-the-hand, heel-clickingly romantic in here, and the Mozart touches so twee, that you may find yourself wishing Wolfgang Amadeus himself would rush in and say something refreshingly…tart. On the other hand, your godmother's going to love every last mouthful, and will recall that oh-so-special duck crêpe just before she remembers you in her will. Unfortunately, if you're coming from downtown and can't squeeze on a cable car, you may have to carry her up the hill. Avoid the crowded cable-car turnarounds, and try boarding a block higher up.

Cafe Tiramisu

As a lone corner of Tuscany flanked by the cuisines of France, Greece and Catalonia, in Belden Place's "Little Europe," Tiramisu sings a different tune. It fulfills the role of a convenient downtown trattoria admirably. The menu is a little staid, in keeping with the some-times austere cuisine of Tuscany, but Tiramisu still satisfies, whether you're in the mood for a full Italian meal or simply antipasti and dessert. The warmth of the

Cost $15–30
Address 28 Belden Place
☎ 415/421-7044
Open Mon–Fri 11am–3pm & 5–10.30pm, Sat 5–10.30pm
Transportation 15, 30, BART Montgomery St
Accepts All major credit cards except Diners

padrone and his small staff should appeal to diners who have landed out-side Tiramisu after running the Belden gauntlet. More soothing in ambiance than its neighbors, it harbors a smallish interior where pretty murals and flattering lighting contribute to a *far niente* respite from the mayhem outside. Downstairs, romantically dim-lit nooks are hidden among the bottles of a wine-lined cave, contributing to the feeling that you have stumbled on a well-kept Financial District secret.

Choose the classics: antipasti and salads change according to season, and make straightforward and reasonably priced curtain raisers, starting at $3 for thickly pomodoro-smeared bruschetta, a tomato and moz-zarella plate, or a bowl of by-the-book minestrone. A beef-and-arugula plate ($10.50) is ample enough to make a main dish. Their Osso Bucco ($14.50), a falling-apart, slow-braised veal knuckle poached in a rich and savory stock of onions, carrots, and celery, comes with mashed potato or a polenta cushion. Workaday pastas like spaghetti or penne pomodoro ($15) decorate the rest of the menu, along with daily specials that come with unusual sauces or combinations: wild salmon or porcini ravioli, for instance. None cost over $15.

With a name like Tiramisu, you can bet on an impressive dolci selec-tion and, in this case, even the over-exposed namesake dessert ($6) does-n't disappoint. In fact, even if you've been enjoying the mussels at Plouf or the paella at B44 next door, it's worth dropping by here for the trademark "pick-me-up" of liquor-soaked ladyfingers layered with espresso-and-mascarpone cream. Other classic Italian desserts are just as good and can be tasted on a changing sampler plate ($6.50) of gelati, diplomatico, zabaglione, and tiramisu—quite a bouquet.

Caffè Macaroni

Perhaps this isn't the *absolute* tiniest restaurant in this city of vest-pocket bistros, but it's definitely a contender. Like so many joints in North Beach, which lies immediately to the north, it's triangular, but it's the only one with spirallini pasta glued onto a ceiling so low that you can pick them off and eat them (but don't). Originally launched by a bunch of Italian waiters on their days off, Macaroni is a Lilliputian slice of Italy. You sit along one intimate table, facing the sidewalk and on public view, feeling a little like a disciple in Da Vinci's "Last Supper." Pedestrians, just inches away, cast wistful glances; as do your successors — there's almost invariably a waiting line. If you fail to get the downstairs table, there's the even tinier, half-moon one upstairs.

Cost £20–35	

Address 59 Columbus Ave at Jackson
☎ 415/956-9737
Open Mon–Sat 5–10pm
Transportation 15, 30, BART Montgomery St
Accepts Cash only

The food isn't especially cheap, but it's invariably good. Favorites are nursery food like ravioli or gnocchi in a series of comforting sauces like wild mushroom or pomodoro. They start at $7.25 and change daily. There's an antipasto dalla vetrina plate that starts at $6 for lunch and features cold titbits such as artichokes, olives, and pieces of mozzarella; it's amplified later as a supper appetizer ($11). Stinco d'agnello al rosmarino ($13.95), or lamb shank, is gorgeously aromatic and succulent. Fish specials feature local petrale and salmon (from $12). To go with an espresso, there's tiramisu ($5), biscotti, and limoncello. Somehow it all adds up, especially when you lash on the mark-up for a decent bottle of Chianti. At the same time, the sense of camping out is fun; the pasta-ed ceilings and tables are just so cramped that the place seems to have been knocked together out of leftover packing cases in an afternoon — and probably was.

It must be added that the waiters help a lot. Genetically programmed to be as flirtatious as possible, they just can't help reminding diners of that skit on "Saturday Night Live" where even the giant pepper mill becomes a come-on. So this is a grand place for a gaggle of girls on a night out, and if the wait's just too long, try their spillover cafe across the road, Macaroni Sciue Sciue.

Campton Place

Tucked away in the back half of a boutique hotel, Campton Place manages to be low-key yet upscale, seamlessly formal to the last silver tea-spoon, yet laidback at the same time. Though the main restaurant is very expensive indeed, you can dine afford-ably in the comfortable bar, with its dark-ly macho wood, and brunches are good value. The adjoining restaurant area exults in new blond wood set against repainted linen and bone walls. Pistachio and pale lavender accents here and there soothe its silver-haired, patrician clien-

Cost $30–150

Address Campton Place
Hotel, 340 Stockton St at
Union Square
☎ 415/955-5555
Open Mon–Fri 7–10.30am,
11.30am–2pm &
5.30–9.30pm, Sat & Sun
8am–2pm
Transportation Market Street
lines, 30, 38, 45, BART Powell
St
Accepts All major credit cards

tele. This is a Parnassus for god-like chefs. Campton's superchef, Laurent Manrique, is Gascon, and his own native gods of feasting still sing loudly—cheeses at diners' elbows include an overwhelming Jean Grogne triple-cream, for instance, a standout on the most pungent cheese cart in the West.

But Campton Place is also known for its outstanding American brunches. The corned beef hash ($14.50), a surprising find in such a temple of haute cuisine, is certainly a draw; unswervingly traditional, it comes topped with tiny flecks of parsley and thyme and irreproachably poached eggs. There's nothing original about French toast of lemon poppyseed bread with jam and whipped cream ($13), or eggs Benedict on a pepperjack biscuit with tasso ham in Hollandaise ($15), but they're plenty comforting and the kindly waiters occasionally add croissants, on the house. Manrique's brunch menu is a venture into American dining that you and your wallet can survive. So too are appetizers in the quiet little bar area. This gourmet bar mini-menu kicks off with oysters (a half-dozen for $12), and a trio of smoked, cured and spiced tartares with warm potato salad ($15), cheek by jowl with Osetra caviar ($48) and, surprisingly, burgers ($14.50). So if you want Campton lite, it can be achieved, just not in the evening, when even the lovely tasting menu, with its amuse-gueules and foie gras plates, comes to $75.

If you need some special cosseting the morning after a night on the town, try the marvelous Pousse Rapière-macerated Armagnac, orange, and prune cocktail ($12).

E&O Trading Company

The mood is Indiana Jones-meets-Pier One Imports, rather than Somerset Maugham in Penang. Paul Ma's design of batiks, birdcages and bundles tries hard to suggest a Pacific trade route, an atmosphere that is somewhat at odds with the usual brewpub racket that reigns downstairs. Frank Commanday's foaming amber and golden craft beers do make this part of the E&O worth visiting, but so do the quieter moorings on the elevated mezzanine,

Cost $12–35
Address 314 Sutter St at Grant
☎ 415/693-0303
Open Mon–Thurs 11.30am–10pm, Fri & Sat 11.30am–11pm, Sun 5–9.30pm
Transportation Market St lines, BART Powell St
Accepts All major credit cards except Diners

where the tables are spacious, and you can squirrel your party away from the live jazz (playing on Thursday to Sunday nights), eyeball the scene below and nibble in peace on modestly priced Pan-Asian "small plates", derived from the cuisines of any of India, Thailand, Vietnam, Cambodia, Malaysia or Indonesia.

Waiters are child-friendly and willing to discuss the trendy menu and its ingredients with patience. The phrase "small plates" sometimes seems suspiciously like a code for "not a lot of food," or even "less bang for your buck." But not here, where chef Glenn Wielo and menu consultant Joyce Goldstein devised clever and innovative, made-on-the-spot wood-oven, grilled or wok-fried appetizers. The E&O works hard on sauces and marinades, and hooray for them! Lamb, chicken, basil beef, or limed-prawn satays ($5.95) come with zippy, tangy peanut, pineapple, or raita dipping sauces. Lemongrass chicken ($13) adorns scented rice and beans. Thai corn fritters ($5.95) are crunchy outside and creamy within. Nan bread ($5.25) is either vegetarian or meat, and it's filling. There's a make-it-yourself lettuce appetizer ($5.95), and some tasty Malabar crab samosas ($6–7).

The food isn't really Thai or Cambodian or Indonesian; it's more like a Californian's dream of those ancient southeast Asian cuisines, accessibly served in colorful, bite-sized Disney cartoon versions. But whatever they are, these dishes are enjoyable, relatively cheap, and served amid an alluring decor in a very convenient location. Everything arrives at the table chop-chop fast, making this the perfect solution for famished shoppers who need to tie on a modestly priced nosebag, especially those with tired feet, a giant thirst, a clamorous family, and too many bags in tow.

Farallon

From the cockleshell porch to the seaweed fronds woven into the cushions, designer Pat Kuleto's decor for Farallon features enough marine motifs to suggest the Little Mermaid on Ecstasy. Jellyfish tentacles and sea-urchin light-fittings dangle over crabs and mussels in the tiled floor. Like Botticelli's Venus on the half-shell, you perch on overstuffed conch banquettes to peruse a mile-long wine list, or gaze at the heavenly vaulted ceiling, formerly the canopy of a Victorian bathhouse.

Cost $25–60

Address 450 Post St at Powell
☏ 415/956-6969
Open Mon 5.30–10.30pm, Tues–Sat 11.30am–2.30pm & 5.30–11pm, Sun 5–10pm
Transportation Market St lines, BART Powell St
Accepts All major credit cards except Diners

SEAFOOD

Farallon diners are often very beautiful people, couples caught up in some dizzy bubble of intimacy. They usually go for Seafood Indulgence ($19.50), a tin turban lavishly studded with oysters, clams, cockles and, for sheer suggestiveness, crab claws, a single solemn scallop, and periwinkles teased out with tiny silver toothpicks. The whole production is spangled with salmon caviar on crushed ice, enough as a shared appetizer to get an "ooh" and "aah," but not to fill a diner from head to toe. Other diners may feel piqued by small portions: prawn handroll ($3.95) is a seaweed-wrapped, sushi-style cornet with ginger-plum brandy dipping sauce, and a mere half-mouthful. When you're hungry, chef Marc Franz's Croque Monsieur ($10.95) is the thing: Black Forest ham with gruyère on Levain is blanketed with a béchamel fluffed with egg—simple and hefty enough as a lunch dish by itself. Main courses like roast king salmon, grilled prawns, or braised wing of skate are offered in season, and there's always a non-fish choice as well, such as a foresty and substantial flank steak in Béarnaise sauce on potato gratin ($21.95).

Franz's dessert chef is Don Hall and his desserts are to-die-for dazzling. Tahitian vanilla bean croquettes ($9) and bourbon chocolate pie with hazelnut sauce ($9) are both made for chocoholics. Other than the decor, it was the wine list that made Farallon's reputation, and dozens are available by the glass at reasonable prices. Forefathers Marlborough Sauvignon Blanc ($6.50) is brassy, while Selbach-Oster Kabinett Bernkasteler Badstube Mosel-Saar Ruwer ($9.50) is delicate and aromatic, notwithstanding the eight-word name. Prices by the bottle start at $30, but the mark-up goes into the hundreds for some rare vintages.

First Crush

First Crush's quirky wine bar targets shoppers or theatergoers in need of some nice food and wine before the next activity of the day. Owner and wine enthusiast Frank Klein has imported Jennifer Biesty, formerly of Bizou and London's River Cafe, to marry plate to glass. She crafts appetizers to go with a choice of 390 wines. They're all available by the very elegant glass, all Californian, and there's a special emphasis on less-known varietals from Sonoma and Napa. Their not-so-secret hope is to teach folks to match food with exciting wines. Recently, staff made over the ground floor with tiny tables and a bar, and now it's sunny and white inside. "Womb in a tomb" is the phrase that used to leap to mind for First Crush's cabernet-red, oubliette-like basement, but it's now repainted a green that's more suitable for private dining.

Cost	$25–40
Address	101 Cyril Magnin St at Ellis
☎	415/982-7874
Open	Mon–Thurs & Sun 5pm–midnight, Fri & Sat 5pm–1am
Transportation	Market St lines, BART Powell St
Accepts	MasterCard, Visa

So far, so good, but portions are often as skimpy as plates and tables; wine definitely comes first. Biesty's menu includes vegetable, fish, duck, and beef plates, plus a soup and salad, followed by entrees if you want a full meal. The wine and food marriages are compelling and sometimes surprising, and they usually work. For instance, should you go for the well-dressed Caesar salad ($7.75), a good choice, they propose a glass of Liparita sauvignon blanc from Napa ($9). With ham and Parmesan and truffle-topped coleslaw ($8.75), the recommendations shift to a crisp white Viognier ($6–8) or a glass of Marsanne ($8–9). If you crave a hamburger, it's a hearty Sonoma cabernet for you ($8), and if feeling the need to tuck into a substantial pork and veal sausage ($8.40), an Unti Dry Creek Syrah ($8) fits the bill. There are sample-sized wine "flights" of three tastes for $11. In no time you'll be mugging up gewürztraminers of Mendocino County's Anderson Valley and sauvignon blancs from Sonoma County's Dry Creek region, and nattering about "forward noses" and "notes of burnt pineapple."

The plates are often awkward to manage on the minuscule tables—why not bowls?—and not always filling. But this *is* the golden age of Californian wines. Carpe diem!

The Food Center

There's nothing fancy about this place, just simple convenience and the opportunity to sample a handful of different Asian and Latino cuisines for a handful of change. It's a nameless basement of food stalls down some rickety stairs that functions as a cafeteria for downtown office drones. Rackety, bustling, cramped, filled with uncleared, messy trestle tables and a choice of everything from lumpia to burritos and from popcorn chicken to tapioca pearl custard and Vietnamese coffee, it's a place to catch your breath and try a little of everything, a lunchtime version of an Asian night market.

Cost $2–10

Address Kearney St at Bush
ⓣ No phone
Open Mon–Fri 11am–4pm
Transportation Market St lines, BART Montgomery St
Accepts Cash only

The quality is erratic, but you won't be cheated and you'll make occasional discoveries. House of Lumpia is nearest the stairs, and sells authentic Filipino lumpia, which are small, cylindrical, deep-fried, meat-filled rolls. They're a sweet-and-sour, crunchy, two-mouthful snack, a cross between egg rolls and miniature sausage rolls, containing minced pork, peas, corn, and carrots, with jasmine rice and sweet orange dipping sauce served on the side. Served in stacks of seven for $5, they're an ideal snack. Taqueria Vallarta peddles straightforward and ample Mexican burritos and quesadillas with guacamole and salsa, starting between $2 and $3 apiece. There's the Chinese New Ocean stall and a Japanese sushi and teriyaki bar called Ichiban, plus a Thai counter called Lee's (not the sandwich chain). Unquestionably the best value in the whole place, however, is found at Viet Number 4 Pho, which sells the national dish of Vietnam. Pho ($4) is a big, colorful, plastic bowl of beef noodle broth surrounded by little additional saucers of shredded herbs, vegetables, and bird chiles. Number 4 also sells good little banh mi (from $2), which are sandwiches of roast pork or meatballs and cilantro, plus delicious Vietnamese desserts like tapioca pearls ($1.50), and Vietnamese drinks.

Needless to say, these stalls are very good value if you're on the trot. Though never mentioned in the local press, they're a find for visitors hunting down a bargain lunch. Curiously, there are still no food stalls at the existing Chinatown night market on Portsmouth Square nearby, though this may change.

Globe

What a surprise the little Globe can be, out here in nowhere-in-particular-land between Telegraph Hill and the Embarcadero Center! Formerly the notorious Barbary Coast of saloons and brothels, this is now home to quiet apartments, law firms, and this small and alluringly dim late-night hangout. Run by chefs formerly at Postrio and other restaurants, it opened on a shoestring in cramped premises that were once a blacksmith's shop, evidenced by the occasional ring on the Globe's brick walls. For some years it's been the place where kitchen warriors from around the city come after they've hung up toques and scrubbed down stovetops. Then they dish the dish with pal Joseph Manzare over his delicious food.

Cost	$15–50

Address 290 Pacific Ave at Battery
☎ 415/391-4132
Open Mon–Fri 11.30am–3pm & 6pm–1am, Sat 6pm–1am, Sun 6–11.30pm
Transportation 12, 42, F, BART Embarcadero
Accepts All major credit cards except Diners

Smoked salmon carpaccio ($9) with chives, capers, and lemon, plus a slurp of dill-speckled oil and crème fraîche arrives in an extra generous portion. Zesty grilled sardines ($7) make another casual starter, while oyster platters (from $9) and romaine lettuce salads ($7) also give you something to nibble on while your next course cooks. Main dishes are downright Midwestern in size: choose from massive pork chops on pepper relish ($9.50), short-rib braised beef stew ($16) with spinach and horseradish potatoes, a Fred Flintstone-sized all-American T-bone steak for two ($36), or aromatic, wood-fire roasted lamb ($18), served with mint spätzle that are neither dry nor pasty. Simple herbed roast chicken ($18) comes with garlicked potatoes and collard greens. A mountainous seafood platter ($21) turns out to be a continental shelf of anything tasty that crawls or swims. Desserts don't disappoint, either: save space for an extravagant espresso pot de crème, or one of the brownies, tarts and pies (all $7). Wines cost around $40, for which you'll find a stellar Storybrook Zinfandel. If the food takes time, it's because the chef does it well.

At lunchtime, Globe is a business haunt. The open kitchen with wood-fired oven, bar, flowers, candlelight and cramped tables is in no way fancy, but it fills up fast. And Globe keeps serving until 1am—which passes for dawn in this town—making it handy if you're out late.

Harbor Village Restaurant

Palatially housed in a big dining room with sweeping views of the Bay, Harbor Village swarms with happy events whenever there's a wedding or promotion to celebrate over tiny cups of jasmine tea. In fact, tea, dim sum and celebration go together like love, sex and marriage. But you can also have a beer or a bottle of very fine wine with a full meal, and a couple may dine in this rather hushed, grandiose setting as festively as a large group. There's an opulence to Harbor Village, with its traditional teak and rosewood screens, koi tanks, silk hangings, Chinese linen, and crystal—not to mention the free parking at the garage below.

Cost $20–50

Address 2nd floor, 4 Embarcadero Center
☏ 415/781-8833
Open Mon–Fri 11am–2.30pm & 5.30–9.30pm, Sat & Sun 10.30am–2.30pm
Transportation Market St lines, 1, 42, F, BART Embarcadero
Accepts All major credit cards except Diners

Harbor Village's dim sum are served at round tables with a Lazy Susan ("a revolving relish tray" as they call them in this P.C. city), and are perhaps the most elegantly presented in the city, nestling in decorative bamboo steamers, and delivered with accompanying exquisite teapots that are continually replenished. Dim sum are priced from $2.60 to $6.50 per serving. The common denominators of all the trolleys are ha gao, or cradling plump prawns; chun guen, or crispy-fried spring rolls of spiced minced pork or chicken; cha xiu bao, or soft and squashy pork bun with a smoky barbecued pork interior; xiu mai, or steamed dumplings; xi jap fung zao, or chicken feet; and the labor-intensive wu gok, or taro dumpling. But Harbor Village also has a full menu of fresher-than-fresh fish taken from the large in-house tanks, including catfish ($25), rock cod ($26), crabs ($36), lobster (from around $35), and geoduck ($36). Peking duck ($38), in its boned and roasted variations, is another specialty. If these prices seem steep, remember that they are banqueting dishes shared among two or three.

Harbor Village is the West Coast outpost of a Hong Kong empire of restaurants and yum cha (Cantonese snack houses), with branches around the world. Its formality might seem almost old-fashioned—like a scene in an early Ang Lee movie—but really it's a calm realm unto itself, and in many ways beyond comparisons.

Harry Denton's Starlight Room

San Francisco does views fabulously, and cocktail hour is the hour for sunset peeking. So if you're craving a view with a martini in one hand and a plate in the other as the sun sinks slowly in the west, the Starlight Room is one sure bet (among many). The mood here is of slightly self-conscious, old-fashioned glamour "between the stars and the cable cars." Friendly, chatty waitresses wear figure-hugging, floor-length gowns. Mirrored walls, ruby-and-gold damask booths, and framed pictures of stars like George Clooney make it all nostalgic in a slightly "Vegas" way. Wraparound windows overlook downtown and the Bay, although the best view is unaccountably hogged by the band.

Cost $20–40

Address Sir Francis Drake
Hotel, 432 Powell St
☎ 415/395-8595
Open Daily Mon–Fri
7am–midnight, Sat & Sun
8am–midnight
Transportation Market St
lines, BART Powell St
Accepts All major credit cards
except Diners

Happily, the drinks and nibbles are not all expensive and the rosemary bruschetta with caramelized onions ($9) is downright delicious—dangerously so. Even more tempting is rosemary pizza with roasted garlic, pesto, goat cheese, and mozzarella ($12.50). Oyster platters ($15 for six, $7.50 for three) include Salutation Coves from Nova Scotia, Coromandels from New Zealand and local Miyagis from Tomales Bay; a half-dozen come on the half-shell with sherry vinegar and that standard cocktail sauce. As for the crabcakes ($14 for three), they're crisped on the outside, well seasoned, and will go down all too fast. Smoked salmon plates ($14) come with capers and dabs of cream, plus baskets of sourdough; prawns arrive with dip ($14); and a throw-caution-out-the-window caviar tray (Beluga $95 per oz) rounds off their all-appetizers menu. If you order a Happy Hour cocktail or spritzer between 4.30pm and 8.30pm, you'll get two or three restorative mouthfuls for a mere $4, and will immediately want another. Martinis start at $6.50 for a modest-sized glass.

The trouble is, you keep wanting more of everything here. But as the sun starts to bathe the downtown skyline in pink, you'll start to feel this place really has its niche: family reunions, business celebrations, honeymooners, company parties, and conventioneers—whatever. All in all, this is a fun place to grab a snack and a cocktail before going on somewhere else.

Henry Chung's Hunan

When *The New York Times* and East Coast foodies discovered Henry Chung's Hunan-style food back in the 1970s and declared it "the best Chinese restaurant in the world," his place kicked the national spice level up several notches. Henry Chung's Hunan has set San Franciscan tastebuds ablaze ever since. Hotter even than the cuisine of Szechwan, food from the Hunan region is rich in smoked pork and game dishes—this fondness for smoky meat was part of the Mongolian legacy left behind by Kubla Khan, and even includes a steak tartare, as described by Marco Polo.

Cost $10–20
Address 924 Sansome St at Broadway
☎ 415/546-4999
Open 11am–11pm
Transportation 15
Accepts All major credit cards except Diners

The restaurant's barn-like decor is no great shakes, the inevitable result of the popularity the *Times* spawned and of the 1989 earthquake, which closed the former premises on Kearney Street. Henry got his recipes from his Hunan-born grandmother and his menu starts with her dinnerplate-sized spring onion cakes ($2); crispy-fried and irresistible, they not only take the edge off your hunger but make you want more. Diane's Special is two onion cakes ($6.50), stuffed with ground beef and other goodies; kids will like them because they somewhat resemble quesadillas, and milder cheese, pork, and veggie variations are at hand. Henry's steamed dumplings ($4.25) are another signature dish, but the hot sauce is so extra-hot (red chile alarms adorn the menu margin) that you'd be well advised to ask for a toned-down version. Hot-and-sour soup ($4.75) is a hot contender for the city's best, but this is an unending debate in San Francisco. What is certain is that this soup originated in Hunan, as did Kung Pao chicken ($8.25). Number 23, the curried tofu ($6.25), is delicious. Chicken curry ($8.25) is ultra-hot, fierce and complex, as is Henry Chung's legendary harvest pork ($7.50) which, in the opinion of most regulars, is the must-try dish here.

These are dishes to get you through the harsh winters of western China, even to try for a Long March. If you ask for milder versions, they'll happily provide. Remember, "medium" is h-h-h-hot! Service is so fast you can hardly unbutton your jacket before your piping onion cake arrives, and it's an actual challenge to spend more than $20 per head.

FRENCH

Jeanne D'Arc

Jeanne d'Arc is a well-kept secret, hidden away in the basement of this slightly old-world, French-accented hotel. Tricked out with antique armor and old pikes, helmets and hangings, this bistro commemorates the life of the French martyr and "Maid of Orléans." The place is discreetly lit, and the low ceiling fosters an intimate atmosphere. The waiter is solicitous, the food is simple and good, prices are modest—and if it seems odd to run a French grill named the "Jeanne d'Arc," that's French humor for you.

Cost $30–50

Address Cornell Hotel, 715 Bush St
☏415/421-3154
Open Mon–Sat 6–9pm
Transportation 2, 3, 4, 38, BART Powell St
Accepts All major credit cards

The restaurant offers a simple, unapologetically French menu, with a prix fixe four-course option for $28.75 that changes daily and seasonally. There is no a la carte. The starter is a hearty soup of the day—perhaps Du Barry or Parmentier—made from fresh vegetables in season served with crispy French bread, followed by a salad of whatever is fresh at the market, from artichokes to mushrooms or a plain salad frisée. Main dishes can on occasion seem mundane, but the sole bonne femme is an outstanding fish *du jour*: wine-poached, mushroom-trimmed, and served with lemon slices. Like the fish, meat dishes change daily, though entrees like steak frites or filet mignon are invariably on the bill of fare. Coq au vin, boeuf bourguignon, or other lusty staples of the French palate are richly simmered, wine-dark stews. Crème brûlée and soufflés fill out the dessert list. It's not the trendiest meal in town, but then Jeanne d'Arc is a little bit like a restaurant in a French city, and it's a Bastille Day favorite.

You'll find your eyes wandering around the room, with its bric-à-brac hinting at the portcullis and halberd. The decor is highly diverting, not just in the restaurant but also in the hotel itself, from the antique elevators to the old, French posters on the walls. Owners Claude and Micheline Lambert arrived here from Orléans nearly forty years ago, and run the Hotel Cornell de France upstairs. All in all, the Jeanne d'Arc is a modest little curiosity, and a boon to the famished budget traveler.

Jeanty at Jack's

(♨) When this 1864 Silver Rush-era restaurant was taken over by chef Philippe Jeanty (of Jeanty's Bistro, in the Wine Country), downtown types were apprehensive. In a city where 140-odd years of business is as good as it gets, fashions are transient and chefs too, and messing with a beloved memory is walking where angels fear to tread. Jack's sank ignominiously when its last owners lost business, and the building—beaux-arts interior and all—was snapped up by

Cost $30–75	

Address 615 Sacramento St between Montgomery and Kearny
ⓣ 415/693-0941
Open Daily
11.30am–11.30pm
Transportation Market St lines, 15, 30, BART Montgomery St
Accepts All major credit cards

a shortlived dotcom. Next came the swan dive of e-commerce, and then along came chef Jeanty. He respectfully left the repainted stucco garlands and black and white floor tiles, but tucked tables into the mezzanine and added more upstairs, where there's a sky-lit attic.

Et voilà! Vestiges of Jack's old-time menu survive in the cooking, which is traditionally French. Beetroot and mâche are everywhere these days, and Jeanty's beet and mâche salad ($8.50) is festively red, and comes dressed with feta and citric vinaigrette, the old-fashioned cress-like greenery making it sweeter than the usual wild watercress. Home-smoked salmon carpaccio ($12.50) is a groaning platter, blander and oilier than usual, and thickly sprinkled with shallots and mini-capers. The died-and-gone-to-heaven winner is a decadently silken duck "foie blond" pâté paired with port-soaked pear slices ($9.50). The tendency to play it traditional returns in the *comme-il-faut* coq au vin ($15.50), so thickly juiced and mahogany brown that you suspect it simmered all morning. Steak tartare ($16.50) is made with the rarest Midwestern corn-fed beef, and comes crowned with raw egg yolk in the shell, plus a sculpted metal cone of delicate French fries. It can be a tad underseasoned—indeed everything's a little underseasoned. Perhaps that's to accommodate businessmen's levels of cholesterol or hypertension? But this is a sweet-toothed diner's menu and portions are lavish. Do go for the ambrosial, twin-layered chocolate mousse brûlée ($8), though the lemon sherbet in a lemon ($7) makes a good mouth freshener.

Study that wine list carefully because there are surprises. Some Alsatians and Rieslings are outstanding, and the $19 pitcher is a deal.

Kokkari Estiatorio

Where else do you find a thousand-year-old amphora in the toilet? Kokkari looks like a Zeffirelli film set rather than a Greek restaurant, and it's a pleasure just to peruse. Tagged "chic Greek," it's an Olympian enclave overlooking quiet Jackson Square. Architect Howard Backen seems to have waved his magic wand to produce a total experience, complete with Herculean stone fireplace, high windows, Persian rugs, and inlaid and oiled wooden tables and chairs. It's both imposing and traditional.

Cost $30–50

Address 200 Jackson St at Front
☎415/981-0983
Open Mon–Thurs 11.30am–2.30pm & 5.30–10pm, Fri 11.30am–2.30pm & 5.30–11pm, Sat 5–11pm
Transportation Market St lines, F, BART Embarcadero
Accepts All major credit cards

These elegant furnishings sit on hardwood floors, accompanied by a soaring wine archive and a giant sand-filled copper timbale, used to prepare the excellent, mud-like Greek coffee. There's nary a whiff of Zorba or plate smashing about the eclectic food and upscale Greek wines.

Chef Jean Alberti's salads are a strong point: the creamiest manouri cheese ($8.95) ever to have romanced orange segments and frisée with figs and toasted almonds; or a classic Greek salad ($9.95), with baby spinach, pears, walnuts, Maytag blue cheese, and nut oil vinaigrette. Avgolemono soup ($7.50) is unusual here—silkily egged, not the usual egg-flecked chicken consommé—with a lemony zing and none of the curdle found in traditional versions. Spanakopita ($8.95) seems a trifle stingy at just two triangles of phyllo-dough, albeit layered with spinach and feta. Kokkari flatbread ($13.95) is actually a pizza with four cheeses. A brilliant moussaka ($19.95) and a vegetarian, well-cumined pastitsio ($17.50) dazzle; but grilled salmon ($17.95) was a smallish portion swamped by rice beans. Asparagus, fava, and pea vines ($16.75) risotto was more of a pilaf of vegetables than a risotto. Desserts include honey ice cream ($8). Retsinas like Malatina disprove all prejudice against the native crush ($18); so does a very holy vintage Agioritikos made by Mount Athos monks ($40). Ask Glaswegian-Italian maitre d' Tonino Dravandi for advice from his bar, where a shorter menu is always available too.

Kokkari is on the expensive side but its authenticity and elegance make this a special place, and the food reaches Parnassian heights that you may not have found on holiday in Corfu.

Kuleto's

Squashed into the side of the busy Villa Florence Hotel, in the heart of downtown, Kuleto's is the reliable standby you wish you'd found earlier. A block up from the cable-car turnaround, it's at the raucous end of touristville and looks noisy. But it has soothing lighting, thanks to Pat Kuleto's tortoiseshell lampshades, plus quieter banquettes upstairs, parallel booths in dark, elegant wood opposite the open kitchen, and a long counter. Its location, near dozens of hotels and the Moscone Convention Center, guarantees that it will be packed with lunching ladies, businesspeople and tourists in equal parts, all trying to bend the hardworking staff's ears; so you may have to park elbows at the counter while you check out their menu. Alternatively, wait in the aspidistra-filled hotel lobby or catch a snack at the smaller Caffè Kuleto.

Cost $15–40

Address 221 Powell St
☏ 415/397-7720
Open Daily 8-10.30am & 11.30am-11pm
Transportation Market St lines, F, BART Powell St, Powell St cable car
Accepts All major credit cards

The menu is fish-anchored, eclectic and cleverly combines Tuscan and Californian cuisines, so it's hard to call it one or the other. Chicken, scaloppine and lamb classics run from around $14, and the fish of the day is always a good bet (from $15). Pastas and risottos are also recommended: they are almost invariably simple but done right, and reasonably priced. Angel-hair pasta in tomato, basil, and garlic ($8.25), and gnocchi with mushrooms ($11) come with homemade focaccia or sourdough, as do penne with lamb sausage, red chard, and ricotta ($9.25), linguine with clams, pancetta, white wine, tomatoes, and cream ($10.25), cheese-and-spinach-filled tortellini in radicchio and gorgonzola cream ($9.75) or, best of all, smoked-salmon-filled ravioli in asparagus and lemon cream sauce ($9.95), a wonderful juxtaposition of smoky fish and tart citrus. Salads are interestingly composed and start at $4.50.

Kuleto's opens early enough for the earliest East Coast visitor, with an excellent omelet shortlist boasting oddities like spinach, mushroom, and goat cheese ($7.50). Fresh-squeezed orange juice ($2.50) is real. Polenta with eggs ($6.95), smoked salmon, cream cheese, and bagel ($8.95), pancakes with fruit ($7.95), and eggs, bacon, or sausage (in this case, Italian) and toast ($8.95) round off the breakfast choices.

BAR MENU

Lefty O'Doul's

You can find half the missing people of the world in this beer-soaked dive. Almost half a century old, the spirit of a baseball legend lives on here— O'Doul's is named after the San Francisco Seals manager and DiMaggio pal, that same green-suited O'Doul whose name is on bottles of non-alcoholic beer. As local sports writer Jeff Carter put it: "It's all about the man in the green suit. He was here at a good time and he had a good time when he was here." Lefty's big, bow-fronted picture window contains a grand piano at which wannabe Frank Sinatras and Franky Laines drone out "Ghost Riders In The Sky" nightly, accompanied by Garry Newman or Maddaline Goepel. To the rear, fans tuck into bar food under a wall of the "greats", from DiMaggio to Babe Ruth, while a large TV overlooks chess games scrutinized by would-be Kasparovs.

Cost $6–15

Address 333 Geary St at Union Square
Ⓣ 415/982-8900
Open Daily 7am–2am
Transportation Market St lines, 38, F, BART Powell St
Accepts All major credit cards

In between the Sinatras and the Kasparovs, there's a long self-service food counter that dishes up Reuben sandwiches, Polish sausages and Greek salads. As watering holes go, the Lefty Hall of Fame has not changed one jot since it was opened in the 1950s by the Greek Bovis family, who also own the Gold Spike (columnist Herb Caen's favorite). It's nothing fancy, but the clientele and singalongs make the atmosphere simpatico and entertaining, so why be fussy? Families with kids are welcomed here, too. The Greek salad ($4.99) is really fresh and tasty, roast beef or turkey sandwiches are edible, the sauerkraut with the Polish sausage ($5.99) unquestionably sour, and navy bean soup ($1.90–2.55) is just that. To wash down your meal, choose from Clos de Bois, Kendall-Jackson, or Mondavi ($4–5), or any of fifteen beers on tap, including Fosters, Guinness and Boddington.

"Where are you now, Joe DiMaggio?" asks the old Simon and Garfunkel song, "Mrs Robinson." But though a lonely nation turns its eyes inside Lefty's they'll see plenty of Joe, and they won't be lonely for long. According to their very jokey and warmhearted manager Marina Bovis, if you're ever in a road accident and wake up with amnesia, just head for Lefty's and you'll know you're in San Francisco.

MacArthur Park

(🍴) In the part of town that used to be the colorful Barbary Coast, this rollicking brasserie overlooking little Jackson Park has wooed and won enthusiasts to its comfortable, fan-backed wooden chairs, informal service and familiar American menu for over thirty years. It's the place of choice for bringing your visiting relations if they are traditionalists who cannot face "vertical food" or any spicy adventures. Despite its upscale location, chef Melissa Miller's menu is down-home American and

Cost $9–35

Address 607 Front St
☎ 415/398-5700
Open Mon–Thurs
11.30am–10pm, Fri
11.30am–11pm, Sat 5–11pm,
Sun 4.30–10pm
Transportation 12, 42, F,
BART Embarcadero
Accepts All major credit cards
except Diners

finger-lickin' tasty, bringing in displaced southerners as well as hordes of after-hours businessmen pining for their mom's kitchen. Not that many moms cook barbecued ribs and chicken as good as MacArthur's!

MacArthur's serves American soul food, the nearest that a white-linen San Francisco restaurant can get to the South. Mesquite-grilled barbecued baby back ribs ($17.50), served with onion rings, are well worth every extra inch and ounce of outlay. Barbecued chicken ($16.50) is served with the same finger-lickin' "Mac Park" barbecue sauce, plus coleslaw and fries—alternatively, order a giant portion of fluffy garlic mashed potatoes ($4.50). The beef hamburger ($10.40) uses top-quality Niman Ranch natural beef. Those with more questing appetites will want to check the grilled calves' liver with caramelized apples, oak-smoked bacon, and grain mustard jus ($14.75). Also recommended are the Maryland crabcakes with red pepper coulis and vegetable medley ($18.25), and the jambalaya with fried okra, jasmine rice, and grilled shrimp brochette ($17.50). It's not easy to be a vegetarian in this Valhalla for carnivores but the salads are hefty and flavor-punchy: the "Mac Park" comes with creamy blue cheese or Dijon dressing ($6.40), while the Caesar is topped with Sonoma Dry Jack cheese and thyme croutons ($7.75/$9.85). The Thai chicken salad ($13.25) features almonds, ginger, and garlic. Cobb salad with smoked chicken ($13.75), and tuna Niçoise with green beans, eggs, potatoes, and tapenade ($15.25) make healthy choices.

Conversely, sinful desserts of the excruciatingly-slow-death-by-chocolate type include Judy's Mud Pie ($5.50). This is American fare to calm the wariest, most fearful diner. And MacArthur Park's barbecue sauce is good enough to justify taking home.

Plouf

Mainly young and restless, Plouf's firm following comes here as much for the scene as for the mussels. Waiters with adorable accents run around in stripey matelot jumpers while the customers sit outside, quaffing blanc de blancs with their moules marinières. Haplessly hip and a little flip in style, it's decked out with fish motifs both inside and outside, and is allegedly Provençal-inspired if anything. But its hardworking American chef dishes up fine fish and chips with aioli and vinegar as well as the ever-popular moules.

Cost $10–35

Address 40 Belden Place
ⓣ415/986-6491
Open Mon–Wed
11.30am–3pm & 5.30–10pm,
Thurs & Fri 11.30am–3pm &
5.30pm–midnight, Sat
5.30pm–midnight
Transportation 15, 30, BART
Montgomery St
Accepts All major credit cards
except Diners

Their chef is a Midwesterner and his fish and chips are not a bad deal for $11. But plump, briny mussels ($13) steamed in a very dry white wine, garlic and parsley broth are what Plouf is best known for, served in baby calabashes with crusty baguette for soaking up winey, garlicky mussel nectar. You can also get them in crème poulette ($13), wearing a creamy shallot and herb dressing. Fries arrive on the side in a little extra pan and also have their own sauce choices, ranging from aiolo to peppered vinaigrette. For a lunchtime snack, doorstop-sized foccacia sandwiches crammed with lamb, goat cheese, onion, eggplant, and aioli ($14) or chicken with bell peppers, cress, and prosciutto ($13) fill a big hole; the goat cheese and walnut croquette on red beets and cress with mustard vinaigrette ($13.40) pleases vegetarians. A giant Caesar salad ($12.50) is almost always on offer too, with other jumbo main-course salads including a whopping ahi tuna Niçoise with croutons, fennel, eggs, beans, mesclun, anchovy, radish, roasted peppers, and sherry mustard vinaigrette ($15). Appetizers include calamari and fennel tempura in gribiche sauce ($7.50), potato-wrapped scallops with fennel and cucumber salad ($9), or crab-cakes with mango sesame vinaigrette ($9.50). Tropical fruit also adorns Plouf's tuna tartare ($12) in the form of mango and papaya pieces.

True to their gallic form, Plouf offers cheese and fruit by way of dessert: Camembert with Port Salut and some pears ($7). Is there something affected about a seafood joint that calls itself Plouf ("splash") and lays on the coolness and the fruity combinations so heavily? *Mais oui*, and it appears to be working.

Postrio

Perhaps Wolfgang Puck's flagship at the Prescott Hotel should be renamed "Poshio." Imelda Marcos came here to be seen in the early 1990s, when this jewel in Puck's culinary crown was already a legend. It's designed to dazzle from the moment you find yourself in the busy, exciting, people-watching bar, to the moment when you float down their Fred-and-Ginger staircase past the giant copper brasserie to mingle with the great and famous all around, ready for your close-up—well, that's the fantasy. Then there's that legendary 800-label wine list.

Cost $30–100
Address Prescott Hotel, 545 Post St
☎ 415/776-7825
Open Mon–Sat 11.30am–2pm & 5.30–10.30pm, Sun 10am–2pm & 5.30–10pm
Transportation Powell St lines, 38, BART Powell St
Accepts All major credit cards

It's designer food. Minuscule wasabe-avocado mousse bites on tuna sashimi ($16) are dotted about on the giant plate in grapefruit and yuzu vinaigrette. They look stingy and surreal as a De Chirico painting, but make a fascinating combination. A salmon appetizer ($15) is a single giant blini with smoked salmon, dilled crème fraîche, a twenty pence-sized dollop of caviar, and a spoon of fine-minced shallot. The signature dish is grilled quail in brown butter sauce ($28), atop a quail egg ravioli that gushes yolk with every forkful, and it's a dilly. Complaints? No problem. Grumble about your salmon in smashed peas, sake-braised salsify, and toasted almond and lavender ($27), and *boum!* A second salmon appears by magic. You can't catch Postrio out. For dessert, raspberry and rhubarb compote in chèvre citrus cream ($9) is a triple-taste explosion; it's also on the dessert sampler ($9.50), along with local cheeses.

Postrio is overpriced but enthralling, serving fabled wines within a highly-charged and glorious environment, with artery-challenging fare angled at surgeons in town for medical whoop-de-doos. So if you happen not to be the former Lady Macbeth of Manila, or on expenses, escaping for under $100 per head means cutting even a modest bottle of Carneros chardonnay ($38). Here's the solution: their bar menu is excellent, so plump your weary dogs down and try tuna tartare with macadamia phyllo ($14), baked oysters in Pernod, spinach, and tomato aiolo ($16), or smoked salmon, red pepper, or wild mushroom pizzas ($12-16). These are all accessible dishes that Postrio's staff probably chow when the surgeons have gone—leaving (we trust) huge tips.

Redwood Park Upstairs

(symbol) The Transamerica Building is a sky-scraping landmark with a low-level bonzoi redwood forest of hobbit-like dimensions at its feet. Since it's such a recognizable tourist haunt, common sense dictates it should have a high-profile restaurant to match, but the space was empty for quite a while, until Fifth Floor and Aqua chef George Morrone came along to supply some gourmet glitz. Morrone's idea is to supply two separate menus for two different pockets and appetites in one. Redwood Park Downstairs, with its enormous abstract wall paintings by Mark Keller, has been set aside for formal diners, while Redwood Park Upstairs offers a shorter menu for the lighter wallet, serving it at the bar counter or at small tables just up a small flight of stairs.

Cost	$15–75
Address	600 Montgomery St at Clay
(symbol)	415/283-1000
Open	Mon–Thurs 11.30am–2.30pm & 5.30–10pm, Fri 11.30am–2.30pm & 5.30–11pm, Sat 5.30–11pm
Transportation	Market St lines, BART Montgomery St
Accepts	All major credit cards

Since this is superchef George Morrone's very personal cooking on display, you can take it that "lighter" is a relative term. Few people on earth rattle the pots more creatively than Morrone, whose fanciful flights turn out as stunning works of art every time. "Upstairs" aims at quick, fresh, and affordable dishes, like a pan-fried petrale ($16), a plate of lobster ravioli ($14), or a mound of perfectly crisped French fries ($9), served with confit or dab of cassoulet plus an irresistible garlic mayonnaise. A spuddy holy trinity brings roasted and chive-sprinkled fingerlings plus a daub of garlic mash and a tuft of French fries with mayonnaise ($12). Seafood bisque ($15), ambrosial with champagne and mustard-cream, arrives with a little secret inside—a tiny baby scallop. The dish is recognizable from Fifth Floor Restaurant's tasting menu, where Morrone built up a cult before Michael Mina lured him to this $4 million sanctum sanctorum. Desserts include Morrone's signature pot de crèmes ($9), in all flavors from ginger to caramel.

This newcomer could not have picked a better spot to open, and the fact is that almost anything Morrone does is interesting, if not necessarily cheap. A year or so ago, however, there would have been no "Upstairs" menu, just lots of main courses priced at over $30, or even $40. More diners can now afford to try Morrone's cooking. It's a sign of the changing times.

Rue Lepic

Rue Lepic is a postage stamp-sized restaurant on the corner of one of the steepest blocks in Nob Hill. The clientele is mainly well-heeled visitors eager for master-chef Michiko Boccara's special French cuisine. It's a little bit of a mystery why the place isn't completely booked solid all the time. Perhaps you could put it down to the awkward location in picturesque "Tendernob," straddling the lower Nob Hill section on its way to the Tenderloin. Spotless and chic, with white-clothed tables, mirrors and seamless service, Lepic offers gourmet cooking at a lower price than many similar places.

Cost $35–60
Address 900 Pine St at Mason
☎ 415/474-6070
Open Daily 5.30–10pm
Transportation Powell–Mason cable car
Accepts All major credit cards except Diners

One special ($42) five-course prix fixe menu includes lobster tail, for instance; in many restaurants one lobster dish alone would cost almost the same. Boccara's cooking is absolutely classical fare that might have come from Julia Child's *Mastering The Art of French Provincial Cookery*. The shellfish bisque, for instance, is made on a terrific stock that must have been the work of hours: clam juice, shrimp tails, cream and butter, all of it gorgeously emulsified into the smoothest of creams before shreds of shrimp and crab are added. Cream of corn soup is mild and sweet, and also made on a deep and rich stock. Seafood pasta comes studded with clams and crab. The mahi mahi is succulent and perfectly cooked, but served with an under-seasoned gratin. Perhaps you can put this under-salting down to Lepic's clientele, which tends to be "mature". Mrs Boccara will blow any healthy intentions, however, by serving crème brûlées to ruin any waistline. Wine comes by the glass in several intelligent choices.

Wine starts at around $6 by the glass, with bottles at around $30. The $42 prix fixe is a no-holds-barred gourmet blow-out, but there's also a $34 five-course menu that has just enough choice to make it ideal for most tastes. Altogether, it's a pretty satisfactory evening out, with lots of pleasure and no hidden surprises—but do watch your step here. Descending to Lepic from the top of Nob Hill is a little tricky in heels. They could wind up trying to catch you as you tumble towards Pasadena...

Sam's Grill and Seafood Restaurant

Unrepentantly "Old San Francisco" in food, style and customer, Sam's Grill has filled the stomachs of generations of good ol' boys for nigh on 136 years. "If it ain't broke, don't fix it!" must be the motto here, because the only thing that's changed in decades is the no-smoking ban, which must have hit the cigar-tooting businessmen who cluster here hard. Sam's is such a living legend that Jack London or Dashiell Hammett probably stood there before them, playing pinochle and yelling for another dozen oysters–although London probably sold the oysters to Sam, while Hammett drank Wild Turkey. Wooden cubicles with little drapes line one side of Sam's for secret deal-making. The rest of the house features molded wainscoting over a tiled floor and comfy booths, all tended to by waiters who are summoned by little bells and are experience and briskness personified.

Cost $10–35
Address 374 Bush St at Belden Place
☏ 415/421-0594
Open Mon–Fri 11am–9pm
Transportation BART Montgomery St
Accepts All major credit cards except Diners

Sam's menu is also resolutely "early Western," with plain, no-nonsense grilled or pan-fried platters of local sand dabs ($14), petrale ($15), king salmon ($16), or swordfish ($19). It's nice to report that they are executed perfectly à point, rarely overdone. But Sam's also sports later American staples like Caesar salad ($4.25), asparagus in mustard mayonnaise ($3.50), creamy spinach Florentine ($3.50), and the Californian Hangtown Fry ($9.50). Named because condemned men en route to the gallows in the Gold Country used to request it as a last breakfast, Hangtown Fry is really just shirred eggs with oysters and bacon—they knew it would take a while to fetch! Crab legs ($13.50) are another nostalgic dish here. Steak or chicken dishes exist, but better keep it simple and stick to the fish.

A couple of token desserts are offered, but regulars aren't dessert fanciers—this is such a male atmosphere that it positively exhales martini fumes. But as a surviving piece of the old city, it's unbeatable. A warning: the place doesn't stay open late, doesn't tolerate fools gladly, and is open only weekdays, not weekends. No doubt the ghosts of John L. Sullivan, Jack Dempsey and Gentleman Jim Corbett have told them to keep out the newfangled world. After all, it ain't broke in here.

Sanraku Four Seasons

Few non-Japanese San Franciscans know about the Sanraku, so when you first lay eyes upon this low-key establishment, a block above Union Square, it's not clear what's going on here or why a line of tourists is forming outside every lunchtime. Peering through the window reveals a mysteriously unadorned interior with few clues other than pine tables, chopsticks and an occasional oriental ceramic; sheer word of mouth is responsible for the line outside.

Cost $15–50

Address 704 Sutter St at Mason
☎ 415/771-0803
Open Mon–Fri 11am–10pm, Sat & Sun 4–10pm
Transportation 2, 3, 4, PM, BART Powell St
Accepts All major credit cards

Sanraku is famous for its specialized kaiseki menu of four or seven plates of zensai, delicacies arranged in a multi-course flight that you reserve ahead and discuss ahead with chef Hiro Hattori. Chef Hiro-san then whips up a custom menu created for your party's tastes and mood. Start with softshell crab or seaweed salad in handmade bowls with sauce. A suinono, or consommé of something like green bean, spinach or bonito, arrives in a mini-kettle with a minute cup to slurp from (yes, you can). Next comes sashimi—raw salmon or mackerel with soy and seaweed—followed by two custom-made sushi of whatever the chef has to hand. Tempura—battered or steamed fried vegetables or shellfish—are followed by a meat dish, sometimes with miso. The meal ends with a tea-scented cube of green mochi, or rice-gluten ice cream, washed down with cups of green tea. The cost will range from $30 to $47, depending on the number of plates that you order. Chef Hilo also serves non-kaiseki meals too, with zensai beginning at $9 and main dishes from $13, but his kaiseki menu is a way to learn how real Japanese food is served. Plates arrive in sequence but grouped in ensembles, so you have the chance to try several things at once.

The Sanraku has thrived here for a dozen years, yet never gets plugged in the local press. Along with the very elegant Hana Zen yakitori bar a few blocks away on Cyril Magnin Street, Sanraku is a number one destination for visitors from Japan. Do they know something we don't?

Scala's Bistro

🍴 Scala's develops into a fully-fledged occasion from the moment you meet a Beefeater in scarlet bloomers at the door. After that, you park yourself onto the list and start angling for a menu. Ear-splitting with chatter, the ground-floor dining room glows with the young and the beautiful. Beneath a gloriously ornate silver ceiling, a giant mural of tropical fruit—heavy on bananas—faces huge picture windows that open onto downtown bustle. Booths cradle nests of

Cost $18–50
Address Sir Francis Drake Hotel, 432 Powell St
☎ 415/395-8555
Open Daily Mon–Fri 7am–midnight, Sat & Sun 8am–midnight
Transportation Market St lines, BART Powell St
Accepts All major credit cards except Diners

beautiful young women wearing timeless black, high-stools balance canoodling duos, and one or two large round tables give groups and families space to yell against the din. Service is brisk yet graceful under pressure.

So it's not all about the food, you understand, but the kitchen won't let you down. Scala's first chef was the much-praised Donna Scala, who took her French-Italian skills and made the menu work, then left it behind when she moved on to the Wine Country, where she and her husband now own Napa's Bistro Don Giovanni. Presentation is lovely here even if portions are small. Squash blossoms ($9.50) burst with fluffed-up, sweet buffalo mozzarella, and their backdrop of tangy, tiny flash-broiled cherry tomatoes is beautifully counterbalanced; a little poem of flavors. Peekytoe crabcakes ($11.50) are made with small, highly prized Maine mud crabs, mild and mushy, on a tasty, piquant bed of roasted corn and chanterelles with thyme aiolo. Squash ravioli ($11.50) balances the sugariness of the pasta with lemon-cream parsley sauce—an eye-opening combination. Risotto with preserved orange is astonishingly good; a salty edge to the orange makes it work ($16.50). Pizzas are fine choices: beefsteak tomato with pesto and mozzarella ($12.50) comes on a wafer-thin crust; a Margherita ($10.50) will get polished off within minutes.

Chocolate cake dessert ($7) came with a melty middle and real vanilla ice cream. OK, it's not cheap, but pick with care and you'll still get out of here alive. But reserve ahead if you've got an anniversary, or just want to celebrate in larger numbers.

Schroeder's

🍴 "Life's too short to drink cheap beer!" says a plaque above the antique rosewood bar in Schroeder's, which goes some way towards explaining why you can pay up to $9 for the most festive of wheaten gold weissbiers on tap here, served in bathtub-sized Bavarian beer steins. A pitcher is only $2.75 extra. A huge, oak-paneled barn that stayed in the Kniesche family for generations,

Cost $12–30
Address 240 Front St
☎ 415/421-4778
Open Mon–Fri 11am–9.30pm, Sat 5–10pm
Transportation Market St lines, BART Embarcadero
Accepts All major credit cards

Schroeder's is a real chunk of old San Francisco, a 1893 beer-and-sausage hofbrau relic of yesteryear—women were finally allowed to drink here only after 1970! The decor is very oompah-oompah, so studiously "Student Prince" that unsuspecting strangers may wonder if Mario Lanza will render "Drink! Drink! Drink!" from the bar. New owners Jena and Stefan Filipcik come from the German-speaking western part of the Czech Republic. They've kept the antique antlers and wood paneling, restored the very jolly 1930s Herman Richler murals, polished the mahogany rosewood bar and oak tables, hired Joe Smiell's polka band in for Fridays, and stuck dirndls on the luckless mädchen of the house.

Schroeder's appetizer list offers sausages of many sizes, while on the bar menu, a small plate of sausages, red cabbage, and sauerkraut ($6.75) hits a minor spot. Under chef Stefan, vegetarian and fish-of-the-day platters have been introduced, plus his own dorschleber ($5.95), or homemade goose liver with cranberries ($5.95). As well as Californifying the old blackboard menu, Stefan churns out a mean schnitzel ($12), with lighter spätzle ($2.50). Potatoes fill the rest of the menu in pancake and spätzle combinations. Vegetarians get käse und spätzle with mushrooms and tomatoes ($11.75) or spätzle with basil and goat cheese ($13.95). Carnivores get authentic sauerbraten or pickled beef ($14.50), veal Stroganoff ($12.75), or Stefan's Lord-take-me-now peppered loin of venison with pears, thyme, and berry sauce ($21.95), the biggest artillery in his all-out effort to seduce the Oktoberfest crowds.

But for many regulars, Stefan's "lederhosen-lite" innovations take second place to washing down any of eighteen Bavarian and Czech beers on draft—rare, chestnut-hued double bocks, Franziskaner, Hefe Weissbier and Czech lagers of legendary crispness and bite.

SEAFOOD

Tadich Grill

At the end of a stressful week, the Tadich Grill is just the place to relax. Regulars know what to expect: old-fashioned San Francisco dining in paneled, curtained booths or off the zinc bar. The food is unexceptional, but there's a deep inner peace in knowing it's always going to be exactly the same, in that unchanging nostalgic time warp where waiters have no specials to reel off and you know you'll never have to hear the

Cost $30–50
Address 240 California St at Battery
☏ 415/391-1849
Open Mon–Fri 11am–9.30pm, Sat 11.30am–9.30pm
Transportation BART Embarcadero, California St cable car
Accepts MasterCard, Visa

words "Hi, my name's Christophe and I'll be your waiter for the night..."

Originally founded by Croatian immigrants in 1849 as a coffee stall for sailors, the only surprising thing about the city's oldest restaurant these days is that over 150 years later they are still cooking sole Florentine, sand dabs and petrale exactly the same way as they always did. The briny allure of those huge heaps of oysters, mussels, clams, prawns, and crabs piled up on the counter is another nostalgic throwback. Now that Jack's has changed, the Tadich is the only true survivor of its ilk. You get exactly the same grilled and broiled catch of the day that new arrivals ordered during the Gold Rush, when they wanted their local fish recently deceased and barely seared in butter on a spitting pan. The menu now allows for three versions of halibut, salmon, and swordfish, plus the local flatfish specialties, petrale and sand dab. Prices range from $15 to $18 per plate. They grill or panfry or broil within full view, adding so-so spinach or broccoli if asked, plus something called branch potatoes that nobody makes anywhere else. Tadich still makes a Crab Louie; anyone on a 1950s kick will enjoy the retro cocktail sauce made from ketchup and mayo.

The Tadich Grill's best suit is its lack of pretension and down-to-earth, gruff service—the waiters take the time to give you a lesson in fileting fish. So stick to the Real McCoy: fresh fish gilded with butter and lemon. The wine list is strong on bone-dry whites, including a nice Bogle by the glass ($5.50).

Waterfront Restaurant

"Food and views," said veteran Chronicle columnist Herb Caen, "that's what San Francisco is about." On the face of it, the Waterfront owns the city's dream location, the setting that film buffs recognize from that scene in the movie *Vertigo* where James Stewart talks to his old pal in the shipping industry. Now released from the eyesore of a freeway that threatened to topple in the 1989 quake, and was demolished, the Embarcadero is bursting with views. So when Waterfront's new restaurant opened upstairs, everybody rushed here to sip and sup beside the bay. The clean and articulate design incorporates not just watery views, but Asian antiques and a seafood menu.

Cost $30–50	
Address Pier 7, Embarcadero at Broadway	
☏ 415/391-2696	
Open Mon–Fri 11am–2pm & 5–10pm, Sat & Sun 5–10pm	
Transportation F	
Accepts All major credit cards	

Prices, however, were and still are high, though the menu changes daily. Bruce Hill's fusion seafood includes appetizers like ahi tuna ceviche with truffle-tangerine dressing ($10.75); tuna and citrus juice are very untraditional choices for this Peruvian dish, which normally uses a dense, white-fleshed fish like sea bass, but it works because of the extra-strong flavors. Salmon tartare ($12) comes with a beet compote, egg, and a whiff of Osetra caviar, crab profiteroles ($12.50) come with fennel, pecans, and Champagne dill vinaigrette, and butternut squash soup ($8.50) with lobster-pear salpicon and curry crème fraîche. Entrees include ahi tuna au poivre with sunchoke purée, wild mushrooms, braised kale, and sweet carrot sauce ($28); honey-soy cured steelhead trout on salad frisée ($28); and pan-roasted Chilean sea bass with braised veal cheeks and brussel sprouts en croûte ($27). There are meats too: Australian rack of lamb ($33), and Argentinian beef tenderloin with red wine-braised lentils, broccoli rabé, Stilton butter, and Merlot demi-glace ($31).

Many locals opt for the lower-priced little cafe below, which has lots of the good points and some of the food. With its little jetty and tables at the back, its counter seating and viewside stools, downstairs has become the preferred spot for casual dining. Once again, San Franciscans are left wondering why lower-priced eateries seem to do better along the Embarcadero, where the view should lend the chance for restaurants to truly sparkle.

Waterfront Restaurant

The Tenderloin

THE TENDERLOIN

N

CALIFORNIA STREET

PINE ST

BUSH STREET

SUTTER STREET

POST STREET

GEARY STREET

O'FARRELL STREET

ELLIS STREET

EDDY STREET

TURK STREET

GOLDEN GATE AVENUE

VAN NESS AVENUE

POLK STREET

LARKIN STREET

HYDE STREET

LEAVENWORTH STREET

JONES STREET

SHANNON STREET

TAYLOR STREET

MASON STREET

COSMO PLACE

MARKET STREET

STEVENSON STREET

JESSIE ST

Thai House Express

Soups

Shalimar

Le Colonial

Grand Café

Naan 'n' Curry

Golden Era Vegetarian

Dottie's True Blue Café

Vietnam II

Saigon Sandwiches

TENDERLOIN

CIVIC CENTER

City Hall

UNITED NATIONS PLAZA

Tú Lan

0   200 yds

Le Colonial

(🍴) Walking in here feels like time travel-ing to another era, and you may feel yourself reaching for your khakis and trop-ical helmet. Le Colonial is mysterious and upscale, without being heavy-handed. Imagine a conservatory reached by sweeping stairs, situated off Taylor Street just a step away from a none-too-salubri-ous back street. (The location is notable, not just odd: the legendary Trader Vic's once stood here.) Fill the conservatory with jungle sounds, teak-shutters on white walls, Moorish tiling, dark-stained bam-boo, and rattan, and populate it with graceful, uniformed waiters and antique

Cost $18–45

Address 20 Cosmo Place
℡ 415/931-3600
Open Mon–Thurs
11.30am–2.30pm &
5.30–10.30pm, Fri
11.30am–2.30pm &
5.30pm–midnight, Sat
5.30pm–midnight, Sun
5–10pm
Transportation 38, BART
Powell St
Accepts All major credit cards
except Diners

collectibles. It's somewhat disillusioning, then, to learn that Le Colonial is a spin-off of a mini-empire devoted to recreating Saigon in the 1940s, with branches in Los Angeles, Chicago, New York, and Philadelphia. If you get over that, then chef Dieu Ho's cooking will charm the credit card right out of your pocket.

Start in the lounge with exotic cocktails like the Asian Pearl ($7), livened up with trailing twigs of mint and cilantro, followed by French-Viet-namese appetizers. Shrimp hoisted aloft on sugar canes make a good start ($6), as does a stuffed pork and seafood "goi cuon" ($8.50); these pancakes are made with rice flour and coconut, and therefore crispier and more golden than more ordinary varieties. Like more or less everything, they come with dipping sauces, in this case a sweet and spicy hoisin and peanut, with fresh chile, sesame, garlic, and sugar. If you're allergic to cilantro, better tell them before you order goi cuon, because like most things on the menu it gets half a cilantro bush as a condiment. Main dishes include bamboo-steamed or banana-leaf-wrapped snapper or bass ($17), and a coconut milk red tiger prawn curry ($16), long-simmered with egg-plant and mango. Stellar lemongrass chicken ($15) or roast duck ($23) also get lots of play on the menu. To finish, try one of Le Colonial's desserts: Vietnamese banana spring roll ($8) or tapioca pearls in coconut ($7).

Lately, they've been offering special menus for less money. But don't use their valet parking unless you're on an expense account. Park instead at the public Sutter-Stockton Garage and walk the three blocks.

Dottie's True Blue Cafe

Jostled by the Vietnamese and Pakistani cafes of the Tenderloin, Dottie's is the lone American diner. A survivor of many years, it's so triumphantly busy that folks start lining up to eat here from the early hours. It's unusually popular with visitors, and small wonder. Heftier in portions and better in value than some other old-time diners around Union Square to the east, Dottie's offers honest

Cost	S8–15
Address	522 Jones St
☎	415/885-2767
Open	Mon & Thurs–Sun 7am–2.30pm
Transportation	27, 38, BART Powell St
Accepts	MasterCard, Visa

American food at low, low prices—even if you do have to wait to peg your seat at its little tables with their traditional, blue, picnic oilcloths and Carolina-shaped salt and pepper shakers.

To do Dottie's properly, you need to take the morning off and combine lunch with breakfast, on an empty stomach. They make their own breakfast rolls, jalapeno cornbread, buns and muffins, as well as strawberry-mango bread for their French toast—a whopping doorstopper that comes with real maple syrup and fruit. A hefty stack of fruit pancakes ($5.95) comes with more syrup. Alternatively, dive into a traditional mixed fry ($6.75) of terrific bacon and eggs with fried bread or an additional tomato. If you want to have your pancake and eat it, you can do both dishes on the same plate with the "Open Road" ($9.95). All simple diner fare, but compare Dottie's brunch to others in spots marginally more salubrious: the pancakes are tastier and larger, the syrup is the real McCoy, eggs are fresh and bright yellow, the coffee is constantly replenished and strong enough to stand an ox in, home-baked bread is included, and the waitress isn't wearing a nylon miniskirt and support hose.

The message is simple: come to Dottie's for a big ol' honest brunch. But you can also morph that menu into a late lunch, because Dottie goes to the trouble of serving wine and beer with staple dishes like the Southwestern omelet of eggs with chile sausage, peppers, cheese, and salsa, plus homemade fries and tortillas. Despite its offputting location in the heart of the "Loin," Dottie's is always filled with backpackers and young tourists, and it's not hard to see why.

Golden Era Vegetarian Restaurant

(🍴) Can everything be recreated in tofu? This Vietnamese vegan restaurant is a shrine to the protean (and protein) wonders of soy, where you can eat everything a normal Vietnamese restaurant serves without any meat, fish or other animal products—yet also minus tasteless white blocks of mush. Even the carrot cake comes without milk or eggs. It goes without saying that vegetarian restaurants flourish in San Francisco, both high-end and gourmet, like Greens, Millennium and Herbivore, or humble, like Boy Choy and Ananda Fuara. But Golden Era is the only place in either category to serve vegan food in a former temple which was converted from a subterranean dancehall. It has gilded chairs and pillars, its own shrine, and inspirational texts such as "If we do not love ourselves we could not love others."

Cost $7–20
Address 572 O'Farrell St at Jones
☏ 415/673-3136
Open Mon & Wed–Sun 11am–9pm
Transportation Market St lines, 27, 38, BART Powell St
Accepts MasterCard, Visa

Service is as delicate and respectful as the food. Vegan appetizers include variations on classics like crêpes with tofu, mushroom, bean sprout, and jicama ($5.95), and tay-ho rolls of tofu, carrot, mushroom, steamed bean sprout, and lettuce ($5.95). Both are as tasty as they are when non-vegan, and big enough for a main course. Imperial rolls ($4.25) come stuffed with lettuce, tofu and the Vietnamese hallmark herbal trio of mint, basil and cilantro, plus peanut sauce; Buddha Buns ($4.75) are soft, steamed bread stuffed with tofu, beans, and water chestnuts; both are great choices. Among the better main dishes are the house rice clay pot of tofu, soy, mushrooms, bean thread, and gingered rice ($7.25), sautéed garlic "beef" ($8.50), caramelized "chicken" in sweet and chile soy ($8.95), and tamarind soy "beef" with vegetarian "shrimp" chips ($7.50). There's even "prawns" in ginger ($8.95). That carrot cake is stodgy; substitute traditional Vietnamese coffee ($2.50).

Golden Era doesn't accept reservations. The clientele consists of both locals and Australian backpackers, dedicated chowhounds from Down Under who have somehow sniffed out their good but affordable vegetarian food. A word on the neighborhood: the funky Tenderloin area is chock-a-block with excellent Vietnamese food at rock-bottom prices, but women may not want to come alone after dark.

Grand Cafe

The Grand Cafe's splendid raw bar and wine list—plus its marble floors and counter, massive pillars, and Arts and Crafts light fittings, booths, and banquettes—may make you feel as though you're Musetta walking onto a stage where the scenery has upstaged your waltz before you have even opened your mouth to sing. But it's a seductive start for any meal. The Cafe's latest chef, Paul Aremstam, previously worked at the Rubicon, and comes fresh from a stab at running a raw bar on a slightly too raw block of the Tenderloin.

Cost $20–50
Address Hotel Monaco, 501 Geary St at Taylor
☎415/292-0101
Open Mon–Thurs 7am–10.30am, 11.30am–2.30pm & 5.30–10pm, Fri 7am–10.30am, 11.30am–2.30pm & 5.30–11pm, Sat 8–10.30am, 11.30am–2.30pm & 5.30–11pm, Sun 9am–2.30pm & 5.30–10pm
Transportation 38, BART Powell St
Accepts All major credit cards

A fish "natural," Aremstam has really perked up the shellfish and fish menu. Fruits de mer platters (from $25) include intense, coppery-tasting Quilcene oysters ($2 separately) with mussels, clams, prawns, and the sweeter, deep-cupped Kumamoto oyster (a local success story—it's a hybrid that took years to develop). Aremstam treats many dishes simply, letting Prince Edward Island mussels ($11), or a truly exquisite wild mushroom tart with truffle sabayon ($12), speak for themselves. There are a few false notes, however, one soup of the day—thin fava bean—was downright unseasoned ($7), and the Gribiche sauce on the asparagus ($10) belongs on fish. As befits a fish supremo, however, Aremstam's skate wing ($19) triumphs, exulting in brown butter and capers on wilted cabbage. Meat dishes feature rabbit, lamb, rib-eye steak, and duck, with prices hovering around the $20 mark. Sonoma duck ($22), for instance, comes in a sour cherry coulis, and is well matched with a superb mashed potato ($4), of petite Kennebecs with oil. Elsewhere chef Aremstam has kept his new broom in the closet. The Grand Cafe's famous banana cream pie with coconut caramel sauce ($7.50) lingers on the menu, its flaky crust still filled with liquor-infused custard on macadamia chips, and topped with cross-sliced bananas. Wines include a spectacular Cuvée Marie ($7 per glass), a white with guts.

Next door, the Petit Cafe serves inexpensive bar-menu versions of the same dishes. But for special occasions, the sheer theatricality of Grand Cafe makes for a real event.

Naan 'n' Curry

When you enter the "Naan," place your order at the counter by the door. It doesn't take long to arrive, because the food is your standard kormas, koftas, tandoors and kebabs. The counterhand jots your order on a scrap of paper that he hands to the man at the tandoor, who prepares it while you find cutlery and a seat at a trestle table inside.

Cost $4–10
Address 478 O'Farrell St
☎ 415/775-1349
Open Daily noon–midnight
Transportation 27, 38, BART
Powell St
Accepts Cash only

Decor is a multicolored, borderline-hallucinogenic paint job, with bare tables, scarves stapled across the ceiling and Taj Mahal holograms. The "Naan" prompts you to wonder who took charge of decorating, and what they were on. It turns out that Pakistani owner Atique Rehman hired a Mexican artist and told him to express himself.

You can bring your own beer—they don't serve any—or help yourself to water or lukewarm chai from the jugs at the back. The "Naan" is anything but antiseptically neat and tidy, but none of that will seem to matter once your food is delivered by one of Atique's headscarved relations. It's the best value in town, probably the hottest too, and definitely the cheapest. As you'd expect, their naan is golden and aromatic. It comes in all the usual flavors of onion, garlic, or spinach, and costs just $1. Vegetable curries are just $4. Chicken curry ($5) is intricately spiced and garlicked, with cream and yogurt stirred into the rich and long-simmered sauce. Chicken kofta with coconut ($7) contains lots of large chunks tenderized to a sweet and spicy hash. Kebabs ($2) come in several varieties, including vegetable, chicken, and beef. Basmati rice pilau ($1) is a meal unto itself, even without meat, glinting with golden saffron specks, pistachios, almonds, and aromatic goodness.

Atique himself is an ascetic-looking pigtailed man in gym shoes and shorts, chopping away at carrots in the back behind a fridge full of Fresca. He has only been open for a year and already yearns to expand. His regulars include anybody from a family of Asians living nearby, to backpackers looking for fiery late-night fodder and businessmen on a quick lunch break. Diehard fans sometimes compare it to the Shalimar, and agree that while both are finds, the vibes are somehow different. The competition gives them both an edge.

Saigon Sandwiches

Saigon Sandwiches exists for one thing more than any other: banh mi. People come from all over the city to this modest hole in the wall, where San Francisco's best smoked-pork Vietnamese banh mi or meat-filled sandwiches are made. There's usually a crowd—and sometimes a foot-stomping mob—from the nearby Civic Center offices, plus van drivers, mail carriers and even City Hall bureaucrats. The endlessly patient women who run the place occasionally take a Zen-like fascination in rearranging their little mountains of rolls instead of dealing with the madding crowds at the counter. They know the customers will all come back again.

Banh mi is indefinable but *banh* means something akin to "snack" or "small roll," according to Vietnamese speakers, while *mi* is "noodles," but also "stall." Over the years, the sandwiches have declined a bit in size, but absolutely not in quality, and they still cost only two dollars, with extra pickles or dressings for fifty cents. Made from golden, pliantly chewy homemade French baguettes, the sandwiches are hollowed out to house several different grilled or smoked meats, from delicious smoked pork to meatballs or liver sausage. They never spill out, though massive clumps of fresh cilantro go on top along with that very red and hot sweet-and-sour dipping sauce made with cane sugar, chiffonéed carrots and bird chiles. None costs more than $2.75. Saigon Sandwiches does sell other banh, like cha gio spring rolls or rice cakes in banana leaves, as well as cane sugar, tapioca, or rice drinks.

Sadly, Vietnamese coffee only comes in cans here; otherwise, you could easily imagine yourself to be in Hanoi or Ho Chi Minh City. A minuscule table or two by the wall permit you to hover briefly, but essentially this is for takeout. You can even phone a party order ahead, then come to pick it up. Although several nearby Vietnamese cafes peddle banh mi—Viet No. 4 in the Food Center at Bush and Kearny, and the Little Paris Cafe on Kearny Street can give Saigon Sandwiches a run for their two bucks—this remains the fastest and probably the cheapest Vietnamese place in the city.

Cost $2–2.50

Address 560 Larkin St at Eddy
☏ 415/474-5698
Open Mon–Fri 7am–4.30pm, Sat & Sun 9am–4pm
Transportation 19
Accepts Cash only

Shalimar

The first thing you notice when you enter Shalimar is the overwhelming nose-blast of garam masala spices. The second thing is the unceasing racket from the open kitchen, a clatter of decibels that combines the rhythmic slapping of nan bread onto the tandoor oven with the chop-chop-chop of the cleaver behind and loud disputes breaking out in Pushtu, Gujurati or Urdu. There is no service and you'll have to ask for your own portions at the counter, where their English isn't good, then help yourself to water and cutlery. But your food will show up in five or ten minutes and then you'll feel better, because it is very good and very cheap.

Cost $10–15
Address 532 Jones St at Geary
☎ 415/928-0333
Open Daily noon–11.30pm
Transportation 38, BART Powell St
Accepts Cash only

Once you grab a laminated menu from the counter, you're in for some honest curries. The menu is hilariously funny as well as short, and their curries are as good as Indian food gets for these prices, and a lot hotter. Chicken, lamb, vegetables, or prawn curries are dished up on the spot, no main course costs more than $5.99 or $6.99, and the nan, in its many onion and vegetable varieties, is irresistibly crisp for $2.50. But if your tolerance for the hot and spicy isn't immense, avoid this temple of spice—it must also be said that the big, black, uncrushed peppercorns in the lamb and spinach curry and veggie korma ($5.99) can be a little crunchy and indigestible. Basmati rice ($1.50) is saffron-flecked, plump-grained, and aromatic and comes with more nan bread, piping hot from the tandoor.

The word about Shalimar must have been out for a while, because the line snakes out of the door and down the block at suppertime. The Shalimar is right on the edge of the Tenderloin, and if you're female you're probably going to feel more comfortable if you come with a friend. The "Loin" is funky rather than scary, but nevertheless not somewhere to linger alone after dark if lost and wearing a camera around your neck. But it definitely harbors some of the best Asian hole-in-the-walls in town outside the Richmond district.

The Tenderloin

Soups

Several Russian Hill writers have a healthy little old daily routine. Every lunchtime they descend from their ivory towers to stroll several blocks down to this cheap and cheerful establishment, with its exuberant brown-and-white checkered trim. Inside it's a prettier pink, with comfy counter seating. It's not rude to call it cheap, because that's what it

Cost $2–8
Address 784 O'Farrell Street at Hyde
☎ 415/775-6406
Open Daily 10am–6.30pm
Transportation 19, 38
Accepts Cash only

used to say in the window, in big letters. "Dirt Cheap," in fact. According to Wayne and Richard at the counter, they changed the message when the vegetable soups went up from $2 to $2.75—definitely not *dirt* cheap, they apologize. The sign now says "Everybody Welcome" instead, and adds the boast "Dedicated to solving all the world's problems one bowl at a time."

The soups change every day, but there are always two vegetarian soups to choose from, usually freshly made potages like potato and split pea ($2.75). You can also pay a swingeing $4.25 for a pretty large portion in a proper soup bowl, with a refill, plus a cup of coffee or tea, and there is sometimes an extra "combo" deal of half a sandwich and half a bowl of soup for $4.75 with coleslaw, carrot sticks, and coffee or tea. The other two offerings are non-vegetarian, and may include soups such as beef barley and chile, minestrone, chicken and lentil, tomato, lima bean and ham, or even lentil and sausage soup, which comes with lots of lentils and big slices of spicy Italian sausage. The most expensive and popular soup in the joint, however, is clam chowder ($4.75), which has plenty of clams and clam juice, lots of celery and a wealth of diced potato; it's available Mondays and Fridays. Generally speaking, the soup chef could maybe use a little more pepper, but there's a big old peppermill on the counter in here along with Tabasco, jalapenos, garlic salt, and a bottomless bowl of those crackers in cellophane.

Soups does serve other things, like Kosher Hebrew National hot dogs ($2.75 with tea or coffee and fixings) or tuna salad ($3.75). It may no longer be dirt cheap, but everybody is definitely welcome.

Thai House Express

It's a familiar quandary for movie lovers. You're attending a movie somewhere along Van Ness Avenue, and you need a bite afterwards to deconstruct the plot and recharge your batteries. Bad news. Van Ness is a dining Mojave of stratospheric rents, so there's nothing nearby that isn't either a high-end steak emporium that melts your plastic into a puddle the moment you glimpse the doorman, or a diner of banal

Cost $6–20
Address 901 Larkin St at Geary
☎ 415/441-2238
Open Mon–Thurs & Sun 11.30am–1am, Fri & Sat 11.30am–2am
Transportation 19, 49
Accepts MasterCard, Visa

and greasy aspect. Your fallback position: head a block over to Polk's strip of clean and affordable Thai places, among which this is indeed the speediest, as the name indicates. Done in industrial cafeteria style, with plain tables and a clientele of disco bunnies, old-timers and drifting moviegoers, Thai House Express is borderline chic.

First and foremost you have to try the house specialty of nuer kem ($6.50) or strips of dried and refried beef ("one-day beef" is the other Thai name), which comes in generous strips, with a spicy-sour dipping sauce to offset the sweet crispness. Thai House larb ($5.95) never lets you down either: ground chicken, pork, or beef are dressed with chile, onion, rice powder, and lemon; it's crisp and not watery, with all flavors present, correct and saluting. Most Thai salads come with a slightly different dressing of chile, garlic, fish sauce, and lime in larb; all the variations are excellent, but chicken makes the cleanest foil for a thinner, sharper dressing. Tom yum goong ($6.95) is an acceptable if predictable prawn-filled broth, with lemongrass, straw mushrooms, and muted galangal. The po-take ($8.95) or hot-sour seafood soup combination is more exciting, but you may find it difficult to develop a taste for those fish balls of compressed bait—large, rubbery and bouncy as rubber eyeballs from a joke shop. Five-spices beef with cucumbers ($5.95), on the other hand, is aromatic and soy-marinated, and it also comes in crispy roast duck version ($6.50). Finally, reserve a spot for the gang ga-ree gai ($5.95), a mild, yellow chicken curry.

Try not to stare at some of the customers, though some of them are exotically attired. Too near the sleaze of Lower Polk to have high prices, Thai House suffers a bit from the location. However, it stays open conveniently late.

Tú Lan

(♨) Inside talk used to be that this was the best cheap Vietnamese place in town, after foody diva Julia Child discovered it back in the late 1980s and declared it to be her favorite hole-in-the-wall. With its dreary non-decor of formica, cramped tables, plastic bowls and encrusted woks, and its location on one of the nastiest blocks in town, Tú Lan is a mecca for dedicated chowhounds, who home in on it like foody missiles, investing it with all the virtues that inverted snobbery can bestow on a truly greasy spoon. Nothing has changed in fifteen years except that the patrons now include backpackers and the food is more erratic. Oh, and Tú Lan have put Julia's photo on their laminated menu, something that may inspire mixed feelings.

> Cost $4–15
>
> Address 8 6th St at Market
> ☎415/626-0927
> Open Daily 11am–9.30pm
> Transportation Market St lines, BART Civic Center
> Accepts Cash only

The turnover of customers is tumultuous, the sheer volume of traffic punishing and the racket just deafening, though this is all seasonal. Small wonder, then, that the food can be hit and miss from time to time. The cha gio ($3.95), or spring rolls, and the cold imperial rolls with dipping sauces ($3.95) are both served with a distinctive cilantro, mint and basil trinity on the side. They come with noodles and are always sure bets. On a recent trip, the green papaya salad ($3.95) had a flat note—an accident with fish sauce? Larb ($5.25), or beef salad with herbs, had a disconcerting tinge too, although it was tremendous on other visits. Fresh fish of the day ($6.75) varies from snapper to tilapia, chile-ed and gingered to a fare-thee-well. The most expensive thing on the short menu is Ten Things In A Pot ($10.95), a pho with everything tossed into a big broth, instead of on the side as condiments.

In the rosy light of memory, most food lovers in this town will swear they had the ultimate spring rolls, green papaya salads, kebabs, curries, and larbs of their lives here, but lately the patrons have mainly been visitors. On the other hand, it can be really good and prices have not gone up much. Perhaps the sudden attention had mixed results on Tú Lan's in-house dynamics. Maybe a foody "coronation" comes with a tainted chalice.

Vietnam II Restaurant

(icon) Decked out in pink, red and gold, with garish mirrors and strip lighting, Vietnam II seems like an outcrop of Chinatown. Its tanks are full of fighting crabs and catfish, and there's a large koi pond where doomed fish swim beside a bamboo forest. It specializes in pho, a comforting dish that food expert Richard Stirling calls "Vietnam in a bowl." Vietnam II's is among the best, and you can buy a steaming bowl for less than $6. Slurping this Vietnamese "penicillin" will open your eyes to a newer and fairer world.

Cost $12–35

Address 701 Larkin St at Ellis
(phone) 415/885-1274
Open Daily 8am–midnight
Transportation 19, 38, 49
Accepts MasterCard, Visa

Take this opulent, slightly viscous and fragrantly herbed beef broth, aswim with tiny spangles of spring onions, slivers of bird chile, and bean sprouts, then add to your large and colorful plastic bowl from piles of chopped mint, Asian basil, cilantro, and dark green chile pepper. It costs $5.38, and no explanation for that 38 cents is forthcoming. Another favourite here is sweet-and-sour prawn soup ($4.45), served in a veritable bath tub of a flowery plastic bowl, with fresh, fat prawns and chunks of Chinese fruits and vegetables—white eggplant, mango, chile peppers, pineapple, bok choy, and melon can be made out between the plentiful bobbing prawns. It's the first choice of local food guru Patricia Unterman, who also favors their salted fish with chicken-fried rice ($4.50), "number 148" as they call it. This is a Chinese rice dish and, again, it's a meal in itself. If you're not a fish eater, try the cha gio ($4.25), a starter of Vietnamese deep-fried imperial rolls with dipping sauce, and move on to pork over rice noodles ($5.25), or com ga nuong chao ($5.55), which is chicken on rice. And now for the sea cucumber ($4.25)! It's an interesting taste as well as an untested aphrodisiac but the texture may daunt the queasy diner. You would also need to be a fearless diner to try the shredded jellyfish ($5.25) which holds promising properties.

As a long-established cornerstone of the Loin's Little Saigon, Vietnam II is one of a row of traditional Vietnamese outlets that once lined Larkin Street, though many have moved further west to New Chinatown.

Chinatown

Alfred's Steak House

As long as there are conventions and businessmen in this town, Alfred's delivers what the red-corpuscled set wants: juicy slabs of corn-fed beef, massive enough for a heavyweight champ. Founded by an Italian waiter in 1928, this landmark steak house has been a fixture of downtown dining ever since. With a menu that has hardly changed—it still does pig's feet, ultra-dry martinis, and over a hundred labels of whisky—Alfred's serves food that vegetarians and San

Cost $15–50
Address 659 Merchant St
☎ 415/781-7058
Open Mon & Sun 5.30–9.30pm Tues–Thurs 11.30am–9.30pm, Fri 11.30am–9pm, Sat 5.30–9pm
Transportation BART Montgomery St
Accepts All major credit cards except Diners

Franciscans almost never see but out-of-towners crave, especially on expenses. From the clubby feel of the mirrors and dark wood paneling, to rich red walls and damasked tables, the interior breathes stability and permanence. Alfred's moved to its current niche under the Transamerica Pyramid in the late 1990s, and some old-timers still grouch about the move, but it's in the right place for its clientele.

Steak is the story, of course, but the list of other dishes begins with a Caesar salad ($7.95 as a lunch dish, $5.75 as a side dish for dinner), modestly proclaimed "the city's best". Freshly made tableside with coddled egg, garlic, and anchovies according to each customer's taste, it's theatrical and lavish. Cut to the steaks: they are of every kind, from a lunch-sized "petite filet mignon" with Cabernet sauce ($15.95), to a New York steak with green peppercorn sauce ($14.95). Alfred's is heavily stocked with malt whiskies, so it's not surprising they serve steak filet tips with Maker's Mark Bourbon sauce ($15.95). For Texans, they fatten up a chicken-fried steak ($12.95), a cholesterol-defying and homey battered slab smothered in thickened gravy juices, served with garlicky mashed potatoes. At dinnertime, a tenderloin "King" steak ($49.95) weighs in at almost a kilo, with "petite" at 8 ounces ($22.75) or "executive" at 10 ounces ($26.75). There's scarcely room for it, but creamy spinach ($5.95) makes the best accompaniment, along with scalloped, nutmeg-topped potatoes ($3.95).

The City Dinner ($22.50, with soup, steak, and Caesar) and Prom Dinner (chateaubriand, martini, and bottle of wine for two; price varies) are Alfred's specials. The wine list starts around $20 and is fruity, with red Zinfandels, Pinot Noirs, and Cabernets to accompany this heroic fare. And who needs dessert?

Brandy Ho's

Brandy Ho's is one of those places San Franciscans take for granted, an authentic old-time Chinatown standby that's bright, noisy and dependable. Business here is almost entirely from repeat diners, for whom "spicy" means outright Krakatoan. Conveniently central but somehow easy to overlook, it offers some of Gold Mountain's hottest food at its kindest prices. Young visitors make for the hugely popular House of Nanking nearby, thus sparing Brandy's for locals with fireproof tastebuds and a yen for harvest pork. Granted, Brandy's is unpretentious as it gets, from its slightly worn tiles and counter, to the rickety little wipe-down tables. But Jack Ho's welcome is warm, and service is swift. Sitting at the counter and watching the cooks smack their woks about with one hand while chopping fearlessly with the other is fun and instructive.

Cost	$6–20

Address 217 Columbus Ave
☎415/788-7527
Open Daily 11.30am–11pm
Transportation 15, 30 BART
Montgomery St
Accepts All major credit cards
except Diners

This is Hunan cooking for the five-spice addict, and it's rumored that Brandy's recipes come from Henry Chung's mother, founder of the original Hunan restaurant on Sansome nearby. So "mild" means hot and "hot" is hotter than Hades; best to tell them to go easy on that chile and, even if you love chile, hedge your bets. Lunch specials are a bargain $5.95 and include Brandy's utterly moreish onion cake, but it's a baby canapé version only. So blow a couple of bucks on extra orders of their regular-sized onion cake ($1.75 each), a frisbee-sized disk of layered and gilded crunch. Stewed beef noodles ($7.50) contain chunks of home-cured beef and home-cured cabbage in an aromatic broth—unpeppered, but with Brandy's trademark, a remarkable flash of star anise. Harvest pork ($6.95) is a house-smoked mound of pinkish, tender morsels that show how well the spices adapt to the honey-glazed pork.

No actual brandy gets drunk at Brandy's, but green tea ice cream ($2) and jasmine tea or Tsingao beer round off dinner. Years ago, Brandy's brother Jack and his wife opened an upscale Brandy's on Broadway, next to the Helmand and up against the strip joints. With its spare decor and faultless presentation, it was classier and pricier. But location or concept or both killed the Broadway Brandy's. Luckily we still have this one.

Empress of China

(icon) Like a rather grand old lady with fal-
tering manners, the Empress does-
n't try very hard. She doesn't have to,
because she's a firm fixture in "Gold
Mountain," the oldest Chinese name for
San Francisco. You could film key scenes
from Amy Tan's "The Joy Luck Club" or
relocate Ang Lee's "The Wedding
Banquet" here—and in fact many local
weddings and feasts do take place at this
1960s relic, because the Empress is undeniably sumptuous. For its enormous decorative mirrors, its stunning sixth-floor panorama above the
hustle and bustle of Grant Street, and for a wealth of sentimental reasons, it remains a popular haunt.

Cost $12–30

Address 838 Grant Ave
(T) 415/434-1345
Open Mon–Sat 11.30am–3pm
& 5–10.30pm, Sun
11.30am–10.30pm
Transportation 12, 15, 45,
BART Montgomery St
Accepts All major credit cards

Old standbys from Cantonese cuisine dominate, and there's a special
emphasis on fish and shellfish, with northeastern and Mongolian meat
dishes as well. Prawns with fresh vegetables ($16) or honeyed prawns
with walnuts ($16) are popular starters, and there's a version with
chicken called phoenix and dragon ($14), a disconcertingly eclectic
combination of chickens, prawns, and walnuts. But set menus are the
rule, and the all-in lunch menu ($11.50) of soup with pork or one other
meat dish is reasonably priced. Alternatively, plump for one or other of
the set menus: the Empress ($13.50) offers three courses, including soup,
pork, and beef, or chicken; the Princess ($17.95) has an additional
wonton; while the Empress Delight ($21.95) offers five courses, with
Shantung smoked chicken and a potsticker. Menu choices include classics, like the Peking pressed duck, but also feature disappointingly
Westernized dishes like almond and cashew Three Princess chicken, or
frankly tourist-friendly dishes like sweet-and-sour pork, barbecued
Manchurian beef, or a not so tongue-scorching version of Szechwan
beef. Barbecued meats like the quail or the thousand-blossom Mongolian lamb are straight classics and make the best choices.

When it opened forty years ago, the Empress was elegant and ground-
breaking, but San Franciscans knew much less about Chinese food then.
Now, thanks to food writer James Baird, that has changed. The Empress
may remind you nostalgically of the first Chinese food you ever ate,
back in the days when the very words "chow mein" and "sweet-and-
sour-pork" sounded exotic to the suggestible infant ear.

Grand Palace

(🍴) Newspaper tycoon and local matriarch Florence Fang's dim sum
palace and restaurant lies in the heart of
Chinatown. With an interesting old
Chinese style interior that incorporates
round tables and gilt-edged mirrors, it
draws a mixed clientele of locals and visitors alike. One of the curious things
about the place is a large street stall of

Cost $10–35	

Address 950 Grant Ave at
Pacific
☏ 415/982-3705
Open Daily 8am–10.30pm
Transportation 12, 15
Accepts MasterCard, Visa

Chinese pornography just at the door; it's also next to a couple of well-
stocked Chinese kitchen equipment shops, much frequented by cooks
searching for woks and cleavers. Which all contributes to the local color.

At lunchtime, dim sum rules, with a good roster of choices, priced per
serving at or around a very reasonable $2.50. The local delicacy of
steamed chicken feet with black bean sauce ($2.20), however, come at a
knockdown price. Steamed and baked barbecued pork buns are squashy
and delectable. Spring rolls and baked egg custard tartlets are offered
with other familiar choices, like the shrimp dumpling (this version
comes with leek), eggplant with shrimp, steamed egg yolk bun, steamed
beef balls, and a rubbery lotus-seed bun. There are also a couple of comparative rarities, such as beef tripe with ginger and scallion, and bean
cake with oyster sauce. Less common delicacies, such as steamed rice
crêpe with shrimp, or sticky rice with chicken in a lotus leaf come at a
higher price—of $3.50. Dim sum is a daytime-only menu here and
gives way to the a la carte menu by 3pm. The evening menu features the
ubiquitous potstickers ($4.50) or moo shu pork ($8.50), but also some
unusual selections, among them deep-fried squid and deep-fried oysters
($8.95), and Cantonese specialties like shredded crab with shark fin soup
($32), or clay pot dishes like eight immortal bean curd ($9.95). But dim
sum is what Grand Palace is known for and it makes a splendid introduction for newcomers.

Although this is not the longest dim sum list in the city, it's impressive
nonetheless, and good value. Most fearless adult diners find it to be an
ideal first-experience dim sum, utterly exotic in ambiance yet not completely alien. Kids, however, are liable to go "Awww, gross!" as soon as
they see the chicken feet.

Great Eastern Restaurant

Of all the great Chinatown establishments, this palace of seafood is the most authentically Cantonese, if hardly the cheapest. As in Hong Kong restaurants, you walk into a large neon-lit room with a back wall lined with fish tanks, and peer into row upon row of finned and scaled marine life of every species, from crayfish to abalone, via scallops, sea cucumbers, sea bass, and jellyfish. Point at the crab or red snapper or lobster of your choice and have the staff fish it out and take it into the kitchen for a speedy dispatch, or take your seat at a big round formica table in one of the gaudy green-and-gold booths while they bring a flapping fish over for your approval. The finny roll call changes daily: do check the list on the wall for the catch *du jour*, sold by weight. If the tanks make you queasy, rest assured that executions are performed discreetly in the kitchen.

Cost $15–40

Address 649 Jackson St
☎ 415/986-2500
Open Daily 11am–1am
Transportation 1, 15, 30, 45, BART Montgomery St
Accepts All major credit cards except Diners

Whole steamed fish of the day is the unbeatable first choice, as are any of the steamed, cracked crab dishes, served as simply as possible with dishes of sweet-and-sour and Hoisin sauce on the side (for sharing, $28). Airy shrimp balls make a yummy starter ($9) as do prawn dumplings ($9); both are also on combination menus. Prawns come jumbo-sized and heavily garlicked in several versions, including one with an ambrosial pink seafood sauce ($9). Seared scallops and prawns ($17) are piled mountainously upon the plate. The fearless diner will wade straight into elaborate jellyfish or sea cucumber combinations, or even cuttlefish.

Be careful not to give yourself away as a complete tourist rube, since the frantic pace in here means that waiters won't be able to second-guess your heart's desire. So if you don't know what to order, walk around the other tables to look discreetly over shoulders, or go for the combination meals. Alternatively, just ask for the freshest fish from the list. Large banqueting tables down below make this a good choice for a party of conventioneers. Not for the picky, perhaps, but it's definitely a real Chinatown experience.

Hang Ah Tea Room

The Hang Ah's big claim to fame, and it's no idle claim, is that it's the oldest dim sum parlor in San Francisco. Nobody knows *quite* how old it is, but the walls are hung with newspaper photographs of faded beauty queens, labeled "Miss Chinatown," going back to the forties and fifties. Since so many places claim to be the "oldest" this or "first" that, you might feel skeptical. But nobody has ever disputed the Hang Ah's boast, because the tiny parlor, tucked away down steps in a back alley, is so visibly ancient.

Cost $6–8

Address 1 Hang Ah St,
Pagoda Place, off Stockton
☎415/982-5686
Open Daily 11am–9pm
Transportation 1, 30, 45
Accepts Cash only

A few wobbly tables are set for dim sum, and the bustling chef-owner tells you what she's not offering today. There's not much choice: the dim sum special menu is short, sweet, and costs $5.95 for the six-item special menu. It starts with familiar ha gao (prawn dumplings), pingpong-ball-sized steamed parcels containing fat prawns wrapped in the thinnest potato-wheat dough. Like the sew mai (pork dumplings), barbecue-filled cha xiu bao buns, spring rolls, potstickers, and barbecued pork rice that follow, it has a homemade taste—not surprisingly, since it was made in-house by hand. No room for fleets of trolleys in here, but these half-dozen dim sum items are tasty mouthfuls, snacks that also come with a filling plate of pork rice, a fortune cookie (a San Francisco invention, from the nearby Mee-Mee Bakery), and plentiful jasmine tea. If, on the other hand, you want a bigger meal, go for the dinner menu—unvarying every night—of moo shu (sweet-and-sour) pork with fried rice, served with a choice of chicken and vegetable appetizers, plus fortune cookie and tea. For just $6.50.

If you want to pull out all the stops, you can add your choice of three dim sum items and a small plate of foil-wrapped chicken, plus a curried beef roll, to that mo shu pork; all of this comes on a combination menu for $7.95. It's guaranteed you won't be hungry afterwards. But be careful who to bring to the Hang Ah: not everyone appreciates alleyways, and this is one place in Chinatown where rigorous modernization appears to have made no inroads—thankfully.

House of Nanking

(🍴) Despite its lack of pretension and obvious need for a paint job, House of Nanking enjoys long queues every night. It's not that the food is gourmet, but Peter Fang's cooking is inventive. In the odd-shaped spot he and wife Lily run single-handed, he's on call to dish it up endlessly, and in a minuscule space. But because it takes so long to get in, people generally relax, open up and have a

Cost $5–25

Address 919 Kearny St at Columbus
☎ 415/421-1429
Open Mon–Fri 11am–10pm, Sat noon–10pm, Sun 4–10pm
Transportation 15
Accepts Cash only

sociable time once they make it to one of the half-dozen or so hanky-sized tables or counter stools. Presumably, this effect comes from sheer relief, or maybe because of those ice-cold Tsingaos drunk straight from the bottle (no glasses supplied). Naturally, when you're so on top of your neighbor that you have to get out of your chair and pick up your plate to let them in and out, you're pally in no time.

But you can have a really good time here, leaving well fed and almost none the poorer. The Fangs strive mightily to keep prices down and to that end they use all the cheaper local ingredients, with everything chopped and fried in front of the madding crowd two feet away from them. Peter Fang gets up every morning and basically invents a bunch of dishes out of his own imagination, using whatever's to hand on Stockton Street; he goes shopping frequently because there's no space to keep another fridge. Nanking starters include his taco-like deep-fried rice pancakes filled with seafood ($4.95), and a Chinese version of salsa made with peanuts ($4.95). Fish soup ($4.95) is a scratch invention that frequently gets onto the menu. Hotter-than-hell Szechwan dishes are made with very non-Szechwan ingredients like broccoli ($7.95) in a tongue-scorching chile gravy. Peter's Shanghai dumplings are stuffed with vegetables and steamed ($5.95); he also makes a chicken version ($7.95) accompanied with fresh, local, black, sweet cherries, and ginger sauce.

The portions are another draw here: the mainly young, generally student-age and one-hundred-percent Caucasian regulars do immediate justice to the mountainous platefuls of rice that come with everything, and then look for more, well aware of the fact that the Fangs give best bang for their meager bucks.

Lucky Creation

Vegans and vegetarians have two choices in Chinatown that omnivores will enjoy too. One is the quiet and reliable Lotus Garden, at 582 Grant Avenue, housed above a shop with a Buddhist temple upstairs. Younger visitors, however, always find Lucky Creation a sparkier environment, with its worn-down jumble of communal tables—you may have to share—and its casual atmosphere. And the food, along with the Tenderloin's Golden Era or the Richmond's Bok Choy, is perhaps the most innovative vegetarian fare on offer anywhere.

Cost $5–10

Address 854 Washington St at Grant Ave
℡ 415/989-0818
Open Mon, Tues & Thurs–Sun 11am–10pm
Transportation 1, 15, 45
Accepts MasterCard, Visa

The recipe for all the clever meat imitations at Lucky Creation is not always tofu, that staple of Lotus Garden and so many other vegetarian places. It's their wheat (or rather a protein derivative from wheat starch) that's used, just like tofu, to make fake chicken, fake pork, and fake beef, even fake seafood. If this stuff has a name, it's wheat gluten. You'll also find mashed and fried taro dishes, some tofu, and different nut dishes on the interesting menu. Clay pot dishes (from $4.95) are their forte, however, and they make a trademark vegetarian version of all the standards, adding lots of vegetables and noodles to the stews. Some diners, however, and not just vegetarians, may prefer avowedly non-"meat" dishes such as the white fungus and corn soup ($2.95), or taro dishes such as mashed taro puffs in bean and chile sauce ($4.95), a curious but delicious combination of bland and hot. Another winner is the specially cured and extra-sharp sweet-and-sour walnuts ($3.95). You can't go wrong, either, with grilled eggplant ($5.95), served in that same bean chile, a mix of gold-crisped skin and creamy flesh allied with the fire and dark intensity of the sauce.

This is a simple, unpretentious and sometimes loud spot, where young vegetarians are likely to be contented (especially with the prices), while other folks may wish they'd found the Lotus Garden's prayer wheels instead. Don't come if you're looking for peace, in other words. Come here if you want interesting food without any hint of animal products, and are prepared to put up with discomfort to get just that.

New Asia

(🍴) This Chinatown palace seats almost a thousand when locals crowd in here at weekends. Huge, happy gatherings eat dim sum from revolving "lazy Susans" loaded with steamer baskets and dipping sauces, replenished constantly from the passing trolleys. The cavernous space, vast chandeliers and slightly glitzy decor of the New Asia makes it look more like a ballroom for "Come Dancing" rather than a home from

Cost S8–20

Address 772 Pacific Ave at Grant
☎ 415/391-6666
Open Daily 9am–3pm & 5–9pm
Transportation 12, 15
Accepts All major credit cards except Diners

home for hunkering down around big tables to stuff yourselves *en famille*. The upstairs balcony is handy for quieter gatherings and gives you an overall view of the hectic, colorful scene. The women wheeling the trolleys tend to speak little English, but you can point at plates or pictures, or even resort to the friendly manager for translations.

Since this is a "yum cha," or teahouse for snacks, you'll get a pot of piping jasmine tea when you sit down, and it will be replenished constantly. Make no mistake, gigantic and gaudy New Asia may be but this is a superior dim sum parlor, and it's justifiably popular. Unlike smaller rivals, it maintains an extra-large staff to man the trolleys, and the list of choices is long. Customers are mainly Chinese American, so you'll find the kind of dim sum that connoisseurs love. In addition to their very fingerlickin' spare ribs in bean sauce (xi jap jing pai gwat), come squashy pork buns (cha xiu bao), tender shrimp dumplings (ha gao), and the deep-fried pork and noodle spring rolls (chun guen) so dear to San Francisco hearts. Chicken feet, or xi jap fung zao, are just that, fried until crispy and served in a sweetish black bean dressing. They look off-putting, but savoring the juicy flavor by sucking is the correct way to attack, and may convert you on the spot. The little egg tartlets, or daad tad, are the nearest thing to a sweet dessert.

All dim sum plates are priced between $3 and $3.50 per portion, and are not served after 3pm. Evening dishes are stir-fries, duck, and chicken standards, and are reasonably priced. New Asia isn't the most upscale or exotic dim sum parlor, nor the oldest nor, for all the chandeliers, the fanciest. But it is the most fun.

R&G Lounge

A block or so off touristy Grant Street is Chinese Chinatown, where life in "Gold Mountain" hasn't changed that much over the decades. R&G fills the pivotal role of community center, hosting vast family groups at long tables in its barn-like basement. Chef-owner Kinson Wong and partner Joe Ling reportedly added their upstairs parlor after an invasion of seafood connoisseurs came in search of the authentic food. Supposedly, they jostled the regulars in their search for fresh lobster and crab, complaining about dangling televisions, glaring lights, and the general lack of atmosphere. So to please the dual clientele, the owners split the house into upstairs and downstairs, issuing double Chinese/English menus with separate pages. The upstairs is their "front parlor," carpeted and tableclothed for those seeking a little more elegance; there's a separate side entrance to the downstairs, especially popular while $5 lunch specials are being served.

Cost $7–15
Address 631 Kearny St at Sacramento
☎ 415/982-7877
Open Mon–Thurs 10.30am–9.30pm, Fri 10.30am–10pm, Sat 11.30am–10.30pm, Sun 11.30am–9.30pm
Transportation 1, 12, 15
Accepts All major credit cards

It's interesting to speculate how different the menus might be, though both feature fresh seafood out of R&G's tanks, prepared very swiftly and usually roasted. If you ask your servers what's good they'll usually direct you to the salt-and-peppered shrimps and crabs. "Salt-and-pepper" frying involves a spice dip of Szechwan pepper (fragrant, lighter) mixed with salt and star anise. Shrimp ($8.50) are dipped into this and served heads and all, while crabs ($13) are roasted or stir-fried. You'll also find the usual potstickers and egg rolls, but it's a shame not to try the shrimp. R&G is famous, too, for its clay pot dishes, and in particular for the five-plus-one-spice oxtail clay pot ($13), and the beef brisket clay pot ($13), stewed gently with star anise and onions.

You won't always manage to luck into the thousand-year egg rumored to be served here, but the two-hour validated parking makes it easy enough to come back and try again. R&G's sister place, Gold Mountain, is a big and bustling dim sum parlor in the Ocean City building on Broadway. "Gold Mountain" was the old Cantonese name for San Francisco, used by immigrants who came to build railways but who first suffered exclusion and even incarceration on Angel Island.

Sam Wo

You don't come to Sam's for fine dining, you come here because it's an ancient landmark beloved by backpackers, boozers, and those on a budget. Time-worn, true, but it's also haunted by the ghosts of the Beat poets who scarfed chow mein here for a dollar, as well as that of Edsell Wong, Sam's long-serving waiter of legendary rudeness. Chow mein is now $4.95. The owner beckons you in through the front door and past the kitchen, where loud whacking noises set the tone. You tumble up steep, narrow staircases to two Dickensian garrets above, with indeterminate orangey pink walls, a few old cut-out calendar pictures and posters, and wobbly tables that all need a folded-up napkin jammed under one leg. Not only is the decor funky, but the food arrives very slowly on a dumbwaiter, heralded by a rude buzzer, and just when you are about to despair. These days the buzzer is the only rude thing around Sam's.

Cost	$5–10

Address 815 Washington St at Grant
☎ 415/982-0596
Open Mon–Sat 11am–3am
Transportation 1, 12, 15, 30, 45
Accepts Cash only

When the food does finally arrive you will feel immediately cheered, even if it's mainly by the amazingly low prices. Chicken noodle soup ($3) is bland but can be doctored up with several soy and chile sauces at hand. Barbecued pork rolls ($2.50) with chopped cilantro and Chinese mustard on the side are a standout. The beef broccoli over rice plate is a mere $4.95 for the standard, quickly stir-fried version, while the fried rice with bits of shrimp in it is also $4.95, and again requires additional seasoning. But since almost all the main dishes are wok-fried noodle or rice-based duck, chicken, or pork stir-fries, and none costs over $5, you will have nothing to complain about. You could be full to bursting, in fact, for less than $10.

Since Sam's is open until 3am, it attracts nightcrawlers who are loudly elated and want the world to know why. Their bumptiousness might be the reason for the eventual death of the long-suffering Edsell, who was older than the century when he joined the choir celestial. But the Beats have conferred immortality upon both Edsell and Sam's, and it will never close.

Tommy Toy's Cuisine Chinoise

As the West Coast's imperial palace of "haute Chinoise," Tommy Toy's exudes an atmosphere of hushed oriental splendor that you're unlikely to find elsewhere in Chinatown, or maybe anywhere else at all. Through ultra-discreet lighting you discern Ming vases, silk hangings, and exquisite antiques wherever you look, and may feel for a second as though you've strayed onto the set of *The Last Emperor*. Tommy Toy's isn't shy of showing off the celebrities that have

Cost $35–60
Address 655 Montgomery St at Merchant
☎ 415/397-4888
Open Mon–Fri 11.30am–2.30pm & 6–9.30pm, Sat & Sun 6–9.30pm
Transportation 1, 15 BART Montgomery St
Accepts All major credit cards

eaten here, either—yes, sigh, another Mick Jagger sighting, folks. You'll definitely feel underdressed if you're not actually in a suit or formal attire here. If the wine list prices make you faint, the ingratiating waiters will take pity and mention the prix fixe and special deals.

As an enthralling hybrid of Mandarin and French, the food is entirely its own kind of art form. It's wallet searing too, but that special tasting menu they'll tell you about is definitely worth it because it includes their most sensational creations. The ballyhooed signature dishes are nothing short of amazing. An exquisite seafood bisque ($15) comes in an antique-looking coconut bowl, topped with a lid of feather-light phyllo; fragrant as summer spray off the ocean. The minced squab ($7.95) come in the form of spring rolls, encased first in lettuce leaves and then in transparently thin rice paper; each mouthful a delight. There's nothing but good to say about the next dish on the special prix fixe menu either, a shredded and tossed pasta of East Coast lobster ($12.95), fried with peppered shiitake mushrooms and pinole nuts on cellophane vermicelli. After that comes a very tender roast Peking duck ($24.95), and after *that* some fried rice—but what fried rice!—and finally some kind of tropical mousse or sorbet ($5.95).

The tasting dinner is $49.50, and an amplified, blowout version is eight dollars more. Tommy Toy's is much favored by out-of-town businessmen, as well as visiting stars, and you can see why. When you want valet parking (only $3.50), discreet lighting and to be generally spoiled to near-death, there's Tommy Toy's.

Yuet Lee

When French film star Gérard Départieu and French minister Jack Lang were in town, they hung out in Yuet Lee for a week, eating until all hours and even cooking here too. A corner diner full of bustle, painted screaming neon green with glaring overhead strip lighting, Yuet Lee is noticeably cheap. Best of all, it stays open until 3am, an ever-ready beacon for late-night clubbers and fun lovers. Despite the manifest unlikeliness of the setting, Messieurs Départieu and Lang maintained it had the very best seafood in Chinatown, and came back to this unpretentious dive night after night.

Cost $6–30
Address 1300 Stockton Street at Broadway
☎ 415/982-6020
Open Mon & Wed–Sun 11am–3pm
Transportation Powell St cable car
Accepts Cash only

The number one thing to do in here is to sit down and hope for service. It will be brisk and cheery, whenever it comes, and you'll get honest recommendations. Yuet Lee offers a section of clay pot dishes in addition to its famous salt-and-pepper prawns ($13.95) and salt-and-pepper squid ($9.95), which are deep-fried until they are tender bites of briny bliss, dashed with diced peppers and topped with lemon. Pepper-and-salt sautéed scallops ($15.50) are another zinger, along with that odd but prized creature, the geoduck clam ($20), which is dished up with "boneless duck feet". As well as the occasional lobster, Dungeness crabs (around $25) are the top choice—in the November to March season. Fished from the tank and steamed, they're served cracked and accompanied by Tsingao beer or giant bowls of well-lemoned tea, or cooked in a clay pot with silver noodles and satay sauce, or stir-fried with a sensational ginger and black bean sauce. In short, this is no place for fish haters or, for that matter, vegetarians, though they may accept the vegetable chow mein ($6), which is standard Americanized fare; it also comes in chicken ($5.75), prawn ($6.50), sliced sturgeon ($6.25), and Chef's Special versions ($6).

Don't on any account mention to the squeamish that Yuet Lee also serves steamed frogs ($18), and many and varied tripe and intestine dishes (from $6). Not everybody will be thrilled by the air of nonchalant chaos, either. The message is clear: bring fearless diners and night crawlers like Gérard and Jacques only.

North Beach

NORTH BEACH

N

FRANCISCO STREET

Albona Ristorante Istriano

Zax

CHESTNUT STREET

Buca Giovanni

LOMBARD STREET

North Beach Playground

GREENWICH STREET

Trattoria Contadina

Church of St Peter & Paul

Washington Square Park

FILBERT STREET

Cobalt Tavern

Moose's
Mario's Bohemian
Cigar Store

UNION STREET

NORTH BEACH

Penal PachaMama

Fugazi Hall

Il Pollaio

Rose Pistola

Calzone

Café Jacqueline

Bocce Café

Capp's Corner

GREEN STREET

Ina Coolbrith Park

North Beach Museum

L'Osteria del Forno

VALLEJO STREET

Finocchio Club

Enrico's Sidewalk Café

The Helmand

Stinking Rose

BROADWAY

City Lights Bookstore

Black Cat & Blue Bar

JACK KEROUAC ST

Tommaso's

PACIFIC AVENUE

Vesuvio's

Café Prague

Coit Tower

Pioneer Park

FILBERT STEPS

TELEGRAPH HILL

STOCKTON STREET

GRANT AVENUE

KEARNY STREET

MONTGOMERY STREET

SANSOME STREET

TAYLOR STREET

MASON STREET

Powell-Mason Cable Car

POWELL STREET

0   200 yds

Albona Ristorante Istriano

Dining at the Albona is like visiting Bruno Viscovi for supper in his own parlor, except for the bill. It's a cozy little room on a rundown block slightly beyond the heart of North Beach, not big enough to seat more than twenty or so, and unabashedly old-fashioned in mood. Smaller tables allow intimacy for the romantic; the rest of the room offers round tables for jolly parties of five to

Costs $30–60

Address 545 Francisco St
☎415/441-1040
Open Tues–Sat 5–10.30pm
Transportation 15, F,
Powell–Mason cable car
Accepts All major credit cards
except Diners

ITALIAN

eight diners. If you fail to reserve, Bruno sends you to the bar next door in the Hotel San Remo for aperitifs and munchies. He calls for you later, then sits you down to tell you what was in the market that morning. Out-of-towners and regulars with gutsy appetites will love the Albona if they appreciate rustic Istrian food with the extra spice that reveals Bruno's Balkan roots.

Bruno's palate originates from Istria, that part of the northern Adriatic that was by turn Venetian, Austro-Hungarian, Italian and, more recently, part of Yugoslavia. His cuisine combines rustic pastas and risottos with game and fish. Former Yugoslavs, the waiters hover gently while Bruno sells you on the de rigueur house appetizer of chifeletti ($13), pan-fried potato gnocchi in a lusty sirloin tips sauce, or simple pomodoro. His chifeletti are renowned: resembling potato balls or croquettes, they are airier than gnocchi, with strong hints of nutmeg and cumin. Brodetto Istriano ($17.25), another specialty, is an Adriatic bouillabaisse. Lamb ($16.50) wears a deliciously spicy cumin sauce, while pork ($16.50) is stuffed with apple and comes with sauerkraut. Albona's risotto is a creamy platonic ideal, especially the prosciutto and mushroom ($13.75). Raviolis ($13.50) arrive in cumin-scented sirloin tips sauce, or sage butter with pine nuts and raisins, or three cheeses. Viscovi also features venison and rabbit on a regular basis, done in the Austro-Hungarian way with juniper berries and honey ($17.75), or alla cacciatore ($16.75), with olives and sweet peppers. Orange and ginger crème brûlées just pass muster ($6).

You can leave contented for $30 per head, but Albona is definitely worth a splurge. A blow-out for two with a couple of great Chiantis will take a hearty chomp out of twice that amount.

Black Cat and Blue Bar

When prizewinning chef and restaurant entrepreneur Reed Hearon, of LuLu's and Rose Pistola, first bought the formerly rundown Black Cat coffee bar—a boho cafe from the Beats era—he made some sophisticated additions, including black cherry booths and mirrored ceilings. Somehow, though, it seemed more about concept than character. So two years ago he tried again, and now the snaking, glamorous length of metalworker Doug Hellikson's new zinc bar is the reigning star. At one end it's a raw bar with shellfish and desserts, at the other it curves into a wood-fired rotisserie. Behind a wall-to-ceiling wine library. Black Cat barmen get plenty of practice at cosmopolitans, Manhattans and martinis, and also debriefing customers. Think of it as a kind of stage, where women in Blahnik heels sit comparing vodka cocktails and fearlessly sampling crustaceans. All you need is Veronica Lake in her blue velvet snood.

Oh yes, the food! Scott Warner's menu is a marine hodgepodge mixed with bistro French. Oysters include tiny, plump, sweet Kumamotos ($1.85 each), Sinku Summer Ice from Japan ($1.95), and Caraquet, a saltier New Brunswick type that's a nickel cheaper than most places at $1.95. You're going to like the half-Maine lobster ($17) and the lavish trio of tartares ($10): tuna with olive-fennel, sea bass with tarragon-lemon, or salmon and cucumber. The calamari-heirloom tomato salad ($10) works because heirlooms are acidic enough to take on the calamari. For main dishes, the rotisserie roasts duck breast with caramelized onions ($24), a decent rabbit with chard and pine nuts ($18), and Watson pork aux chanterelles ($24). Fish of the day ($17–23) runs from salmon to halibut and back again plus a fat-tailed monkfish they call loup de mer ($27).

Cynics say that the Black Cat has been Pygmalionized so often that, on its ninth life, it doesn't know if it's Fifties Beats, fin-de-siècle, Parisian belle époque, the Venice Lido, or whatever. But a cinq-à-sept aperitif and appetizer is still very pleasant here. Another moment to savor is dessert hour, with profiteroles and hazelnut cake ($6–7). They even throw in fortune cookies with quotes from Ginsberg and Ferlinghetti!

FRENCH/SEAFOOD

Cost $20–45

Address 501 Broadway at Kearny
☎ 415/981-2233
Open Daily noon–2am
Transportation 12, 15
Accepts All major credit cards except Diners

Bocce Cafe

The principle charm of the ever-green Bocce is its outdoor patio at the back, a not-so-secret hideaway of overhanging vines and fairy lights that lures young and restless funseekers out on North Beach's rialto on pleasant nights. There's nothing sophisticated about it, but the approach to Bocce is appealing: a trellised passageway leads from an unmistakably Italian red, white, and green gateway to a roomy, warm-tiled interior where everyone feels at home and there's plenty of room.

Cost $7–30

Address 478 Green St
☎ 415/981-2044
Open Daily 11am–11pm
Transportation 15
Accepts All major credit cards

Bocce's menu isn't sophisticated either, but it's wholeheartedly Italian. Lunchtime sandwiches ($6.50) are thick and filling, with sausage, chicken, and vegetable. Supper starts with minestrone ($3.95) and bruschetta ($3.25), or a carpaccio of thin-sliced raw beef in olive oil and capers ($5.95), or mussels bordelaise ($7.95), or mozzarella caprese ($7.95) with tomatoes, basil, and oregano. The antipasti ($11.95) delivers a handsome platter of mozzarella, roast eggplant, sliced bologna, and mortadella, with assorted roast peppers. The rest of the menu is utterly simple and homey. Pasta ($6.95) comes in ample portions. Pick from fettuccini, penne, spaghetti, or rigatoni, with a choice of sauces—Bolognese, roast garlic, primavera, zucchini, sausage with marinara, alfredo, pesto, carbonara, feta cheese, or mushroom cacciatore. Scaloppine, lasagne, salmon, and chicken dishes begin at a modest $12. A traditional cioppino ($18.95) is the most expensive item, a mighty stew of crab, prawns, salmon, calamari, clams, and mussels in a marinara sauce, served in a copper calabash with pasta on the side. This is a foolproof place to bring an unadventurous palate. Children, if they don't want spaghetti and meatballs ($8.95), will plump for ravioli in a cheese and meat sauce ($10.95). House Chianti classico begins at $15 a bottle or $4 per glass, while pinot grigio begins at $16 per bottle for a modest Veneto, and there's a sparkling prosecco ($22) as well.

The unchanging, honest nature of the food brings people back to Bocce Cafe. But on a romantic, balmy night, there's more than just the food to like about it. The garden just the other side of the windows beckons with its vines and lights and sturdy metal tables, a piano tinkles on the night air, and this feels like a grand place to be.

Buca Giovanni

Village-like and more laid back than touristy Chinatown or Fisherman's Wharf, North Beach is still the traditional home of good times in San Francisco. Plenty of old holes earn the tag "North Beach landmark," so what exactly does Giovanni do to distinguish his *buca*, or cave, from other familiar haunts? The answer is that he helps you beat the fogged-over blues. This is a cozy, romantic hideaway for warming yourself over rustic, lusty Piedmontese, or Tuscan dishes like rabbit stews. You'll see why the Buca hangs onto its regulars easily.

Cost $15–45
Address 800 Greenwich St at Mason
☎ 415/776-7766
Open Tues–Sat 5–10.30pm, Sun 4–10pm
Transportation 15, 30, Powell–Mason cable car
Accepts All major credit cards

Lucca-born Giovanni Leoni carved the restaurant from the basement of an old bakery back in the early 1970s, and the establishment pre-dates the food fads of subsequent years. So this isn't the kind of food to keep you thin, but it's extremely satisfying. Some dishes are resonatingly good. Upstairs is the tiny prep room where starters like beef carpaccio with capers, arugula, and truffle oil ($8.25), green-lip mussels from New Zealand in rosemary, wine, and tomato sauce ($8.25), bruschetta ($5.95) and assorted antipasti ($9.25) are whisked below, past a couple of extra tables near the entrance. To follow, come the aforementioned baby rabbit stews, one of them grappa-stewed and justifiably legendary ($15.95); another is "con nereb" ($18.95), with olives, sage, and polenta. (One question: why must it always be "baby rabbit?" Why not "fulfilled, super-annuated and suicidal rabbit?") A dozen or so pastas include excellent homemade raviolis, among which the one filled with ricotta and spinach in sage pomodoro ($14.95) is particularly good, as is the one filled with wild mushrooms and veal in a pepper and walnut cream sauce ($16.95). The usual panna cotta or tiramisu follow for dessert, plus an especially good torta di lemone with berries and cream (all $6.95).

Until quite recently, Leoni raised his own rabbits along with herbs and vegetables, and roasted his own coffee. Nowadays the kitchen belongs to Brooklyn native Michael Alfieri, but Buca Giovanni hasn't started doing anything newfangled. On a chilly summer's evening, it's hard to imagine anything more cheering than a brisk stroll down Columbus Avenue for an aperitif, before heading downstairs to this cozy cave.

Cafe Jacqueline

Can you never have too much of a good thing after all? And is a feast actually much better than enough? Chef-owner Jacqueline Margulis has come up with a unique twist upon the "do one thing and do it well" maxim. Nothing could be cuter than her little spot, with its white linen and red roses, soft lighting and plank flooring—unless it's her clever menu. At this postage stamp of a cafe off Grant, she has invented a three-course menu entirely based on soufflés, designed to suit her oven and her limited space. Airy and lofty and feather-light from starter to main dish to dessert, all her soufflés come to share, and they are all made on the spot. Just one or two soups or salads precede them, items that take the same time to eat that a soufflé takes to rise.

Cost $30–50

Address 1454 Grant Ave at Green
℗ 415/981-5565
Open Wed–Sun 5.30–11pm
Transportation 15, 30
Accepts All major credit cards except Diners

The obvious starter is a gruyère soufflé that wraps you in an enticing waft of smoky, milky cheese and egg before you even lay eyes on it. It's served with crusty baguette and costs a somewhat puffed-up $20, but feeds two. The gruyère soufflé is a kind of basic building block on Jacqueline's menu, which also contains variations like vegetables, herbs, crab, artichoke, or porcini mushrooms, as well as more recherché items that rise to a teetering $30 in price. The dessert soufflé has to be pre-planned to arrive in time, but nobody will resist the dark or white chocolate version, oozing melted chocolate from deep within and served with cream. Fresh peach, strawberry, and other fruit soufflés are also on offer, while the liquor-enhanced numbers like Bailey's or Cointreau ($30) are standouts.

The fact that each soufflé feeds two makes Jacqueline's an idyllic rendezvous *à deux*, especially after a pleasant meander around North Beach on a sunny Sunday afternoon, with the prospect of another one back under the stars. The final check will indeed be fluffed up, and not quite so airy-fairy, but by that stage you'll have stars in your eyes and be feeling entirely at one with the world.

Cafe Prague

(🍴) If cafes exist to stimulate intellectual curiosity and conversation, the curious, slightly surreal decor of Cafe Prague can only help. It exudes the tradition of Eastern European coffee houses, and feels like somewhere Kundera would come to write. Murals of the Charles Bridge, mirrors, a stopped clock on exposed brick walls, books in English and Czech left lying around the room—it

Cost $7–20	

Address 584 Pacific Ave at Columbus
☎ 415/433-3811
Open Daily 8am–midnight
Transportation 15, BART Montgomery Street
Accepts Cash only

all contributes to the unbearable hipness of being, and the general impression that this is the place to bring your laptop and kill the better part of a day in highly literate company. The cafe even keeps Czech newspapers. Plus there's all the beer you can handle, including Pilsner Urquell.

North Beach has its many legendary Italian cafes, like the Caffès Roma, Puccini, Trieste, and Malvina, all serving espressos and desserts, and all ideal stops before or after a meal. But the Prague is different, not just because it's Czech but because it's an all-rounder that serves lunchtime specials, soups and salads, dished up by the pleasant women at the counter. It even attempts crunchy muesli for breakfast, along with other brunch fare. Soups may include a shrimp bisque ($4.50) and organic tomato gnocchi ($3.50); they change daily and always feature one vegetarian option. Sandwiches are large; ordering a tuna melt ($7.95) brings a large plate of six-grain sourdough topped with lots of tuna and cheese, with salad on the side. A few good, simple salads ($4.50/5.75) come in two sizes. At weekends, you'll find eight or more Czech specialties posted on the blackboard behind the accordionist, from Gulás ($12)—flushed with fresh paprika, heavy with pork, and served with doughy dumplings—to fish dishes ($12–18) such as roast salmon or a prawn risotto. The Czech owners are at pains to get organic vegetables in season for their pastas and risottos. Among desserts, apricot strudel ($5) is a standout.

Come by weekend evenings if you want to try one of the impromptu Czech dinner menus, or to let your tastebuds find out exactly what a Staropramen Starobrno is (clue: think Czech national beverage), or even to hear live Czech accordion music.

Calzone

Calzone has its suspect touristy side, but it earns its popularity honestly. It has more than a couple of redeeming features, the most evident one being that it's a pleasant, easy-to-find place to wait for somebody at a sidewalk table with a Campari or espresso in one hand and a couple of postcards in the other. The eternal carnival of Columbus parades in front of you, which is not unentertaining. Another virtue is that you can order filling food here until all hours, and the bar is open later still. So if you find yourself with a raging appetite for pasta after listening to blues at the Saloon or some other local *boîte* in the midnight hour, Calzone's is a good solution.

Cost $15–35
Address 430 Columbus Ave at Vallejo
☎ 415/397-3600
Open Mon–Thurs & Sun 11am–1am, Fri & Sat 11am–3am
Transportation 15
Accepts All major credit cards

You can, of course, get calzone here. These are glorified pizza pockets, Italian-style empanadas that come filled with practically any kind of ingredient, from cheese or spinach to smoked chicken, ham, or beef. The smoked chicken is a tasty option. They solve a modest hunger pang but are a tad steeply pegged at $10.95. That's at the snack level, but there's also a short list of larger appetizers, such as a plate of stuffed Portobello mushrooms ($7.95), or roast garlic ($7.95). The assorted and varied pasta plates start at around $12; the angel hair with clams ($13.95) is particularly good. For dessert there's (yawn) tiramisu ($6) and, of course, a full selection of really good espressos and cappuccinos.

Calzone is pitched at visitors, but it can make other claims. Locals find it convenient, it's fun for people-watching, and the lighting upstairs is mercifully more dim than below—borderline romantic in fact, and great for big parties and reunions. The service is another plus: always swift, ever friendly. And this is about the only place in the neighborhood that can fully cater for a party of, say, over a dozen starving nightcrawlers on the trot who happen to be more in the mood for pasta with Chianti than, say, moo shu chicken and jasmine tea. That's enough of a claim already.

North Beach

Capp's Corner

When the Beat poets were looking for pasta at Tommaso's or jug wine at Mario's Bohemian Cigar Store, they were used to a very different world of dining. Nothing shows more how food has changed over the last half-century than a trip down Columbus Avenue and its side streets. But the old, family-style Italian joints in North Beach still soldier on, among them this venerable haunt. The hostess here is the famous ex-stripper Magnolia Thunderpussy and yes, her welcome is warm. Capp's exudes a gen-

Cost $12–25

Address 1600 Powell St at Green
☏ 415/989-2589
Open Mon–Thurs 11.30am–2.30pm & 4.30pm–10.30pm, Fri–Sat 4.30–11pm, Sun 4–10pm
Transportation 15, Powell–Mason cable car
Accepts All major credit cards except Diners

uine whiff of the 1950s, with its checkered tablecloths, long tables and wood-paneled walls hung with framed photos of visiting celebs like "Cassius Clay" and Rudolf Nureyev.

Family-style is the best way to describe Capp's prix fixe, four-course, steal-of-a-deal menu ($16.95). You start with minestrone (and yes, it will remind you of your mother's) or an iceberg salad with dressing on the side; then there's ribsticking spaghetti, meatballs, or lasagna; followed by chicken and beef choices; and finally striped spumone ice cream. The price falls to $15 if you drop the salad and soup course. An a la carte menu is also on offer at lunch and dinner, with such fancy items as roast pork in a creamy gravy ($15.50) or pan-fried catch of the day ($14). For a family on a budget this is the way to go, because the kids aren't going to complain about having to eat "fancy food" and there won't be any surprises. It's hardly gourmet, though people do salivate over their pasta al pesto ($9), and they've added more Chianti varieties to the wine list.

But if you have a large party of out-of-towners to entertain, including kids, bring them here and you'll go home full and feeling somehow richer. Capp's is also a no-brainer for a meal before or after "Beach Blanket Babylon," the institution of a show playing next door. Nobody knows how old Capp's is, but when they opened they painted the lyrics to Dorothy Fields' new song, "The Sunny Side of the Street", across the door. They painted it over a couple of years ago, but somehow you'll find yourself humming anyway.

Cobalt Tavern

(icon) Time was when this was the Washington Square Bar and Grill, where movers and shakers hung out to play pinochle on the counter. Venerable columnist Herb Caen came to "the Washbag" to see his pals Ed Moose and Peter Osborne, and the barman was Frank McCourt's brother Michael. Now the old lady has been completely revamped in shades of electric blue, with sophisticated tableware and whiffs of modernism in the pictures. New chef Guy Ferri has put a dashing new menu into place, with daily and seasonal variations, plus a well-considered wine list and nightly doses of live jazz. So why has it taken this long for nostalgia-mongers to get used to cool blue in place of hot reds, to cute boy waiters instead of Michael and those nice girls who called you "hon"?

Cost $20–50	
Address 1707 Powell St at Union	
☎ 415/982-8123	
Open Daily noon–midnight	
Transportation 15, 30, 45	
Accepts All major credit cards except Diners	

Ferri was a graduate of Stars, under Jeremiah Tower, and his new regime has something extra in the way of Stars-style glamor. Along with oysters on the half-shell ($1.95 each), there's white bean soup with pancetta and pesto ($6) and exciting salads like heirloom tomatoes with warm crostini and black olive tapenade ($8.50). The Napoleon of salmon tartare with crispy wontons ($8.50) is a mini-tower stacked with crunch, a hint of chile fire and delicious cucumber. Filling options are the confit of duck with braised French lentils and rhubarb compote ($9.50), a cod brandade gratin ($7.50), and wild mushroom strudel with greens ($8.50). For entrees there's wild king salmon ($18) and an interesting sweet pea risotto with wild mushrooms, tomatoes, lemon, and white truffle oil ($16). Grilled steak, roast pork, chicken, and leg of lamb make more conventional mains. Wine by the glass starts with an Australian Chardonnay, Oxford Landing ($5), on a short, interesting list that includes Wild Horse, a Malvasia from Monterey ($27), and Cakebread Sauvignon Blanc from Napa ($38).

All things must pass and it's time to stop grieving for the Washbag: Osborne has moved over to the ballpark and MoMo's, while Moose is the other side of Washington Park. Diners have come around, and while it's still early days, Cobalt seems to be creating its own fan following.

North Beach

Enrico's Sidewalk Cafe

With its tables corralled on the sidewalk offering terrific live jazz and a warmed-up view of passers-by, and its sweeping, glowing interior that includes a great semi-circular bar at one end, Enrico's has a classy elegance all its own. Yet it's also surrounded by seamy sex clubs. As such it's an authentic piece of San Francisco history—since 1958 it has held its own against the rising tide of porno joints on this strip. It was once frequented by those ever-thirsty Beats, too.

Cost $20–50
Address 504 Broadway at Kearny
☏ 415/982-6223
Open Mon-Thurs & Sun 11.30am–11pm, Fri & Sat 11.30am–12.30am
Transportation 15, BART Montgomery
Accepts All major credit cards

In true continental fashion, longstanding regulars like to come here for the bar menu rather than the full a la carte, because there's a terrific array of cocktails, and the bar staff are amiable, knowledgeable and unfailingly swift.

Their recently revamped menu is interesting, as long as you don't have a raging hunger for huge mounds of pasta. Appetizers like bruschetta with smoked salmon and goat cheese ($12) and a tapas plate of paprika-ed papas bravas ($6) are openers you can also nibble at the bar. Also available are salmon or beef carpaccio in balsamic dressing ($10), an array of simple antipasti like roasted garlic ($10), and a raw bar outside with oysters on the half-shell ($12). A fine array of pastas like Portobello lasagna with wild mushrooms ($13.50) is matched with gourmet pizza options on focaccia bread ($10–12), some with fancier toppings like goat cheese and pear with walnuts. The rest of the menu features regular meat and fish entrees such as monkfish with sweet ravioli in mushrooms and ginger ($21) or grilled lamb shanks with smoked bacon in pomegranate sauce ($24).

The dessert and cheese choices are also tempting enough for a quick snack if you don't want to stay for the whole meal, and the wine list has some rarer French and Spanish labels as well as a broad Californian selection (from $6 a glass). At Enrico's you get the feeling that it's really about the atmosphere and the music and the hipster quotient. But it's never less than a carnival, so bring a bunch of friends.

The Helmand

An interesting and somewhat out-of-place restaurant joins Enrico's amid the porno clubs on this slightly sleazy strip of Broadway. The fact that The Helmand serves authentic Afghan cuisine has done nothing but enhance its upscale reputation, however. The atmosphere inside, moreover, is the opposite of the scene outside. It's a haven of peace, cocooned with carpets and antique hangings, with solid wooden chairs and unfailingly gracious service. The food is a revelation to anyone with no idea what Afghan food is about, and it's relatively reasonable in price.

Cost $20–45

Address 430 Broadway at Montgomery
℡ 415/362-0641
Open Tues–Thurs 5.30–10pm, Fri & Sat 9.30–11pm
Transportation 12, 15
Accepts All major credit cards except Diners

The main story is lamb or chicken dishes, marinated and then charcoal-grilled, as in Arab cuisines. Afghans, however, use the subtler spices of tandoori cooking, along with lentils, flat bread, and basmati rice. The list of interesting starters has to begin with the mashawa ($3.95), or yogurt soup livened up with a wondrous carnival of different beans and pieces of grilled beef. Aush ($3.95), another soup, contains thread-noodles in a yogurty blend, this time with a drizzle of meat sauce for garnish. Aushak ($4.95) is the Afghan version of ravioli: jumbo pillows with a vegetable filling, served with a ground-meat sauce and a form of raita, or minted and spiced yogurt dressing. The kaddo borawni ($4.95), or roasted pumpkin, comes dressed in a garlicky yogurt or a kind of beef sauce. Samosa-like turnovers, or borownee (from $6.95), are filled with meat or vegetables. Lamb can come several ways: large, lavishly-spiced meatballs ($15.95) wear a spicy tomato and onion dressing; kebabs ($15.95), which exude a delicious hint of smokiness, are marinated in raisins and onions, and served with roasted eggplant or on a bed of jasmine rice. Desserts (around $5) include spicy rice puddings like burfee, a sweetened ice cream. Coffee is in tiny cups, and cardamom-scented, Turkish style.

The roots of The Helmand's cuisine are part Indian, part Arab, and part Persian. The ingredients come from all three regions but have acquired their own subtle distinctions, hard to pin down at times and even harder to describe. It's worth reserving ahead, as more diners have been coming here in recent times—perhaps to express a sympathetic and intelligent interest in Afghan culture.

North Beach

Mario's Bohemian Cigar Store

Mario's is a tiny snippet of a cafe, and famous as yet another hallowed Beat haunt. It has been here longer than anyone can remember, and so what if the waiters aren't real Italians anymore? That's never an issue in this town, where race and ethnicity are so kaleidoscopic that nobody's worried. As for the food, it would be worth coming a long way for one of their eggplant focaccia sandwiches, or the caffè con Vov.

Cost $6–15

Address 566 Columbus Ave at Union
☎ 415/362-0536
Open Daily 10am–midnight
Transportation 15, 30, 39, Powell–Mason cable car
Accepts All major credit cards

Well-herbed focaccia comes from the Liguria bakery, where it has usually sold out by lunchtime—probably to Mario's. It's hard to choose but most people give the cigar to the eggplant sandwich ($6.50). Slices of eggplant are grilled lightly and tossed in rosemary, salt and oil, spritzed just enough to give a golden-brown to the outside and a sweet creaminess within. They're so unwieldy that you'll tame one with difficulty and several napkins. Sandwiches come in a meatball variation too, as well as with a mild Italian sausage filling ($7.25), served with a lusty garlic-tomato sauce and a slice of gruyère. The grilled chicken sandwich comes with a slice of mustardy Vella Jack cheese from Sonoma. Salads and gourmet pizzas with wafer-like crusts and very fresh tomato and herb toppings round out the menu, along with polenta plates. To follow the whopping focaccia sandwich, which is big enough for a meal by itself, there's a very squishy, ultra-creamy tiramisu ($4.25) plus all the usual Italian coffee variations—with the additional eggnog kick of Vov if you desire. Vov is a yellow, egg-based Italian liquor that has the effect of mellowing out the coffee as well as sweetening it. If you want to be both wired and mellowed simultaneously, give it a try.

You can still buy cigars here, too. At one point the owners got carried away with all this longstanding success and opened a bigger place up on Russian Hill's Polk Street. It was too comfortable, well stocked, and elegant, and everybody preferred to come to this funky little dive instead.

Moose's

As much a city landmark as proprietor Ed Moose's former spot across the square, the legendary, now-departed "Washbag," Moose's attracts the same happy-go-lucky movers and shakers, thanks in no small measure to the owner's big, welcoming grin. Nightly live music and a pretty location overlooking the park help the atmosphere too. Despite a ban on cell phones, Moose's is a loud and bustling spot, with plenty of clatter from the kitchen. If you need to mellow out, ask for the "Vitamin V" vodka Martini—the much-missed *San Francisco Chronicle* columnist Herb Caen invented it, and it's still served here. A dining room upstairs caters parties, with comfortable round tables, and otherwise offers a bit of peace and quiet.

Cost **$15–25**
Address **1652 Stockton St at Washington Square**
☎ **415/989-7800**
Open **Mon–Wed 5.30–10pm, Thurs 11.30am–2.30pm & 5.30–10pm, Fri & Sat 11.30am–2.30pm & 5.30–11pm**
Transportation **15, 30, 39, Powell–Mason cable car**
Accepts **All major credit cards except Diners**

The menu is thoroughly eclectic and changes constantly. It's an old-fashioned offering of chops, burgers, grills, and fish of the day, but also has some contemporary fusion flourishes. The Mooseburger ($8.75) is a hangover from the good old days at Ed's old place—a crusty baguette cradles a whopping chunk of minced sirloin, lightly seasoned and surrounded by enough fries and coleslaw to sink the weak; it's faultless. Starters are much more vegetable-oriented and depend on what's in season. Around these parts, asparagus begins in February and artichokes in March, and nobody can get enough of them: steamed, braised, in vinaigrette or aioli ($6). Few San Franciscans eat steak nowadays, but the New York steak ($30) is well over half a pound of some healthy animal. Many variations of seafood pasta come and go, including the fabled version with clams and another with lobster (from $19.50). The wine list is long and has a very generous selection of glasses (from $6).

San Francisco is a happier place because of Moose's, and it would be pretty difficult not to have a good time here. It is, however, a loud, partying spot where people come to celebrate special occasions rather than enjoy intimate meals *à deux*, and it's not really the best venue for children.

L'Osteria del Forno

Rare is the hour when you don't see optimists standing outside this sliver of Northern Italy, faces rounded with hope at the gorgeous smells emanating from its wood-burning oven namesake—an oven almost as big as the Osteria itself. Hopefuls wait up to an hour at peak times. Run by two Italian-born women, Wally and Susanna, this place's charm overflows its pocket-hanky premises. Your only possible problem might be the no reservations and no credit cards rule.

Cost $10–50	

Address 519 Columbus Ave
☎ 415/982-1124
Open Mon, Wed–Thurs & Sun 11.30am–10pm, Fri & Sat 11.30am–10.30pm
Transportation 15, 30, Powell–Mason cable car
Accepts Cash only

But it's worth it. The sure, just-like-*nonna's* touch of Wally and Susanna's cooking has never faltered since the Osteria opened in the mid 1990s, though now it leans toward high-volume wood-smoked pizzas. They dub their mean Campari-Champagne cocktail a Shakerato ($4.50) and were among the first to serve carpaccios of wafer-thin, caper-studded salmon, or beef with arugula ($7.50). Plates of speck ($7.50) and Piedmontese pancetta ($7.50) are just as tasty. Divinely thin-crusted pizzas ($2.50-3.75 per slice) have conventional toppings: mozzarella; pancetta and red onion; pomodoro; garlic and anchovy. Crespelle stuffed with prosciutto or roast porcini ($11), and roast beef, lamb, or pork of the day ($10 as a plate, $6.50 as a sandwich) lead the handful of entrees. There's a short wine list, strong on rollicking dolcettos from Piedmont. The few desserts include the chocolate "salami" Bolognese ($4), a chocolate dessert made in the shape of a sausage. But why not selflessly relinquish your seat to the hungrier tourist staring through the window and move on to one of the local bakeries or cafes for dessert? Or to Mario's Bohemian Cigar Store, just down Columbus Avenue at Union, for caffè con Vov?

There's a trick to getting in here. Try coming between 3pm and 5pm, when the wait is down to 15 minutes. Four years ago, in an effort to burst into a bigger place, Wally and Susanna moved to the Mission and opened the superb Vineria. But though the food rocked and the wine list rolled, they gave it up because little L'Osteria was enough work on its own.

Peña PachaMama

Deprived fans of the fascinating and under-appreciated cuisine of Bolivia finally have a place to come: here, to this interesting little night-spot run by Eddie Navia, star player of the Andean armadillo-shell guitar known as the *charanguita*. With partner Quentin, Eddie is the founder of a local Andean band called Sukay, which plays here along with the Bohemians and other Latino bands. Navia's place makes an entertaining night out, with music and food that most find rich and unfamiliar, and with that notoriously great Bolivian beer to wash it down.

Cost $7–25

Address 1630 Powell St
☏ 415/646-0018
Open Wed–Sun 6–11pm, Sun 10am–3pm
Transportation 15, 30, Powell–Mason cable car
Accepts All major credit cards except AmEx

Salteñas ($4.50) are the staple empanadas or meat-filled pasties of Bolivia, and are far more interesting than the usual doughy pockets. They have a uniquely Bolivian personality, being made with a curried and extra-eggy pastry, with chicken, olives, carrots, and potatoes inside: four or five bites of pure Andean atmosphere. The name suggests they come from Salta, the Argentinian city in the Andes, yet they are so Bolivian that you can't get them anywhere outside the Andes—except here at Peña PachaMama. The bocadillos ($6.50), a platter of "little mouthfuls", offers one salteña plus stuffed yucca fritters and a dollop of papas a la huancaina; a fair culinary introduction. Main dishes include pacho pollo ($11.95), which is a chicken stew served with greens and potatoes, and Bolivian salpicon ($12.95), a rich-juiced beef brisket simmered with freeze-dried potatoes—another Bolivian specialty and not as bad as it sounds. Picante de pollo ($10.95) comes with garlic rice, while the vegetarian papas rellenas ($9.50) is a temptingly tasty platter of stuffed peppers. Desserts include cantuta iced ice cream ($5.50), made with fresh vanilla bean and served with fried, fruit-filled tortillas. The irresistibly sweet alfajores ($5.50) are a light, eggy shortbread served with dulce de leche.

Peña PachaMama features Chilean wines like Diablo ($25) plus Paceña beer and homemade sangria ($4.95 a glass; $18 per litre jug). But don't forget the "national" cocktail of the Andes: a Pisco Sour, a blend of Peruvian or Bolivian brandy whipped up with lime and ice. Peña PachaMama are currently petitioning for a license to serve it along with their nightly line-up of Latino bands and musicians.

Il Pollaio

"Do one thing, but do it well!" is the motto at Il Pollaio, a piece of old-style North Beach that has remained in the same little spot between the Gold Spike and Michelangelo forever. Inside, dozens of chickens await a dusting of oregano or rosemary marinade and a garlicky basting. They are grilled on the spot over hot rocks, beneath Chianti bottles that were probably festive looking when José Castellucci first drank and hung them up some time back in the seventies. The Castelluccis are Argentinian Italians, very friendly people who know how to deal with meat. They also roast steaks, lamb, pork, Italian sausages, rabbits, and even eggplant. So Il Pollaio pulls in all the North Beach regulars and old-timers. If the DiMaggio brothers were still around they'd probably be in here nightly, collecting takeouts for the missus.

Cost $5–20

Address 555 Columbus Ave at Union
☏ 415/362-7727
Open Mon–Sat 11.30am–9pm
Transportation 15, 30
Accepts MasterCard, Visa

Everything is made while you wait, so order a glass of burgundy ($4), or even a bottle ($15). Soups ($2.50) are made daily, should you feel the need for minestrone or lentil. A half-chicken ($4.50) can be eaten in or taken away; the combo ($6.75) comes with a side order of salad or fries, or you can have an entire bird to yourself ($8) and order fries separately ($2). José's salads ($4.75 as a side dish) come in various versions, including bean, mixed greens, and coleslaw; they're undressed—they hold the mayo—but there's some left out on the counter. Chops ($10), either pork or lamb, are juicily basted in a special mix, and are never overdone; ditto the steak ($13.50). Rabbit ($13.50) pretty much has to be ordered, then awaited for a half-hour or so.

The main attraction of Mr Castellucci's rotisserie, other than the charming Mr Castellucci himself, is the idiotically low prices. The entire Italian community of San Francisco comes here. While you wait, take a chair beside the locals and look out at the carnival on Columbus Avenue, with its wonderful view of the Church of SS Peter and Paul behind it, and remember the story about how the parish priest refused to marry Marilyn Monroe to Joe DiMaggio there because she was divorced. The old-timers are probably still shaking their heads over that one.

Rose Pistola

For a while after it opened, Rose Pistola was the most talked-about place in town, and the paper was filled with news of its superchef owner, Reed Hearon. Five years ago, he won the coveted James Beard "Best New Restaurant of the Year" award, and seemed poised to change the profile of North Beach food. Flagship of Hearon's restaurants, Rose Pistola still exhibits his "North Beach nouveau" recipe in action: the big, elegantly spare dining room has a sitting

Cost	$20–60

Address 532 Columbus Ave at Vallejo
☏ 415/399-0499
Open Mon–Thurs & Sun 11.30am–3pm & 5.30–11pm, Fri & Sat 11.30am–3pm & 5pm–midnight
Transportation 15, 30
Accepts All major credit cards except Diners

area, the long bar comes with a menu, the kitchen is cheerfully open, the wine list is long, with an emphasis on whites, and there are plenty of fishy appetizers. Service is friendly and attentive, and you can sit at a tiny bar table or relax in one of the booths—though you'll have to wait for the latter or reserve. Middle-aged couples dominate the bustling scene; it's a good choice for anniversaries.

The appetizers shine more brightly than main dishes here, and are available on the bar menu from 5.30pm to 7pm. The calamari salad ($9.95) comes lightly seasoned with lemon and pepper and is freshly made, though the portions are a little smaller than you might hope. Mussels "Maria" ($8.50) are steamed in Noilly Pratt with fresh tarragon, while a chopped salad ($5.50) surprises with quirky combinations. Smoked trout and frisée salad with tangerine and grapefruit segments ($7.75) is delicate and delicious, while ris de veau terrine ($10) and confit of duck leg ($15.70) also rise to the occasion. For main courses, the whole grilled fish of the day (from $14.50) or honeyroasted quail plus four spices ($16.50) are served with garlic spaghetti. Other Ligurian classics include chicken-in-a-brick and rabbit ($22), plus a flash-seared rib-eye steak in red wine ($26). All dishes change daily, and are served with chutzpah and more than enough bread—and very good bread it is too.

The sheer pretension of some of the names on Hearon's menu may annoy: anyone fancy a "tarte fine à la forme d'Ambert emincée de bavette aux poivre vert et haricots beurre" ($9)? But this is people-watching central, and even if it's only for appetizers at the bar, Rose Pistola is always an experience to remember.

The Stinking Rose

The true garlic capital of the world is Gilroy, a couple of hours south of San Francisco by car: if you love garlic very much and have no qualms about your breath, California is the state for you. But you don't have to be a vampire or out on a first date to harbor doubts about the Stinking Rose, a tourist magnet that no restaurant reviewers include and most locals avoid—although they do like

Cost $12–40	
Address 325 Columbus Ave at Broadway	
☎ 415/781-7673	
Open Daily 11am–11pm	
Transportation 15, 30	
Accepts All major credit cards except Diners	

the owners' other places. But visitors and seekers after a one-off "experience" may well enjoy the Stinking Rose for its atmosphere of general mayhem, as well as its whacky decor of ruby-velvet-draped cubicles and garlic paraphernalia—it boasts "the longest garlic braid in the whole world". It positively reeks of informal good cheer, and the food isn't bad either.

Thanks to an inventive and wide-ranging menu, it's possible to have a very complete if garlicky repast, starting with—of course—a garlic potato and onion soup ($5.95) or a hell-raising bagna cauda ($4), the hot Italian dip made from pounded anchovies, garlic and olive oil, heated fondue-style. Roasted garlic bulbs ($4) are always sweet and delicate, utterly different from the fresh variety. Main courses feature forty-garlic roast chicken with garlicky mashed potato ($13.95), garlic-encrusted baby back ribs ($21), at a swingeing price, or pasta such as gnocchi in a brilliant garlic-brie sauce with pine nuts and asparagus ($12). The garlicked prime rib ($29.95) comes with roasted garlic bulbs on the side and the tag "scares women and small children." But the proof is in the pudding—and if you are brave enough, the Stinking Rose's garlic ice cream ($2) will leave you in no doubt that garlic can be a three-course meal. Service is brisk and friendly.

It's hard to get your head round the ice cream—it just tastes wrong. Like the avocado or cheese ice creams available at Mitchell's ice-cream parlor, it makes the grade as curiosity, not as an "aha!" epiphany. Much like the Stinking Rose itself.

Tommaso's Ristorante Italiano

Just like Tosca's, Vesuvio's, Speck's, Mario's and City Lights, Tommaso's has never changed much and never will. As much a part of North Beach as its bars and Beat myths, Tommaso's is an authentic landmark where families come to feed together at the same trough. Celebrities haunt it too—the story goes that Francis Ford Coppola insisted on making his own pizza here. The Crotti family have run this restaurant since 1973, using the same pizza oven that their predecessors, the Lupos, brought with them from the Old Country when they opened in 1935, and that oven has lost none of its much patina-ed tang. There's usually a short wait at the bottom of the stairs, and the earlier you come the better, they say.

Cost	$20–40
Address	1042 Kearny St
☎	415/398-9696
Open	Tues–Sat 5–10.45pm, Sun 4–9.45pm
Transportation	15, BART Montgomery Street
Accepts	All major credit cards

There's nothing out-of-the-way about the food. It's all honest and always the same, and that's its charm. Unfussy, no-nonsense pizzas with a score of toppings, spaghetti, lasagne, and scaloppine are served in a cellar with kitschy little wall murals, tablecloths, and cozy booths. Wood-fired pizza began here at Tommaso's long before it was chic and upscale, so you'll find it dependable. Crusts are thin and toppings classical: there's mozzarella and tomato, mushroom, pepperoni, and variations of several cheeses ($13–17.50). Ask for their antipasto plate of marinated roast red peppers ($6.25), fresh from the oven; otherwise it's asparagus, broccoli, or beans, as fresh roasted vegetables is a seasonal specialty. Try the "coo-coo" clams ($9.50), very simply presented with oil, spices, balsamic, and a pinch of oregano. The rest of the menu is just plain, reassuring comfort food, from the spaghetti and meatballs ($11) to the veal parmegiana ($17), mushroom-stuffed calzone ($16–21.50) and manicotti in marinara ($11). There's a short but useful wine list of hearty California Zins plus any number of gulpable native Italian Chiantis, Barberas, Sangioveses and dolcettos that might take your fancy. Dolci include tiramisu, cheese-cake, cannoli, and spumone (all from $5).

After you've sacrificed your warm spot to the next horde of regulars, get back onto your feet and stroll out along Broadway and Columbus to walk off that pasta and find a nice cafe for a nightcap. Wherever you look there's temptation!

North Beach

Trattoria Contadina

Trattoria Contadina is another cozy, family-run North Beach evergreen, where the staff are so kind that they practically take out adoption papers for you on the spot. The place has ambiance in spades. Tables are positioned close together in true trattoria style, and the setting is warm and wood-lined. You would be well advised to book ahead at the weekend, as this is a popular place for birthday parties. Part owner Dirk is a very hands-on *padrone*, an accomplished promoter for Salvatore Parra's regional food.

Cost	$15–35

Address 1800 Mason St at Union
℡ 415/982-5728
Open Daily 5–10pm
Transportation 15, Powell–Mason cable car
Accepts All major credit cards except Diners

Start with a generous portion of that unbeatable Tuscan classic, carpaccio di manzo ($6.95), which is a thinly sliced filet mignon with arugula, Parmesan cheese, extra virgin olive oil, and capers. Fresh mozzarella, basil and tomato ($6.95) is another favorite, as is the homemade soup of the day ($4.95). To follow come the usual pastas and risottos—fettucine with smoked and fresh salmon in cream sauce ($13.95) is a winner. After that, if you have room, Contadina does meat well. There's often a grilled steak ($16.95) with shaved raw onions, lots of lemon, and a snow pea, squash, and cauliflower medley; or lamb chops with polenta ($17.95), featuring five French-cut chops done just right. The constantly changing veal scallopine dishes, like vitello con porcini ($21.95), come highly recommended. But perhaps the favorite dish among regular patrons is chef Parra's house special fettucine ($12.95), which comes tossed with chicken, tomatoes, peas, and a hint of creamy Italian cheese, and is served in portions that are heroic in size.

To follow, there's good, strong coffee and desserts such as chocolate torta with fresh whipped cream ($4.50), which comes from the divine Victoria Bakery a few steps away, and zabaglione ($3.50), an absolutely ambrosial yellow fluff. Once upon a time you could find this Italian staple everywhere, but nowadays it's quite hard to get, because it's labor intensive and easily curdled. Understandably, very few cooks want to stand over a double pan of egg yolks and Marsala, stirring the zabaglione for twenty minutes. But how nice that someone still does!

Zax

Not quite North Beach, but above the main drag of the Wharf, Zax is near touristville without being the least bit touristy. Run by a Mark Drazek and his wife Barbara, Zax is a classified secret, a miniature supper club for hip locals. The food is changeable and adventurous, the clientele is young, the lighting is kind and the room is a soothing petal-pink. The wine list is small but perfectly informed.

Cost $10–35

Address 2330 Taylor St at Columbus
ⓉⓉ 415/563-6366
Open Tues–Sat 5.30–10pm
Transportation 15, 30, Powell–Mason cable car
Accepts MasterCard, Visa

Drop by Drazeks to try the house specialty, their fabled twice-baked goat cheese soufflé ($9); it's a gold-domed toque that combines a crunchy top and an infinitely creamy interior, and is served with a Walforf-style salad of celery, Granny Smith and fennel bulb in cider vinaigrette that's puckeringly sour but crunchy, and goes brilliantly with the soufflé. Their warmed frisée lettuce with smoked bacon and poached egg ($6.25) is another discovery; it isn't always on the menu, but take advantage when it is, because it's heavenly. Other starters may include steamed mussels in garlicked nectar with roasted tomatoes ($8.75), or a mixed salad with blue cheese, walnuts, and sherry ($6.75) that's simple and tasty. Zax constantly changes fish dishes according to what's in season: swordfish ($21.95) is an ideal choice for a "puttanesca" variation with olives, capers, and roast peppers, plus arugula rather than anchovy. Portions are very lavish, presentation hearty. Non-fish-eaters can choose from a Niman Ranch stew or a pork porterhouse or a Petaluma roast chicken (from $19; prices change seasonally). These rustic and simple dishes all come with fine, fresh greens on the side. The sweets are tartes and galettes that change daily, along with homemade ice cream.

The wine list is another story: it's reasonably priced, and mixes some less-known California "finds" with some fine New Zealand whites and Argentina Malbec. Almost all are priced in the twenties, and many are available by the glass (from $6). The beer is a rhapsody to the finest: try Anderson Valley Poleeko Gold, Chimay, Red Hook, Anchor Steam, or Pilsner Urquell (from $4). Valentine's Day is an extravagant glory in Zax, where soft colors, soufflés, and overall pinkness make it a natural for romance.

Fisherman's Wharf & the Waterfront

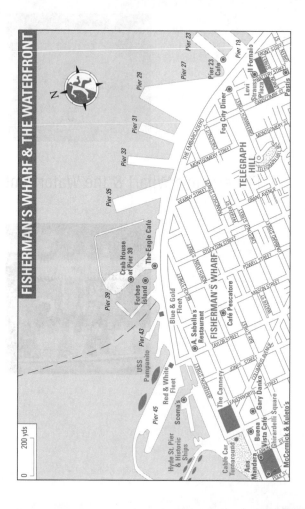

FISHERMAN'S WHARF & THE WATERFRONT

A. Sabella's Restaurant

Antonio Sabella emigrated from Sicily in 1871 and settled here to fish the Bay. Back in the 1920s his family began this seafood restaurant, and they still run Sabella's today, four generations later. While some places in Fisherman's Wharf undoubtedly do peddle tourist fare, and the area is a carnival of tat in places, it originally became popular for seafood and views, and you can still find decent, reliable food at places like this. So if you have visiting relations with a yen to see the Wharf and try the local fish, Sabella's, with its big windows, fireplace and cavernous dining hall, is a traditional catch.

Cost $20–50

Address 3rd floor, 2766 Taylor St

☎ 415/771-6775

Open Mon–Fri 5.30–10.30pm, Sat 4–11pm, Sun 4–10.30pm

Transportation 15, 42, F, Powell St cable car

Accepts All major credit cards

The menu has been pretty much the same for the best part of a century. Start by scrutinizing the most obvious choices: the Sabellas keep everything crustacean and finned in the giant saltwater tanks at the back, and they change the water daily. The cioppino or local seafood stew ($22 for a tureen) is bobbing with clams, crabs, and crayfish, and there's a solid bouillabaisse ($19.50). Dungeness crabcakes ($12.50) vie for attention with a crab-shrimp Louis ($14.75) that incorporates other crustaceans from the tank. Monterey calamari ($8.25) are rings sautéed in the pan. Fresh farmed abalone in a beurre blanc ($52.75) come at a whopping price, but wild abalone's getting hard to find, and they at least grow them on the spot. Local fish start with the Bay petrale ($17.95), grilled simply with lemon. And when you've licked the last finger and wiped the last trace of butter off your lips, there's a dessert cart with items like blueberry and raspberry tarts (from $5.75).

All this is entertainment enough for most people, but if you do crave more, they sometimes run a mystery-dinner theater program, with Colonel-Mustard-in-the-Conservatory plots. Sabella's isn't cheap, and most San Franciscans never come here except when they have out-of-towners in tow, but they've now added seasonal prix fixe lunch deals at around $19.50 for three courses (rising to around $29.50 at night), which might change a few minds. The place might not be trendy, but with judicious choices to avoid higher prices, the honest fare and ambiance merit a visit.

Ana Mandara

Entertainers Don Johnson and Cheech Marin's exquisite restaurant frames Khai Duong's French-Vietnamese cuisine perfectly: it's the most escapist dining experience in San Francisco. Most people believe that whatever it takes—reserving ahead, parking qualms, $75 bottles of wine—it's worth it for Duong's thrilling fusion fantasies. Despite the touristy Ghirardelli Square surroundings, Ana Mandara raises expectations from the moment you arrive. Tropical greenery, teak-shuttered windows, antique sculptures and plashing waterfalls all evoke Indochina under the French.

Cost $30–65

Address 891 Beach St at Polk
☏ 415/771-6800
Open Mon–Thurs 11.30am–9pm, Fri & Sat 5.30–10.30pm
Transportation 10, 19, 30, 47, 49, Powell St cable car
Accepts All major credit cards

But beware of the blue-mauve lychee-scented cocktail "specials" ($7) that resemble innocent Coolaid but conceal a lethal vodka one-two punch, as they may color your judgment! To start, try an oyster and water spinach appetizer ($10), or green papaya with prawns and jellyfish in chile vinaigrette ($7), or banana blossom with chicken and grapefruit salad ($7), or striped bass ceviche ($14); all are strikingly artistic as well as distinctly flavored. Soups ($7) are hot-and-sour variations with crab, lobster, or mussels. For entrees, a celebrated dish is the wok-sautéed halibut ($20) with little mounds of chiffonéed dill and scallion, dotted pho-style around the platter. Equally characteristic is banana-leaf-wrapped snapper or bass ($20), which comes in an herbed coconut dressing or a miso shiitake sauce. A lobster tower in rice, avocado, and daikon sprouts ($28) looks almost too sculptural to eat. Veal shanks with clove basil ($22) arrive in tangy tropical salsa. Do all these little extra bits add up to a sense of overkill? Just a little bit; yet it all looks like art, never gimmicky or too busy. Crispy mango spring rolls with coconut vanilla cream in mango sauce ($4) and mung bean gateau ($4) conclude.

To follow the killer cocktails, Larry Stone has assembled a mile-long wine list with mark-ups to match. A small smoking patio adjoins the upstairs cocktail lounge, where deep sofas permit you to enjoy a fine jazz combo as graceful hostesses ply back and forth in Ao Ba Ba silk skirts. Of all the top places in San Francisco, this leads the "most splurge-worthy" category.

Buena Vista Cafe

The Buena Vista has a firm spot in local lore, and not just because it appears in a Meg Ryan movie. In the weepie *When a Man Loves a Woman,* Meg goes into rehab after a scene at the Buena Vista where she says she wants to be as "cool as they are!" pointing at a tourist couple. Much as it ought to be, Meg's ensuing recovery is no way connected to the cafe's more historic claim: to have served America's first Irish coffees! According to legend, San Francisco journalist Stanton Delaplane once enjoyed the drink at Shannon Airport, where barman Joe Sheridan had created the recipe. Warmed by his discovery, Delaplane worked tirelessly to recreate the drink with Buena Vista bartender Jack Koeppler. The secret: pour the coffee in a glass with a spoon, then add the mellow whiskey generously; next turn over your spoon (the one that was already in the glass, to prevent it from cracking) and carefully pour the whipped cream over the back until it looks like a thick lid. Drink and repeat.

Cost $10–25
Address 2765 Hyde St at Beach
☎ 415/474-5044
Open Mon–Fri 9am–2am, Sat & Sun 8am–2am
Transportation 10, 19, 30, 47, Powell St cable car
Accepts Cash only

Whatever else the folks who warm themselves here try, they always praise that coffee ($5.50), which is robust and stiff enough to get the heart back in you after a blowy afternoon on Alcatraz. Food is equally simple and laid-back. Breakfast lasts all day and includes eggs done every which way but loose (starting at $5.95). Eggs Blackstone on muffins comes with smashed tomatoes and homemade hollandaise sauce ($8.25). A thickly sliced and spiced French cinnamon toast ($6.95) and a creditable corned beef hash with eggs ($7.95) are more filling. The patti melt sandwich comes with lots of onions ($7.95) and a giant Reuben on rye with Swiss cheese and sauerkraut ($7.75) makes another great lunchtime stopgap. The most expensive item is the rib-eye steak ($14.95), and one of the most popular is a kitchen-table version of macaroni and cheese special ($8 when available).

The staff may be rushed but there's always someone to chat to. Wood trimmings, yellowing newspaper clippings on the walls, old-timey lamps, and the eternal view over Hyde Street Pier's tall ships complete the scene, making the Buena Vista a friendly spot for a pause.

Cafe Pescatore

Generally overlooked because it's neither in North Beach nor on the Wharf, Pescatore is really an annex to a boutique hotel. Perhaps that's why the bathroom is through the lobby of the adjoining Tuscan Inn, making the trek there something you might make if trying to duck your half of the check. Inside, it offers a little lunch patio with outdoor tables and planters, perfect for a snatched business lunch or a quick respite between attractions—the Coit Tower and Alcatraz, say. Inside, you are greeted by a table groaning with a bountiful display of the day's antipasti. A large, brass-trimmed bar gives way to a cozy but modern back room with a friendly atmosphere. It's a great place to be huddled on an overcast day.

Cost $10–25
Address Tuscan Inn, 2455 Mason St at North Point
☏ 415/561-1111
Open Mon–Fri 7–10.30am & 11.30am–10.30pm, Sat & Sun 7am–3pm & 5–10.30pm
Transportation F, Powell St cable car
Accepts All major credit cards

A short and very informal menu starts with good salads: the Caesar ($5.95) is particularly ample, if a tad bland, while the insalata mista ($5.50) offers mixed greens, balsamic vinegar, Gorgonzola, and caramelized walnuts. Individual pizzas come in three versions: a simple Margherita of tomatoes, mozzarella, and basil ($8.50), a filling Rustica with sausage ($9.50), and an addictive Quattro Formaggio—four cheeses—with a smattering of prosciutto ($8.50). The linguine con vongole ($13.50) is the usual clams prepared in a wine and clam juice reduction, but staff will happily add more to it on request—sun-dried tomatoes, for example. To follow up, a homemade tiramisu ($3.50) and bread pudding ($3.50) beckon. If you're full, the usual espressos and cappuccinos should get you up and moving again. Several well-chosen Chiantis and dolcetti are reasonably priced from $4.50 to $7.50 a glass.

All told, the Pescatore is a modest yet useful little eatery where the check is never going to be huge. So if you do elect to search for the restroom and your date wonders if you skipped, at least it's not going to be a major loss. It's also very child-friendly. There's another big plus to the Pescatore: despite being on the cusp of the two touristvilles of North Beach and Fisherman's Wharf, both restaurant-heavy neighborhoods of the city, it unfailingly turns up parking spots. A bit of a mystery, that, and never one to ignore in this town.

Crab House at Pier 39

Sturdy, sweet and red as a blood orange at sunset, Dungeness crab epitomizes San Francisco's ocean heritage. Thanksgiving Day is usually the first time that locals roll up their sleeves and go out in search of a fine old mess of crab; after that there's a couple of months to get down to the Wharf to pick it up fresh. Unfortunately, the Dungeness is in decline, and sometimes the crab fishermen strike. But since Fisherman's Wharf is the third most-visited attraction in America (after Disney World and Disneyland), it's no surprise to find a zillion vendors hawking crabs al fresco along the sidewalk.

Cost $10–50	

Address Pier 39, Fisherman's Wharf

Ⓣ 415/434-2722

Open Daily 11am–9pm

Transportation 10, 15, 39, 47, F

Accepts All major credit cards except Diners

Yes, it's touristville, but if you want to sit down and butter all your fingers and clothes in warmth and comfort, the Crab House is a place of rampant good cheer, with a chef who used to be a star sommelier and captain at the late, legendary Ernie's—Andrea Froncillo. Crab House looks bleakly modern outside, but inside it has a fireplace, warm nautical trim in cherry wood, and a view of hundreds of sea lions. It caters to visitors who are chilly after a ferry trip or a visit to Hyde Street Pier and need warming up. No prizes for guessing the number one attraction on Andrea's menu. But considering how some places can gouge the visitors on the Wharf, the $32 that Crab House charges for a two- or three-pound "Killer Crab," roasted in "secret garlic sauce" isn't that bad. You get a half-order for $17.95, a couple of dollars less than suburban fishmongers charge for fresh-from-the-Pacific crabs—which is how they should be. A mean crab cioppino ($19.75) is bisque-like in its creamy intensity. There are hot crab melt sandwiches of crab meat with cheese on sourdough ($12.90), crabcakes ($9.95), and a crab cocktail ($9.75) in that red, spicy seafood sauce.

You could also buy a crab from a vendor's cart on a cardboard plate ($6.99 per lb) and take it to the pier's end to dismember in front of jealous California sea lions. But you'll have a blazing fire in here!

The Eagle Cafe

AMERICAN/SEAFOOD

The Eagle dates to 1928 and has hardly changed since the Depression years, when the local longshoremen and fishermen hung out here to drink and grab the odd bowl of soup. Beat scene hangers-on took to it a couple of decades later, when it was still across the road on Jefferson, near where "Ripleys Believe It Or Not" rules now. After the Pier 39 development began, the

Cost $12–25
Address Pier 39, 2nd floor, Fisherman's Wharf
☎ 415/433-3689
Open Daily 7am–5pm
Transportation 15, F, Powell St cable car
Accepts Cash only

Eagle was granted a preservation order, and it walked across the street to its current perch—lock, stock, and barrel. Now it's marooned among the pier attractions, with Disney-style glitz all around it, but you can still call this aged dockside dive on the Wharf an authentic landmark of old-time San Francisco. Nowadays the Eagle is a tourist haunt rather than a working cafe, but the welcome's warm, the tea's hot, and corned beef and cabbage rules on Fridays.

Their clam chowder isn't bad either, a smallish cup of creamy soup with seafood and potato bobbing in it ($3); there's a larger version too ($5.75). Breakfasts are what the Eagle really does best, and the popular choice is corned beef hash and fried eggs sunny side up ($7.95). But someone's also doing something creative in the kitchen, and things are looking up on the menu these days: pancakes ($4.95) are winning more praise than they used to a few years back, and the meatloaf ($7.95) is getting a positive response as well. There's no doubt the drinks are more popular here than the food, however. They always have been, in no small part because they're so much cheaper than anywhere else around the Wharf.

Frankly, the Eagle's a pleasant little respite for a bit of old-style funkiness. It's just calming to come up for a bowl of chowder and a Bloody Mary, or a cup of tea, before you wander out among the crowds again. Whether touring the Wharf or squiring visitors around the Pier 39 attractions, it's good to know you can always duck inside here for a drink and a bit of peace and quiet, and look out through the bright blue windows past the jetties and the seals, and across the Pacific towards Hawaii.

Fog City Diner

Folks who balked at the prices used to wonder why a passer-by with a major jones for a BLT or a burger would want to come to this glorified, neon-lit caboose, just because it looked retro. But that was ten years ago, and Fog City has triumphantly outlived the carping. Designer Pat Kuleto's dining car trimmed in neon and chrome still looks cute, inside and out, and the prices no longer look unreasonably high—no more than you'd expect for a restaurant that starred in a Visa commercial (and still doesn't take American Express). Kuleto picked the darkest wood and leather for the seating, and custard cream for the walls, which are hung with big animal abstracts by painter Wayne Ensrud.

Cost $10–35
Address 1300 Battery St
☏ 415/982-2000
Open Mon–Thurs & Sun 11.30am–11pm, Fri & Sat 11.30am–midnight
Transportation 42, F
Accepts MasterCard, Visa

Now for Samuel Ramirez and Jose Torres' new "diner food," which has downsized one menu section into "small plates," with less in the way of teetering sandwiches than there once was. Diner it may be, but some creative Latino-fusion notes sing on the menu, and the trendy offerings include tongue-scorching burritos and quesadillas. Burritos come with fillings such as sweet-and-sour mu shu pork, red pepper and hoisin sauce ($7.50), and there's a quesadilla with roast Anaheim chile, tomatillo salsa, and pumpkin seeds ($7.95). There are still a few sandwiches, including one with roast vegetables ($10.50) and another with the fish of the day ($12.50). Further small plates run through reliable crabcakes in a sherry cayenne mayo ($10.75), and the ubiquitous tuna carpaccio ($8.75). Dip into the oyster bar, too. As befits a diner so near the wharf, they offer an enormous Dungeness crab cioppino ($18.95) plus a daily salmon dish ($17.50), not forgetting Szechwan pork chop in apple-peppercorn chutney ($17.95), and a straightforward steak and fries ($23.50). Kids will love their own options, including a hot dog with chile on the side.

Families en route to and returning from the Wharf will have no complaints. No, it's not especially cheap, but it's all fun, and the cholesterol-bubbling rich sweets that follow—such as a chocolate fudge brownie a la mode ($5.75), brûlée-o-day ($5.95) and vanilla pudding in chocolate sauce ($5.50)—further enhance well-being.

Forbes Island

Forbes Island is a curious phenomenon. Tourist tat is what most people expect when they learn about a floating island restaurant. But how cynical! San Francisco has other floating restaurants but only one floating island. Ex-coastguard and carpenter Forbes Thor Kiddoo used to live and work as a builder of floating homes, and began to work on a Captain Nautilus-style marine home in the mid-1970s. By 1980, Forbes Island had become a 100-foot-long islet with real palm trees, a waterfall, a Tahitian-style dining room, a lighthouse with a viewing deck and an underwater saloon. Diners phone the island from H Dock, under the Eagle Cafe, to catch the "tiki boat shuttle" out to the island.

Cost $35–65
Address Pier 39 at Fisherman's Wharf
☎ 415/951-4900
Open Wed–Sun 5–10pm
Transportation 10, 15, 39, 47, F, Powell St cable car
Accepts All major credit cards except Diners

Forbes Island is more than just a curiosity. It offers a romantic evening that you should enjoy with the right person—or people. But it all comes oh so slowly, and you may pine for your food through several baskets of the (excellent) Acme baguette and unsalted butter. Start with fresh oysters on the half-shell with a hot, cayenned sauce ($12), or foie gras served with butter-tossed pear halves and currants ($12). Chef Paul Irving has a tiny galley to work in but always manages a catch of the day. Roast duck ($24) comes with a contrastingly zesty pomegranate, cherry and orange sauce, accompanied by mixed wild rice, squash, asparagus, and carrots. A rack of lamb ($26) is baked in herbs with roasted potatoes on the side. Chocolate mousse, lemon sorbet, and a cream and berry vol-au-vent are frequently on the dessert list (all $8), but isles flottantes is the obvious choice—these meringue icebergs arrive in gentle caramel, surrounded by berries and chocolate drizzle. Irresistible.

Forbes has launched $35 all-inclusive menus, with rather fewer choices. Superior menus appear on special occasions, like the Valentine's Day menu of vegetable pistou, spinach and goat cheese salad, gravlax and mahi-mahi, poussin, or filet mignon. In case that doesn't sound amorous enough, the dessert choices include passion fruit sorbet on mango coulis. It comes with Champagne included and costs $65—a little pricey, perhaps, but cheaper than a trip to Tahiti.

Il Fornaio

Part of the expanding West Coast chain started by a director of the Williams-Sonoma kitchen equipment stores, Il Fornaio has been around since 1988. It has several locations in the area, including the pioneer branch down on the Peninsula, in Palo Alto. Though corporately separate, they borrow heavily from a related chain of bakeries—also called Il Fornaio—with branches all over Italy. A working bakery, with artisanal breads made in-house (the name means "the baker"), this restaurant has proven its own recipe for success with its acido baguettes, Pugliese, ciabatta, and dessert breads, baked at their pleasant grill. There's also a rotisserie, and pasta and pizzas are served both outside and inside. The San Francisco location is on the waterfront at Levi Plaza, opposite the museum dedicated to the famous Levi's jeans. You can visit Coit Tower, descend Filbert Steps, take a peek at Gold Rush-era jeans, then recuperate over a meal, all in half a day.

Cost $25–40
Address 1265 Battery St at Levi Strauss Plaza
☎ 415/986-0100
Open Mon–Thurs 7am–10pm, Fri 7am–11pm, Sat 8am–11pm, Sun 8am–10pm
Transportation 30, 42, F
Accepts All major credit cards

Il Fornaio isn't a fancy place, yet it somehow manages to look it, thanks to terracing, French windows and warm mahogany wood. Inside, white-linen calm reigns along with that gorgeous smell of baking bread, and staff are helpful and friendly. If you grab a table outside on a blowy night, you'll find the terrazzo warm enough, thanks to outdoor heating. The menu is pasta-based and not overpriced. Their outstanding, chewy bruschetta ($4.95) complements hearty penne and linguine pastas in changing seafood and sausage variations ($10–15.95). Polenta ($7.95), in wild mushroom and pomodoro versions, is a standout, along with the lobster-filled ravioli with lemon-cream and shrimp topping ($16.95). Pizzas (from $9.95) start at a bargain price, while herbed Maine lobster ($16.95) is equally good value. Mesquite-grilled meat ($17.95) and rotisserie chicken ($14.95) plates are rustic and Tuscan in inspiration, and porterhouse steak ($25) arrives juicy and rare. If the selections are a bit unimaginative, they're also dependable; any of the seafood pastas will blow you away.

Unsurprisingly for a specialty bakery, breakfast gets raves here: the usual egg omelet and eggs Benedict ($6.95–8) are enthusiastically greeted by early birds, who get croissants and pastries as part of the deal.

Gary Danko

FRENCH

Few places are more serious about food than Danko's. As befits a celebrity chef's finest creation, this is one of the city's prime destinations for gourmands, and it books out many moons ahead. Gary Danko is the former chef from Viognier who teamed with the Ritz-Carlton's Nick Peyton to take over a former French restaurant on the Wharf. It's a consistent chart-topper and the city's food writers never tire of explaining why his food just blows all competition away.

Cost $50–150

Address 800 North Point St at Hyde
℡ 415/749-2060
Open Mon–Wed & Sun 5.30–9.30pm, Thurs–Sat 5.30–10pm
Transportation 10, Powell–Hyde cable car
Accepts All major credit cards except Diners

The tasting menu hits those highlights and lets you hang onto the family heirlooms too. This is your chance to eat food that will introduce you to a new world.

Either ask for the set menu of three ($55) or four ($64) or five ($74) courses, or put your own meal together for about the same outlay. You choose from eight appetizers, five fish dishes, six main courses, the cheese cart, and a list of eight desserts. All dishes are also available a la carte, but the tasting menu brings five set dishes and a flight of matching wines. A star acolyte of Madeleine Kammen, Danko has a very traditional French style of cooking. Among the appetizers, a pinkish, velvety, luscious, and sensual lobster bisque comes straight from the classics, and there are two foie gras dishes. Other starters disclose Asian touches, ahi tuna with nori, enoki mushrooms and lemon-soy dressing, for instance. The tasting menu may start with oysters with leeks, salsify and osetra caviar (served with a light white wine from the Vienna woods); then move on to black bass with apples, cabbage, and tarragon; followed by soy-glazed beef filet with an eggplant-pepper marmalade; then a farmhouse cheese selection and, to top it all, a warm apple crêpe with calvados ice cream.

One of the very best moments of the prix fixe is when your cheeses arrive, and you get a wonderful wafting gust of some of the world's finest Vacheron triple-creams and Crottins, plus a running commentary from your always informed, generally relaxed waiters. It's also worth noting that you can walk in here to eat at the bar without making a booking.

McCormick & Kuleto's

AMERICAN/SEAFOOD

Most native San Franciscans regard Fisherman's Wharf as a protected reservation for tourists, but that doesn't mean good food is scarce in the vicinity, and seafood and views abound at this often-overlooked family restaurant in the old Ghirardelli chocolate factory. The Sunday brunch makes a sound-value choice for families on a mission to keep children busy, and lunch and supper deals also feature regularly. The adjacent Crab Cake Lounge is their handy raw bar, and it has the same view plus a short but affordable menu of oysters, crabcakes, sandwiches and pizzas.

Cost $15–35
Address Ghirardelli Square, 900 North Point St
☎ 415/929-1730
Open Daily 11am–11pm
Transportation 30, 42, Powell–Hyde cable car
Accepts All major credit cards except Diners

Tables are not cramped in Pat Kuleto's interior, which incorporates sweeping windows with views of the bay complete with Alcatraz and surfers. You can reserve, but probably won't wait for long anyway, and there's free parking. Amid lots of starched linen and dark wood, the waiters are old-school twinkly and smiley, which is another plus. A special children's menu (from $7.95) affords succulent chicken strips, fries and salad, or spaghetti in herbed tomato sauce, at trimmed down amounts and prices. Adults can lash out on a terrific oyster menu which features piquantly metallic Sinku Summer Ice, wee coppery Malpeque Bays or Salutation Coves, and New Zealand Coromandels. A sampler ($11.20) educates you about oysters. The brunch menu features traditional Hangtown Fry ($7.80), complete with oysters, eggs, bacon, and potatoes. Crabcakes ($12.70) and smoked salmon eggs Benedict ($10.25) stuff you as fully as an entree would, and the hollandaise sauce is unusually spicy and tangy. Traditional Wharf dishes like clam chowder ($3.95) and Dungeness crab ($14.75) join a very long list of fresh fish from as far away as Hawaii and Maine; most are done simply.

The wine list is long and it isn't cheap: California Zinfandels start at an inexcusable $40, while the chardonnays start at $30 but rise rapidly to a 1999 Cakebread Chardonnay at $69—also too steep. The reserve list is purely academic. But there are other pleasures than wine at Fisherman's Wharf: walk off your meal on the Hyde Street Pier and you'll be pleased you ventured here—even if you're a local.

Pastis

If you ever feel the need for an authentic piperade à la Basquaise, this is one place to find that zestiest of tomato, pepper, and egg Basque sacraments. The Pastis version comes with poached eggs, rather than scrambled, and slivers of Serrano ham, and if owner Gerald Hirigoyen's own celebrated salt cod "al Pil-Pil" isn't on the menu, this is your best bet for tasting his native Basque fare. After that, chef Isabelle Alexandre's food is all over the map. At this backstreet brasserie, you can tuck a stool up to the long zinc bar or take your Pernod and your plate outside to eat on the little entrance patio on Levi Strauss Plaza.

Cost $15–40

Address 1015 Battery St at Greenwich
☎ 415/391-2555
Open Mon–Fri 11.30am–3pm & 5.30–10.30pm, Sat 5.30–10.30pm
Transportation F, 12, 15, 32
Accepts All major credit cards except Diners

As a former chocolatier, and owner-founder of SoMa's Fringale, Bayonne-born Hirigoyen brought his native charcuterie—Bayonne ham and sausages—along with his love of desserts. He has also taken on some bright and burgeoning young talents at his kitchen, and since he's usually banging the pots at Fringale, he does not shackle the larger Pastis into a new-French or even new-Basque menu, but lets things evolve at their own pace. After the cod brandade peppers ($8.50), another Basque appetizer is seared oxtail ($9), a surprising choice but don't knock it until you've tried it. Main dishes get more French, and include steak and pommes frites ($22), roasted squab ($19), and classical duck ($20) with a nicely crunchy skin. A word must be put in for the solicitous care put into vegetable side dishes, from the perfect garlicky French fries to the green beans, the peppers (again), and many others. Since patisserie is respected here, you can safely try the lemon tart ($6), and Manchego and Idiazabal cheeses also appear from time to time.

These are slightly lower prices than Fringale, attractive enough to make it worth a little saunter down Filbert Steps of a late afternoon, even if it does seem off the main drag. Pastis is a short walk from the Wharf, too, which is very handy for a ferry.

Pier 23 Cafe

🍴 Far and away the best reason to come to this glorified fish shack is its sprawling deck overlooking the waters of the Bay, along with the nightly live music, which ranges from jazz to rock. The ultra-gourmet Tuesday and Saturday farmers' market (alternating between Levi Strauss Plaza and opposite the nearby Ferry Building at the time of writing) makes another splendid reason to visit.

Cost $15–25
Address Embarcadero at Greenwich
☎ 415/362-5125
Open Mon–Tues 10am–midnight, Wed–Sat 10am–2am, Sun 10am–10pm
Transportation F
Accepts MasterCard, Visa

Notoriously, San Francisco is sunnier in winter than in summer—remember that old Mark Twain crack about the coldest winter being summer?—so outdoor seating is a bit of a risk on Pier 23, but it comes with a view, especially when the fog has lifted. On a sunny day, opting for fish tacos or cracked crab plus a bottle of Corona on the waterfront is a no-brainer, and a considerably better choice than your own backyard.

You'll often find Pier 23 hosting a wild office or birthday party, with numb wage slaves downing potent Margaritas or Screwdrivers. Perhaps in order to stand up to bartender Noel's admirable cocktails, the Pier's seafood menu is hearty rather than gourmet. But it supplies party ambiance in spades, and the food rarely disappoints if you keep it simple. Appetizers include a plain chilled artichoke with dill mayonnaise ($5.85), hot garlic prawns ($9.75) or prawn quesadilla ($9.50), and roasted garlic with Cambozola ($8.75). After that it's crab and shrimp all the way, with a whole oven-roasted crab with lemon garlic and parsley ($25), and variations on seafood cocktails (from $8.25). "Catch of the day" usually includes the local petrale served with vegetables and rice in a citrus sauce ($14.25), blackened salmon ($13.25), or halibut ($14.25). Of these, petrale takes the biscuit, the reason being that it's a relatively lean and tender, large-flaked flounder found up and down the whole West Coast. It's usually pan-fried or grilled, and the less done to it the better.

With so much seafood, omelets may seem like an afterthought. But they're enormous and beautifully done here, and weekend brunch is an ideal time to find sunshine along the waterfront. With its sizeable outdoor deck, bay views and accommodating tables, this is a fine spot to spend a liquid Sunday afternoon.

Scoma's

Al and Joseph Scoma opened Scoma's forty years ago as a cafe for fishermen, and it still sits at the end of Pier 47, halfway to Alcatraz and heaving slightly among the fishing tugs. The menu stars a *Little Mermaid*'s casting call of salmon, halibut, crab, lobster, clams, mussels, snapper, and scallops (they've dropped abalone and bass). The very high turnover of fresh shellfish and seafood is brought into the restaurant's receiving station, which you can visit, via its own boats. Inside, the decor is borderline cafeteria-bleak, but since you're surrounded by the great bowl of the Bay, it hardly matters.

Cost $15–50

Address Pier 47, Fisherman's Wharf
℡ 415/771-4383
Open Mon–Thurs & Sun 11.30am–10.30pm, Fri & Sat 11.30am–11.30pm
Transportation 10, 30, F, Powell–Hyde cable car
Accepts All major credit cards except Diners

Dishes may be unsophisticated but they are plain and fresh. Begin with clam chowder ($4.25/6.25), which is made on a thick, creamy roux, and follow with fresh Dungeness crab served with drawn butter, or displayed on a bed of iceberg lettuce as Crab Louis, along with Scoma's own Crab Louis relish, a kind of mayonnaise with additions that they say are their own recipe. The summertime dish of petrale comes blamelessly doréed in a pan after a quick trawl through some egg—interestingly, they use salad oil rather than butter to fry it. Sand dabs, snapper, salmon, Alaskan halibut (flown in specially twice weekly), and any other finned specimens get the same treatment; prices vary from $15 to $55 per entree according to season and market. They also do a brisk traffic in pan-seared steaks, while for dessert, there's that ubiquitous and iniquitous tiramisu ($7.25). Your best bet is the prix fixe dinner menu ($35), or the seasonal prix fixe lunch ($20).

Serious food critics don't come to Wharf restaurants, but that never seems to affect Scoma's, which relies entirely on out-of-town trade and word of mouth, as well as the custom at its own fish depot. It's a pleasant sunny day's outing amid the seals and boats, and you can see why visitors love it, despite the minimal decor and high prices. It makes an easy trip by car, too, as you can avail yourself of the Wharf's subsidized parking.

Nob Hill & Russian Hill

NOB HILL & RUSSIAN HILL

CHESTNUT STREET

Lombard St. Hill

San Francisco Art Institute

LOMBARD STREET

N

GREENWICH STREET

VAN NESS AVENUE

LARKIN STREET

HYDE STREET

LEAVENWORTH STREET

JONES STREET

TAYLOR STREET

FILBERT STREET

Antica Trattoria

Zarzuela

UNION STREET

RUSSIAN HILL

MACONDRAY LANE

Le Petit Robert

GREEN STREET

Frascati

Yabbie's Coastal Kitchen

Pesce

I Fratelli

Ina Coolbrith Park

VALLEJO STREET

Freusier Octagon House

BROADWAY

POLK STREET

Powell-Hyde Cable Car

Allegro Ristorante Italiano

BROADWAY

PACIFIC AVENUE

PACIFIC AVENUE

JACKSON STREET

WASHINGTON STREET

VAN NESS AVENUE

East Coast West Delicatessen

LARKIN STREET

HYDE STREET

JONES STREET

TAYLOR STREET

SACRAMENTO STREET

Grace Cathedral

Swan Oyster Depot

CALIFORNIA STREET

Crustacean

California Line

Nob Hill Masonic Center

PINE STREET

Grubstake

LEAVENWORTH STREET

BUSH STREET

Modern Thai

0   200 yds

Allegro Ristorante Italiano

There are lucky Russian Hill residents who simply walk here every day for supper. It's that kind of place: small, local and family run, with a quietly modish kind of elegance and a very faithful bunch of regulars that includes writers, intellectuals and political heavy hitters. Allegro never advertises and is rarely written up by the press; there's not a lot of room in this intimate trattoria and it

Cost $10–30
Address 1701 Jones St at Broadway
☏ 415/928-4002
Open Daily 5.30–10pm
Transportation Powell–Hyde cable car
Accepts All major credit cards except Diners

doesn't need any more business—it's probably as simple as that. It's easy to understand why folks come back here all the time, because the staff just fall over themselves to make you happy. Only your own mother might spoil you more.

A fresh salad makes the best starter here. Radicchio alla griglia ($5.95) is tossed in garlic and olive oil. Allegro's own version of a ceviche is renamed bocconcini allegro ($6.75), and includes grilled peppers with marinated calamari, plus basil and—an unusual note—mozzarella. Allegro is known for pasta, risotto, and in particular, gnocchi. The Allegro gnocchi ($10.95) are straightforward little dumplings, coated with basil or tomato sauce, with lashings of fresh parmesan and black pepper on the side; almost austere but pretty unbeatable. The penne arrabiata ($9.95), or "angry pasta", comes in a pungently peppered sauce—not all the pastas match their sauces ideally here (orecchiette with chickpeas and eggplant?), but this one does. Allegro's most requested supper dish is a simple pollo al mattone ($11.50), or "brick" chicken, where a half-chicken is grilled under a brick and turns out as juicy and as cozily surrounded by mounds of mashed potato and grilled vegetables as you could hope for. Several veal scallopini and steak dishes appear as main courses, along with the fish of the day. Bistecca Russian Hill ($17.95) is the most expensive item and, like the other main dishes, it comes with additional fresh vegetables.

Nobody would complain about these hardly gouging prices. Since Allegro seats fewer than fifty, and has a reasonably wide-ranging menu for its size, it must be one of the last great philanthropic institutions of the city.

Antica Trattoria

Antica Trattoria's popularity at weekends used to make folks wonder if Russian Hill felt deprived of restaurant choices. Despite the clusters of new eateries in this area, reservations are still essential, though there is less tension about getting a table than there used to be, and less tension about getting to it in time, probably because traffic and parking issues loom far less large on Friday nights than they did back in the old days. The hostess used to (rightly) caution diners on the phone that they might have to vacate the table for the next party if late. But things have relaxed inside Ruggiero Gadaldi's upscale, neighborhood Italian, where mature and well-heeled diners loll around white-clothed tables in the austere elegance of the half-paneled room. They have no trouble finishing their meal in complete *dolce far niente* comfort these days. The welcome is warm, and there's no parking panic—the Gadaldis have introduced their own.

Cost $25–60
Address 2400 Polk St at Union
☎ 415/928-5797
Open Tues–Thurs & Sun 5.30–9.30pm, Fri & Sat 5.30–10.30pm
Transportation 19, 41, 45, 47, 49
Accepts All major credit cards except AMEX

Waiters take the trouble to coach diners on food, and point out the appropriate and complementary wines. Start with antipasti ($9.75) and bruschetta ($5), both ordinary but fine. Risotto ($12.50) has been known to be cooked somewhat past the critical point, but that's the kind of thing that happens on crowded nights. Fusilli with steamed vegetables ($11.50) is perfectly finished, if ordinary. The striped bass ($17.50), on the other hand, is succulent and unspoiled, done simply with steamed zucchini—and perfect that way. For dessert there's tiramisu ($5), and it's pleasant enough, if not the homely confection of mascarpone and Tia Maria of your dreams. Panna cotta with fresh raspberries and strawberries ($5) may please you better.

Although it has seemed uneven, Antica Trattoria earns universal acclaim from local critics. One thing is certain: the situation improves on weekday nights. Along with Pesce, which Gadaldi also co-owns, Antica now valet-parks for diners at the nearby Alhambra gym for $10. Truly, a sad fate for the most beautiful single-picture movie house in the city, a veritable poem of faux-Moresque rococo, but it puts Antica within reach.

Crustacean

With its showy, well-stocked bar, 270-foot-long exterior glass wave, maritime wall murals and elevator adorned with a large, pink, neon crab sign, Crustacean certainly makes a splash. It draws crowds at weekends and expects a certain spiffiness in its clientele, all of whom seem prepared to wait for the pleasure of cracking some crabs while their credit cards melt. This is the upscale, uptown sibling of Thanh Long, the An family's rollicking crab house way out west in the Avenues, where locals have been cracking crab for generations. In 1991, Diana An's children opened this neon marine wonderland, which has Vegas glitz and buzz in spades, along with a dress code: no T-shirts or jeans allowed, it's linen and bibs!

Cost	$35–85
Address	1475 Polk St at California
☎	415/776-2722
Open	Mon–Wed 5–10pm, Thurs–Sun 11.30am–4pm & 5–10.30pm
Transportation	1, 19, 47, 49, California St cable car
Accepts	All major credit cards

It's all about the Dungeness crab ($33–35) here: roast, "drunken," or sweet-and-sour. "Drunken" means poached in three wines with spring onions and spices, "sweet-and-sour" means Asian-style, but the trademark of Crustacean, the single dish that made its name, is the garlicked roast crab, best eaten with their celebrated garlic noodles ($9.25). The noodle recipe, identical to Thanh Long's, is so secret it has to be made elsewhere and brought here under wraps—it seems that the secret is about a pound of butter per noodle, and almost as much garlic! But crabs aren't the only specialty of the house. Vietnamese cha gio rolls ($8.25) are stuffed with crab and pork, and either deep-fried or served "imperial" style—cold, with cellophane noodles. There are fat marinated satays of giant shrimp and chicken ($9.25). Shrimp-stuffed squid with mushrooms ($10.25) comes in a delicate nectar of spices and nuoc mam dipping sauce. But face it: a messily orgiastic meal of crab is what most people want at Crustacean, served with linens rather than plastic bibs amid a sophisticated ambiance. For desserts, try the celebrated lemon sorbet in half-lemon bowls ($6.25), a nice party-capper.

Remember to reserve, though you may still have to wait for the food. But if your wallet is on a diet, take it on a trip out west to Thanh's instead. Oh, and parking? Forget it.

East Coast West Delicatessen

Opened in 2001 to comfort all the homesick New Yorkers, East Coast West Deli looks borderline bleak from the outside. But that's just an affectation. On the inside, the decor may also be on the sparse side, but the handsome tiles, the photos of Billie singing the blues and the warm atmosphere encourage you to stick around and give the sandwiches, bagels and gefilte fish the time of day.

Cost $8–20

Address 1725 Polk St at Clay
☎ 415/563-3542
Open Mon–Fri 10am–9pm,
Sat & Sun 8am–9pm
Transportation 19
Accepts MasterCard, Visa

The acid test has to be potato latke ($10), or "potato pancakes", as they're styled here. They come authentically buttery: golden and crispy on the outside and soft on the inside. If you're really hungry, order a "pancake delight" ($10), which adds sliced pastrami and corned beef on top of two pancakes, with a few pickles on the side. It's all undeniably filling as a brunch dish. But then again, maybe a nice chicken soup with matzo balls ($11) is a more traditional choice, the body-building aroma of chicken reinforced with chewy dumplings. Corned beef sandwiches ($10.50), heroic in size and served on a credible rye bread, are nicely done. If you're into making a mess, order the smoked salmon, herring or whitefish platter (all $10) and make your own sandwich—tool around with your lump of fish in a heap of capers, iceberg lettuce, sliced onions, cream cheese, and bagels, and build yourself a brunch. Stuffed cabbage ($10.50) is another heart-warmingly traditional choice, in which minced beef is mixed with diced onion and wrapped up inside a steaming cabbage leaf. Any number of smaller items can be added to the plate. Chicken livers ($8) are not an over puréed pâté or sandwich paste, but have a rougher texture that you only get from a manually chopped liver. For afterwards, it's no contest: go for the cheese-filled blintzes ($5) or light dessert pancakes with applesauce on the side ($5). There's also a noodle pudding-style kugel with lots of candied fruit ($4).

All in all there's only one complaint, and it's that nobody's rude in here, in the true New York deli style. But since there's not much serious competition—aside from Moishe's Pipic and David's—East Coast West is likely to enjoy a long run.

Frascati

Frascati is no longer your friendly little Italian on the corner. These days it's your pan-Med corner bistro—but still affordable, and often overlooked in favor of flashier Polk Gulch buzz spots. When incoming owners Rebekah and Rich Wood took over the old trattoria, they hung onto the name, the famed chocolate bread pudding, the Russian Hill faithful, mustard walls, and higher-than-usual $15 corkage, as well as the ting-a-ling of passing cable cars.

Cost $35–50
Address 1901 Hyde St at Green
☎ 415/928-1406
Open Daily 5.30–10pm
Transportation 41, 45, Powell–Hyde cable car
Accepts MasterCard, Visa

They've added a wine bar and wooden floors, though the outdoor seating is gone (no permit). The food is as much French or Spanish as Italian. In the bustling kitchen, which you can see from the mezzanine tables, new chef Mark Pollard adds modern touches to what was once a traditional trattoria menu.

Pollard has subtly introduced a few new flavors, so those fabulous Prince Edward Island mussels now come with oregano broth and chorizo ($8.50), while bruschetta arrives near pizza-like, with prosciutto and pears ($9). Perhaps the most likable appetizer is sautéed green beans with ricotta ($7). Their cheese plate offers milky Valençay goat cheese, a triple-cream from Burgundy called Explorateur, a Fourme d'Ambert bleu, and an aged sheep cheese known as Le Lezevou. It's a pretty safe bet that there's a Francophile cheese-nut around here! Of several decorous salads, roast beets with orange, arugula, and goat cheese in hazelnut vinaigrette ($7) is turning into a regular. Lobster bisque ($7) is infused with tarragon and crème fraîche. Pasta courses ($7–9) include porcini tagliatelli, gnocchi with peas and beans, and a couple of risottos ($7 starter, $13 main), one with quail and the other a frisky primavera-style lemon-asparagus number. You can add lobster tail to the risotto at a bargain $21—a bequest from Frascati's old menu. A choice of roast chicken ($18), pork tenderloin ($19), grilled saddle of lamb with a chop ($20), or wine-braised lamb shank ($19), wraps it all up, with pan-roasted halibut ($18) or salmon ($21) as finned options.

Black and white chocolate bread pudding ($7) is a signature, inherited from the previous chef-owners, so give it a go. Cell phones are "confiscated and made into soup," warns the menu.

I Fratelli

Sometimes it seems as though the lucky inhabitants of Russian Hill and Nob Hill think they're living in Naples. They conduct life entirely from neighborhood trattorias, waving joyously at each other as they disembark from the Hyde Street cable car. The occasional French chef sneaks in, but with I Fratelli, Frascati and Allegro perched above the Broadway tunnel, and other Italian places further down the slope, Russian Hill is taking more than its share of the annual pasta harvest.

Cost $12–30
Address 1896 Hyde St at Green
☎ 415/474-8240
Open Daily 5.30–10pm
Transportation 41, 45, Powell–Mason cable car
Accepts All major credit cards except Diners

There's nothing amazing about I Fratelli's food, but it's generous, and the brothers or *fratelli* in question—John and Peter—are entertaining enough to turn the place into one constant party. Their bruschetta ($3.95) is toasted and garlic-rubbed, with sliced tomatoes, Parmesan, and fresh herbs. If you prefer, there's a simpler garlic bread. Prosciutto di Parma ($5.75) is a classic Italian appetizer but only available in season here, which is a good sign. Ceviche ($6.75) isn't particularly Italian, but gets a special dispensation since Russian Hill lies at the heart of a city that loves raw fish to a fault; the marinade isn't bad, and you'll find rock shrimp as well as chilled calamari in a kind of vinaigrette sweetened with red onion and tomatoes, with lots of cilantro on top. A beef carpaccio ($7.90) is triumphant with big caper buds and Parmesan flakes. A grilled vegetable plate ($6.75) is a mixture of eggplant and peppers lightly tossed in oil, with little crunchy corners. Among the pastas, "birthday fettucine" ($13.90) comes with andouille, tasso, chicken, shrimp, and a creamy roux—it's like a jambalaya served on pasta instead of rice. Several veal dishes come in a number of different sauces, beginning with a simple piccata ($16.90). Dolci include cheese flan with berries ($6), and fine old Fonseca ports to wash them down.

Unpretentious, and well signposted on a corner blazing with light, I Fratelli does well for a modest neighborhood place. Come Friday you'll find the joint already jumping with a large cast of locals, often with children in tow, hovering over the blue-checked tables and enjoying their Chianti with the good humor that seems rampant in this little Naples by the Bay.

Grubstake

It may look a little tacked together from the outside, but Grubstake boasts a cute deck, adorned with just one plastic table, next to what looks like a mural-splattered train caboose. The inside looks like a railcar diner, complete with period windows, because half of Grubstake is just that: it was built from a historic dining car that once ran on the Key Route electric trains from Berkeley. It opened in 1937 as the Orient Express diner, and it's now mainly taken up by a bar—the dining half out front was added on 35 years ago. A very mixed crowd of locals, some very old and some very young—Grubstake is child-friendly—hangs out here for burgers, breakfasts and the unique Portuguese Corner menu. In fact, Grubstake serves the only Portuguese food in the city.

Cost $5–25
Address 1525 Pine St at Polk
☎ 415/673-8268
Open Daily 5pm–4am, Sat & Sun 10am–4am
Transportation 19, 47, 49, California St cable car
Accepts All major credit cards except Diners

The owners are unhurried, friendly, and yes, mainly Portuguese, though many dishes originate closer to home. The chile-rubbed chicken wings ($5) are good and spicy, while jalapeno poppers ($5) sound surprising and are, in their way—they turn out to be crispy fried peppers, not eye-popping and not bad. A series of burgers with historically inspired names like "Claim Jumper" and "Gold Rush Blue" are very inexpensively priced (from $5), though more of an effort could be made with the uninspired buns. The dishes on the Portuguese menu, on the other hand, are more interesting. A crispy fried trout ($12) served "com todos" with potatoes and vegetables is perfectly delicious. So too are Portuguese-style costelatas a Alentejana ($9.50); these lamb chops are seasoned with wine and a garlicky bite and served with slightly dry, peppery mashed potatoes—great comfort food. So head for Grubstake's Portuguese Corner, or come for the filling weekend brunch menu of omelets, pancakes and variations like "Mountainy Man"—three eggs and ham. All brunch items are priced under or around $5. Espressos and cappuccinos are good here too, and they serve a Portuguese vinho verde ($14).

But far and away the potent selling point of Grubstake is its late hours. Bar-hoppers and night-crawlers know that they can come here way past 3am for decent, filling Portuguese food.

THAI

Modern Thai

(🍴) Sometimes you wonder how all the Thai places along Polk Street manage to do it. A cluster of great Thai restaurants flourishes in a few down-at-heel blocks, and the resulting competition produces some of the most interesting food for the smallest outlay. All the restaurants are usefully near the movie theaters too. First and foremost is Modern Thai, with its very agreeable outside patio—for balmy nights—and an interior that includes vaguely Victorian touches, like the "Venice of the Orient" photos of Bangkok, dating from around 1900.

Cost $8–20

Address 1247 Polk St at Bush
℡ 415/922-8424
Open Mon & Wed–Sun 11am–10pm
Transportation 19, 38
Accepts All major credit cards except Diners

Teak-brown colonial chairs, white linen with fresh flowers and plum walls have transformed what was once an Italian trattoria. Otherwise, there are no special extras to hike up the prices, although a bunch of magazines adorns a large harmonium (for playing hymns?) Crab or prawn pad Thai noodles ($6.25) have an extra tamarind and palm sugar sweetness, and make a robust starter. Chicken satay ($6.95) is three hefty skewers loaded with peanut sauce, plus a cucumber salad. Som-tum ($5.95) is a green papaya salad, and comes very hot indeed, thanks to the chile-lime dressing; it's possibly just too hot, but excellent value nonetheless. Several fish dishes give a choice of very different spicings: salmon with Thai choo-chee red curry coconut sauce ($12.95), fried trout in a chile tamarind sauce ($10.95), and trout steamed in a banana leaf ($9.95) are all sensational. Roast duck curry with Thai basil and coconut ($8.95) is another standout. Sticky rice ($2) and mango ($2) are the desserts of choice. The red and white house wines are a mere $2.50 per glass: cheap but still gulpable.

This is just one of several good, bargain Thais around Polk Gulch. Chai-Yo, a Thai noodle spot at 1331 Polk Street, specializes in really traditional Thai cuisine, with dishes such as pork blood soup. One Asia, on Larkin Street, is a relatively fancy-looking place that's cheap, but earns plaudits. Then there's Little Thai at 2065 Polk, higher up; you won't believe your luck in there either. But Modern Thai is a favorite, if only because you can sit outside on a warm night, and because it's super-handy for everywhere.

Pesce

When owner Ruggiero Gadaldi opened another seafood joint near his thriving Antica Trattoria, there was an immediate cheer on Russian Hill. This is a smaller, stripped-down version of its parent, with a hotly beating Italian heart with a passion for seafood as its driving force. You might even prefer the informal atmosphere. A blackboard of daily spe-

Cost $10–25
Address 2227 Polk St at Vallejo
☎ 415/928-8025
Open Mon–Sat 5–11pm
Transportation 19
Accepts MasterCard, Visa

cials dangles on a string at the door, advertising a fresher-than-fresh seafood menu that pulls in a happy crowd. As a bar-cum-cafe with a serious seafood menu, Pesce has an undeniably individual flavor, and while it doesn't have much in the way of decor—tables are the bare, rickety minimum—it somehow compensates by being richly atmospheric.

A yeasty crowd of local roués and their girlfriends perch at the counter and grab the menu board as it passes around the joint. Dishes change regularly, but you might find a bacalao plate ($8), a traditional tapas variation on brandade that's like cod fishcakes and pretty satisfying. In winter, local petrale ($13.50) are very good here—basically, Pesce's kitchen just introduces a fresh fish that was swimming earlier that day to a brief liaison with butter. Grilled salmon ($14) is a little more serious, and broiled tuna ($15) is accompanied by side orders of vegetables. This is one place to try the traditional cioppino ($18). Pesce's version really delivers a classic, with lots of flavorsome salmon and cod and sea bass in a true fisherman's stew, crowned with crab legs and served over massive mounds of polenta. Halibut is poached and dished up in a spicy broth. Crabcakes are large-flaked and generously proportioned, and come accompanied by a tartare that's loaded with olives and capers.

One warning: don't come here if you're looking for vegetables or meat. You'll find yourself out of luck if you try to find street parking too. But in an adroit business move, the Gadaldi crew has taken over the Alhambra, and now all the restaurants along Upper Polk can use it for valet parking for a flat $10 fee. It's a brilliant solution to the parking problem, and has caused a new Upper Polk "restaurant row" to blaze into being overnight.

FRENCH

Le Petit Robert

The French community of San Francisco dates from the nineteenth century, when it launched Boudin's Bakery and ran churches, hospitals and restaurants, and this city is still full of Frenchmen with a mission to feed. But lately the busiest missionary from la belle France has been Pascal Rigo, owner of Chez Nous, Galette and Panissimo Bakery, and baker of more

Cost	$15–30
Address	2300 Polk St at Green
☏	415/922-8100
Open	Daily 10am–11pm
Transportation	19, 41, 45, 47, 49
Accepts	MasterCard, Visa

tarte Tatin than you can throw your croissant at. In this attractive Russian Hill cafe, you'll find a long, wood-floored room with a high ceiling, and tables that invite you to plonk down a newspaper beside your coffee and sauçisson sandwich. There's a small bar and lots of bustle, so don't come in here for a quiet tête-à-tête.

Chef Robert Cubberly has been lured from Fog City Diner to do the mix-'em-and-match-'em small-plates thing, and the food is quite serious, if small in scale. Interesting soups change daily, and may include a simple but good soupe a l'oignon ($7), wearing Swiss cheese. The sauçisson charcuterie plate ($9) comes with tiny pickles and Dijon mustard. Salads change daily too, and can be light, like mesclun with pomegranate or candied pecans ($6.50), or fussy, like frisée with sautéed potatoes, smoky bacon, and a few bits of duck confit ($8). A fresh and simple leek salad ($8) comes barely parboiled, with a mustardy vinaigrette, and can usually be found on the menu in the right winter months. Cod brandade ($8.50) is a small piece of cod on a heap of mashed potatoes. The message may be that we're all eating less nowadays. But if you really need to feed the beast, and don't want to add three small plates together, then go for a grande assiette like steak frites ($15), gigot d'agneau ($15), or duck cassoulet ($13.50), swimming with beans and Toulouse sausage. These main dishes also change daily, and make Le Petit Robert more than a cafe.

For dessert, there's a pot de crème with praline ($7), which comes in a pretty little recycled jar. But it's the celebrated tarte Tatin ($7) that wins top votes—it's an apple pie turned on its head so the buttery outside is topmost and the apple below, and utterly delicious.

Swan Oyster Depot

Time-travel rarely gets more nostalgic than at Swan's, an antique whose faithful followers have only two gripes—that the five Sancimino brothers don't stay open all night long, or at least into the evening (for some reason these guys like to go home) and that they only take cash. All that aside, and notwithstanding the long wait for the rather creaky bar stools to free up, nothing could be more pleasant at this Edwardian temple to bi-valves. A couple of giant wall charts showing fish of the world will help you kill time. Hey, this place hasn't changed in ninety years: you expected to make reservations?

Cost $7–25	

Address 1517 Polk St at California
☎ 415/679-1101
Open Mon–Sat 8am–5.30pm
Transportation 1, 19, 47, 49, California St cable car
Accepts Cash only

Once wedged in at the counter, you'll have a basket of fresh sourdough bread, some beer or wine, chunks of lemon, one Sancimino brother and a bottle of Tabasco in front of you, plus those old-fashioned crackers that come in little packets. A dozen oysters will cost just under $14 in bills and they'll be from nearby Tomales Bay or Hog Island—most probably from Johnson's Oyster Farm. They're so fresh that as they slip down your throat, having given up their all a second earlier, you'll find yourself pondering if this is murder, pure and simple, as food writer MFK Fisher once claimed, or just heaven, with the essence of the ocean in every oyster. People who didn't "get" oysters before should come here for a sudden conversion experience. You can eat other things, of course: the clam chowder ($4.25) is creamy, full of good stuff and famous for winning a "world's best" award, while the crab Louie ($9.95) and other salads are simple, old-fashioned, and unfussy to the point of being undressed. You request the vinaigrette or mayonnaise dressing yourself.

That's that for Swan's menu, but there are a couple of bonuses. The AMC multiplex around the corner in the former Cadillac building is short on affordable eating options before movie matinees; so here's one. Attention-starved San Francisco ladies like to come down to Swan's for cheering company, the alternative being the seven Lucca brothers' deli on Valencia Street. This is a terrible town for women in some ways but, all told, it's a terrific town for oysters.

Yabbies Coastal Kitchen

On Friday and Saturday nights, Yabbies looks very seductive indeed. Flooded with laughter, and filled with urban professionals hoping for roistering and oystering, it's a really fine-looking slice of architectural design, from its glassy tiles to the clever little oyster bar and Persian-design cushioning on the wall seats. Up at the classy end of Polk, there's enough polish in its setting to lure in passers-by, who check the long and stylish wine list then stay to check out the oysters. Even if you weren't looking for something deliciously fishy, you'd have plenty to eyeball over a martini or a cosmopolitan at the well-stocked wine bar.

Cost $15–35
Address 2237 Polk St at Vallejo
☎ 415/474-4088
Open Mon–Thurs & Sun 6–9pm, Fri & Sat 6–10.30pm
Transportation 19, 41, 45, 47, 49
Accepts MasterCard, Visa

Yabbies is apparently the Aussie name for those mini-crayfish that pinch your toes when you're paddling. Something like them appears in their splendid raw bar, which also features several varieties of oyster, including rare Washington and British Columbia types ($1.95 each). There are also solid, sunset-pink Dungeness crabs, plus fat prawns, clams and New Zealand mussels, all displayed wantonly about a little glassed-in tub of ice. A definite Aussie glow warms the menu, which carries Australian wines and includes a blazing Oz-style version of cioppino ($19.50) with lots of chile. The chef here used to be Mark Lusardi, who carried an experience of Thai and other Asian food over into spice management, and added oodles of chile and cilantro. He has now rolled on but, it seems, his legacy continues. Yabbies makes the seaweed-cured Hawaiian tuna called "poke," ($10.25), a form of ceviche unique to the islands. Some main dishes are featured, including Thai snapper with teensy Manila clams ($17.75), mahi-mahi grilled with sesame-and-mushroom noodles ($17.75), swordfish with a puttanesca sauce ($18.75), salmon grilled au naturel ($18.25), and prawns with basil, red chile oil, and ginger ($17.25). A couple of chicken dishes are on tap for non-fish-eaters.

Yabbies is a fun dating spot, or maybe even a fun place to find a date. Service is friendly and the general atmosphere is one of bonhomie. With Swan Oyster Depot at the other end of Polk Street, Russian Hill is spoiled for bi-valves.

Zarzuela

As faux-Madrid tapas hotspots go, Zarzuela's is one of the oldest of scores around town. It's also one of the best partying spots on the hill. You can't really miss it: the egg-yolk yellow awning is right on the corner. A zarzuela (seafood stew) is always on hand here, even if the music track is not always real Zarzuela (another meaning of the word that signifies a Spanish potboiler opera, complete with blood-and-guts plots). But every-

Cost $15–35

Address 2000 Hyde St at Union
☎ 415/346-0800
Open Tues–Thurs 5.30–10pm, Fri & Sat 5.30–10.30pm
Transportation 45, Powell–Mason cable car
Accepts MasterCard, Visa

thing's as authentically Spanish as chef-owner Lucas Casco can make it. As one of the first to launch tapas in San Francisco, he's done his best to turn this into a real copy of Madrid's Puerto del Sol tapas bars, though his carefully dressed tables with hand-decorated ceramics are a little bit spiffier than the originals. The only complaint around here is the waiting, because they don't take reservations—oh, and they could use some parking spots too.

First things first: they bring black Spanish olives and a solid levain-style bread to the table when you first arrive. Jugs of sangria come next, and then a list of the tapas of the day, which changes frequently. A Spanish bruschetta-style bread with tomato topping ($3.75) is a plain but healthy start. Mushrooms sautéed in garlic and white wine ($5.50) are another popular kick-off, along with the classic tortilla española ($3.50) and the equally familiar spicy shrimp with aioli ($6.75). Poached calamari ($6.75) and a chilled plate of escalibada ($8.25), a delicious mess of grilled and roasted vegetables, are two further classical choices, as are the boquerones con piquillo of anchovies with peppers ($5.25) and the duck leg ($8.25). Sometimes Manchego cheese is available, a nice slice, and there's often Serrano ham too. Cakey desserts ($4.50) such as angel-cake and cheesecake will sweep you away.

For a party paella ($14.95 per person) to share among a table, you'll need to drop a hint ahead of time because it takes a good half an hour or more to cook. It's well worth the wait, but remember that they'll add a 15-percent group surcharge. Or give their house special of zarzuela ($14.95) a go. It couldn't be a more appropriate order.

North & Central

The Marina, Cow Hollow & Pacific
Heights
p.128

Japantown, Fillmore & the Western
Addition
p.153

The Richmond
p.171

The Civic Center & Hayes Valley
p.199

The Haight Ashbury District & Cole
Valley
p.219

The Marina, Cow Hollow & Pacific Heights

THE MARINA, COW HOLLOW
& PACIFIC HEIGHTS

Ace Wasabi's Rock & Roll
Izzy's Steak & Chophouse
Sushi
Cozmo's Corner Grill
CHESTNUT ST
LOMBARD ST
Plump Jack Café
Bistro Aix
GREENWICH ST
Balboa Café
FILBERT ST
Eastside West
Crissy Field

St Francis Yacht Club

San Francisco Bay

Municipal Pier

Greens
Marina Green
MARINA BLVD
Magic Theater
African American Cultural Society

Palace of Fine Arts & Exploratorium
JEFFERSON ST
BAKER STREET
MARINA
BEACH STREET
Mexican Museum
NORTH POINT STREET
FORT MASON
Presidio Museum

FUNSTON AVE
PRESIDIO BLVD
Baker Street Bistro
Meze's
See inset
LOMBARD ST
COW HOLLOW
GOUGH STREET
OCTAVIA STREET
FRANKLIN STREET
VAN NESS AVENUE

Curbside Too
Liverpool Lil's
Lhasa Moon
GREENWICH STREET

WEBSTER ST
The Brazen Head
FILBERT STREET
Perry's Sports Bar
UNION STREET

N

Café de Paris L'Entrecote
Betelnut Pejiu Wu
Charlie's
GREEN STREET

LYON STREET
Rose's Café
FILLMORE ST
VALLEJO STREET
BROADWAY

PACIFIC HEIGHTS
BUCHANAN ST
PACIFIC AVENUE
Haas Lilienthal House
Spreckels Mansion

BAKER STREET
BRODERICK ST
JACKSON STREET
Alta Plaza Park
Jackson
WASHINGTON ST

PRESIDIO AVENUE
SPRUCE STREET
WASHINGTON ST
CLAY STREET
STEINER ST
Fillmore Trattoria
Lafayette Park
CLAY STREET

SACRAMENTO STREET
Sociale
CALIFORNIA STREET
Ella's
SACRAMENTO STREET
CALIFORNIA STREET

0   500 yds

Ace Wasabi's Rock and Roll Sushi

Since the same guys that launched Tokyo GoGo own this happening place, it probably comes as no surprise to learn that it's no run-of-the-mill sushi bar. It's a throbbing izayaka, or cocktail bar, with live entertainment, sumo wrestling on a TV screen, happy hours, and a "sushi cam" that relays pictures of you popping raw fish in your mouth to your friends. Oh, and lots of sushi. The soundtrack is of deafening rock music

Cost $10–30
Address 339 Steiner St at Chestnut
☎ 415/567-4903
Open Mon–Thurs 5.30–10.30pm, Fri & Sat 5.30–11pm, Sun 5–10pm
Transportation 22, 28, 30, 43
Accepts All major credit cards except Diners

and braying young professionals; don't come here for a tête-à-tête. Come here for fusion and confusion, and always read the specials on the board above the counter.

There's great sushi to be discovered here, washed down with special cocktails made from rare and wondrous sakes such as iced blackberry and raspberry ($4), a sake punch smoothie ($5), and the famous onoko-roshi sake, which is much prized and hard to get. Wacky sushi combinations include the Flying Kamikaze ($10.50), which is spicy tuna, albacore, and asparagus in ponzu sauce; the Three Amigos ($10.50), which is tuna, yellowtail, and eel with cucumber and avocado daubed with wasabe tobiko; and the spider roll ($9.75), which is fried softshell crab, avocado, and lettuce. Ace Wasabi's is so fusion-oriented that they go so far as to call their other creations "Japanese tapas." Some of the more charming ones are a spinach noodle cake in spicy peanut sauce ($5.95) and a hotter-than-hot wasabe potato salad with tamari honey-marinated salmon. Endamame ($3.50) and spicy beans ($5.50) will please vegetarians, although the portions are small. Potstickers come in ahi or hamachi with a chile sauce ($8.25). Satays are also wildly inspired: try the large, rare shrimp in vinegar ($7.95); tofu in garlic miso ($3.25); or chicken teriyaki ($3.75). Duck duck ($9.75) turns out to be a kind of duck sushi in a spinach and daikon salad, and not a bad idea.

When you get bored there's always something to look at in here, from sumo to bingo. But you won't get bored, though possibly somewhat deafened or a little annoyed by the insistent hipness factor. If you can handle all that, however, this place is fun.

Baker Street Bistro

If you happen to be near the Presidio on a warm night, stroll up here to check out chef Jacques Manuera's unpretentious but sweet bistro. Baker Street is tucked away off the main drag, which makes it all the nicer to take a table on the sidewalk and savor the twilight moment when the waiter comes by to light the candles. Enjoy escargots or pâté over a glass or two of well-selected wines and, if you like what you see, follow up with some simple country dishes.

Cost $15–30

Address 2953 Baker St at Greenwich
℗ 415/931-1475
Open Tues–Sat 7am–2pm & 5.30–10.30pm, Sun 7am–2pm & 5–9.30pm
Transportation 28, 41, 43, 45
Accepts MasterCard, Visa

The menu changes nightly, and there's always a pâté; the duck liver ($4) is a handsomely fluffy, mousse-like dollop with little pickles on the side. Escargots ($6.50) are almost a meal in themselves, tossed with mushrooms and shallots in an intense white wine reduction, then dished onto a heap of well-parsleyed angel-hair pasta. If the chef puts the regular mousseline of scallops ($7) on the menu, go for it, because it's a subtle, cream custard-style affair, served with very fresh and garlicky prawns—you'll be licking your fingers shamelessly. A Bay Area influence appears in the strong ginger brunoise sauce that adorns the dish of chicken breast ($9.75). There's always rabbit on the menu, such as the plump Sonoma rabbit in Dijon mustard sauce with pasta and vegetables ($10.75). It's available both a la carte and on the prix fixe menu and is very enjoyable, as are the veal blanquette de veau ($10.75), lamb ragout ($10.75), and steak ($13.50), which comes with steamed potatoes and vegetables. Among the desserts, poached pears ($4), crème brûlée ($5), and crème caramel ($3.50) are welcome, and there's usually a nice cake or vacherin on special.

The four-course prix fixe ($14.50) is one of the best deals in the Marina. That's saying something, as this part of town has several good French places, including the nearby Curbside Too, Cafe de l'Entrecôte, and Bistro Aix. And come Christmas Eve, New Year's Eve and other big major holidays, chef Manuera turns into a local philanthropist when he puts on a $45 lobster and foie gras multi-course feast. A welcome respite from turkey.

Balboa Cafe

Years ago this clubby landmark was the heart of the Marina singles scene, a known point of the Bermuda Triangle. Back in the twentieth century, bachelors came here of a Friday night, never to be seen again until Monday. A few years back, Gavin Newsom and the Getty boys took over this corner opposite their PlumpJack wine empire and Eastside West cafe. They lightened up the decor with "American bar" wood and brass, comfy chairs and a whiff of spiffiness. The linen is starched and impeccable, even if the service is no longer starchy older guys but gorgeous young women in white coats. The singles scene continues of a weekend, but on weekdays it's suits and an older crowd—you'd never know a body ever met a body over a glass of rye, other than to thrash real estate deals out.

Cost $15–50
Address 3199 Fillmore St at Greenwich
☎ 415/921-3944
Open Mon–Wed 11.30am–10pm, Thurs–Sat 11.30am–11pm, Sun 11am–10pm
Transportation 22, 28, 30, 41, 45
Accepts All major credit cards except Diners

The Balboa's owners have kept the menu classics. Their "thing," the dish they've always been known for, is the acclaimed hamburger ($9.50), a pleasant but virginally unseasoned cobble-stone of ground beef between two wagon wheels of flavorless tomato on a crispy baguette, with very skinny, crisp French-style unseasoned fries on the side. You might find the pork barbecue version ($9) more flavorful. Gravlax ($9) is another regular favorite around here: Balboa's is sweetish—you'd never know it had lain in salt and fennel for three days; three accompanying potato cakes were stingy mini-medallions. Homemade artisan bread is a strong point too, but the kitchen seems to forget the seasoning again: have the anti-salt police been in? Generally the food is fine, just not as jammed full of taste as it might seem with a few drinks sloshing around inside you on a Friday night. The dinner menu offers risotto ($14), herbed chicken ($18), steak frites ($27.50), and Peeketoe crab Napoleon ($18.50).

The wine list is a lot more interesting than this standard comfort fare. In fact, the food furnishes an excuse to explore Balboa's large and questing cellar of rare New Zealand Sauvignon Blancs, Australian Syrahs and Californian everythings. At $7 a glass, you won't be robbed if you want to try several.

Betelnut Pejiu Wu

"Pejiu wu" translates from Chinese as "brew house" or "pub," while betelnuts are the stimulating Areca nut and Betel leaf with lime that southeast Asians and Pacific islanders chew. This comes only as background to what is one of the more frenzied dining experiences in a town that offers plenty of frenzies. Betelnut is a hallowed shrine of pan-Asian food that presents only one real problem, and that's getting a table. So lively is the scene here than just getting to the bright red bar and finding an empty stool while you wait is a challenge.

Cost $15–40
Address 2030 Union St at Buchanan
☎ 415/929-8855
Open Mon–Thurs & Sun 11.30am–11pm, Fri & Sat 11.30am–midnight
Transportation 22, 41, 45
Accepts MasterCard, Visa

Slow revolving fans and rattan walls bring a whiff of tropical Penang. It's a stage for showing off cocktails with lemon twists and things to twirl: from the inevitable Singapore Sling ($5.50) of gin, cherry, and lemon, to the dangerous Tsunami ($5.50) of amaretto, Southern Comfort, and "exotic juices". The Betel Juice ($5.25) does not in fact contain betel, just white rum and pineapple with Midori, but there are more sinister combos, like "Bloody Mary's Chewing Betel Nuts" ($5), which is just too darned hot to handle with its bird's eye chile and garlic. After that, you dive into a very long list of pan-Asian tapas such as stupendously fiery, chile-crusted calamari ($6.95), chicken satay with Indonesian peanut dip ($5.95), and salt-and-pepper Gulf prawns ($7.95). This sort of finger food will soon sweep all the bars in town. Vegetarians may choose a bowl of country-style miso with oishi vegetables and tofu ($6.95) along with a deep-fried mound of chile-crusted green beans ($7). There are several good noodle dishes and a few familiar and unfamiliar salads like the green papaya ($6.95), which is perfectly Thai in seasoning, and the Japanese "tako" salad of squid, cucumber, and Asian pears ($8.95). For the very hungry, there's barbecued chicken ($12.95), barbecued Mongolian beef ($12.95) served with crumbly "old man" sesame biscuits, and char-broiled pork ($11.25), which comes with green onions.

This is truly pan-Asian food, ranging from Indian nan bread to hibachis grilled Korean-style and the Mongolian barbecue. But Betelnut's so consistently popular that you'll probably be too busy looking at the cooler-than-cool people to ponder much.

Bistro Aix

Bistro Aix is just a stone's throw from the Bermuda Triangle, as the yuppie cruising nexus of the Marina is known, due to the mysterious disappearances that take place in bars there nightly. But Bistro Aix is set back from all that sad hurly-burly, managing to maintain a dignified restraint. Its quarters are pretty and artsy, and there's a pleasantly protected and heated patio where the New York Museum of Modern Art has been

Cost $15–35
Address 3340 Steiner St at Chestnut
☎ 415/202-0100
Open Mon–Thurs & Sun 6–10pm, Fri & Sat 6–11pm
Transportation 22, 28, 30, 45
Accepts All major credit cards except Diners

kind enough to loan a spectacular mural version of Van Gogh's famous canvas "Starry Night"—so that's why it disappeared a year or so ago! Seriously, John Beard's bistro is one of those places that seem to have taken the classic French brasserie formula and got it right, in an easy-going and fun way.

"Aix" presents a pretty wide set of choices that change daily. It always begins with a soup, such as their celestial chard and cranberry beans ($4.50), the risotto of the day ($7.95), or a homemade gravlax plate ($7.95). But the real specialty is the classic steak pommes frites ($17.95), which arrives with sautéed potatoes and a large knob of butter. Other favorites are the top sirloin burger ($8.50) and the roast half-chicken with mashed potatoes combination ($15.95). All are drop-dead delicious. Of several fish dishes that are always on offer, the ahi tuna with spinach ($18.75) is a standout. These entrees can be ordered separately but are also featured dishes on the $14.95 two-course menu, along with a pasta choice such as shellfish risotto, where they are accompanied by soup or salad. Desserts like the homemade sorbets are an additional $6 but you're unlikely to find any room.

A fairly limited but clever wine list offers a dozen or so red and another dozen white wines by the glass, well selected and well priced, with a couple of half bottles in each category, mainly French. Decent beers like Späten are on tap. Unlike so many other places that try to overdo (or underdo) their French bistro food, this is good, uncomplicated stuff, and very nicely presented.

The Brazen Head Restaurant

This clubby, pubby neighborhood supper club is almost too secret to mention aloud, let alone put in a guide. A haunt of politicians and newspaper hacks, it was named for the oldest pub in Ireland, the 1666 haunt of Emmet and Fitzgerald that got *its* name from a red-head of ill repute who lost her head at the Battle of Limerick. Anyone who knows the original can tell you that similarities stop there. The best thing about Eddy Savino's Brazen Head isn't its notoriety, it's the secrecy. Clippings may deck the walls but they never advertize, there's no sign and they disdain reservations. You'll be plonked on a barstool and plied with simpatico barman-talk while they wait for regulars to slope off into the night and free up a table.

Cost $15–40
Address 3166 Buchanan St at Greenwich
☎ 415/921-7600
Open Daily 5pm–1am
Transportation 22, 30, 43
Accepts Cash or debit cards only

The fare is not exactly traditional pub fare either (in the original Brazen Head you'd be lucky to find a cellophane-cheese sandwich). It's even too gourmet to be haute pub cuisine. On the other hand, it reads like a cook dreaming up a menu from what's available and what they'd like themselves. Hearty homemade soups may include soupe à l'oignon with gruyèred toast ($4.95), or lentil soup with curry and ginger ($4.95). The very garlicky snails ($7.95) are another regular dish. Rich, thick-flaked crabcakes ($9.25) come with an equally chunky herbed mayonnaise, and the Brazen Head has possibly the strongest-seasoned Caesar salad in town ($4.50). The steak au poivre ($24) is always enjoyable; it's rubbed with garlic, seared in butter, flamed in brandy, then smothered in a sauce made from pan juices reduced with cream and served with potatoes au gratin—a cholesterol zinger for a certain kind of what-the-hay mood. The recipe works less well on chicken ($18), but it's still dreamy with those potatoes, tenderly layered with butter and cream.

Even if no table is vacant, you'll be just dandy at the Brazen's horse-shoe counter. In fact, it's perfect for a late-night meal à deux, with George Shearing chords wafting off a tape and the smell of steaks flam-béing in the kitchen.

Cafe de Paris l'Entrecote

Few places feel more old-time than Cafe de Paris. This Union Street fixture is so comfortably retro that just coming in to look around is a nostalgia spree. If you prefer to sit outside, the pleasantly sheltered sidewalk seating makes a nice lunch or twilight resting place. The number one pride and joy here, however, is the entrecôte sauce invented by Monsieur Freddy Dumont in 1941, using a secret recipe of a dozen ingredients; it's chock-full of garlic and butter.

Cost $25–50

Address 2032 Union St
☎ 415/931-5006
Open Mon–Thurs
11.30am–11pm, Fri & Sat
11.30am–2am, Sun
11.30am–10pm
Transportation 22, 41, 45
Accepts All major credit cards
except Diners

The number two pride and joy here is chef Bruce DeFalco, who says he is a nouvelle cuisine enthusiast, though you'd never know it from his golden, crispy, addictive pommes frites—the number three pride and joy at Cafe de Paris. It's too bad they don't serve these at the sidewalk tables. Indeed, there are folks who want to order the fries as an appetizer without the accompanying hamburger—in vain. Instead, there are nicely presented but rather conservative seafood extravaganzas that include oysters ($9.95) and steamed mussels ($13.95), as well as various assortments of shellfish. Snails ($8.50) and duck confit ($9.95) come with the Cafe de Paris entrecôte sauce and Cafe de Paris vinaigrette, both of which can also be bought to take home. Onion soup ($7.50) is served with a pleasantly lavish amount of gruyère, and a salade Niçoise ($14.50) uses fresh tuna along with the house vinaigrette. Does anywhere else in town serve ris de veau ($13.95) in Madeira wine sauce? Or steak tartare ($11.95) mixed tableside with egg? This menu is so eloquently conservative that whenever it does sound a rare note of wild abandon you wonder if you're dreaming. Yet it does have these moments, as with the crevettes "sauce Punget" ($10.95), a dish of soy, sesame, and ginger-marinated jumbo shrimp on skewers, with a divine marmalade horseradish dip; or the pricey rosemary prawns ($20.95), served in tomato and ouzo and accompanied by a slice of feta cheese in phyllo crust.

You'll hear much about the entrecôte sauce (maybe too much?) but there are other lures to the Cafe de Paris. One of them is music: don't forget to ask about their French *chanson* and jazz nights.

Charlie's

Charlie's is owned by young Michael Schwab, of the Charles Schwab brokerage family, which gives you something of a clue to the Manhattan-like upscale ambiance. The zinc-accented interior is as trendy as the young clientele, with dangling TV screens that play Sean Connery's "The name's Bond—James Bond!" bits over and over.

Cost $10–30

Address 1838 Union St at Laguna
☎ 415/474-3773
Open Daily 5.30–9.30pm; brunch Thurs–Sun 11am–3pm
Transportation 41, 45
Accepts MasterCard, Visa

A very happening bar scene makes this a cramped place to eat at the best of times (the smoking patio is no better), but the young and beautiful elite don't mind this sacrifice to the cause.

It's an ambitiously broad menu. Starting with brunch: the chicken club sandwich ($9) turned out to be bacon and fried egg with tomatoes and butterball lettuce, served on sourdough bread with mesquite kettle chips. It was chunky and filling: a keeper. French toast with caramelized bananas ($8) and huevos rancheros ($9) are all you could want for a Sunday morning start. The garden omelet ($9) comes with green onions, peppers, goat cheese, wild mushrooms, and Charlie's sautéed potatoes. Moving on to lunch, the Caesar salad ($8) is a winner, with entire hearts of romaine lettuce, giant Parmesan flakes, and a creamy dressing with a nice lemon-anchovy tang. Other appetizers are also up to snuff: day-boat scallops ($12) come with sesame-soy ponzu and a tangle of frisée. A duck confit and prosciutto salad ($12) arrives tangy and sharply highlighted with blood oranges and goat cheese. Huckleberry-glazed foie gras on a brioche ($14) comes with a sweet quince confit. The Asian chicken salad ($11) is a sesame-crusted grilled chicken breast with a won bok salad of a particularly light bak choy; it's a smoky-tinged meal in itself, and good value. Main courses at dinner include Niman Ranch New York steak with two eggs done any style ($25), with more of those popular "Charlie's potatoes". Maine lobster ($24) is stylishly sculpted with avocado and tomatoes. Very intense chocolate puddings fill the dessert fix ($7), along with crème brûlée.

Chef Garret Martindale manned the pans in some heavy-hitting kitchens before he was lured here. At Charlie's, he successfully walks the tightrope from brunch to supper, and from all-stops-out mains to sandwiches. He deserves a quieter arena and a solid following.

Cozmo's Corner Grill

🍴 Cozmo's is living a charmed after-life. Ten years ago it was Marina Joe's, a funky old dive at the heart of the Marina that had been around forever, and where the testosterone level was so high you kept expecting Frank Sinatra and the boys to walk in. Several subsequent reincarnations bombed from bad luck, bad timing, and sheer hubris. When Steven Levine, the chef–owner of Spear Street's Cosmopolitan Cafe, took over this notorious spot, he made the space feel welcoming and roomy, and turned it into an overnight success. With exposed brick walls, a big wine rack, an open kitchen and a hugely comfy sports bar with a bunch of dangling TVs, the testosterone level has shot back up again as well.

Cost $10–35
Address 2001 Chestnut St at Fillmore
☎ 415/351-0175
Open Mon–Thurs 5.30–9.45pm, Fri 5.30–11pm, Sat noon–5pm & 5.30–11pm, Sun 10am–3pm & 5.30–9.45pm
Transportation 22, 28, 30, 43
Accepts All major credit cards

It's an inviting place for casual passers-by to wander in for a bite and a beer while they watch the game. The menu offers fusion gestures here and there, from ahi sashimi ($5) to tea-smoked duck ($4.50) and braised artichokes and mushrooms in aiolo ($4.50). Portions are generous and sometimes mind-blowingly pretty. Chef Levine borrowed some trademark dishes from the Cosmopolitan, including a creditable Niman Ranch house hamburger ($9), served with dynamite fries—this is one place to head for when you crave a hamburger. A few dishes are signature standouts, particularly the goat cheese gnocchi and herbed potato gnocchi with truffle oil and pecorino Romano ($14), the grilled pork chops ($16), and the braised lamb shank plate ($16). The frisée salad ($6.50) comes with Chioggia beets, goat cheese and a coronet of runny poached egg, and you might find yourself ordering it at every visit.

For children—of all ages—there's only one dessert in here, and that's the vanilla malted milkshake ($6), served with warm chocolate chip cookies straight from the oven. The cookies take a quarter of an hour to bake, so order them as soon as you arrive. Cozmo's is handy for Crissy Fields, Fisherman's Wharf, and the Presidio, and the owner seems to have realized that, in this neck of the woods, parking can make or break a restaurant. Happily, they validate parking tickets here.

Curbside Too

If you've ever dreamed of having your own little bistro *du coin*, it would probably look just like this absurdly cute cable-car diner with just enough room for 28 gourmands sucking in their breath. Opposite the Presidio gates, and a stone's throw from the Golden Gate Bridge, it's the second in restaurateur Antoine Ralliaume's three-bistro mini-empire. Curbside has mock-flock walls with bric-a-brac like pink candelabras; its window bears the ghostly image of the Eiffel Tower. One-man host Michel Saga is everywhere while standing still, and could hardly be more French if he were exclaiming "Ooh la la!" in a Feydeau farce.

Cost $15–35

Address 2769 Lombard St at Lyon
☎415/921-4442
Open Mon–Fri 11.30am–2.30pm & 5–10pm, Sat & Sun 9am–3pm
Transportation 28, 29, 41, 43, 45
Accepts All major credit cards

Scratched onto the chalkboard above Michel's head are daily appetizers ($6–7) like warm goat cheese salad, escargots du Curbside, and asparagus soup. Next, choose from chicken, lamb, seafood, a couple of steaks, and vegetarian entrees. Whatever has just been caught will be fish of the day ($13–20): typically mahi-mahi, sea bass, salmon or halibut. Ahi tuna in lemon butter ($19) is seared chunks on a big white plate, engulfed by a mandala of feuilletéd zucchini, tomatoes, asparagus, and potato scallops. The same artful hand creates the "vegetarian platter" ($13), with Zen-like veggies on a rice timbale. Chicken breast is stuffed with crab velouté ($15); crabcakes ($13) are generous. Steak frites or sirloin in "bleu cheese" ($17) are delicious, and so is filet mignon with green peppercorn sauce ($20). All are reminiscent of the sort of simple dishes you'd find at a French bistro. Curbside is known for its desserts ($6), so nibble on zesty orange-lemon tart or profiteroles smothered in chocolate fondant sauce—a guilty pleasure for the health-obsessed.

Bringing your own wine costs $10 corkage, but Alderbrook Red Zinfandel ($29) and a decent 1997 Chablis ($46) aren't bad value. Curbside house reds are serviceable at $5.50 to $7.50 per glass. If their tiny lot is full, there's plenty of parking in the Presidio, especially if a romantic twilight stroll through eucalyptus beckons. Don't forget the first Curbside Cafe, 2417 California at Fillmore (☎929-9030), and the new Curbside Bistro, 1345 Bush at Larkin (☎923-1375), in the Alliance Française, which has "un petit accent Normand".

Eastside West

Eastside West opened with the millennium in what the *Bay Guardian* aptly calls the "Heteroyuppieland" of the Marina District. Scott Dammann's place is all about its raw bar and seafood, but its 125 wines, live jazz, and laid-back brunches on the back patio vie for attention too. This particular corner may be a little less trendy than some, and the people who eat here may be merry rather than cool, but Eastside West is still full of people shooting oysters at unearthly hours. Its cocktails, including julep mojitos and ruby red daiquiris worthy of Hemingway, are impressive, and so are its oyster combinations.

Cost $8–30

Address 3154 Fillmore St at Greenwich
☎ 415/885-4000
Open Mon–Wed 5–10pm, Thurs & Fri 5pm–midnight, Sat 10.30am–3.30pm & 5pm–midnight, Sun 10.30am–3.30pm & 5–10pm
Transportation 22, 28, 43
Accepts All major credit cards

It sounds pricier than it turns out to be. The ample raw bar serves shellfish and seafood plates, ranging from a daily ceviche of snapper or some other white fish tossed in avocado salad and trimmed with baked tortilla strips ($8.50), to chilled steamed mussels ($7.50) and Dungeness crabs (around $30). Seafood platters include a $78 mother-of-them-all, with crab, ceviche, oysters, shrimp, mussels, and clams, piled on one of those silver whoop-de-doo tureen things. The price actually seems about right once you dig in, because there's plenty of food to go around a table of four or five. Chef de cuisine Christopher Pastena supplies other dishes with names as long as he can make them. The "warm baby spinach and duck confit salad with cranberries, pixie mandarins and Laura Chenel goat cheese" ($8.50) sparkles like a counter at Tiffany's and tastes better. The "grilled voodoo baby back-rib teepee with maple sweet potatoes" ($18) is yummy beyond belief. One of the desserts is those Rice Krispie treats ($6) you learn to make at your mother's knee, and it comes served with a warm walnut brownie and homemade ice cream. It sneaks ahead of the pecan whiskey tart with bourbon ice cream ($6.95).

Eastside West is never boring, and more or less affordable. The clientele may hail from "Yuppie Heights" (as locals dub the apartment-dwellers up the nearby hills of Pacific Heights, Presidio, and Union Street) but it could be recommended to anyone in search of a seafood blowout, or looking for a Champagne dinner on a Chardonnay budget.

Ella's

🍽 It was sometime back in the last century that Ella's won its laurels as one of the city's best neighborhood brunch spots, and it has clung to that crown tenaciously. Ella's is so beloved that it was recently able to expand, acquiring blue awnings under which you can line up for brunch, and a guava-pink interior. It's all on the strength of chef-owner Don's fresh-squeezed juices, home-baked pastries, rosemary-perfumed chicken hash, and buttermilk banana pancakes, though a supper menu is also served during the week. The hash and pancakes alone make addicts out of Pacific Heights and Laurel Heights residents, so it's no surprise that you'll face quite a wait for the weekend brunch—sometimes 45 minutes or more.

Cost $10–30

Address 500 Presidio Ave at California
☎ 415/441-5669
Open Mon–Fri 7am–9pm, Sat & Sun 8.30am–2pm
Transportation 1, 2, 3, 4, 43
Accepts MasterCard, Visa

One of the best things about Ella's—when you do reach a table—is that fresh-squeezed blood orange fruit juice ($2.50). It's a pity that blood oranges are generally only in season during winter months, since they're so much stronger and fruitier than the ordinary kind. After the juices, it's the Earl Grey tea, freshly brewed in real pots, that wins local votes. Omelets are fast and fluffy, and the accommodating staff will deliver your bacon either extra-crisp or regular, and your eggs creamy or well done, exactly as you request. Ella's buttermilk pancakes ($5.50) come with the banana actually mixed in, yet are airy and light. And the chicken hash with rosemary ($7.50) is one of the best breakfasts around: golden and crisp on top, aromatic and soft within. Brunch ends at around 2pm at weekends. At teatime, the buns are homemade, and deliciously sticky; the coffee torte is elaborate. There's a homey supper menu after that, featuring plain dishes such as grilled salmon ($9.50), roast chicken, the occasional meatloaf, and similar rib-sticking fare. The chicken potpie ($10.75) is legendary for its delicately flaky and gilded crust that conceals succulent pieces below. Sadly, they do not cook supper at weekends.

The residents of Pacific Heights seem to treat Ella's as a personal club. One tip: if you come by yourself, you'll be less likely to wait, because you can always just grab a barstool.

Greens

Greens is as much about its sweeping and undeniably cool bayfront view as its organic produce. When vegetarian film stars make movies in San Francisco, they always wind up at Greens, which is run by the Marin Zen Center's Green Gulch Farm. Whatever you eat will come from their garden, which you can visit on the other side of the Golden Gate. Carved from an old

Cost	$20–45
Address	Fort Mason Building A
☎	415/771-6222
Open	Mon 5.30–9.30pm, Tues–Sat 11.30am–2pm & 5.30–9.30pm, Sun 10am–2pm
Transportation	28
Accepts	All major credit cards except AmEx

warehouse at Fort Mason, a former army base that's now part of Golden Gate National Recreation Area, Greens has an impressive decor. Zen-like paintings and driftwood sculptures complement the satiny-smooth tables and chairs, and it's all set against the horizon of water and sky, and a jaw-dropping view of the Golden Gate Bridge. The clientele is mixed in every possible way, although diners tend to be older, and exude the impression that they consider themselves very cool.

A quarter of a century after it opened, Greens still sets the benchmark for American vegetarian restaurants, even if the food, while never disappointing, also never quite enthralls. Founder Deborah Madison's Sunday brunch made the place famous, with its door-stopper tofu sandwiches ($8.50) and buttermilk hazelnut pancakes with nectarines, crème fraîche, and syrup ($9). Heroic pita pockets come with feta, kalamata, and hummus ($8.50). Salads (from around $9) are huge, and may feature goat cheese and arugula with beets, or mixed lettuces with kumquats and pistachios. Dinner main courses include dishes such as ravioli stuffed with peas and pinoles ($18.75) and a curry of coconut and Thai spices ($17.75). The prix fixe Saturday night menu ($45) is a good place to start, and may include wonderfully eclectic dishes such as Mediterranean phyllo cakes of layered seasonal vegetables, or a prettily striped vegetable terrine, or Mexican-style turnovers stuffed with corn, black beans, and onion-pepper dice. Ginger crunch with plum sherbet ($6.25) or apricot and blackberry sorbet with ginger shortbread ($6.25) are good cappers.

Service is so obsequious you may want to give the waiter a group hug. Madison herself has long since moved to Santa Fe, leaving her creation in Annie Somerville's hands. Maybe all San Francisco has moved on a bit, but Greens is still special. Book way ahead!

Izzy's Steaks & Chop House

Izzy's name says it all. At this long-established, straightforward but very comfortable bar and grill, you can count on meeting A1 Steak Sauce bottles on every table, along with French's and Grey Poupon mustard, bottles of Lea & Perrins Worcestershire sauce, and ketchup. With any luck, the waiter may forget to call your uncle from Chicago "hon." As a stately pleasure dome for carnivores, Izzy's is a bit of an institution, drawing a large number of commuters who head home to Marin County after dinner. Its popularity is easy to figure out: although San Francisco has its share of steak house chains, one that exists purely for locals is harder to find. That's why Izzy's has a firm niche in the hearts of transplanted Midwesterners and New Yorkers who miss their pound of steak—although seeing as they live in San Francisco now, they want it to be organic and wholesome, and preferably from the Niman Ranch.

Cost $15–35
Address 3345 Steiner St at Chestnut
☎ 415/563-0487
Open Mon–Sat 5–10.30pm, Sun 5–10pm
Transportation 22, 28, 30, 43
Accepts All major credit cards

Simpler is invariably the better way to go at Izzy's, where two possibilities are usually under consideration: "medium" or *"really* well done." Establish your orientation on that particular spectrum for a sirloin, T-bone or filet mignon and add the regular side dishes of choice: a baked Idaho potato, split across the middle and oozing sour cream and chives or butter, or a gratin oozing much the same but in layers. The price is an inclusive $23 for all of the above, and includes really smooth and creamy spinach or caramelized carrots and baked onions, and a starter mini-salad as well. The steak au poivre, in a demi-glace of cognac and cream, is a couple of dollars more.

There's nothing wrong with the rest of the menu of backribs, tenderloin, and chops, they're just not steak, which is what Izzy's is best known for. The people who come here come often and order the same thing every time. Where they find to park is another story, though there are a couple of public garages nearby. As for the service, it's old-school brusque rather than twinkly. Sometimes that can be a bit of a relief, as you might suspect it is to Izzy's regulars.

Jackson Fillmore Trattoria

San Francisco's neighborhoods are blessed with many trattorias serving casual Cal-Ital fare. Run by hard-working young owners and buzzing with locals chowing elbow to elbow, they usually serve better food than their older North Beach cousins, and seem more casually festive than downtown places. Jack Krietzman's Fillmore hangout is one such notably unglamorous foody mecca. (Check the front of the line 22 bus to find the inspiration for its name.) Resembling a grocery from the outside, with eight squashed and noisy tables, lots of people waiting, laid-back service and dishes that sometimes run out early in the evening, Jackson Fillmore is all about the food.

Cost $10–50
Address 2506 Fillmore St at Jackson
☎415/346-5288
Open Mon–Thurs & Sun 5.30–10pm, Fri & Sat 5.30–11pm
Transportation 3, 12, 22, 24
Accepts All major credit cards

In fact, it's a zoo. Meals for two can easily close in on $100 including wine, making Jackson Fillmore less than a bargain, but the free bruschetta steeped in tomato salsa rocks and rolls you the moment you luck into a table. Antipasti can be uninspired, aside from the unexpectedly amazing chilled and shelled peas with flaked Pecorino ($6.75). Rabbit ($11) is a house specialty: rolled in crunchy crumbs and fried in butter and oil with garlic and fresh twigs of rosemary, it's to-die-for tasty. Eggplant Parmigiana ($10.75) and herbed roast chicken ($11) are rustic and plain in a good way, and don't let you down. Gnocchi ($12.75) are the best in town, and this is definitely a gnocchi town—several different cheeses with bits of smoky chicken are mixed into a basic dough. Sea bass in a lemon-parsley sauce is perfect, though the sauce can be under-seasoned. Desserts are well worth saving room for: zabaglione ($5) is possibly the fluffiest on earth, and gets even better when chocolate fudge is added; you'll want seconds. The wine list is fairly priced, but at $23, it makes more sense to order a whole bottle of Pinot Grigio than individual glasses at $7.

Reservations are only for groups, and the wait is annoying but there are usually seats at the counter. A recipe for happiness would be to sit at the bar with an out-of-town buddy to catch up on a million stupid breakups while you order gnocchi, rabbit, and Pinot Grigio. Then order crocus-yellow zabaglione. Twice.

Lhasa Moon

If hundreds of Tibetan restaurants lined the Marina, perhaps it would be a more spiritual place. Stockbrokers would spin prayer wheels instead of heading for the nearest watering hole at dusk. Since Lhasa Moon is the only Tibetan restaurant known to most citizens of San Francisco, it wears the label "Marina antidote" quite proudly, offering live Tibetan music, photos of the Dalai Lama and Himalayas, and occasional prayer texts around small tables. The food is simple, like the restaurant itself, but when chef Tseten Paljor and co-owner Tsering Wangmo get a little singing going, it's quite an evening. Just don't be in a hurry.

Cost $8–25
Address 2420 Lombard St at Scott
☎ 415/674-9898
Open Tues, Wed, Sat & Sun 5–10pm, Thurs 11.30am–2.30pm, Fri 11.30am–2.30pm & 5–10.30pm
Transportation 28, 30, 43
Accepts All major credit cards except Diners

Tibetan food bears similarities to Chinese, with its wok-frying and steaming, but also uses Indian aromatic spices. Start with a cup of salted butter tea, perhaps the single most Tibetan item on the menu, if not in the culture. It is indeed salty, and tastes slightly fermented, so it takes getting used to (but perhaps not so much as it would in Tibet, where the butter would be made from yak milk). Chubby Tibetan dumplings called momo ($7.50) are like little pouffes stuffed with bak choy, cabbage, herbs and chopped meat, and are served with a dipping sauce of chile and soy on the side. Jhasa khatasa ($4.50) is spiced medallions of chicken. Fat griddle cakes called shabhaley ($8.50) are crammed with the same kind of fillings, then flattened, sliced, and served with the same chile-soy sauce. Lephing ($8), a white, gelatinous cake made from a mung bean extract, is topped with another fiery soy sauce. At home, Tibetans eat potatoes and daikon, since potatoes grow at high altitude. You'll find plenty of them here, although the owners admit they've adapted dishes to local tastes. Potatoes are served with spinach in the dish called shogok ($4.50), and in shogok mgopa ($8.50), a beef stew.

Co-owner Tsering Wangmo is a dancer and has written her own cookbook. The fact that she grew up in a southern Indian refugee camp may prompt you to wonder exactly how many small neighborhood restaurants in this city are run by ex-refugees. It turns out that in diverse San Francisco there are at least four or five...perhaps more.

Liverpool Lil's

Opposite the Presidio gates, and not far from the Palace of Fine Arts, this vaguely hippy version of an English pub looks as though it might sprout horse brasses, but usually gives wall space instead to sports heroes like Joe DiMaggio, a one-time patron of the place. It hasn't changed since the halcyon days of 1973, when it opened as the only

Cost $10–20	
Address 2942 Lyon St at Lombard	
☎ 415/921-6664	
Open Daily 10am–midnight	
Transportation 28, 30, 43	
Accepts MasterCard, Visa	

halfway decent dining option for many blocks around. These days, Liverpool Lil's always shelters a few old-timers breast-feeding their pints in front of a muted TV, while lunching ladies hover over martinis with a good book. By early evening the back restaurant is filled with the older Pacific Heights crowd—small wonder, then, that martinis accompany burgers and fries here as often as well-groomed grandchildren. Liverpool Lil's is definitely child-friendly, which is something to remember if you're taking the kids to the Presidio. Later on, a few dating couples drift in.

Liverpool Lil's really does try to serve authentic pub cuisine, and it succeeds, far better than it may even know. There's no menu, and the nightly specials of beef, chicken, and fish are all in the $15 range, and come in a special deal with garlic bread, a soup (such as onion), or a well-made, generous, old-fashioned salad. Salads include a Cobb (butterball with ham and boiled eggs), a Niçoise (tuna, anchovies and eggs), and a Caesar (romaine hearts with anchovies, garlic, Parmesan and coddled egg). Salads or baked potatoes are either included in the deal, or served separately ($7.95). A stodgy steak and kidney pie ($9.95) has chopped beef and tarragon under its pastry, which sticks to the roof of your mouth in just the right way. Lamb chops with Crosse & Blackwell mint jelly ($15.95) are redolent of a million British Sunday lunches, and the fish and chips ($8.95) of a million Saturday soccer matches. Prescott pork chops ($8.95) are two fat, breaded chops with fried apple slices and mashed potatoes.

Locals maintain that for over 25 years the mixed vegetables that accompany almost every dish have been so underdone as to have been scarcely introduced to a gas flame. That may seem curiously unBritish, but then this is California.

Mezes

🍴 Two gaily colored, narrow rooms attempt to bring the Mediterranean to the Marina, together with a Greek "tapas" or small plates menu, and Greek wines served by waiters that just ooze schmooze and charm. Painted in sunny yellow and Aegean blue with the odd primitive mural, Mezes also has a less noisy upstairs room for when you're look-

Cost $10–50

Address 2373 Chestnut St at Divisadero
☎ 415/409-7111
Open Daily 5–10.30pm
Transportation 28, 30, 43
Accepts MasterCard, Visa

ing for somewhere for a chat. "Mezes" means the kind of food you share around a table over a glass of raki or ouzo, and that's what you do here. But be warned: don't come if you're really hungry!

Grilled octopodi ($9), or octopus, and kefalograviera ($9), or fried sheep's cheese, are equally good starters, and are served with sliced-up lemon and a spritz of oil. Also full of flavor are the kolokithokeftedes ($9.95), which are fried zucchini and potato cakes served with the creamy, garlicky yogurt dip called tzatziki. Spanakopita ($6.95), or phyllo layers stuffed with spinach, feta, and herbs, is a Balkan staple; here, it comes in two fairly stodgy slices, both of which are tasty enough, if a little on the heavy side. Known in Turkish as "the priest fainted," Melitzanasalata Imam ($8.95) is half a grilled eggplant stuffed with mixed peppers and feta cheese, and served with pita. It's quite delicious, though it seems pegged a little high for what is, after all, just well-grilled veggies. Also a bit pricey is the arnisia paidakia ($16.95), which is four minuscule marinated and grilled lamb chops, served with a few slices of roast potato. For dessert, after the honeyed phyllo pastries with clotted cream ($5.95) there's only one choice, a yaorti e meli ($5.95), the yummy and healthfully sour live yogurt with fresh honey that so many Greeks eat for breakfast.

A carefully selected wine list includes a special of the evening at $7.50 a glass, and an excellent retsina ($5), plus the ouzo that is traditionally drunk with appetizers. Mezes means "snacks," nibbles plates that permit a steady stream of drop-ins to graze and sip. And this is the correct spirit with which to patronize Mezes: casually. Just don't come when you're starving, or be prepared for a far bigger bill than anticipated.

Perry's Sports Bar

This good ol' sports bar is swamped on football nights, when the tailgate party is in full swing and the many draft beers on tap are flowing like Niagara Falls, along with the testosterone. Despite a cameo in Armistead Maupin's *Tales Of The City* as a singles scene, the ambiance is old-fashioned American bar bonhomie: checkered blue cloths at round tables with bentwood chairs, dark wainscoting, little cafe curtains, and a whiff of ketchup and steak sauce on every table. It makes most people nostalgic for the bar they went to on the East Coast some time in the 1980s. There's at least one blaring TV, and often a large-screen game going on.

Cost $13–30

Address 1944 Union St at Laguna
☏ 415/922-9022
Open Mon–Fri 11am–11pm, Sat 2–11pm, Sun 2–10pm
Transportation 41, 45
Accepts All major credit cards

But if you think Cliff and Norm are going to sidle up and buy you a Rolling Rock, you're wrong. As well as brewskis, Perry's drinks include swanky vodkas and gin martinis, and there's sangria ($4). Happy hour runs from 4pm to 7pm nightly, and martinis are half price on Thursdays. Yes, you can chew on buffalo wings, onion rings, potato skins, and chile in cups. But you may well find a soft spot for the corned beef hash ($9.95); Perry's chef is Scott Gorenstein and his hash is a golden-domed cake of smashed potato, long-simmered onions, and meat tenderized with thyme, parsley, and pepper, nailed by perfectly poached eggs that peer balefully from the top. The Caesar salad ($5.50) is pretty exemplary: a romaine heart comes with gutsy, well-anchovied dressing; you can also have it with a grilled chicken breast ($7.95). Fish and chips ($12.95) is a nostalgically battered lump of crispy cod with thick fries, but it's only available on Fridays as the day's Blue Plate special.

But despite the no-nonsense menu, this isn't a blue-collar home from home. It's a social club for the guys (and dolls) who come singly or in bands to watch soccer and golf on satellite TV, seeking occasional fuel in the form of burgers—or crabcakes or quesadillas. Matches are sometimes early, so Perry's serves granola with non-fat milk and several Mexican dishes for brunch. This is California after all, and that's as near to fusion as Perry gets.

PlumpJack Cafe

The big story at Gavin Newsom and Billy Getty's place is all about the wines. They launched a showcase for Californian wines at PlumpJack Winery, then opened a restaurant to go with it on the corner. The allure of the place is that you can bring the wines in at next to no corkage and drink them here at shop price, a lure that works like a charm. The bacchanalian theme is very underscored in the faux-renaissance, silvery-sheened decor, which tucks away all manner of playful wine racks and wine holders and pieces of wine library above the heads of the happy diners, all of whom are soon in vinous good form. Many of the wines require a bit of gymnastics on the part of the staff, in fact.

Cost $25–50

Address 3127 Fillmore St at Filbert
☎ 415/563-4755
Open Mon–Fri 11.30am–2pm & 5.30–10.30pm, Sat 5.30–10.30pm
Transportation 22, 28, 45
Accepts All major credit cards except Diners

All these bottles mean that you get a sommelier along with the territory, and he coaxes you towards some memorably great mid-range bargains, mainly nosey Zinfandels and Cabernets and Pinot Noirs, at virtual retail cost. You can get a good Russian River or a Bonny Doon for as little as $17, while glasses start from $6. Meanwhile, the menu was crafted by mover-and-shaker James Ormsby, a celebrity chef who specializes in seafood. The menu is relatively short and sweet, and starts with simple antipasti like beet salad ($5) and steamed mussels with orange-mint bruschetta ($9). Caesar salad sings of anchovy ($7; $12 with chicken). Other starters include a summer vegetable terrine ($19) and ahi Niçoise salad ($15). The hefty, hearty hamburger ($15) is a keen favorite here, served on focaccia that's already juicy with a bit of pomodoro sauce and heaped with caramelized onions. Southern fried chicken breast ($18) comes with creamy polenta, braised greens, and sherried Hen o' the Woods mushrooms. Duck dishes have featured lately, such as the Maple Leaf Farms duckling trio of grilled breast, crispy leg, and grilled sausage ($24), served with sweet potato purée, spinach, and huckleberry sauce.

PlumpJack has toned up its interior decor lately, and it now seems to be more of a business hangout for expense account dining. There's a private room for company parties, and a distinctly discouraging look on the face of the hostess at the door.

Rose's Cafe

Like the promising youngest kid who wants to try everything at once, Rose's has everything: from breakfast pizzas and focaccia to roast chicken and pasta. Owner Reed Hearon broke momentarily from his North Beach flagship Rose Pistola to take a crack at this former Il Fornaio spot, and Rose's tries to build on the casual bakery-cum-cafe idea, with some pleasantly heated terrace seating and a few sidewalk tables out front. Outside is good for whiling away a sunny afternoon over the wines, which are available by the glass. Inside, a room of chrysanthemum yellow, with bright red-and-blue glass chandeliers, is a fun lunch spot by day and a romantic dining room by night.

Cost $7–25	
Address 2298 Union St at Steiner	
☎ 415/775-2200	
Open Mon–Thurs 7am–10pm, Fri 7am–11pm, Sat 8am–11pm, Sun 8am–10pm	
Transportation 22	
Accepts MasterCard, Visa	

The wood-fired pizza oven is on from dawn's early light, baking the focaccia and pizza dishes that are Rose's trademark. Thin focaccia is doubled like a torte and sandwiched with Italian Fontina cheese—the yummiest version ever of a grilled cheese sandwich ($6.75) and perfect for a quick breakfast or lunch. Breakfast pizza ($6.75) is also plate-sized: a thin crust is crowned with bubbling ham, cheese, and eggs. Come lunchtime, a flurry of colorful salads makes an appearance, full of unexpected, jewel-like colors and tasty surprises. One of the zingiest is arugula with goat cheese ($7.95), served with a bruschetta smeared with fearsome piperade. House soups such as minestrone ($4.25) are rustic and always changing. Other sandwiches may entice you into calorific excess—house focaccia is deliciously present in a grilled salmon or grilled chicken sandwich with sun-dried tomatoes and aioli ($7.95), and there's a great steak sandwich with caramelized onions, arugula, and Gorgonzola ($9.95). Grilled salmon and chicken dishes also make an appearance later on, for supper, when a steak frites ($12.95) is also available, with good fries.

Homemade sorbets and gelati ($2.50) are refreshing finishers to a meal, along with assorted homemade cookies and biscotti, good cheese, great wines by the glass, and two really fine ports. Casual it may be, slow service and all, but Rose's is a pleasant pause after promenading the length of Union Street.

Sociale

Few places come more picture-pretty or pleasing than this garden bistro, which opens onto a heated, brick-inlaid courtyard off the street. It's almost a postcard. Eating prosciutto and drinking Chianti outside makes you feel like you're on holiday, and it's no punishment inside the apricot- and lemon-sherbet-colored interior either, a setting as spring-like as a Fragonard. A minute but well-stocked wine bar in the corner supplements the seating, which is padded and decorated with Provençal prints.

Cost $10–25
Address 3665 Sacramento St at Spruce
☏ 415/921-3200
Open Mon–Sat 11.30am–2.30pm & 5.30–10pm
Transportation 1, 4, 33
Accepts MasterCard, Visa

"Made from fresh fruit daily," proclaims the menu about the MentaLimone and FruttaLimone drinks ($3.50). They turn out to be refreshing homemade mint and peach lemonade, respectively, though both are rather diluted. If you order the fussy but festive spring salad ($7) for your appetizer, the waiter will be happy to split it for two; it has fennel, apple, and dried cherries on baby greens, and is topped with Gorgonzola and candied walnuts—an everything-coming-at-you mix of produce in a rather too sweet dressing (the vinaigrette seems to have more honey than balsamic vinegar). The Portobello mushrooms stuffed with sausage and chard ($7), however, are excellent, as are the fresh mussels in puttanesca sauce on crostini ($9), and you could hardly fail to enjoy the simple-but-perfect fried olives ($6). Panini include a really beefy steak sandwich ($10) on an excellent Il Fornaio baguette, grilled just right with onions, arugula, and roast tomato—no complaints here. When it comes to the main dishes, Sociale bake a mean "brick" chicken in truffle-mashed potatoes with chard ($11), and their take on fish and chips ($10) elevates this humble dish into cod filets served on a fine salad with garlic potatoes. But it's the risotto that has won hearts here, a true primavera with asparagus and leeks ($14). For dessert, the cannoli ($7) is a highlight: creamy with chocolate flakes and nuts, and wholly satisfying.

The young waiters are eager to please but never intrude, and this spring-like spot is much patronized by returning customers, mainly locals. Laurel Heights lost a couple of good neighborhood Italian restaurants not long ago, so when Sociale opened last year it took off right away. Small wonder that it's humming.

Japantown, Fillmore & the Western Addition

JAPANTOWN, FILLMORE
& WESTERN ADDITION

Alamo Square Seafood Grill

The lucky folks of Alamo Square—"Historic Alamo Square," as the city likes to call it—have their very own village bistro. It's one of the better ones, with a loyal local following that doesn't care if nobody else ever hears about it. Cheap and casual, that's Alamo Square, a small and no-frills seafood grill where the catch of the day will always be fresh, and even the Kir is better, and cheaper,

Cost	$25–50

Address 803 Fillmore St at Fulton
℡ 415/440-2828
Open Mon–Sat 5–10pm, Sun 10am–2pm & 5–10pm
Transportation 5, 22
Accepts MasterCard, Visa

than most. It's tiny, with pale apricot walls over a long cushioned banquette. In atmosphere and flavor, it straddles the border between Hayes and Haight, with a tiny bit of Gallic flavor all its own.

Candidly, theirs is an ordinary menu, but it offers extra here and there. Salmon, snapper, swordfish, and tuna are always on the menu and Alamo took a page from the Hayes Street Grill, where first you pick your fish and then you pick your sauce, a mix and match, tailor-made approach for $13.50 a piece. The sauces are: herbal, wined Béarnaise, buttery beurre blanc or beurre rouge, a garlicky aioli-like Provençale sauce, and a mousseline sauce with lime that's like a tarter, creamier Hollandaise. A real bouillabaisse ($4.75) has lots of clams and mussels and some large flakes of snapper. The spinach salad ($5.25) comes irreproachably dressed in real Champagne-shallot dressing, really roasted walnuts, and poached pear. A traditional Niçoise ($6.95) comes with fresh ahi tuna, lovingly presented. Moules farcies ($6), or baked mussels, reek appropriately of garlic. A crunchy jicama and corn salad accompanies the crabcakes with a creamy lobster sauce ($6.95), and is almost generous enough for a main dish. There are just a few meat dishes, such as a good oven-roasted chicken in jus with sautéed mushrooms ($9.75) and steak in a classic Béarnaise ($12.50).

Alamo's all-in prix fixe ($11.50) is one of the best deals in town—if they were just three blocks closer to the Gough-Laguna blocks of Hayes Valley, they'd be stuffed to the gills with French horn players. As it is, the villagers get to keep their precious secret. One final accolade: the wine list is good, starts in the teens, and much of it is in the twenties.

Benihana

Of course Japantown has its touristy side, with its kitsch sushi places like the one where the sushi floats past in little boats, and with its exotic boutiques and antiques stores, and exquisite truffle and bakery counters—not forgetting the cinema, bowling alley and sake bars. Should all this not immediately appeal, Benihana is likely to please any bored children you may have in tow, because they can sit around and watch a teppanyaki chef at work at close quarters. It's a performance art of dazzling knife-play, and delivers a sizzling barbecue for instant eating.

Cost $15–45

Address Kinetsu Building,
1737 Post St at Fillmore
☎ 415/563-4844
Open Mon–Thurs
11.30am–2pm & 5–10pm, Fri
11.30am–2pm & 4–11pm, Sat
11.30am–11pm, Sun
11.30am–9.30pm
Transportation 22, 38
Accepts MasterCard, Visa

The interior of Benihana is filled with happy families, all sitting around chefs in red toques and kimonos. They are bent over hibachi cooking tables, which seat up to eight folks. The chefs slice away at fresh vegetables in a frenzy of balletic activity, with a speed that might seem positively surreal—unless you're used to it from shows like TV's "Iron Chef." While the chef is setting up steak, chicken, vegetable, and seafood teppanyaki dishes, bowls of soup, salad, and other side dishes materialize. The flashing knives act of the chef really impresses the younger set as he starts to fool around a little bit, flipping bits of steak and chicken and prawn, then catching them. The choreography is impressive, but the food is perhaps more the point for adults, who can sit back to eat barbecue and drink sake and Sapporo. As you'd expect, this is child-friendly food that does not challenge the tastebuds. All-in options include soup, salad, and dessert (from $15.75), with a special children's menu (from $9). There's also an all-you-can-eat prix fixe ($19.95), which brings sushi plus a series of steaks and surf-and-turf stalwarts.

The art of tabletop teppanyaki cooking is centuries old, as is the development of knife skills, but this particular form of performance art began in the 1960s, when chef Rocky Aoki introduced it to a place on Broadway, and watched it spread. Next to the sea lions at the Wharf, you can enjoy great success in taking young visitors to Japantown, thanks to entertaining places like this where kids can enjoy spectacle and food together.

Brother-in-Law's BBQ

When you're hit with a hunger for that rib-sticking Southern soul food, walk through the Western Addition until you reach the block where Louisiana native Eugene Ponds' barbecue has been watering the mouths of locals with terrific aromas for two decades. Brother-in-Law's has just two modest little tables, although it's blessed with parking.

Cost $8–15	
Address 705 Divisadero St at Grove	
☎ 415/931-7427	
Open Tues–Sun 11am–10pm	
Transportation 24	
Accepts MasterCard, Visa	

Despite a location near the notoriously non-carnivorous Haight-Ashbury District, people flock from all over town to Brother-in-Law's for Eugene's barbecued chicken, beef brisket, and back-ribs. Don't confuse it with Brother's Korean Restaurant in the Richmond: that's another popular barbecue, but because it's Korean you take the meat to your table and do it yourself. At Brother-in-Law's, they do it for you!

This is simple food served in a small and homey place where regulars overflow into the adjacent parking lot to dine off styrofoam. Start with Eugene's baby back-ribs ($11.75) or the chicken, either half or whole ($6/11); both come with their appropriate sweet-sour sauce and are dished up in a whopper of a container, with plastic cutlery supplied. Sliced beef and beef brisket ($8.25) come tenderized by marinating and long simmering in the legendary barbecue rub, with hot or super-hot sauce on the side. The cost for everything is between $5 and $10, excluding side dishes; these include salted and vinegared collard greens, a chunk of corn bread, and baked beans or potato salad. You can also get a double-combo, or "two way," that includes two meats with two side dishes for $11.95. The portions are so prodigious and the meat so juicy that you would be well advised to come in your oldest trousers and keep plenty of paper napkins on hand. For dessert ($4), there are cobblers like peach pie and sweet potato pie, but they're not always "on".

Despite the nearness of the Haight, don't bring vegetarians here—the greens and potato salad won't begin to assuage their sufferings, in fact they'll worsen them. If desserts are off today, give a thought to gospel singer Emmit Powell's place nearby at 511 Hayes Street. Locally, Powell's has the sweet potato pie vote, though it has to be said that Brother-in-Law's beats all opposition on the barbecue front, with the exception of the pricier Memphis Minnie's.

Cafe Kati

If you are a foodie in search of the blow-you-totally-away ultimate in fusion food, put this one somewhere on your list for its quirky, cheeky creativity. The food is an East-meets-West affair starring Kirk Webber's vertical food; you may want to frame it. You'll need to book ahead, and you'll certainly have to keep a little pocketful of "oohs" and "aahs" at the ready. It can get cramped and loud in

Cost $25–100

Address 1963 Sutter St at Fillmore
℡ 415/775-7313
Open Tues–Sat 5.30–10pm
Transportation 2, 22, 38
Accepts All major credit cards except Diners

here at weekends, when the buzz attracts an upscale, all-black-wearing crowd who find it easy to walk here or park at the nearby Kabuki.

The house favorite appetizers are the best choices because they're quickly made and better priced than the mains, although they change often. Even the Caesar salad ($7.95) comes vertically stacked, towering on its leaves as a kind of monument to crispy romaine lettuce. Webber uses phyllo pastry a lot, in particular to make a goat cheese and Portobello mushroom Middle Eastern-style pie ($13) that comes with a sweet-sour plum sauce and bing cherry vinaigrette. Ahi tacos ($7.95) are a take on the fish taco, adding endamame, daikon radishes, and wasabe. Fat prawns ($8.95) are rolled in peanut sauce, then grilled and served on a bed of green papaya salad with extra mint and chile. Vietnamese spring rolls ($7.95) are refreshingly filled with mango as well as lettuce, rice, and carrots. Choosing from the entrees menu will seriously increase your bill. The red wine sauce—and the price—that accompanies the tuna ($25.75) may seem a little strong, but it is delicious when mopped up with mashed potatoes and onion rings. Kati's well-known vertical food theme continues with a towering, double-cut Beeler ranch pork chop in herbed crust that soars from a base of melted leeks and spätzle ($22.95). The sticky desserts could be framed: butterscotch pudding ($6.50) comes totteringly and fancifully finished.

The wine list makes an interesting read, but that might be all you can afford to do. These are among the highest prices around for wines, and also for main dishes, so stick to the interesting appetizers. The timing sometimes goes wrong here, so be prepared for a wait.

Caffè Proust

Stuck on the other side of the Panhandle, and more Western Addition than Haight in flavour, the slightly bohemian Caffè Proust is one of the prettiest cafes in town, as well as the most artistic. The "hopelessly unofficial" headquarters of the Marcel Proust Support Group supplies a relaxing bouquet of pasta, draft Guinness, and lots of Californian reds and whites. There's a bohemian, vaguely intellectual ambiance, and a fairly constant entertainment roster. It's definitely the one bright spot in this residential neighborhood, and rejoices in a roomy corner location with enormous wraparound windows that make it into something of an aquarium. The regulars worked on the place themselves, putting out a Marcel Proust zine and producing the wall art that's always much in evidence.

Cost $8–20
Address 1801 McAllister St at Baker
☎ 415/345-9560
Open Mon–Wed & Sun 5–10pm, Thurs–Sat 5–11pm
Transportation 5, 24
Accepts All major credit cards

So it's not just about the food, you understand. But the simple menu isn't bad and the daily specials can be better than good. A stunningly fresh calamari salad ($8) goes down well with a pint of porter, or you might enjoy an orange and walnut salad with Gorgonzola ($8), washed down with an Italian soda. Being Caffè Proust, they also supply an alternative vegan version, served without the Gorgonzola ($8). The fries are chunky and good here, and are also sold separately ($5), garnished with mayonnaise and sprinkled with romano—an inspired idea. Of their regular pastas, spaghetti Bolognese ($12) is always on the menu, along with fettuccine ($12) in marinara, pesto, or vongole sauces. Pasta is served in friendly portions, with lots of Parmesan and pepper available to taste. Parisian steak frites ($14) is excellent; if you lived on the next street, you'd be here several times a week.

Just don't come here if you can't stand the works of Marcel Proust, because they're quoted here and there and at least a handful of the people here look as though they might in fact have read them, or are able to pretend they did so convincingly. In case you were wondering, yes, they do serve madeleines here, for a dollar apiece. However, you might be more interested in the five-dollar zabaglione pie in a chocolate hazelnut crust.

Chez Nous

When Frenchman Pascal Rigo launched his first "Mediterranean mezes" place on Fillmore, people still hadn't heard of tapas, and the novel idea took off right away. Chez Nous is narrow as a hallway, painted aqua and crammed with tables, which are hard to get (they don't take reservations). When you do finally sit, the food is good, the service very helpful and the noise a sign of this restaurant's continued fashionability. Putting up with the hassles is your choice, but you can weight odds in your favor by coming early or sending someone ahead to nail you some barstools for the wait.

Cost	$10–25
Address	1911 Fillmore St at Bush
☎	415/441-8044
Open	Tues 5.30–10pm, Wed & Thurs 11.30am–3pm & 5.30–10pm, Fri & Sat 5.30–11pm
Transportation	2, 3, 4, 22
Accepts	MasterCard, Visa

The bread and baked goods are all divine here—Rigo owns Panissimo nearby, and uses his own organic flour from San Francisco's oldest mill, also part of his mini-empire. Despite the name, Laurence Jossel's food is more Greek than French. You'll meet mezes like warmed marinated olives ($3.50) or spreads ($3.50) such as tarama (roe), melitzanosalata (eggplant), or tsatsiki (cucumber-garlic), served with crackers. Roast potato wedges ($5) come with a bean aiolo on the side, and the Spanish tortilla ($5.50) comes appropriately sliced, filled with layers of potatoes, and served at room temperature. Two more Mediterranean specialties are the little trademark lamb cutlets sprinkled with lavender salt ($9) and the grilled Monterey calamari in a fennel, orange, and olive salad ($8.50). Along with chocolate pot de crème ($6), you can finish with a Greek yaorti e meli ($6), a dessert of yogurt with raisins and honey plus a sprinkling of pistachios.

Rigo's Bay Bread empire began near here, and has spread to the Breton crêperie Galette, across the road; La Boulange de Polk, with a second branch in Cole Valley; and Le Petit Robert, on Polk Street. Rigo seems to know instinctively what San Franciscans want when they don't want full-course dinners. You may have dark suspicions about the small-plate philosophy he pioneered—doesn't it really mean "less food for more dough?"—but this food is not only good, it also answers another local desire: the need to sit in a cafe and try to look like decadent Euro-trash.

Florio

(🍴) All is dark and intimate at Florio behind its photogenic checked curtains and Art Nouveau lettering. But the sombre wooden furnishings are offset by a lively bar scene, and celebrations are usually in progress at a couple of large round tables. Professionals from "Yuppie Heights" descend here for special occasions, or simply to people-watch over cocktails, either cozying up to the bar or imbibing at one of the sidewalk

Cost $10–35	

Address 1915 Fillmore St at Bush
☏ 415/775-4300
Open Mon–Thurs & Sun 5.30–10pm, Fri & Sat 5.30–11pm
Transportation 1, 2, 3, 4, 22
Accepts All major credit cards except Diners

tables. The crowd could be described as fortymumble or thereabouts, and the menu lists mainly testosterone-pleasing French brasserie classics.

The cioppino ($19) is the one non-French exception on the menu. This old-fashioned San Francisco shellfish stew is a classic that stars a very large cast of Dungeness crab, clams, mussels, prawns, and snapper, all in a saffron- and chile-laced stock. It's very much a party dish, and Florio's is one of the best in town. Less grandiose appetizers include a tasty and dainty brandade of salt cod set on arugula with olives and roast peppers ($6), and a charcuterie plate ($9) with an unusual mixture of prosciutto, chicken livers, Serrano ham, tasso ham from Louisiana, soppressata, and a few cornichons for garniture. But perhaps the most interesting appetizer is the frisée with a poached egg, lardons, fromage blanc, and vinaigrette ($8); in fact, Florio's may have been the first place in town to serve this very feisty mix. They also do a plate of ruby-red beets prettily contrasted with seasonal greens and cracked walnuts ($9). The most wholesome dish on the main course menu is oxtail ravioli ($15), and there's a justly popular roast chicken with pan juices and mashed potato ($19, $35 for two). Classical French steak frites comes with sauce Béarnaise ($24, $38 for two) and the pork tenderloin ($18), another great favorite, comes on a bed of caramelized apples. Fish dishes may include petrale or sea bass (from $20). The cheese selection ($6) is a fine assortment of four, one of which is invariably Gorgonzola, and desserts ($6) are sorbets or gelati.

Be prepared to knock knees with your neighbors, as tables jostle in the gloom. Still, strolling down here for cocktails and a meal is certainly an attractive proposition.

Galette

As a piece of faux France dispensing buckwheat pancakes at warp speed, Galette joins an already numerous army of new crêperies in town. Run by the owner of Chez Nous, it looks like an Alpine après-ski lodge crossed with Tintin's den, with a few tossed-in references to Brittany, home of the crêpe. At this useful location, and with fairly low

Cost $8–20

Address 2043 Fillmore St at California
☎ 415/928-1300
Open Daily 11.30am–11pm
Transportation 1, 3, 22
Accepts MasterCard, Visa

prices, it operates at high volume and density, with just about enough room between elbows. It's a suitable place to take kids, and also very convenient for a pit stop while shopping or en route to the movies.

Main course buckwheat pancakes run from a bargain $4 to $6, and you pick from savory fillings like ratatouille, spinach, simple gruyère cheese, chicken in different sauces or the hot merguez sausage; there's a daily special too. Generally speaking, the simpler the filling the better at Galette: occasionally you meet an under-heated element with the more complicated fillings. Galette does better with dessert pancakes. The Crêpe Nutella ($4) is one of the cheapest items, but it's hard to resist the deliciously unhealthy Crêpe Liègeois ($9), which is soaked with chocolate ice cream and crème Chantilly; the Banana Split ($9), with caramelized banana, coconut, lychee, cassis, and Chantilly; or Poire Belle Hélène ($9), with pear, caramel, chocolate, and Chantilly. There's a *spécialité de la maison*: Cannelles de Bordeaux ($6), which are small chocolate cakes about the size of kidney stones, served with chocolate ice cream. There's also a short extra menu, with fare like bouillabaisse ($9)—which isn't bad at all—and salads (around $6), but pancakes is what Galette is all about.

Beverages are not a strong suit. A $4 glass of Côtes du Rhone is brutal, but what do you expect for $4 a glass—something a French person would drink? Kir Breton—cider with cassis—costs $3.50 and is very sickly indeed. The service is, well, authentically French: "non!" or "bof!" are heard more frequently than "oui!" But if you have a Nutella crêpe-shaped hole in your tummy and are dashing off to a French movie at the Clay, you might just overlook the service.

La Méditerranée

🍴 Like its sibling off the Castro, La Med serves a bunch of Middle Eastern mezes, or appetizers, but it has a livelier scene with a really buzzy feel. It's about as wide as a passage, though the ceiling is high and they do their best in the evening with cushions and garlands of tiny white lights. Whereas the Noe Street branch is a comfy pit stop for shoppers, you might go as far as attempting the occasional date here.

Cost $5–20
Address 2210 Fillmore St at Sacramento
☎ 415/921-2956
Open Mon–Thurs 11am–10pm, Fri & Sat 11am–11pm, Sun 10am–9.30pm
Transportation 22
Accepts MasterCard, Visa

Sure, it can be cramped if you come at peak time, and the acoustics can be clattery, and sometimes you wait, but on a balmy night you'd describe Fillmore's "Med" as atmospheric.

Chef-owner Levon does a generous bowl of lentil salad ($7.95). His cold cucumber and yogurt soup ($3.95 cup, $5 bowl) is lightly minted, and thinner than a raita or tsatsiki. There's always a soup of the day ($2.50/$3.50), which might be something like tomato finished with cream, and a quiche of the day ($7.75) too—expect something along the lines of creamy salmon. Levant sandwiches ($8.50) are Middle Eastern lavosh, roll-em-ups made on flat bread with fillings of falafel, cream cheese, and tabbouleh. That's a lunch and a half, but if you need something even more filling, there's a similar mix on the vegetarian Middle Eastern plate ($8.75), which also has spanakopita, or Greek spinach and feta pie, along with cheese in phyllo pastry and dolmas. Lebanese specials include lule kebabs ($9.25), and Lebanese kibbeh ($9.25), or lamb with cracked wheat and pine nuts. A celestial pomegranate sauce is poured over drumsticks to make chicken pomegranate ($9.25), served with rice. Levon's phyllo specialties include a Moroccan cilicia ($9.25) of cinnamon chicken, almonds, raisins, and chickpeas. There's a beef version called a Levantine meat tart ($9.25), and a series of karni ($9.25), or cheese vol-au-vents.

Fruit and cheese ($8) make a fine lunch on the tear. The homemade baklava goes down well, but the epitome of sensuous Middle Eastern sweets arrives in the form of the datil amandra ($4.95), dates and nuts rolled in phyllo and served warm with a dollop of stiffish crème fraîche on top.

Mifune

Mifune has carved itself the little niche of quick noodle fix, and as a drop-by place for a noodling interval before or after a hot tub or something at the Kabuki, it's a convenient choice. Most of the repeat customers don't need any encouragement to slurp their noodles. And how else would you gulp down those steaming bowls of mountainous fat white or thin buckwheat noodles? But just in case you don't get the point, they supply only chopsticks, and the menu urges you to drop all dignity and make whatever slurping noises you need to in shameless abandon. The booths in Mifune's minimal design owe their cozy, slightly cramped and closed-off feel to those high, blue, flap-hung ceiling curtains. It's all you need for canoodling.

Cost $5–15

Address 2F Kintetsu Mall, 1737 Post St at Webster
☎ 415/922-0337
Open Mon–Thurs 11am–9.30pm, Fri & Sat 11am–10pm
Transportation 22, 38
Accepts All major credit cards

The story is simple. Noodle dishes come in many variations on home-made udon (fat, round, white flour) or the stronger-tasting soba (thin, pale brown, buckwheat). There are hot and cold varieties, and dozens of different dressings and accompaniments, from sliced teriyaki chicken and beef, to natto, sliced vegetables, and miso, or anything else a vegetarian might order. Prices start at around $5, with additional charges for dressings. If you order the noodles with a small salad and a side of sushi, plus tea, you'll pay just $7.95 at lunch. For alternatives to noodles, Mifune have a brace of ramen dishes, such as shellfish ramen ($5.75), and donburi plates such as beef donburi over rice ($4.50). They also serve tempura, teriyaki, and sushi selections, but most people come here for just one thing, and they slurp it with gusto. Dessert is green-tea ice cream ($2.50), to go with the nichon cha green tea.

There have been carpings about the service, and the spanking turnover certainly means that it's rushed in here. But the words brisk and efficient might seem more appropriate, a matter of getting down to the business in hand. A note on "J-town" dining: with its mix of high-end and low-end, touristy and non-touristy dining, and the availability of validated parking, there's truly somewhere for everyone.

Perlot

Lavishly reappointed in high Edwardian style, the Hotel Majestic is the dowager of Japantown. A survivor of the Great Quake of 1906—it was just south of the Van Ness Avenue firebreak—it has known many a facelift. Its latest makeover has brought with it a culinary renaissance under the guidance of new chef Christopher Steinbock, and the ambiance is an immediate plus. The

Cost $25–70

Address Hotel Majestic, 1500 Sutter St at Gough
ⓣ 415/441-1100
Open Mon–Sat 7–10.30am & 5.30–10.30pm, Sun 7am–2pm
Transportation 1, 2, 49
Accepts All major credit cards

charitably lit dining room is toned in apricot and gray. Pianist Donald Asher softly tickles "You Do Something To Me" in the background—in fact, he plays any pre-1955 request, and trying to catch him out is something of a pastime around here.

The three-course prix fixe menu ($45) changes weekly, and offers a half-dozen choices per course. One excellent starter might be a large charcuterie plate ($16), which sports rabbit rillettes on melba toast, a homemade terrine with pistachios, and a trio of cheeses from Cowgirl Creamery that send most diners reeling—triple crème, Sophia, and sheep's milk. The celestial Canadian Fox Island mussels ($10) are lightly steamed in a shallot, tomato, and white wine broth that interferes minimally with their essential perfume. If you're looking for a good piece of steak, the grilled rib-eye ($25) is a fine specimen. A cannelloni of lobster, shrimp, and mascarpone ($23) brings a brace of large pasta tubes stuffed with sweet, creamy shellfish to the table. Other main courses frequently seen on the menu are monkfish with polenta and wilted greens ($22), blue-nose sea bass ($24), and rack of lamb ($26). For dessert, a very intense flourless triple-chocolate torte ($7) is so rich that it makes the other offerings on the menu—perhaps fresh raspberry and blackcurrant sorbets—quite redundant. It's almost impossible to taste more than three small mouthfuls before going into chocolate shock.

The wines feature a very reasonably priced Cakebread ($7 per glass), and a half bottle of Testarossa, among a wide-ranging selection of Californian varietals. All told, this is excellent value for excellent food, and the atmosphere pushes it into the class of places for a special date.

Pizza Inferno

"Acid rock" is the only way to describe this demented little Japantown pit-stop right on Fillmore Street. The paint job is way over the top: neon green fights angry red and black graffiti over the ceiling, floor, bar, and tables. The wait staff, by way of contrast, combine mellow, laid-back charm with sympathetic service. But the main reason for coming here is the Happy Hour (4–6.30pm) and their special "twofer" extra pizza after 10pm. At this useful location, in the middle reaches of Fillmore Street, that's pretty much a steal of a deal.

Cost $10–25
Address 1800 Fillmore St at Sutter
☎ 415/775-1800
Open Daily 11am–midnight
Transportation 2, 3, 4, 22, 38
Accepts All major credit cards except Diners

Inferno specializes in devilishly thin crust, square pizzas, with unusual gourmet and yuppified toppings such as wild mushrooms with caramelized Roma tomatoes ($9.95), goat cheese with walnuts ($9.45), and calamari, clams, and shrimp ($9.95)—that combo may be a mite too crustacean for some tastes. Despite their small, flattened dimensions (about eight inches), the pizza squares manage to sock a curiously intense, flavorsome punch, and they're big enough for more than just one person. Since they start at $6.95 and the wine list includes passable half-liter carafes of Chianti ($9), you can split an Inferno pizza and add a nice little Caprese or Caesar salad ($3.95) plus wine for two and pay only $20—a cheap date indeed! That's more or less it for the Inferno, except to add that it's especially handy before or after a movie at the nearby Kabuki Theater because of the happy hour bargains.

Inferno isn't somewhere to get carried away over, but the service is genial, and the pizza offerings are none too shabby—plus you can have a decent movie thrown in on the next block to boot. The Kabuki—which, despite the name is simply a movie theater—is part of the Japan Center complex, which has validated parking and a more relaxed atmosphere than many downtown theaters. Sometimes you might find yourself in Japantown and more in the mood for pizza than sushi, and it's nice to be able to slip away for a slice or two before the show.

Rasselas Jazz Club

Amazingly cool live jazz with fear-somely hot Ethiopian food–it may never offer a fork, but Rasselas offers the fieriest of combinations known to man or woman! Known more as a jazz nightclub than a restaurant (the bar is open till midnight, and till 1am on weekend nights), Rasselas nevertheless offers good Ethiopian food. There are now two branches around the Fillmore: this big old dive near Divisadero, and a smaller, newer place in the Western Addition (1534 Fillmore St, ☎415/346-8696). Both feature no-utensil food at amazingly low prices, though only the Divisadero Rasselas has an actual dining room and the decor is slightly funky. Few places can offer good food at these prices, and few come more interesting either. The California Rasselas is endearingly like a dark sitting room, with settees that appear to have come from the Salvation Army–and why not?

Cost $10–25

Address 2801 California St at Divisadero
☎415/567-5010
Open Daily 5–10pm
Transportation 24
Accepts All major credit cards

In case you're still unfamiliar with the aromatic stews of East Africa, you should know that they come with the useful addition of injera, an unleavened spongy bread that holds the rich, spicy juices while you convey food to your mouth in little parcels. The best deal for vegetarian jazz heads is the veggie combo, or kik alecha ($12.50), which centers around a hellaciously hot, puréed yellow lentil and root vegetable stew with lots of delicious yam in the mix, plus the classic Ethiopian berbere spice. There's also plenty of that good old injera to counteract the heat, and some greens known as "gomen," which are mustard and collard leaves long-simmered in onions and peppers. Such a combo, at $12.50, would keep two jazz-lovers listening happily. The classic lamb and chicken dishes of Ethiopian cuisine are here too, including yebeg wat ($11.75), a rich and fiery lamb stew, and doro wat ($11.75), an equally spicy chicken version. Kitfo ($10.75) is a steak tartare that's cured in berbere spice.

Next door, a few tables are ready if you want to sit for you meal, but you can take your plates with you to listen to the music while you eat— the sofas won't mind. There's beer to soothe your burning mouth, and baklava ($4) for dessert.

Sapporo-Ya

You could easily miss Sapporo-Ya, because even its ancient noodle mangle at the door doesn't exactly shout its presence aloud. Tucked into a corner of the Kinokuniya Building, the big Japanese mall next door to the Kabuki, it has an unpretentious, low-key vibe, with just a few nondescript tables and a smaller side room that looks invitingly tranquil. Sapporo-Ya's specialty is the soba fix or, more specifically, a deep super-bowl of noodles that's perfect for making your very own *Tampopo* movie before or after the movies. The ambiance is more soothing than the pulsating Mifune or any of the flashier sushi bars.

Cost $5–15

Address 2F Kunokuniya Building, 1581 Webster St
☎ 415/563-7400
Open Mon–Sat 11am–11pm, Sun 11am–10pm
Transportation 22, 38
Accepts All major credit cards except Diners

The number-one selling point is their homemade noodles and, as the noodle grinder at the doorway testifies, Sapporo-Ya has been making its own Hokkaido noodles for over twenty years. Hokkaido noodles are an acquired taste. Some folks find their rustic flavor a little strong, others like them inordinately. You can sometimes spot waiters from other Japantown places, noodling away in peace. Choices are simple, and the standout here is the huge clay bowl of piping-hot ramen ($4.95–13.95), which comes with ten different accompaniments, from carrots, spinach, and bamboo shoots to miso with barbecued pork or some kind of seafood; there's also a tempura ramen with fresh vegetables. Bury your face in the heat from the noodles and go in there with your chopsticks. Sapporo-Ya is also known for another specialty: the southern Japanese rice-flour and egg pancake known as an okonomiyaki, traditionally cooked by families on little grills; this is probably the only place in town you can get it. The pancake's mix of egg and rice flour has the effect of making it thin and very crispy, and it is served with various vegetables, meat, or seafood. Try the fried shrimp, or the thin-sliced beef dressed in a pungent shoyu sauce ($10.95). You can also order okonomiyaki with fried noodles ($11.95). Cold Sapporo beer washes it all down.

The ramen here is darker, decidedly rougher in texture and more flavorsome than some people are used to. But according to the photo on the wall, Chris Isaak likes it, so who'd disagree? And don't forget the free parking.

Takara Sushi and Seafood

Like other parts of San Francisco, Japantown has its ra-ra touristy joints, but it also has modestly priced backstairs dining known only to discerning locals–and very few non-Japanese San Franciscans know about Takara. Semi-hidden away at the rear of the secondary mall building, its interior is unfussy, with traditional Japanese floor seating, a sushi counter and wooden tables. The food is equally simple and faultless. When you arrive, you are given a hot towel for your hands and a choice of utensils.

Cost $20–40

Address Japan Center, Miyako Mall, 22 Peace Plaza #202, Post St at Webster
☏415/921-2000
Open Daily 11am–11pm
Transportation 2, 3, 4, 38
Accepts All major credit cards

On weekdays, the little sushi bar is usually less populated than the small Western-style wooden tables. Try the nigiri combination ($13.50) of halibut, tuna, yellowtail, salmon, and four other sushi, or the takara special ($16) of tuna, eel, sea bream, and salmon, plus five others; both are good value. Singly, the sushi dishes range from $3 for geoduck to $4.50 for crab. The non-sushi menu includes shabu shabu ($6.50), which is dishes of meat poached in broth; nabi sukiyaki, or ponzu-simmered beef ($7.50); and fat udon noodles ($4.75). Agedashi tofu ($4.50), deep-fried in hot dashi or bonita stock, is silky and delicate. There are a couple of unusual extras as well: zosui ($7) is a rice porridge, congee-style, while ochazuke ($7.50) is a special tea-over-rice meal, where nori is crumbled and tea poured over a rice dish; both are traditional fast-food fuel, and probably new to most *gaijin*. Takara's specialty, however, is their "iron pot" dinner ($19), a multi-dish banquet that starts with an appetizer such as a piece of sashimi and a savory cup of custard, and continues with miso soup, a bowl of pickled vegetables, rice, salad, and a main dish of poached meat or seafood in a decorative iron pot. It concludes with two green, chewy, tea-flavored mochi, or rice-flour ice cream squares, which come from the exquisite Yamada Seika bakery, nearby on Sutter Street.

Like other Asian meals, all courses arrive at once—except for the green mochi. Their excellent sake costs $5 for a small carafe. If you find your taste for it grows, you could always move on to M's, a fascinating sake bar on the lower floor of the Miyako Mall.

Zao Noodle Bar

"The way of the noodle is long and narrow," says the creative Californian mind ensconced in the kitchen at this bargain noodle bar. At Zao, diners get their quick noodle fix from steaming bowls large enough to bury your face in. The founder of this growing empire is likeable local chef Adam Willner, an alumnus of Il Fornaio who opened the first Zao in Palo Alto a few years back. Now he has a mini-chainlet

Cost $10–15
Address 2406 California St at Fillmore
☎ 415/345-8088
Open Mon–Thurs & Sun 11am–10pm, Fri & Sat 11am–midnight
Transportation 1, 3, 22
Accepts MasterCard, Visa

going, dedicated to the philosophy of the noodle as the (rather wobbly) staff of life. Zao offers endless permutations, from the Chinese ribbon-like flat noodle to the Vietnamese translucent rice noodle and the Japanese buckwheat soba noodle in broth, which Adam has rebaptized as "zao mein" pan-fried noodles.

You get a spoon along with chopsticks to fight your way into one of those giant bowls. Vietnamese rice noodles ($6.95) are almost like a salad, with a riot of green beans, bak choy, tofu, and carrots, plus sour soy-lime sauce. The vegetables all look spectacularly fresh and healthful—and are, in fact, sometimes almost raw. Zao "surf 'n turf" ($8.88) is another bottomlessly deep bowl, this time using the flatter Shanghai noodles with sweet-sour chicken, prawns, greens, red peppers, and squash, in ginger-garlic chile. Most slurpable are the pad thai with prawns ($8.75), for its tamarind sweet-and-sour sauce, and the tiger prawns in curried coconut sauce, which comes with the admonishment "One Ocean, One Earth, One Bowl." (Words to live by!) Zao's menu offers one or two non-noodle items, too. Satay skewers arrive in three flavors: Thai chicken in peanut ($5.50), Korean beef in peanut ($5.50), and veggie mushroom with yakitori sauce ($4.95). For dessert, try mochi rice ice cream and banana rolls.

Beverages are a treat here, which is nice, since so much of the food is spicy. The coolers are delicious, especially the ginger-orange ($2.50) and the Thai-spiced iced tea ($2.50). There are also decent beers, sake cocktails like "Demon Killer" ($5.50), and acceptable wines. Branches of Zao can be found at 820 Irving St, in the Sunset, 2031 Chestnut St, in the Marina, and 3583 16th St, in the Castro.

The Richmond

Angkor Wat Cambodian Restaurant

On his 1987 tour, Pope John Paul II sped past the city's first Cambodian restaurant in his Popemobile, maybe disappointed by the blanket of summertime fog. His Holiness did, however, order their takeout chicken and pineapple soup. Perhaps he should have slowed down and relaxed into the silken, floor-level cushions at this showcase for the subtleties of Khmer cuisine. The soup remains popular for its sweetness and mildness, qualities that spare tender digestions. Now called simply "the Pope's Soup," it's a refined consommé with coconut, basil, and galangal, and without soy or fish sauce.

Cost $20–35

Address 4217 Geary Boulevard at 6th
☎ 415/221-7887
Open Mon–Fri 11am–2pm & 5–9.30pm, Sat & Sun 5–10pm
Transportation 2, 38, 44
Accepts All major credit cards

Angkor's food is intricate and irresistibly presented. Perhaps their carpet likes it too? It could do with a shampoo and scrub. But it's a shame not to sprawl on cushions, chat with the maitre d', Tha, and look at the temple art from ancient wats. Regular tables exist for people who don't sprawl well. Go for the confusingly named lott ($5.95), which is miniature chicken, peanut, thread-noodle, and chestnut-stuffed rolls in lime sauce. Cambodian crêpe ($5.95) is made with crispy rice flour, filled with sprouts, white noodles, cucumber, and chicken, and tossed in basil, mint, and cilantro. It's smaller than La Vie's or Angkor Borei's lacey plate-sized cakes, but veggie variations are available as well. The seafood Haamok ($7.95), or mixed shellfish and fish custard in a banana leaf, is a curious-tasting delicacy that takes two hours to steam. Other favorites are Joanna's famous catfish ($12.95), poached in a complex broth of coconut with sweet bean curd, lime, and chile; and five-spice shark ($12.95), which comes with a subtle touch of oyster sauce. Cambodian curry ($11.95) is milder than an Indian, and is spiced with star anise, lemongrass, galangal, cinnamon, cumin, and nutmeg, and served in a coconut shell. Wine prices are fair, starting at $14.50 per bottle; corkage is $8. Desserts ($3.95) include "flaming banana" and smooth and creamy jackfruit crème.

Angkor Wat's Joanna Sokheun Suong and Keith Dan opened the city's first Cambodian place in the mid 1980s, when Pol Pot's holocaust was a fresh memory, and their first restaurant became a way to help those back home. They now publish their own cookbook, on sale here.

Brother's Korean Restaurant

It's a carnivore's ball at Brother's. "Strictly functional" is the way to describe the decor, or lack of it, but judging by the crowds that wait at the door every night, the important stuff—meat—is just right. A "coal man" patrols tables to add live coals to your very own table grill. Above diners' heads are 1950s-style extractor fans, but the aroma of cooking meat lingers alluringly anyway. Even

Cost $15–35
Address 4128 Geary Boulevard between 5th and 6th
☎ 415/387-7991
Open Daily 11am–3am
Transportation 2, 38, 44
Accepts MasterCard, Visa

those who don't feel an urge to rend mounds of pork, beef, and chicken-en—the latter is a sop to Westerners, since Koreans stick to pork or beef—seem to enjoy the do-it-yourself, party aspect of Brother's, and it's well suited to families or gangs of friends.

The all-inclusive pork and beef bulgogi (set meals) start at $15.95 at dinner. Generous banchan, or small plates, are included in the price, and are served by speedy and motherly staff. They begin with a delicious hot Korean soup served from a metal pot, and continue with a dozen or more plates of tofu, kimchee (pickled cabbage), rice, mixed vegetables, bean sprouts, vinegared cucumber, bean curd in broth, and assorted pickles and peppers that rapidly swallow the available table space with a host of jostling flavors and textures. Staff are happy to keep the banchan coming, but meanwhile, you get to choose if you'd like to cook your own meat on the grill or get it readymade. A pile of salad leaves appears with the meat—you can pack your own choice of flavors into each lettuce leaf, roll it, and tuck in. A Korean specialty beer called Cass is crisp, full, and ideal for washing it all down. Lunch specials include portions of kal bi (ribs), bul koki (beef), or bul tok (pork), priced at a reasonable $7.95.

Some visitors complain that this is "American Korean" cuisine. But other Korean barbecues are even more Americanized, and they flourish—New Korea House, in Japantown, and the original Hahn's BBQ, on Polk Street, are among them. Korean families flock in large numbers to Brother's, and another branch, one block up at 4014 Geary, between 4th and 5th Avenues (☎ 415/668-2028), takes in the overflow.

Cafe Riggio

A former haunt of impresario Bill Graham, Riggio's is a holdout from the days when Mayor Dianne Feinstein and Joan Baez ate cheek by jowl with Graham's rock bands. When Chicago-born John Riggio opened up, back in the 1970s, he was ahead of his time with baked cacciocavallo cheese starters and scaloppine dishes that are still his specialties. These dishes were labeled as "Nuova Cucina" back then, and likewise, the jester mural, red ceiling, yellow walls, ceramic plates, and glass loggia seemed bohemian at the time. They're just familiar now, but this Chianti-soaked spot still pulls them in because of its unpretentious atmosphere and "just-like-nonna-made-it" portions.

Cost $20–45

Address 4112 Geary Boulevard at 5th Ave
☎ 415/221-2114
Open Mon–Thurs 5–10pm, Fri & Sat 5–11pm, Sun 4.30–11pm
Transportation 2, 38, 44
Accepts MasterCard, Visa

You'll find some of the padrone's antipasti too button-busting by half: mozzarella and tomato salad ($6.75) and garlic bread ($3.75) fill you up fast. Sautéed formaggio all' arginera ($6) comes hissing in its own skillet. You'll get a whiff of anise in the insalata di calamari marinata ($6.50), which is marinated squid on spinach, and lavish enough for an entree. Minestrone soup with Parmesan ($2.75/$3.75) is lighter. Pasta (from $11) is all over the Italian map, from fettucine to cappelline, and from ravioli to spaghetti with steamed baby clams ($16). Veal specialties include scaloppine della casa ($16), which comes with roasted garlic, sun-dried tomatoes, and mushrooms; scaloppine alla Marsala ($15.50), with mushrooms; and costalette alla Milanese ($16), or breaded puttanesca-tangy cutlets. Veal also comes in the ever-popular piccata sauce($15.50), sautéed with lemon, wine, and capers; or as that comfort-food classic, alla Parmigiana ($14). The piccata wins hands down, though children and those with fearful palates go for the Parmigiana. If you haven't already undone a few buttons, tiramisu ($6.00), homemade cannoli ($5), and berries with zabaglione ($6) compete for your waistline with chocolate torte ($5) and New York cheesecake with raspberries ($5).

The wine list isn't amazing but offers safe wines at a reasonable mark-up, including Seghesio Sonoma Zinfandel ($35) and MacRostie Carneros Chardonnay ($35). Super Specials are a deal here, at $19.95 for Caesar salad or minestrone plus main dish, pasta, and zabaglione. If you've a couple of kids on your hands after rollerblading in Golden Gate Park, Cafe Riggio makes a family solution.

Chapeau!

(icon) This cozy golden- and brown-toned bistro is the apple of Philippe Gardelle's proud eye, and the darling of the Richmond District. The owner busts his Parisian guts to make a dull block into a warm little corner of France, and someone did a cute paint job here, with Fragonard-like touches such as stenciled garlands swagging the walls. A former waiter who came to San Francisco on

Cost $20–35

Address 1408 Clement St at 15th
(phone) 415/750-9787
Open Tues–Thurs & Sun 5–10pm, Fri & Sat 5–10.30pm
Transportation 1, 2, 28, 38
Accepts All major credit cards

holiday, then stayed to work here, Gardelle's personal mission is to convert San Franciscans to good French food. With chef Jesse Frost, he has cleverly managed to infuse the menu with extra inspiration. The word is out, so you'll need to book in advance.

Frost has helpfully produced a series of prix fixe menus for all budgets, plus a wine glossary to teach us what to drink, and all diners get a free cup of soupe du jour with toast as a starter. The three-course prix fixe menu ($19) is available before 6pm, Sunday to Thursday, as is a longer five-course menu ($35). Dishes change daily, but there will often be a soup, such as soupe à l'oignon ($4.50 separately), which is served with an Emmenthal-speckled baguette, enough for a meal in itself. A ramekin of brandade of cod ($8) is another stunner, as are the superb duck confit "Garbure" with cabbage and bacon ($8.50), quail salad Véronique ($12), and foie gras Torchon with prunes ($11). A trademark main dish is cassoulet à la Toulousaine ($15) of haricots blancs, lamb, duck, and sausage. Vegetarian choices include fettucine with wild mushrooms and butternut squash ($24), and vegetarian mille feuille ($22). Chapeau is justly praised for coq au vin ($16), served on clouds of fluffy potatoes, and there's rollicking steak au poivre ($19). Desserts include meltingly warm chocolate cake ($6) and profiteroles ($6).

Another reason to dine here is the fairly priced wine list, diplomatically split into New World and French sections. Favorites include Rabbit Ridge Sonoma County Zinfandel ($25), and some outstanding Pinot Noirs at under $30. It may all add up, but Gardelle's place is well named: "chapeau!" *with* exclamation point is French slang for "congrats!"

Cheers Cafe

(YI) Mornings can be notoriously dreary in "Fog City" and the Richmond District is the grayest spot of all, poking halfway into the Pacific mists. So what can you do when you want to cheer yourself up and it's too early for Asian spices, Russian dancing or Irish bars? Cheers is an option, with brunch served until 3pm. Despite the name, it's not a bar, nor is it part of the chain of airport cafes based on the 1980s TV series—though it does

Cost $7–20
Address 127 Clement St
ⓉＴ 415/387-6966
Open Mon–Thurs 8.30am–9.30pm, Fri–Sun 8am–10pm
Transportation 2, 33, 38
Accepts All major credit cards except Diners

have a counter where you can linger over a drink. The day starts early here, and the yard at the back is the reason: trellised and covered from the elements, and pleasantly laid-back, it's a weekend hangout with people coming and going on their way to do their shopping on busy Clement Street.

Cheers' food is mainly Mediterranean, with a dash of nouvelle Californian and extra pinch of cilantro, ginger, and soy here and there to prove this really is the Richmond. Starters include the antipasto plate of tomatoes and mozzarella ($6.25). Some pasta dishes excel, like the generous gnocchi with prawns ($8.50), while pizzas include one with a rich topping of roasted eggplant, bell peppers, tomatoes, and onions ($9). Try the grilled chicken ($10.95), and the various mixed salads, including one with goat cheese ($6.75); these are healthy alternatives to the ever-popular grilled sandwiches ($4.99). The best dessert is warm pear tart with almond cream, ice cream, and caramel sauce ($5.25); a real waist-buster and a half. The modest wine list has no surprises, but wines are available by the glass ($4.50–6.50).

Cheers recently changed owners and has undergone a bit of an identity crisis in the aftermath. There's an after-work crowd who come in here at around 5—6pm, then traffic slows dramatically. At weekends, when it's nice to sit in the back chatting with the cheery if somewhat disorganized staff, it's a hangover hospital for the temporarily impaired. Why not gingerly assail a Mimosa ($3.50), an omelet (from $6.25), French toast ($6.95), or a fruit salad ($6)? Or fresh-squeezed orange juice ($3.25) with club sandwiches and lots of fresh coffee?

Clémentine

🍴 For those who crave reliable French classics, served by charming Parisian *garçons*, Clémentine is a major lure. It draws locals and out-of-towners alike to Clement Street's restaurant row, with its fairy-lit, tree-fronted, fancy exterior. After-work office birthday parties and older diners come here at aperitif hour to catch prix fixe deals; later, the clientele morphs into lovey-dovey couples, but the ambiance remains reas-

Cost $20–45

Address 126 Clement St between 2nd & 3rd
📞 415/387-0408
Open Tues–Thurs 5.30–10pm, Fri & Sat 5.30–10.30pm, Sun 5.30–9.30pm
Transportation 2, 33, 38
Accepts MasterCard, Visa

suringly conservative. Formally the site of Alain Rondelli's eponymous restaurant, Clémentine owner Didier Labbé is formerly of L'Orangerie in L.A. and L'Arpège in Paris. He has adapted the layout and now hangs a changing exhibition of French paintings. A wraparound mirror at eye level sheds light above the long, cozy banquette and affords diners a sneaky look at everyone else. Co-owner Laurent Legendre is a graduate of Postrio, while the attentive wait-staff are from Paris, Dijon and the Savoie—fine credentials all.

The Early Bird Special (5.30–7pm) offers a whittled-down three-course menu for $19.99, including expertly put-together duck salads ($7 a la carte) that triumphantly mix raspberry vinegar and frisée leaves with succulent duck. Carrot soup, however ($5.50), is as gloppy as baby food, and can be underseasoned. Clémentine comes into focus with its carpaccios ($6.50), which are more Californian than French: salmon with juniper berries and laurel, or beef with Parmesan, thyme, and capers. Sautéed foie gras with port and rhubarb ($10) is blameless, as are main dishes like rack of lamb ($17.50), porcini ravioli ($13.95), and quail ($16.25). The truite aux amandes ($13.50) comes in a generous portion, although the rather innocent farm-raised trout needed lemon and salt to sing, and the crushed almonds are softened in butter rather than toasted. Boeuf Bourguignon ($14.50) is comforting and richly juicy. Desserts ($6) are worthy pain perdu (French toast) and a delicately made frangipani tart made with pears. The wine list offers sedate Sauvignon Blancs and good Merlot varietals, both French and Californian ($5.50–7.50 per glass).

To sum up, Clémentine is the kind of place you might take your well-behaved aunt for a Champagne dinner, if you were hoping to inherit.

The Cliff House

The legendary Cliff House has existed in one form or another for 140 years. Back in the 19th century and later, it was a favorite excursion for San Franciscans at weekends, who would come to take the waters and drink in the ocean air. In recent decades, it has been the butt of some local cynicism, since the food has seldom rivalled the views of sunset over the Pacific, or of the Seal Rocks—whose seals have mostly moved on to Fisherman's Wharf. Happily,

Cost $15–40	
Address 1090 Point Lobos Ave	
☎ 415/386-3330	
Open Mon–Thurs 9am–3.30pm & 5–10.30pm, Fri–Sun 8.30am–4pm & 5–11pm	
Transportation 18	
Accepts All major credit cards	

changes are underway. Owners Dan and Mary Hountalas have rejigged the menus in the three dining rooms, which are fresh from restoration. There's now a distinct possibility of having a decent meal here.

The Cliff House still feels old-timey. There's a blazing fire in the bar, and it remains a nostalgic place for watching surfers. Start with the tried and true, which is still what they do best. The mixed oyster selection ($9.90 for a half-dozen, $17 per dozen), comes on a seaweed "ocean salad" with sesame and chile, and is particularly good value. Crisp and praiseworthy Caesar salads ($7.75) are made with fresh anchovies and plenty of real Parmesan, and grated with a flourish by kindly waiters at the new seafood lunchroom. Dungeness crabcakes are presented with roast red pepper aioli; you get two as an appetizer ($12.95) and three as a main course ($19.50). Along with the hefty broiled burger with onions and fries ($9.75), served with or without cheese, there's a crab Ben Butler sandwich ($17.95) on sourdough bread with salad. The night menu retains its old shrimp and crab Louis dishes, along with some walloping steaks and simple, local fish dishes, but the mahi-mahi ($19.75) has now acquired an up-to-date chipotle aioli, and the squash ravioli ($17.95) comes with a wild sage-infused beurre noisette.

The Cliff House goes fusion? This intriguing thought is swiftly dispelled by a glance at the lavish and traditional brunch menu, with its eggs Benedict ($11.95). They're certainly a better buy than the Champagne brunch ($42), but then the setting—with the surf crashing against the ruined Sutro Baths—is worth a splurge.

179

Coriya Hot Pot City

🍴 If you want to introduce an unlikely group of people to each other in casual surroundings, take them down to Coriya Hot Pot City All-You-Can-Eat Hibachi (to give it its full name) and tell them to bring empty stomachs and their oldest trousers. It's a raucous, rollicking scene here at the Clement academy of Taiwanese barbeque, and there's plenty of bang for your buck too. Other hibachi and shabu-shabu joints around town also make for bargain fun, but Coriya is the lodestar of the West for Asian youths. Always hopping with parties power-noshing their way through Himalayas of fresh meat and fish, it's a landmark—except on Wednesday lunchtimes, when it's shut. This is a hands-on, slap-happy, roll-up-your-shirtsleeves kind of place, and solo diners are barred.

Cost $10–25	

Address 852 Clement St at 10th
☏ 415/387-7888
Open Mon, Tues, Thurs & Sun noon–midnight, Wed 5pm–midnight, Fri & Sat noon–1am
Transportation 1, 2, 38
Accepts MasterCard, Visa

In front of you as you enter is a fake waterfall in front of a counter of fresh tubs of marinated chicken, pork, beef, and lamb—enough to make a vegetarian swoon—plus shrimp, octopus, lobster, crabs, and even sushi. Herbivores get carrots and cabbage with tofu and eggs, and there's a total of over fifty choices. If you so wish, you can stay all evening and try every one, though most people retire after a few hours. A hell-raising chile sauce is the final stop before you head to your table, with its individual stove and hot broth, to start grilling or poaching. Perhaps the best thing about All-You-Can Eat, aside from the fact you really *can* eat all you can eat, is the price. For the lunchtime session and after 10pm, you pay $8.99; it's $9.99 at weekends and $10.99 in the evening. Within the Richmond's tradition of Asian do-it-yourself buffets, the more the merrier is the rule, and there's a $20 minimum per party.

Do-it-yourself barbeques originated in Mongolia, but Taiwanese Coriya draws on several traditions. Known as "steamboat," Hainan Chinese broiling is done in fish broth, and is similar to Japanese shabu-shabu. If you don't know what's for dessert, ask the Asian teenagers at the neighboring table. Tapioca, sago, and rice pudding come in improbable technicolor hues. Whatever your poison is, you can't bring your own, but try Tsingao beer and you'll do fine.

India Clay Oven

Many a homesick British tourist, dreaming of the vindaloos of home, has huddled over a mashed-spud-and-peas samosa in this Outer Richmond joint, tearfully grateful to be handed a basket of pappadums. But San Franciscans have caught up fast on Indian food in the last decade, and this Sikh-owned business is rapidly expanding its kingdom (branches include Tandoori Mahal, at 941 Kearny St, and the India Garden Restaurant, at 1261 Folsom St), though owner Nemal Singh swears he has changed nothing in the ten years since it opened. These Outer Richmond blocks are morphing into a diners' delight, and it's partly because of India Clay Oven's popularity. Dim and a bit pokey by day, when locals throng the lunch buffet, it becomes discreetly candlelit after 6pm, when the place subtly acquires romantic touches—even fresh roses on linen.

Cost S8–15	
Address 2435 Clement St	
☏ 415/751-0505	
Open Daily 11.30am–2.30pm & 4.30–10pm	
Transportation 1, 2, 29, 38	
Accepts All major credit cards	

Not to be confused with the Indian Oven on Fillmore Street, this is the only Indian restaurant at the far end of Clement Street, and it pulls in the crowds. It's no mystery why, since the lunchtime all-you-can-eat buffet offers twenty dishes for a mere $6.99. Come here when you're hungry for standard Indian fare. Chapattis, parathas, and filled nan breads are ample ($1.50–2.50), while pakoras, samosas, and vegetable fritters are spicy and punchy ($3–4.95). As for the curries ($8.95–10.95), some may like it hot but watch out for the vindaloos, and stick to tandoori and milder kormas if you can't take a heavy dose of chile. Vegetarians can survive with ease here, particularly on veggie korma with cheese and nuts ($6.95), or a classic side dish like aloo mattar ($6.95), which is potatoes with peas, onions, and tomatoes. Red and white jug wines start at $16; the corkage fee if you bring your own bottle is negligible.

Indian desserts ($2.50) like gulab jamun (fried batter in syrup), rice puddings, and salty-sweet kulfi are available, but Indian stickies don't ice the cake for every spice lover. So for guiltier pleasures, grab a cleansing mouthful of their aniseed candy then stroll on to one of the Russian delicatessens or Geary Boulevard cafes for a pastry and coffee.

Jakarta Indonesian Cuisine

This temple of Indonesian spiciness has passed the five-year mark, making Jakarta an institution of the mini-restaurant row north of Golden Gate Park. It has won a faithful following for its artistry and ambiance, not to mention the warmth of its owner, Nisman Thahar. The sight of Nisman in his batik shirt may be enough to woo you to the ten-plate rijsttafel—a relic of the showy banquets of the colonial Dutch—at $42 for two people. Jakarta's interior is filled with light, and shadow puppets frolic on the snowy walls alongside pictures of a Balinese Selamatan, or celebration feast.

Cost $20–30

Address 615 Balboa St at 7th
Ⓣ 415/387-5225
Open Tues–Sun 5–10pm
Transportation 21, 31, 44
Accepts All major credit cards except AmEx

Indonesia changed forever with the arrival of the spice trade and the Dutch colonists who craved cloves, nutmeg, mace, ginger, coriander, cumin, fennel, dill, caraway, turmeric, and cinnamon. Jakarta tries hard to show how different islands use variations to build a theory of spiciness. Whether or not you're new to them, the Javanese satays, Sumatran crispy rice-cakes, and Balinese peanut dips and gado-gados (literally, "mixed up, mixed up") are all worth having, and the drinks and sweets also merit discovery. Start with kerupuk ($2.25), a crunchy prawn cracker; or the Jakartan bakwan ($4.50) of crispy prawn cakes with peanut sauce. For seafood, try otak otak ($3.95), which is mini quenelles of fish mousse in banana leaves; or the cumi cumi isi ($4.95) of squid stuffed with prawns. Ayam panggang bumbu Bali is a scorching grilled chicken in "exotic Bali BBQ Sauce," and comes in two versions: grilled breast ($9.50) or half-chicken ($9.95). Thoroughly rubbed in hot chile and minimally spritzed in oil, both are fiery. More subtle is the gulai udang ($12.45), or prawns relaxing in a nutmeg- and cilantro-scented milk bath. Five heavily loaded skewers of sate sapi ($9.25) wear a peanut sauce of extraordinary density, spiked with coconut, peanut, garlic, shallot, chile, and hard-to-find Indonesian palm sugar.

Jakarta's star dessert is kue dadar susudara ($4.25), a thick coconut coating around a fist of shredded ginger, embroidered with guava, ginger, and crème anglaise. Also riveting is kue lapis legit ($4.25), a many-layered cinnamon cake compressed into perfectly pinstriped triangles. Can you bear to nibble such artistry?

Kabuto Sushi

In a town of powerful celebrity sushi chefs, where people seek out sushi artistes much as they would Prince or Bono, Chef Sachio Kojima is one of the most compelling to watch. He creates sushi like a being possessed, and even when he isn't magicking wildly imaginative combinations out of thin air he imparts a certain spirit to his place. He's a performance artist with no time to spare on any details other than creating edible art from raw fish—the tattered carpet, tatami mats, horrid lighting and lack of glamour are actually reassuring. You have a choice of floor-level seating with gaily colored Japanese-style back supports, formica tables under glaring neon, or a prized seat at the coveted counter, where you can watch Kojima at work up close.

Cost $35–50

Address 5116 Geary Boulevard between 15th & 16th
☏ 415/752-5652
Open Tues–Sat 5.30–11pm, Sun 5.30–10pm; closed first Tues & last Sun of the month
Transportation 28, 38
Accepts All major credit cards except Diners

A special kabuto omakase dinner ($50) is offered that includes an endless succession of sushi, plus a dazzling choice of raw nigori that runs from quail egg to sea urchin and includes ninety kinds of rolls, in addition to unusual items like nasu dengaku, or baked eggplant. It's not cheap: most portions cost $6–8 if served separately, so half a dozen choices will push you near the cost of the omakase menu. Start with custard-like uni ($6), or sweetish and delicate urchin. Mirugai ($6), or giant clam, and toro ($8), or tuna, are faultless. Salmon roe with quail egg ($8) makes a great combo, and isn't easily found elsewhere. Standouts include the spicy tuna and salmon skin rolls, softshell crab wrapped in tuna or salmon, and the huge slices of hamachi. Beef teriyaki ($8) and a tender cucumber salad with a nori topping ($6) round out options, and there are interesting tapioca concoctions for dessert (from $6).

Kojima-san's best advertisement is the faithful crowd of devotees with whom he's on first-name terms. He's such a kick to watch that people show up by 6pm, knowing service will slow down dramatically on busy nights, so it's important to get there early. Yes, the place is drab, but you won't care if you can get one of those counter seats.

Katia's: A Russian Tea Room

🍴 Katia's was one of the first Russian restaurants to open in the Richmond District after Perestroika, though chef-owner Katia Troosh says it took a while for local Russians to drop by. Katia herself is from San Francisco's community of Russians from Harbin in Manchuria, many of whom wound up in the Bay Area after World War II, and who still congregate in cafes like the nearby Cinderella. Katia's corner restaurant is a graceful leap up in the world. Her small

Cost $15–45
Address 600 5th Ave at Balboa
☏ 415/668-9292
Open Tues–Thurs 11.30am–2.30pm & 5–9pm, Fri 11.30am–2.30pm & 5–10pm, Sat 5–10pm, Sun 5–9pm
Transportation 21, 31, 33, 44
Accepts All major credit cards

but lively dining room has tall, fan-shaded windows, seats thirty, and resounds to resident accordionist Alex Paskin, whose repertoire ranges from "Stranger In Paradise" and "Those Were The Days" to "Frosty the Snowman." Katia has been known to sing along, and diners sometimes join in. Her waiters are her husband George and their daughter and, like Katia, they treat returning customers as family. But everything goes at an oh-so-Russian pace: don't come here for lightning snacks.

Katia's borscht ($5.50) is unconventional but deservedly famous. Made on light chicken stock, it swims with beets and celery, with chives and a hint of other herbs, plus sour cream. Russian babushkas tell you that a beef bone with marrow makes the right stuff for borscht, but Katia's speaks for itself. Elsewhere, Katia cleverly liposuctions Russian mainstays down into lighter versions for appetizers, or "zakushki," starting with plates of mini-bites like lacy blini ($4.50), eggplant caviar ($4), beet and pickle potato salad ($4), and piroshki ($2.50), which are pastries of beef, cabbage, or mushrooms. To follow, try the beef Stroganoff ($9.95), chicken Kiev ($9.95), or the house extravaganza, a giant blini with sour cream, smoked salmon, roll-mop herrings, and salmon caviar ($16) that will sustain two. Katia's special knack for pavlova ($4.50) wins the prize of them all; along with her borscht, it's really worth crossing town for.

People who wouldn't like Katia's must exist. Among them would be those in a hurry, on a super-tight budget, or who believe Russian food is inherently unhealthy. But anyone with the time will have a diverting night here. Katia's makes a grand introduction to the Richmond District's Little Russia by the Bay.

Khan Toke

🍴 Every moment seems dreamlike in this lost pocket of ancient Thailand. Outside, the place is small and dull brown, but once you walk through the door, it's as though Dorothy suddenly woke up in a Thai version of Oz. Leaving your shoes by the door, you pad softly in your socks past antechambers into a large rear dining room where floor-to-ceiling windows run around a temple garden complete with cupolas, bird cages, and spirit house. You loll upon cushions along banquettes, beside sunken tables with wells for your legs, and there's temple art and Thai silk everywhere. Screen-hung private chambers for banquets and weddings open beyond. Waiters in classical dress move with the noiseless grace of dancers. The mood is of timeless relaxation, and there's as much to taste as to see.

Cost $12–30
Address 5937 Geary Boulevard between 23rd & 24th
☎ 415/668-6654
Open Daily 5–10pm
Transportation 2, 29, 38
Accepts All major credit cards except Diners

The same family has run Khan Toke for a quarter of a century, and if you want to learn about classical Thai food, co-owner Malati Fasudhani offers thoughtful details on the menu. Appetizers include seafood crêpes ($6.25), crunchy fishcakes ($5.95), familiar Thai spicy prawn soups ($5.95), and satays of chicken and beef with peanut dipping sauce ($6.25). There's a delicately seasoned pad thai, plus nut and ginger salads ($5.95) that you roll into a leaf to make mouthfuls. Main courses are rich Thai basil-coconut curries, from the eggplant in spicy yellow sauce ($7.95) to the "red" meat curry with beef and yams ($7.95). Seafood curry ($10.95) comes with prawns or other shellfish, and is rosy and fiery, with cilantro, chile, coconut, lemongrass, galangal, and a fish sauce tang. These dishes all pursue the Chinese-influenced ideal of combining sweet, sour, salty, bitter, and hot tastes. Bananas in coconut milk ($3.50), and a dish of delicious black sticky rice ($4.50) boiled in sweetened condensed milk with a tiny pinch of salt and served with mango, are pleasing desserts, and can be followed with iced Thai coffee or tea.

The prices are higher than at most Thai places, but once you've eaten here it will always be at the back of your mind. Don't come here alone; part of the pleasure is introducing someone to this place.

King of Thai Noodle House

🍴 This almost literal hole-in-the-wall may be bare bones, but on a good night it dishes some of the best "fuel" food on Clement Street, and at some of the keenest prices. King of Thai used to have a picture of Thailand's jazz-loving monarch on the wall, out of respect, but now there's a TV instead. As local noodle joints go, few are tinier or more authenti-

Cost $4–10

Address 639 Clement St at 7th
ⓣ 415/752-5198
Open Daily 11am–1.30am
Transportation 1, 2, 4, 38, 44
Accepts Cash only

cally like a Bangkok noodle stand than this, and not a night goes by when it doesn't sport a line stretching outside the door. Owned by Thai cook Ane Csaisana, it's definitely width challenged—to call it eight feet would be stretching it. It barely squeezes in twenty people, yet it's mushroomed into a local success story with branches all over town, including one three blocks away.

The name says it all. As you flatten yourself alongside the open kitchen, heat wells up at your face from the open grill, but you can watch while the chef stir-fries your noodles ($6.20) with bak choy, eggplant, or broccoli, or hotter-than-hell chile in his well-worn wok. In fact, King of Thai's food may be simply too Hades-hot for some people, but it's justly famous for its beef and duck soups ($5.50). Cooks are stalwarts who handle white-hot woks, churning out pad thai ($5.25) all day long. Just occasionally the food is so hellaciously hot, even for those with fire-eating palates and spice-craving tastebuds, that you simply can't finish. No problem: tell them and they'll tone down the spices. Even the green papaya salad ($5.95) can sometimes be too hot, so you'll need to proceed with caution.

There's not a lot of choice, but odds are that you'll do fine with whatever you get. If you lived within a couple of blocks you'd come here every night, and luckily there's some chance of doing just that, as the Csaisanas run several other branches as well: 346 Clement St, in the Richmond; 156 Powell St, downtown; 1418 Haight Street in the Haight; 1541 Taraval St, in the Sunset; and 3199 Taraval St, in the Outer Sunset.

Okina Sushi

Since the 1980s, literally hundreds of sushi joints have opened all over San Francisco, and the fish cure has not lost its grip on the citizens. Since discovery is the beginning of the end for sushi-hounds, this is one place most food writers never mention, for fear that popularity could dissipate its mysterious magic. A small yet impeccable parlor of three

Cost $20–45
Address 776 Arguello Boulevard at Cabrillo
☎ 415/387-8882
Open Wed–Sat 5–10pm
Transportation 5, 31, 33, 38
Accepts Cash only

tables and four counter stools, this paradise revolves around the immense charm of proprietor and gifted artist Akio Matsuoka, and the food provides "aah!" and "ooh" moments all the way. It's not the cheapest sushi in town—this is sushi for entertaining prospective in-laws or marking some kind of personal milestone—but chef Akio-san puts such an emphasis on presentation that watching him work is a pleasure. His platters laden with sushi are so breathtaking to look at that you almost can't bear to demolish such works of edible art.

When you do, however, you see the point of sushi with immediate clarity. Since sushi and sashimi are the only things on the menu—aside from great sake—there's nothing much to say about them, other than that they are as exquisite and fresh as they could possibly be without actually squirming on the plate. Even the pickled ginger is peculiarly tasty, and the sweet-vinegared rice is neither too sticky nor too dry, and it's fresher than at other places too. Chef Akio's combinations are the usual ones—unagi ($3.50), sashimi chirashi, ($8) and nigiri ($2–4.20)—and he pulls no gimmicks, nothing Californian and wacky, no crazy ingredients or combos. He does, however, know how to use elegant understatement, such as showing off sushi on an antique plate that might come straight from the Meiji dynasty. There are dazzling samplers, too.

In the sushi-loving Richmond there's a parlor for every occasion: cheap lunches, family teas, quick late-night snacks, posh business lunches, romantic trysts. Okina Sushi is for small parties of no more than four, but it's also a place you can visit alone. Plank yourself down at the counter, ask what fish was at the fish market that morning, and just watch.

Pacific Cafe

Fun, cheering and usually filled to bursting, this merry little fish joint in the foggiest part of town has wooden booths, pumpkin-orange walls, kindly lighting, great attitude and fresh seafood on a menu that changes with the catch. Warmhearted hostesses hand you a free glass of wine while you wait. And then wait—with your name scrawled on the wall—up to half an hour. But even if they didn't offer free wine and souvenir abalone shells, you'd still put up with it; and when your fish arrives you'll feel blissfully happy. This cafe has been crammed since it started up over a quarter of a century ago, and from the moment it opens at 5pm every table is spoken for.

Cost $20–40
Address 7000 Geary Boulevard at 34th
☎ 415/387-7091
Open Mon–Thurs & Sun 5–9.30pm, Fri & Sat 5–10.30pm
Transportation 31, 38
Accepts All major credit cards

The catch of the day is scratched onto the chalkboard above the kitchen hatch, behind which a loud clattering of pans is both seen and heard. Starters include a chunky clam chowder or a creamy salmon bisque ($3 cup, $4.95 bowl), calamari vinaigrette ($6.75), and chock-full-of-goodness shellfish cocktails ($4.95–8.75), good and hearty. The best main choices at Pacific are unspoiled local fish done very simply with no frills, such as petrale ($15), salmon ($17), sea bass ($17), generous crabcakes ($18), halibut Parmesan ($18), red snapper ($15), and even the endangered—now farmed—abalone ($34). Shrimp Louisiana ($15) is sautéed in herbs and wine, while sole ($15) comes stuffed with crab and shrimp, plus a superfluous sauce. The tuna plate ($18) offers wasabe butter on the side. Desserts include a decent chocolate torte ($4), and like the rest of the food here, they're nothing extraordinary, just plain yet good.

The wines are equally plain, though you won't care after the second or third at these prices. Choose from a modest Geyser Peak Chardonnay ($18), Chateau Sainte Michelle Sauvignon Blanc ($16.95), or Round Hill Merlot ($14.95); all are available by the glass for around a bargain $5. Pacific Cafe is a fine idea for dropping by earlyish with a raging, ocean-whetted appetite, on your way back from Ocean Beach, the Legion of Honor or the coastal trail, or from just watching the sunset off Point Lobos rocks.

Singapore Malaysian Restaurant

🍴 On Clement Street's restaurant row, a basic rule of thumb is that the less prepossessing a place, the tastier the meal and the nicer the surprise when the bill arrives. This undiscovered jewel at the heart of New Chinatown is nothing much at first sight. Situated next to a shop selling plastic Japanese Godzillas, it looks humble and authentic, perhaps like a Malaysian village canteen. Frazzled plants in the window, batiked cloths and kites serve for decor, belying the warm smile of Seong, who comes from Penang and is only too happy to explain everything about the three cuisines of his peninsula. The clientele isn't stuffy at this easy-going home-from-home, where everybody shares.

Cost $12–20

Address 836 Clement St at 11th
☎ 415/750-9518
Open Mon, Wed & Thurs 11.30am–3pm & 5–10pm, Fri–Sun 11.30am–10pm
Transportation 1, 2, 38
Accepts MasterCard, Visa

The cuisines of Malaysia and Singapore—Malay, Straits Chinese, and Tamil—coexist discreetly on Seong's menu, as they do over there. Peanut and red chile coconut sauces are staples, while appetizers are mostly satays and peanut-dressed salads. Rojak ($5.25), a Malaysian salad of cucumber with jicama, pineapple, and bean sprouts, coated in spicy-sweet sesame-sprinkled prawn sauce, is a perfect start for a spicy meal, as it cleans out your palate. Roti prata ($3.95), or Indian fried bread, is a double layer sliced like a pie, served Malay-style with peanut chile sauce. Otak otak ($3.50) is a labor-intensive dish of delicate mini-mouthfuls of fish custard, grilled inside smoked banana-leaf parcels. Of the twenty entrees, the obvious leaders are kari ayam ($7.50), or chicken curry with potatoes in a fiery coconut sauce, and daging rendang ($8.95), or tenderized chile beef with lemongrass, lime, and coconut. Another smash hit is sambal kachange panjang ($5.95), a sauté of green beans with lemongrass, prawns, and chile in fish paste. Pepes ikan ($12.95), or snapper grilled in banana leaves is Seong's "special" dish, at his top price, and is best with the unmissable ginger rice ($1.50).

Sweetish Malaysian iced coffee and tea ($1.50) accompany hot-weather fruit salads like bu bo cha cha ($2.25) of yams, taro, and bananas in coconut. Not a lot can be said for Seong's wine list, but at $10–14 a bottle or $2.95 per glass for Sutter Home or BV Chardonnay, you'll deal. Alternatively, bring your own (corkage $6).

Le Soleil

San Francisco is a haven of traditional Vietnamese food, but no run-down of Clement Street's restaurant row would be complete without this sunny and affordable standby, with its large tropical fish-tank and friendly waiters. Le Soleil boasts more bright notes on its menu than many neighborhood places, and there's something refined about the presentation and service. The room is pretty, too. The menu is topped by a very long list of inspired and ultra-fresh appetizers, and even the trad Viet pho soups—with their extra plates of mint, cilantro, herbs, nuts, and condiments on the side—have an extra zing and delicacy, and maybe a touch of colonial-era formality.

Cost $7–20
Address 133 Clement St at 3rd
☎ 415/668-4848
Open Mon–Thurs & Sun 11am–10pm, Fri & Sat 11am–10.30pm
Transportation 1, 2, 38
Accepts All major credit cards except Diners

The appetizers are relatively low-priced as well as full of flavor. Among them are traditional classics like the paper-thin cold imperial rolls with a dipping sauce ($4.75), the hot-and-sour soup ($5.25), and of course the pho ($6.75). There's also a seafood soup ($5.25), accompanied by many side plates of condiments. If you're not in a soup mood at all, try the fragrant raw beef salad, or larb ($5.25). Clay pot dishes start with lemongrass chicken ($6.95), or Saigon-style sweet-and-spicy barbecued pork ($7.25), and there's a nice clay pot of jumbo shrimp ($7.25). Le Soleil's signature dish is something called beef luc lac ($7.45), which is grilled, marinated beef on a salad of greens and tomatoes. Among some interesting desserts here is a deep-fried ice cream ($3.50), gorgeously caramelized without and melting within. Try it as part of the multi-course special menu ($15.95), which also includes the imperial rolls, the shrimp, the hot-and-sour soup, the lemongrass chicken, and tea. Alternatively, just share around a number of appetizer dishes. Wines are available by the glass, and don't forget the capper of sweetened-milk with an inky-black Vietnamese coffee ($2.50).

Is this the most amazing Vietnamese food in town? No, but it's really quite good, and it's also unpretentious, fresh, and cheap. Small wonder that locals flock here. You can further ease the burden on your pocket with the prix fixe menu, and get a simple primer in the basics of traditional Vietnamese food as well. Sometimes life is good.

Straits Cafe

Even if the dew is off its Somerset Maugham-inspired tiffin, and the palms are drooping, the raffia tired and the pillars scuffed, this Raffles-on-the-Bay has weathered a decade, and is alive and throbbing. Fancier and more expensive than the Asian specialty houses along Clement, Balboa, and Geary, it's still jam-packed at weekends. Its Indian, Chinese, southeast Asian, and Indonesian curries, flavoured with coconut, basil, and ginger, seemed intoxicating to San Franciscans when owner Chris Yeo opened Straits; that was back when Singaporean food was still unknown in the city, but the restaurant has kept its fan base since.

Cost $18–35

Address 3300 Geary Boulevard at Stanyan
☎ 415/668-1783
Open Mon–Thurs 11.30am–3pm & 5–10pm, Fri & Sat 11.30am–11pm, Sun 11.30am–10pm
Transportation 1, 2, 33, 38
Accepts All major credit cards except Diners

One dish here stands alone as the simplest, most delicious creation in the entire city. It's Yeo's roti prata ($4–5.25), a swirling, cabled plait of crispy, Indian-style, unleavened, oil-fried bread that's as moist and aromatic inside as it's crunchy outside; when hot and dipped into fiery curry sauce, it's flat-out sensational and you will order a second, even a third. What's the *je ne sais quoi*, you may ask? The answer is simply flour, butter, water—it's all in the folding. At Straits Cafe they fold the dough and simply hurl it onto a flat griddle that's spitting with ghee. The herbed spare-rib soup ($4) comes a close second, but isn't always available. The sample platter ($12) is another hit: satay, har gao, and samosas—all three cuisines of Singapore on one plate. Those without fire-roasted tastebuds can try nasi goreng ($9.50), a Malay veggie paella that's full of mini-surprises, or the Straits beef ($11), stir-fried pieces of beef tossed in oyster sauce and served on spiced taro fritters. Duck Kapitan ($18) is smoky duck in lemongrass chile on a pondom crêpe, and has been much emulated around the Bay Area. Salmon on banana leaves ($16) is finished in lemongrass and chile, while shellfish curry ($15) is a basil and coconut potpourri.

A youthful crowd trudges up here with devotion to order the same favorites. You forgot to book and have to wait? Grab a bar stool and really twirl the umbrellas on those gin and cherry brandy Singapore Slings ($6.75).

The Richmond

Sushi Boom

🍴 Such is the passion for raw fish in this town that you can find elaborately presented sushi amid fancy surroundings in every nook and cranny. But sushi-lovers can also luck into the very same blissful bites of perfect fish at bargain prices in a number of new finds such as Sushi Boom. This small and immaculate sushi bar, right on Geary's main drag, charges rock-bottom prices that won't burst anyone's piggybank. Were it not for the fact some of the staff are Korean, you could be in Tokyo.

Cost S8–15

Address 3420 Geary Boulevard at Stanyan
☎ 415/876-2666
Open Daily 11am–midnight
Transportation 38
Accepts MasterCard, Visa

Nobody seems to speak much English, but smiling servers in kimonos demonstrate the different kinds of bento boxes pictorially, along with various donburi, teriyaki, udon, and kushikaki combination plates, and sushi and sashimi. Sit at the counter to watch the chef, or at one of the small tables to admire the china and attention to detail. The atmosphere is informal and chatty, and non-fish eaters, vegetarians, and solo diners are likely to be happy with Sushi Boom's ambiance too. For a cucumber, tuna, and California combination sushi ($8.95), a wooden tray bears six small sushi apiece of each kind. Predictably, crunchy and clean is the verdict on the first, but the California salmon and avocado with a hint of sesame really sings. Beef teriyaki ($9.95) stars well-marinated strips, grilled and served in a plum-tinged sauce with an elegantly carved orange, deftly sliced to reveal perfect flesh, then carved into sections and served with salad. Combined with tempura and California roll portions, it becomes a bento box ($12.95). Lunch deals are bargains: tea, miso soup, two nigiri sushi, and six perfect vegetarian sushi ($7) is faultless.

As a technique, sushi-making is almost a millennium old. Back in the 1820s, Hanava Yohei of Edo tried placing slices of fish into balls of rice, wrapping them in seaweed to make portable Japanese fast food, but he was adapting what was already an ancient technique of fermenting fish in rice. His sushi stalls were so successful that they flourished up until the last world war. Today, San Francisco has an unassuagable hunger for sushi, and fortunately there are oceans to choose from, including this cut-price find.

Taiwan Restaurant

With its small tables, back room and grilling window at the front, this might be the Taipei equivalent of fast food—if it didn't make a point of serving Chairman Mao's favorites, including the saucy "General Tsuo's chicken." Beyond that, it's comfortable and simple, and you can't quarrel with the rock-bottom prices. The pace is brisk, and the place so plain and pink that you might wonder if it was decorated by a six-year-old Maoist with a thing for pink plastic.

Cost $7–30

Address 445 Clement St at 6th
☎ 415/387-1789
Open Mon–Thurs 11am–10pm, Fri 11am–midnight, Sat 10am–midnight, Sun 10am–10pm
Transportation 1, 2, 38
Accepts MasterCard, Visa

Taiwan Restaurant and its North Beach twin are the only Taiwanese establishments in the city, and Taiwanese specialties for you to peruse include sweet rice ($2.50), crisped turnip cakes ($2.95), seafood vermicelli ($4.95), and stir-fries such as pork with preserved meat, oysters, and soybeans ($4.50). The estimable and well-priced General Tsuo's chicken ($5.95) comes in a fruity sweet-and-sour sauce, and is ideal fuel for a long march. Perhaps rice and noodle items are made in batches earlier in the day, as they have a tendency to turn pasty by evening; the turnip cakes go flat, too, though they're still tasty. In addition to its specialties, Taiwan is the number-one dumpling house on Clement Street, and locals come from streets around for traditional ju yug bao ($3.50), or steamed pork and veggie-filled "laughing rolls". The spanking takeout trade keeps the pork buns rolling across the counter, while regulars fill chairs and tables at the back, tucking into xiu bao ($1–4.25), which are great fists of golden donuts rolled in sesame seeds; crunchy with taste, they're the perfect teatime snack. Later on, intrepid diners can attempt exotic treats like shredded jellyfish with cucumber ($5.95), and heart-warming soups like the petals of pork bowl ($4.75), followed by dishes for sharing among the family such as Shanghai thick noodles ($4.50), crispy chicken ($7.95), and spicy green beans ($4.95).

You won't find fine wine or boutique beers here, since Taiwan is a no-frills joint, but you can bring your own for no corkage. There's an obvious reason why New Chinatown families congregate here for huge meals of multiple courses, scarfing them down joyfully from uplifted bowls.

Ton Kiang

Creamy table linen that must have been starched and pressed by Hakkinese angels, some of the friendliest waiters along "County Geary," cleanliness that's right up there with godliness in big, sunny rooms, and Su Wong's dim sum: no wonder a beaming clientele of Irish laborers, Chinese grannies and businessmen think they're in heaven as they stack up the plates. Meaning literally "touch the heart," dim sum are unpretentious Cantonese snacks charged per steamer basket. But where do you find the widest choice: in Chinatown, downtown Oakland, or New Chinatown? That's a familiar San Francisco debate, and it always results in paeans to the Wongs' modern palace on Geary.

Cost	$10–25
Address	3148 Geary Boulevard
☎	415/752-4440
Open	Mon–Thurs 10.30am–10pm, Fri & Sat 10am–10.30pm, Sun 9am–10pm
Transportation	38
Accepts	All major credit cards

The Wongs are Hakkas, the nomadic Chinese people who triumph with rustic specialties and clay pot dishes such as salt-baked chicken ($9) or "drunken" wine-sauced chicken with stuffed bean curd and pickled greens ($8.50). But their dim sum is so dependable, at any time of day, that it's an insult not to partake. The menu for two people ($28) brings you nine plates of dim sum. The menu is strong on ha gao ($3), which is three shrimp dumplings of whole, extra-fat shrimp with spinach, garlic, and basil, rolled in papery-thin wontons. Fresh crab claws ($5) or Dungeness crab crêpes ($3) are also excellent. Vegetarians have to ask for non-fish options such as garlicky pea-vine shou mai ($3), and nol mai gai ($3), or sticky rice bundles in lotus leaves. Proprietress Su Wong's homemade wu gok ($3), or taro dumplings, can be vegetarian or non-veggie because she grinds, proves and kneads her own dough, and will make both. She also spins deft "Cal" veggie variations, using sugar pea tips, eggplant, asparagus, or mushroom dumplings in garlicky batter.

Hakka cuisine is becoming increasingly hard to find these days, even in Hong Kong, so Ton Kiang may be some of the best available anywhere. What's more, the quality here is reliable, and reliability is an underrated virtue, in restaurants as in cars and lovers. Granted, you wait a few minutes at peak times, or twenty minutes at weekends, when huge families descend, but you'll avoid it if you arrive for an early lunch or late dinner.

Traktir

If you ever feel lonely and can't afford a plane ticket to Moscow, there's always Traktir, way out here on Balboa. A pocket of utterly ethnic bonhomie in an airless, homey room, it's decorated with just the occasional poster, plus the usual blaring TV above the corner bar. Eating here feels like visiting a

Cost $10–20
Address 4036 Balboa at 42nd
⊤ 415/386-9800
Open Wed–Sun 5–10pm
Transportation 33, 38
Accepts MasterCard, Visa

Russian friend in their kitchen, and if you've never done that, don't knock it. You could bring the Russian Army Ensemble with their balalaikas and beg them to play "Kalinka," and it could hardly get more Russian. Every night is Bring Your Own Vodka night, and every table drinks from its own bottles. Not that there *are* many tables, there may be just one banqueting table of locals celebrating someone's birthday, or simply celebrating, plus a few satellite tables that soon weld themselves on. Strangers are usually welcomed and quickly find themselves joining in.

Although chef-owner Mark is from Moscow, there's a friendly pan-Slavic take on the menu, which isn't strictly Russian. Start with the straightforward and unadorned chopped chicken liver ($5.95), which is just like Bubba made. Authentic Russian pelmieni ($9.25) and pirozki ($9.25) are also on the menu, sturdy little pastry or potato dumplings swimming in a richly herbed chicken broth that are guaranteed to fill and warm. Of their several chicken dishes, the Kiev ($9.25) is an ordinary, fine piece of chicken stewed in onions and peppers, but it's not as distinguished as the heavier native dishes. Plates of crêpes with fruit and cream ($3.50), and one or two other sweet delicacies supply the *coup de grâce*. It would be difficult to speak volumes about the wine list, because it would require fluent Russian, but it's safe to say that the house white and red ($4.50) goes down, and that there are some interesting Georgian wines and bubblies too.

Come here in a spirit of pan-Slavic brotherhood and perestroika, even if you're an obvious outsider, as you'll be treated warmly and given fast service. The thing to remember is that they truly don't mind you bringing your own bottle, and you can eat those pelmeni until they come out of your ears—for ten dollars per head.

La Vie

(icon) Yet another colonial French-Vietnamese roast crab place in the Richmond? San Francisco's New Chinatown is one of the best places to eat trad Viet in all its fascinating variety, but La Vie has its own niche in local hearts, because it allows you to enjoy the principles of Vietnamese cooking in a theatrical way. The French influences of Vietnam's colonial-era cuisine and the artistry of the country's classical cooking are distinct, and La Vie's staff are happy

Cost $15–35
Address 5380 Geary Boulevard at 22nd
☏ 415/668-8080
Open Mon 4–10pm, Tues–Thurs & Sun 11am–10pm, Fri & Sat 11am–10.30pm
Transportation 31, 38
Accepts All major credit cards except AmEx

to point them both out at this calm, relatively affordable haven on Geary's main drag. Owner Daisy Tang conjures every dish from its elements like a magician, with an emphasis on presentation and a delicate ability to show off key ingredients.

La Vie's pièce de résistance is the elaborate roast crab ($35.95), which arrives sputtering with ginger, pepper, and garlic in a giant wok. It makes delicious if alarmingly messy work for two or three. No less of a signature production is flaming beef in rice paper ($10.95) with prawns, basil, cilantro, and oyster sauce, flambéed tableside with a burst of flame. Equally spectacular is lemongrass chicken, which is turned into spring rolls, or cha go ($7.75), by rolling it into tissue-thin, satiny-white wrappers and dipping into a nuoc cham of chile, garlic, fish sauce, and carrot. Vegetarian choices are potstickers ($5.75) and hot-and-sour soup ($6.95). La Vie's crêpe ($7.25) is a stunner, and also comes in vegetarian form: a crispy yet fragile rice-flour pancake embraces a lavish mound of tofu, mushroom, and bean sprouts (or shrimp or chicken), flamboyantly truncated in two with a mini-forest of mint, basil, and cilantro on the side, plus dipping sauce. La Vie's Han, a true performance artist, should be awarded the tiara for finest crêpe in town.

To make your night, order authentic Vietnamese coffee ($2.50). It comes in a tall glass with a long spoon, in an inch of sweetened condensed milk into which black and bitter drops drip oh so slowly from a curious metal contraption. After a few minutes, you briskly mix and down this sweet, intense, magic potion; pesky but worth the wait.

Yoshi-san's Monkichi

(🍴) In a town where most restaurants lock up firmly after the weekend, a good sushi parlor that opens on Monday and goes out of its way to please children and vegetarians is pure gold. Normally, kids don't go for raw fish and wasabe, and that's putting it mildly. But this little corner place near the California Palace of the Legion of Honor serves child-friendly specials with child-sized chopsticks; wherever you look origami monkeys entice budding sushi-sans. Twentyish Yoshi-san and his wife Nanna run Monkichi, and it's Nanna who makes the origami animal chopstick holders for kids to play with.

Cost $8–20

Address 200 23rd Ave at California
☎ 415/876-1834
Open Mon, Wed–Thurs & Sun 5–10pm, Fri & Sat 5.30–10.30pm
Transportation 1, 2, 38
Accepts MasterCard, Visa

Monkichi's is notable for the imagination of Yoshi's vegetable and fruit sushi, crafted in front of your nose from a list that includes kampyo (gourd), ume shiso (plum), gobo (burdock), oshinko (pickle), and natto (fermented soy), all at a rock-bottom price of $2.30. A veggie roll called My Back Yard ($3.80) explodes with greenery. Not all is herbivorous, however: finned and crustacean sushi ($4–4.50) are tempting too, from Kamikaze (tuna, avocado, onion) and Hanna-chan (tuna with pickled radish and tobiko) to a pick-me-up Power Shot (tuna, onion, and garlic), plus all the unusual and usual giant clams and flying fish roe you could want. There's even the rare poison caterpillar ($7.50) and special fatty tuna ($7.50), when available. Inaro or tofu skin, anyone? It's delicious. Best of all, prices are modest. Even the whopping 49ers roll, a magnificent stripy bolster of golden tobiko (flying fish), red salmon, and green avocado that curves into the cushioned poetry of local football colors is only $8.50.

Yoshi, this Hokusai of sushi masters was formerly at Osame, and also with legendary "Iron-chef" Kevin-san at Ebisu—high kudos indeed! Come around six, take a seat at the counter, look over what he picked up in the fish market earlier, and ask him to choose. Alternatively, take the combination dinner plate ($10.50) with a glass of sake or plum wine (from $3). Yoshi's place makes a perfect capper to an afternoon amble down the coastal trail or the well-kept secret of China Beach, where you can stroll past the villas of the rich and super-rich.

The Civic Center & Hayes Valley

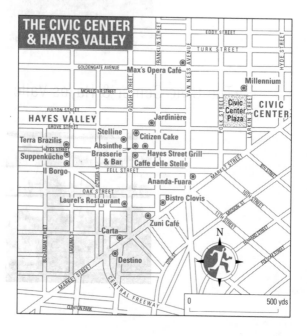

THE CIVIC CENTER
& HAYES VALLEY

EDDY STREET
TURK STREET

GOLDENGATE AVENUE
Max's Opera Café
Millennium

McALLISTER STREET

FULTON STREET
HAYES VALLEY
Jardinière
Civic
Center
Plaza
CIVIC
CENTER

GROVE STREET
Stelline
Terra Brazilis
Citizen Cake
Absinthe
Suppenküche
Brasserie
& Bar
Hayes Street Grill
Caffe delle Stelle
Il Borgo

FELL STREET
Ananda-Fuara

OAK STREET
Bistro Clovis
Laurel's Restaurant

Carta
Zuni Café

N

Destino

MARKET STREET
CENTRAL FREEWAY

CLINTON PARK

0   500 yds

FRANKLIN STREET
VAN NESS AVENUE
GOUGH STREET
POLK STREET
LARKIN STREET
HYDE STREET
HAYES STREET
OCTAVIA ST
BUCHANAN ST
LAGUNA ST
MARKET STREET
MISSION ST
11TH STREET
FOLSOM STREET
HOWARD STREET
10TH STREET

Absinthe Brasserie and Bar

Absinthe really does make the heart grow fonder. The bar is positively effulgent with vermouth, pastis, and Jazz Age cocktails, though sadly it does not yet serve the infamous "green fairy" it is named after. But with its copper cocktail tables and rattan cafe chairs, this morsel of the Rive Gauche goes all out to look like a spot where Rimbaud might meet Verlaine for "just the one." Even if only two tables beckon outside and the Toulouse-Lautrec poster reminds you of a million studio apartments, it succeeds in breathing upscale Bohemian chic. All of which fits the increasingly artsy Hayes Valley, a neighborhood where concert- and opera-goers grab bites before and after a dose of culture. The dining room offers comfort, with plum walls and white linen, but you can also just drink at the bar, enjoying the fumes.

Cost $10–60
Address 398 Hayes St at Gough
☏ 415/551-1590
Open Tues–Fri 7.30am–3pm & 5pm–1am, Sat 10.30am–3pm & 5pm–1am, Sun 10.30am–3pm & 5–10.30pm
Transportation 16, 21, J, K, L, M, N
Accepts All major credit cards

On the short, balanced menu, bar food is sometimes startlingly good, and chef Ross Brown goes all out to impress with the raw bar and shellfish. There's about the best selection of oysters in town ($2–3 each), with six or more varieties, including juicy Fanny Bay (from British Columbia) and tiny, intense Quilcene (from Washington), all served with rose mignonette and walnut bread. Seafood platters for two ($25) boast crab, shrimp, mussels, cockles, and more oysters. Still on that bar menu, but also available in the dining area, are herb-ricotta dumplings ($12), airy quenelles brought down to earth with morels, then picked up with Parmesan flakes. Along with stuffed squash blossoms with mozzarella, sweetcorn, chickpea, and tomato ($12), and a Provençal-style pissaladière pizza of anchovy, onions, and olives ($11), comes a zingy Niçoise-type salad with olives and peppers ($9) that's simple and good. Main dishes are black risotto with squid, scallops, mussels, and clams ($18), sand dabs with polenta ($20), duck-leg confit, old reliable coq au vin ($18), and rib-eye steak ($25).

None of this comes cheap, of course. But this is well-thought-out personality food, and for true lovers of oysters Absinthe is decidedly worth the splurge. Among several pleasant surprises is the comparative affordability of wine by the glass: a flowery Sancerre is just $3.75 and bottles begin at $22.

Ananda-Fuara

🍴 In the slightly marginal blocks around the Public Library and City Hall, low-cost cafes seem to thrive, and here and there you'll find some of the city's best ethnic food as well. Ananda Fuera starts off ethnic and winds up almost spiritual. This is where to come if you want to find out if tofu-scrambled eggs taste like scrambled eggs or not. The answer is no, not really, but most of the food, available both vegetarian and vegan, is both tasty and filling, and none of it is overpriced. The setting is spookily immaculate, almost antiseptic, except for the inspirational Buddhist texts everywhere. You'll see owner Sri Chinmoy around the place, and waiters wear blue and white to match the sky-blue walls, painted with clouds. Somehow it's all a slightly surreal combination.

Cost $10–20

Address 1298 Market St at 9th
☎ 415/621-1994
Open Mon, Tues & Thurs–Sat 8am–8pm, Wed 8am–3pm
Transportation Market St lines, F, BART Civic Center
Accepts MasterCard, Visa

If you want soy-based foods, look no further, but there are other options as well. Try the samosas with chutney ($3.75) or the falafel sandwich ($5.50), served in a wheat chapati with lots of beans and tahini; both are authentic, if a bit stodgy. The "chicken patty" ($5.50) is actually soy, served on a bun and looking like an edible but also resistible fast-food patty. Scrambled tofu eggs ($5.35) come with decent grilled potatoes and rather bland toast. The rest of the menu hits various cultural notes, from burritos to ravioli, but that doesn't disguise the fact that this is a temple of tofu. There are also some tasty salads, including a nice Greek salad ($6.50), and one called Infinite Bleu ($6.50), with blue cheese—which was perhaps inspired by the ceiling. Enjoy it with the Balinese Goddess ($3.50), an iced coffee with lots of whipped cream and a ball of ice cream. The lassi ($2.25) is worth trying here too, in a rose and cardamom version of the yogurt drink.

Interestingly enough, two of the city's best-known vegan options are just one block apart, but this simple, straightforward place could not be more different from the opulent, downright extravagant Millennium, over on Golden Gate Avenue.

Bistro Clovis

Truly Lilliputian and utterly French, Bistro Clovis offers an alternative to the Italian and seafood choices around Hayes Valley as a pre- or post-concert meal. It gets a loyal crowd, and competition is fierce around here. On the plus side is the Rive Gauche atmosphere, helped along by the blackboard listing the nightly samplers and specials. Prices are pretty reasonable, and there's never a wait. "Never a wait" sounds like a bit of a mixed accolade, if you're wondering where the other diners went, but the staff do their darnedest to pretty up the place, and it's always had its faithful followers.

Cost $15–40

Address 1596 Market St at Franklin
☎ 415/864-0231
Open Mon–Fri 11am–3pm & 5–10pm, Sat 10am–11pm, Sun 5–10pm
Transportation Market St lines, BART Civic Center
Accepts All major credit cards except Diners

The menu changes from time to time but certain dishes are now familiar friends. Soupe à l'oignon ($4.25) is robust and curative, while the house pâté ($9.50) comes from the real cognac-infused class, and is accompanied by caramelized onions. Salade tout simple ($4.25) comes with a classic vinaigrette. Clovis often do vegetable terrines, and sometimes fish or meat terrines as well—even a wild boar terrine, when wild boar can be had. The meaty and tender halibut en papillote ($14.50) comes steamed in herbs and vegetables, and gives off a fine perfume when released from its parchment bondage; from time to time, halibut is replaced by salmon or another fish. Cassoulet comme-il-faut ($17), braised rabbit ($12), and spiced duck breast ($19) are other frequent main course choices. The jury may take some time out on the occasional miss here, but dishes such as the boeuf daube ($16.50), or beef stew in a rich sauce over noodles, get a positive vote every time. Desserts are invariably fine here as well, from the tarte Tatin ($5.50) of sweetened apple and flaky crust, topped with melting vanilla ice cream, to the crème brûlée with ginger ($5.50), which has a really pretty crust. Every night the brûlée gets a different, interesting flavor, ranging from anise to orange.

A board on the wall and handwritten sheets list the wine specials *du jour*, which fly the flag for French regional labels. Prices are in the lowish teens for a selection of three wee glasses, which arrive on artists' palettes along with finger food.

Il Borgo

Il Borgo can't seem to make up its mind whether its cuisine is northern or southern Italian, but its indecision proves a diner's delight. Certainly, there's no questioning its Italian credentials: the owner is a former Milanese who once co-owned Umbria, downtown, and the small staff is entirely Italian. Everyone is eager to please—they're so well liked that neighbors stop by just to say hello. The casual interior, with its mock streetlamps and laundry hanging on a line, is whimsical. A block off Hayes Street's bustling restaurant row, Il Borgo is an excellent place to keep in mind before a performance at the symphony or opera nearby. It's the least expensive Italian option in the neighborhood, and in many ways the best.

Cost $12–30

Address 500 Fell St at Laguna
☎ 415/255-9108
Open Tues–Sun
5.30–10.30pm
Transportation 6, 7, 21, 66, 71
Accepts Cash only

The excellent home-baked bread is a good start. Just four appetizers and four salads are on the menu, including lustily dressed bruschetta ($5.75), with tomatoes, garlic, and fresh basil. The first-rate insalata del Borgo ($7) is rather extravagantly made entirely of radicchio leaves, with lumps of excellent Gorgonzola cheese, pine nuts, and a light olive oil-based dressing. Pizzas ($9.50–11) can be split between two as an appetizer here, and they're as authentic as any in Italy, perfectly baked in a wood-burning oven, with thin crust and fresh toppings; the Margherita is the simplest and yet one of the best. Pastas are made in house, and it shows. The triangular ravioli are superb, and there's a sublime special ($11) with chicken and mushroom filling and a porcini mushroom and cream sauce. Penne all'arrabbiata ($9.50) is also excellent. Of the meat dishes, you may prefer those in thin slices and a sauce to the grilled options: veal piccata ($14) and pollo pizzaiola ($12) are always piquant, but the simple roast chicken ($12) can be disappointing. There are always a few seafood options, as well.

The wine list is short, Italian, and fairly priced. Desserts ($4) are not a high point, but there's a house-made tiramisu and a sometimes idiosyncratic but acceptable homemade cannoli. This is a wonderful place to bring a large, casual group: call ahead and Il Borgo can easily accommodate sixteen people, serving family-style.

Caffè delle Stelle

This restaurant tries to do for the Tuscany of the soul what Absinthe Brasserie, across the street, does for jazz-age Paris. Sunflower-yellow walls cheer up a dreary day, as does the equally cheery staff. It's nowhere near the same league, culinarily speaking, as Absinthe, but it's priced a lot lower, and there are free jugs of ice water with lemon slices. Like all the other eateries along this hot-and-happening little strip, it caters to people on their way to or from the symphony, ballet or opera. When you need to shovel down pasta *rapido* before a four-hour dose of "The Ring," Caffè delle Stelle will be more than enough to fortify you through at least the second act.

Cost $12–25
Address 395 Hayes St at Gough
☎ 415/252-1110
Open Mon–Sat 10.30am–3pm & 5–10pm, Sun 5–10pm
Transportation 16, 21, J, K, L, M, N
Accepts All major credit cards

While mainly good, the cooking can be erratic. Not to worry, though, because the Caffè offers much to redeem the occasional misfire, and its starters are pegged from $6.50, pastas from $9, and main dishes at $11. Of special note among the appetizers is a stuffed purse of cabbage ($8), a well-conceived package of tomato, cheese, and mushroom delight that exudes earthiness. Smoked salmon plate ($6.75) is tissue-thin, with capers and lemon. Soccuti ($9), or pumpkin-stuffed ravioli in browned butter, are usually done well everywhere, but there are reports of the Caffè managing to underseason the pumpkin and even undercook the ravioli. In the past, a Gorgonzola, walnut, and Chianti risotto ($11) has been dry instead of creamy, with crumbled rather than blended cheese, and it's rather overpowered by the Chianti, which seems ill-chosen. On the other hand, simpler pastas are usually flawless, including gnocchi prepared with salami and Fontina cheese ($9.75), or any pasta of the day, such as spinach and cheese ravioli ($9.75).

Sticking to a few starters so as not to miss the overture might be safer. Despite the occasional miss, the pavement tables along the wide-windowed frontage, and the *Venus* de Milo and Botticelli within, will always put you in the mood for a bosomy pillow of pasta and Verdi, as will the pace, buzz, and enveloping bonhomie.

Carta

What a fun idea this menu seemed when Carta first opened, several years ago! The cooks are food explorers who dish up a different cuisine every month or two. With its near-Castro location and, that rarest of things, an adjacent parking lot, this place deserves to be busier than it is on weekday nights, though it fills up at weekends, when there's live entertainment. Tables along wide windows face Market Street, but if you happen to be facing the other way, you'll just see large wall-canvases of equine backsides—sorry!

Cost $20–60

Address 1760 Market St at Gough
℡ 415/863-3516
Open Mon 11am–3pm, Tues–Fri 11am–3pm & 5–9pm, Sat 5–9pm, Sun 10am–3pm & 5–9pm
Transportation Market St lines
Accepts All major credit cards except Diners

Service is helpful, which is just as well since there's a lot of explaining to do. "Middle Europe" month featured Hungarian goulash, Polish dumplings, and Czechoslovakian pork. When the menu was "Best of the Mediterranean," however, you might have thought the "random samplings of the Mediterranean" was more accurate: gnocchi resembled small semolina balls rather than the cupped mini-dumplings of Italy, the pasticcio was a pasta pie unlike anything met before under that name, and the warm chocolate pudding cake was mousse-like and nothing like a cake. When they focused on Spain and Morocco, however, Carta excelled with Andalucian tapas and Moroccan couscous. So the trick to this restaurant seems to involve a certain amount of luck in choosing a cuisine they happen to do especially well. Less given to surprises is the weekend brunch menu, which is reliably good and loaded with updated versions of classics like French toast. Prices change with the menus, but almost all appetizers and mains cost around $8 or $9.

The chef is more than willing to serve smaller versions of main dishes at appetizer prices, so you can also put together an interesting if expensive meal that way—although the cost may spiral, especially if you add a glass or two of well-chosen wine. Carta is probably a good buy only if you take the prix fixe plans ($19.95 or $29.95) that may be on offer as part of regular seasonal promotions. That way, the surprises remain only culinary, which is as it should be.

Citizen Cake

Mouths fall open when they come here, then water uncontrollably. Ex-Rubicon patissier Elizabeth Falkner's place is sky-high in concept, custom-built for spiritualizing sugar. Waiters were painted with chocolate from the waist up at Citizen's launch, which no doubt added excitement when they finally got home—if they got home. Not only has she turned the notion of a dessert cafe into an adventure, but she has built an industrial ark to house it, a Swedenborgian cathedral of steel and cement, with Lucite chairs, a vast wood oven and a retail bakery peddling the most exotic ganaches ever concocted by Falkner's unfettered imagination. Is this about decadence or what?

Cost $10–35
Address 399 Grove St at Gough
☎ 415/861-2228
Open Tues–Fri 8am–10pm, Sat 10am–10pm, Sun 10am–9pm
Transportation 6, 7, 22
Accepts MasterCard, Visa

Thankfully, Falkner's straight lunch menus are sound enough to carry the high expectations raised by desserts. You can breakfast, lunch, and dine here, as well as eat cake all day long. For breakfast, Citizen serves savory scones and croissants, cinnamon rolls and granola, while lunch is served from 11.30am to 2.30pm, and features toasted sandwiches such as pork with Havarti cheese, pickles, and jicama orange salad ($12.25), a Croque Monsieur ($11) that never tasted better, or a "Mediterranean" of peppers on focaccia with ricotta and tapenade (£11.50). Pizzas are thin and made to order, and come in either a provolone version or as the daily special, which might be something exotic like potato with blue cheese and caramelised onions ($10). There's a $35 prix fixe dinner on Sundays, too.

Citizen Cake's desserts are good enough to carry this excitement. Patissier's Sara Cameron and Shuna Lydon's cakes have names like Retro Tropical Shag ($5). After Midnight is excruciating death-by-chocolate, with hazelnut crunch and whatever else drives diabetics into shock; equally shocking is the bite of salt that offsets sweet. One choice is "hazelnut on chocolate, gianduja pot de crème, hazelnut ice cream, and espresso vinaigrette," which sounds insane, yet it's a heavenly marriage that, yes, comes with a lick of salt ($8.50), as does corn blueberry parfait with blueberries, blueberry sorbet, and yellow doll watermelon ($8.50), served in a tall glass with a tortilla strip.

The Civic Center & Hayes Valley

Destino

🍴 At this fairly new bistro, lots of gold mirrors and gay colors conjure up a festive mood in spite of the cramped confines and the location in an otherwise rather lonely part of Market Street. Destino is run by a Peruvian and Swiss duo, but the cooking is determinedly described on the menu as "Nueva Latina." Choices begin with a shortlist of

Cost $12–25
Address 1815 Market St at Valencia
☎ 415/552-4451
Open Tues–Sat 5–11pm
Transportation 26, F, J, K, L, M, N
Accepts MasterCard, Visa

the Peruvian classics so dear to Latin American hearts, and continue with some nice new inventions with—since they have Swiss ancestors, after all—lashings of good cheese on everything.

Start with the crispy pork and olive empanadas ($5.50) in a very Peruvian cinnamon-garlic aioli, or a variation called arepas ($5.50), which are crispy-fried, stuffed with goat cheese and meltingly tender. Other starters include a nice hearts-of-palm salad with roast tomato vinaigrette ($5.50), and anticuchos ($5.50), outstandingly smoky and juicy grilled beef hearts served as kebabs that come with a little cup of hotter-than-hell dressing on the side. The portion is hefty, Peruvians will pronounce them the real thing, and they're certainly a contender for best-in-town. Peruvian ceviches ($6.50) of lime- and chile-marinated bass, fresh calamari, or shellfish are also good choices to start; they come in pretty glasses and are served with a creditable aioli. Papas bravas ($4.50) take on a slightly Swiss note from the strongly spice-accented melting cheese sauce that tops the potatoes like a quilt. Among the main courses, Chilean sea bass ($11.50) is perfectly broiled, and is served with peppery black beans and a very smoky chipotle-based sauce that is a nice contrast to the sweet, white flesh of the fish. A Niman Ranch steak ($12.95) also gets an appropriate sauce, this one of chimichurri. Duck dishes make other good main dish choices, particularly the beer-marinated confit ($13.50). Cheese ($6), or glorious pumpkin donuts ($6) follow.

The short wine list includes several Chilean and Argentinian wines, which are largely unremarkable but pleasantly low-priced (from $16). Service could not be more helpful or friendly, as the owners go out of their way to explain dishes to their customers. With its interesting menu and intimate surroundings, Destino makes for a nice find; slightly adventurous diners will especially enjoy it.

Hayes Street Grill

Nobody has ever found anything rude to say about the Hayes Street Grill, the favorite watering hole of symphony musicians and opera stars. Food writer Patricia Unterman's place will never let you down, yet nor will it completely bowl you over, or launch you into a new food universe. With its faultless fish classics and soothing, plain decor of wood and brass and cream walls, it will never frighten you with vertical food, or throw you one of those wasabe-raspberry coulis combinations that might make your mouth bust right out in hives. But the lunch crowd who work in the nearby government offices don't want "tall" food, and nor do the opera- and symphony-goers who come here of an evening, sometimes toting large French horn cases.

Cost $15–40
Address 320 Hayes St between Gough and Franklin
☎ 415/863-5545
Open Mon–Fri 11.30am–2pm & 5–9.30pm, Sat 5.30–9.30pm
Transportation 21, 47, 49
Accepts All major credit cards

When you don't want to be astonished into inarticulate "oohs" and "aahs," and merely crave a perfectly executed, reliably fresh piece of fish, or perhaps a hamburger of humanely farmed and faultlessly organic Niman-Schell pedigree beef that you surmise expired from sheer ecstasy and old age, this is the place. If you like to wash it down with a simple Sauvignon Blanc or Pinot Noir and you're not in the mood for fighting palm pilots and spandex, Hayes Street Grill will console you. Start with crabcakes ($8.50), justly popular for their size and meatiness, with just a whisker of seasoning, or try the very tasty grilled quail salad ($9). After that, beam directly to the grilled seafood du jour ($18), although you could also check over the grilled and roast meats on the menu. Once you've chosen from a shortlist of six of so fish of the day, select from as many sauces; it's generally best to opt for the simple lemon and butter. If you don't care for grilled fish, try Asian-marinated poussin ($19) or the house-made whiskey fennel sausages ($18). The Grill's French fries are as gilded, dry, and crisped as they ought to be.

Desserts can be distinctly praiseworthy here. There's a routinely successful crème brûlée ($6), and the chocolate pound cake with Jack Daniels and chocolate-chip ice cream ($7) makes one resounding ending to an evening—just forget about joining Weight Watchers.

Jardinière

🍴 People can't stop themselves from sighing with pleasure when they walk into Traci des Jardins' place. Pat Kuleto's inverted Champagne-glass interior, with its brushed metal balustrades interrupted by champagne buckets, is a captivating architectural metaphor for, well, love of bubbly. It guides you to a mysteriously black, oval bar, encased by bottles, that's spectacularly spotlit and garlanded with fairy lights. An upper circle with tiny tables for two is suspended on the next floor, its brick partially dressed with burgundy velvet drapes; above that is another, higher realm. A jazz pianist tinkles. A sweep-all-before-you, Fred-and-Ginger staircase leads up to the dining area. If you're a little wary about the cost, however, shimmy up to that black, marble-topped bar, and get a cocktail and a bar menu.

Cost $12–75
Address 300 Grove St at Franklin
☎ 415/861-5555
Open Mon & Sun 5–10.30pm, Tues–Sat 5–11.30pm
Transportation 21, 49, BART Civic Center
Accepts All major credit cards except Diners

More or less anything you pick is going to be delicate and exquisitely presented, but the series of salads, such as the baby artichokes with toasted bread and Crescenza cheese ($14) or arugula with Roquefort and endive ($10) are almost too pretty to disturb. The crabcake with citrus salad ($15) comes with little bits of crystallized orange and lemon, and is also a little sweet, despite that trim. The terrine of creamy foie gras ($20), with a little dish of sweetened pear compote and slices of toasted brioche resting beside it, is almost like a dessert. The frog-leg tartlette with morels and ramps fricassee ($17) is too disturbingly heaven-like to permit analysis. If you want a bigger plate, des Jardins does a trademark pan-roasted squab with peas, carrots, ramps, and porcini ($28), surrounded by a jammy puddle of pan juices and dried cherries. The Thai snapper ($30) is another famous production, this time mixing des Jardins' favorite Asian vegetable, bak choy, with a yazu broth.

A renowned six-cheese sampler is available at the bar ($12). You could just sit here with that and a cocktail for some of the night, or go to the other extreme and dive into the entire tasting menu ($75). If you bring in a bottle that's not on their list, they don't charge corkage; but once you've seen the enormous list you'll realize that it's not an easy trick to pull off!

Laurel's Restaurant

(🍴) This charming Cuban spot dishes up authentic Havana-style *comidas* to the rhythms of the much-loved Buena Vista Social Club boys, but it still doesn't get the attention it deserves, perhaps because Gerardo Privat's restaurant is on a residential block. It's easily missed while driving down Oak Street, but well worth a visit. Savvy efforts have been made to lend it an interesting and spacious feeling inside, with clever use of mirrors, angled banquettes, and tables.

Cost $6–25
Address 205 Oak St at Gough
☎ 415/934-1575
Open Mon–Fri 11.30am–2pm & 5–11pm, Sat 5–11pm, Sun 5–9pm
Transportation 5, 21, 49, BART Civic Center
Accepts MasterCard, Visa

Havana-born chef Reynaldo Naranjo, who used to cook at Nordstrom's, has weighted Laurel's menu toward seafood, and he hits all the Cuban classics on a long and loving menu. His version of tostones con mojo ($4.50), or fried green plantains dressed in a luscious garlic emulsion, is a generous, reassuring serving of six good-sized tostones. Ripe plantains are used in the softer and sweeter maduros con mojo ($4.50) version of the dish. The tamal de puerco ($6 lunch, $7 dinner) is a little unusual in that the corn husk is unwrapped, revealing a large and tasty serving of tender pork nestling in cornmeal, accompanied by tomatoes and salsa. Reynaldo also makes a true fufu con ropa vieja ($8), or mashed plantains with long-simmered beef stew. Black garlicked prawns ($13.50) come in lemon butter with tostones and rice, while coctel de camarones ($8), or prawn cocktail, is accompanied by fried yucca. House paella ($18) bursts with prawns, calamari, mussels, chicken, sausage, and more. Crab entrees come in many forms, including rolls, salads, or sandwiches ($8). Reynaldo always offers rabbit Havana-style ($10) and also the national dish of picadillo ($10), which is peppered ground beef with rice, tostones, beans, fries, and tomato salad, and excellent value. Sweets ($4) are flans or custards: choose from coconut, guava, or chocolate.

The Cuban sandwich is a noble classic. But Reynaldo had to give up on Cuban sandwiches of ham, cheese, and pickle pressed inside a torpedo-shaped bun and grilled—apparently recipe variations are too often disputed. But he and Gerardo (who's Peruvian) do serve Cuban (-style) beer, a frisky Hatuey ($3.50) that's actually made in Puerto Rico. Otherwise, Reynaldo's food is about the closest you can get to Havana in this city.

Max's Opera Cafe

Every branch of the Max's mini-empire has some distinguishing feature; the one at this ultra-popular branch is the grand piano, which often accompanies the waiters on such standards as "Memories" or "Bess You Is My Woman Now." You may relish these impromptu performances, though sometimes for the wrong reasons, but you're likely to relish more or less anything at Max's. Opinions differ as to just how authentic a New York deli this might be (with its plush banquettes, bar seating,

Cost $5–30
Address 601 Van Ness Ave at Golden Gate Ave
☎ 415/771-7300
Open Mon & Sun 11am–10pm, Tues–Thurs 11am–11pm, Fri & Sat 11am–midnight
Transportation BART Civic Center
Accepts All major credit cards except Diners

and huge windows it's too comfortable to be the real thing), but that doesn't matter. It's a great place for a pre-performance nosh, there's enough variety on the menu to please anybody, and the long glass case of New York specialties you pass on the way in helps you make up your mind.

The theme is New York delicatessen food, and the homemade rye bread is a good start, even if the bagels are predictably inauthentic (baked, not steamed). All portions here are cornucopian, so consider splitting your sandwich with someone else at the table. Their chicken soup ($3.75 cup, $5.75 bowl) comes with pretty good matzo balls, and you'll also find a filling borscht ($3.50/$4.50) with diced brisket, sour cream, and chives. More strenuous choices lie ahead. Vast and unwieldy corned beef and pastrami sandwiches ($11.95) spill across a platter; far too big to fit in your mouth, they come with a choice of dressings, plus dill pickles, coleslaw, potato salad, and chopped egg, and they're served on nine different varieties of bread. The Reuben ($11.95), with all of those sides plus sauerkraut, is equally enormous, while the chopped liver ($6.50) is among the best in town—tied with East Coast West Delicatessen's and Traktir's—and authentically hand-chopped, not just puréed. But not everything is Noo Yawk-style sandwiches in here. A creamy plate of polenta ($10.95) takes on flavor from barbecued sweet peppers.

But perhaps it's the chocolate chip cheesecake ($6) you're really pining for? Desserts are as colossal as everything else. The macaroon ($3.75) weighs nearly half a pound; dipped in a vat of chocolate, it's enough to keep an army on the march.

Millennium

Vegan goes *very* upscale at this small, out-of-the-way hotel restaurant, where a gourmet chef and menu attempt to reconcile the best of produce with a strong gospel of no animal products—not even a whiff of Camembert or crème fraîche. Millennium is now almost a decade old, and during that time has lured many diners to its soothing blue-and-white interior for the famous "Aphrodisiac Night" suppers, held on the Sunday night nearest the full moon. The idea of the five-course prix fixe aphrodisiac menu began a couple of years ago, and it leans heavily on luxuriously over-the-top chocolate desserts, most of them involving no serious threat to the cholesterol and none of them actually involving butter or cream.

Cost $15–75

Address Abigail Hotel, 246 McAllister St at Larkin
☎ 415/487-9800
Open Daily 5–9.30pm
Transportation 19, BART Civic Center
Accepts All major credit cards except Diners

But the a la carte menu is seductive already, from the interesting quiches and crêpes to the all-raw dishes. A veggie antipasti plate ($7.95 for a big plate, $4.95 as a side or starter) comes artistically heaped with grilled roast peppers and tomatoes, plus little mounds of legumes in vinaigrette, with focaccia and aioli alongside. Satsuma roll ($8.95) is an Asian cabbage parcel stuffed with Satsuma mandarins, burdock root, carrot, kimpura (a kind of sea kelp), and sprouts with basil and shiso, all steeped in a strongly gingered and limed peanut vinaigrette. Main dishes show Asian and Latino influences: plaintain torte ($8.95) is a many-layered wheat tortilla cake sandwiched with plantains in creamy tofu-cilantro sauce, with a salsa containing watermelon dice and red peppers. Rosemary polenta ($6.25) is grilled, well-herbed wedges drenched in a puttanesca-style sauce of capers and olives. Celeriac ravioli ($15.25) is a completely raw dish of mushroom and walnut terrine served with slices of celery root and cashew cream, tapenade, and avocado.

You can choose two from among these on the Aphrodisiac Menu, which starts with a shared appetizer, a small salad, and a sorbet. Dessert comes with "chocolate almond fudge midnight," or banana brûlée dessert, or another similar choice. Five courses cost an affordable $39, so consult your astronomer (or Millennium) and book; it attracts plenty of yearning couples. The meal is consummated with a herbal "love potion" nightcap.

Stelline

A casual sibling to nearby Caffè delle Stelle, Stelline is a great place to grab dinner before the symphony or opera, just blocks away, but be sure to reserve ahead. The noisy dining room is painted a cheery yellow and lined with wine bottles, tomato cans, and other Italian food bric-a-brac; it's a cross between a small town trattoria in Italy and the sort of East Coast spaghetti parlor that famously has red-checked table-

Cost $15–30
Address 330 Gough St at Hayes
☎ 415/626-4292
Open Mon–Fri 11.30am–2.30pm & 5–10pm, Sat & Sun 5–10pm
Transportation 21
Accepts All major credit cards

cloths—except here the checks happen to be green. You'll have no choice but to stick to simple, familiar dishes, which is probably just as well as there's no real flair to the cooking. That said, everything is flavorful, filling, inexpensive, and competently prepared.

Entrees come with soup or salad, so you may or may not want an appetizer. If you do, there's a slightly grainy polenta ($4.25), topped with garlicky pesto—even better if you mix them together—and Gorgonzola cheese. Caprese salad ($5.50) of fresh tomato, mozzarella, and basil is another good choice, and the white fava bean soup ($3.50) is especially delicious. Among the eight or nine pastas that follow, spaghetti alla puttanesca ($8.75) comes loaded with olives, capers, and basil, plus an appropriately spicy pomodoro sauce—just hope your companion doesn't mind garlic on your breath. Menu specials may be dishes such as cheese tortellini ($9), which are cooked perfectly al dente. Of the non-pasta choices, sautéed chicken breast piccata ($9.75) fairly drips with butter, lemon, and capers; served over spaghetti, it's satisfying, if not subtle. You'll find one or two seafood dishes as well, and the red snapper with capers ($11) is the most expensive item on the menu. Wines are as simple and hearty as the food. Order by the glass and you won't pay more than $5 for Chianti, Pinot Grigio and other standbys.

Don't miss the first act on account of dessert, as there are only three choices, all dull. If you're in a wacky mood, order spumoni—three flavors of ice cream with those kooky dried cherries found in fruitcakes. Espresso is excellent, however, and will keep you wide awake for Tosca's tragic finale.

Suppenküche

There's more than a touch of *The Student Prince* about this würsthaus. With its bare walls, and long pine tables and benches, it even bears a passing resemblance to Breughel's picture, "The Wedding Feast". Roisterers here put away everything from smoked pork chops and venison to a plateful of potato pancakes while working their way through the huge range of specialty beers on tap. Patrons share tables with complete strangers, and you could easily imagine a whole group bursting into song. The place is run by Thomas Klausman; owner Fabrizio Wiest even maintains a website (www.suppenkuche.com) that features a history of his hometown, Mengkofen, going back to the eleventh century.

Cost $5–15

Address 601 Hayes St at Laguna
415/252-9289
Open Mon–Fri 5–10pm, Sat & Sun 10am–2.30pm & 5–10pm
Transportation 5, 21, 22, F, J, K, L, M, N
Accepts All major credit cards except Diners

This is one of a handful of places that preserve German cuisine intact, and hard-to-find classics include käsespätzle ($11), which is egg noodles topped with cheese and onion butter sauce, and potato pancakes with applesauce ($9.50). On weekend mornings, the critical importance of the potato in German cuisine is properly saluted on the Suppenküche brunch menu. If you have a fancy for nutmeg- and caraway-tinged dishes, you'll find more than a hint in the meat dishes. The choice of traditional wursts, schnitzels, and roast meat is wide, and portions are exceptionally generous. Pork dishes (from $13.50) may be accompanied by red cabbage or sauerkraut, with more than a hint of clove, apple, vinegar, and black pepper. More variations of sausages and potato come aplenty on both brunch and dinner menus, while the venison and veal dishes are accompanied by housemade spätzle, the potato and egg noodles that adorn plates all over Germany and Switzerland. There's always a fish of the day as well, such as sautéed trout in lemon butter sauce with bouillon potatoes and spinach ($14.50). For dessert, sinful Black Forest cake ($5) completes the surfeit.

The beer selection is another reason to visit Suppenküche, with pitchers priced at a reasonable $11, and two-liter boots at $14. Each beer is served in its appropriate individual glass, just as in Germany, and there are twenty on tap: hefe weizen, pilsner, oktoberfest, dunkles, helles, bock beer, and schwarzbier, plus two Belgians—Leffe Blond and Mardesous Abbey.

Terra Brazilis

With two Brazilian restaurants within samba-ing distance (Canto do Brasil is just around the corner on Franklin), it's inevitable that people will compare. But aside from a musical touch to Canto's folksier ambiance, and some fascinating Bahian dishes at the more upscale Terra Brazilis, it's hard to come down on either side. Comparisons aside, Terra's corn-yellow and brick walls adorned with modern canvases, and its big windows and rustic trestles make it welcoming on a gray day. So does the house sangria, served by the glass ($5.50), and the sugar-cane cocktails called Caiporuvas (a version of a Caipirinha). There's space for parties, too.

Cost $15–35
Address 602 Hayes St at Laguna
☎ 415/241-1900
Open Tues–Thurs & Sun 5–9.30pm, Fri & Sat 5–10.30pm
Transportation 21
Accepts All major credit cards except Diners

Michael Cook's menu mixes the flavors of the Latin diaspora, from tropical tapas to the cuisine of Salvador, in Brazil's Bahia province. It begins with starters such as mixed Iberian olives ($4) or bolinhos de bacalhau ($6.50), which are balls of deep-fried salt cod and potato, and eaten as finger food. Crab-filled piquillo peppers in salsa verde ($8.50) are divinely fiery, while yucca fritters ($5) are a snack dish that can sometimes be stodgy—not these, however, which come moistened with chimichurri fire-spiked peanut sauce. A Portuguese cheese sampler ($8) entices with fresh figs and cashews. Feijoada ($8 starter, $13.50 main) is the national dish of Brazil, a long-simmered black bean stew bobbing with smoked garlic sausage, ham, dried beef, and manioc flour; it's hard to make it authentic outside Brazil, but Cook meets the test head on. Bahian-inflected dishes here include the mussels in chile-coconut nectar with limes ($8.50), and carneiro vatapa ($15.50), which is an enormously rich, textured ragout of lamb with butternut squash in peanut-coconut cream; a dish for voluptuaries. Chicken served in a tamarind and green machucho stew ($16) tastes even more tropical, while tuna ($18) gets an orange-chipotle marinade, and comes with a crunchy Mexican jicama-cucumber salad.

The wide-ranging wine list is strong in local Zinfandels, Rhone varietals, and Sauvignon Blancs (including several from New Zealand), priced from $4.50 to $9 by the glass.

Zuni Cafe

Oddities of space, shape and profile have always helped Zuni's popularity. Perched on an edgy Market Street corner, with its sharply triangular profile filled floor to ceiling with windows, it's always ablaze with light and filled with noshing diners. Chef Judy Rodgers helped make it a pioneering Cal-fusion establishment, but back in the days when Zuni began, it was just a small place that won over food writer Elizabeth David and prospered accordingly. Back then, a fondness for oysters and salmon and focaccia seemed cultivated and decadent rather than simply the human condition. Though Zuni has been going for a quarter of a century, their wood-oven food is still exciting, and their brunches are never anything less than showy.

Cost S15–40
Address 1658 Market St at Gough
☎ 415/552-2522
Open Tues–Sat 11.30am–midnight, Sun 11am–11pm
Transportation F, 6, 7, 26, 71
Accepts All major credit cards except Diners

The menu changes daily, but begins at the raw bar with every type of Pacific oyster you can lay your hands on (from $1.95 each); Zuni may very well win the contest for leeriest oyster bed in town. After the oysters, it's all hail to their Caesar salad ($8.50), gleaming with viscous, lemon-tangy, eggy dressing, and made with real anchovies and giant Parmesan flakes. Zuni may win the Caesar contest too. After these firsts, Zuni is known for its roast meats, especially the oven-roasted chicken on a Tuscan salad ($35 for two). This is a trademark dish for celebrating couples out on their anniversary or birthdays, and it entails a longish wait. Fish of the day, such as Zuni's equally famous salmon with smoked bacon ($20), is also satisfying. You're going to be happy with the signature hamburger ($10.99), too, though it's only served at lunch or late at night; rare and tender beef comes in two layers of chewy, rosemary-flecked focaccia, with salad and great fries on the side.

Forget pretentious tall food that lures foodies into parting with their ephemeral bucks. Call this food Cali-Itali, Cal-Med, or just call it a good old feed, it doesn't matter. Be warned, however, that the service is liable to be slow if you eat here during the early-evening rush hour; just remember to warn them if you're in a hurry.

The Haight Ashbury District & Cole Valley

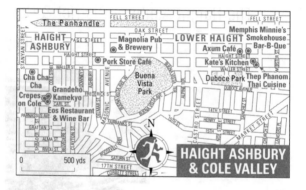

Axum Cafe

The Lower Haight has its own strip of cheerful eateries that offer unbeatable bang for the buck to the students and punks in this hood, and the Axum is a favorite. The cafe is named for Ethiopia's pre-Christian city, as seen in pictures, hangings, and posters on the restaurant's yellow-rinsed walls. That color is offset by gold-fringed light shades, which sport Ethiopian motifs, and red curtains. Like the older Massawa, nine blocks higher up, this dingy but sympathetic little Ethiopian restaurant specializes in the feisty, berbere-spiced stews of East Africa, and whatever you order will come with injera, a flannel-like bread that suburbanites have been known to flop across their laps, mistaking it for napkins. There are no forks, unless you demand them. Filling injera with sizzling cubes of hot-spiced beef or lamb is the mandatory skill for eating Ethiopian.

Cost S8–15
Address 698 Haight St at Pierce
⊕415/252-7912
Open Daily 1–10.30pm (Wed from 5.30pm)
Transportation 6, 7, 66, 71
Accepts All major credit cards

Vegetarians can get by just fine in here with a sampler of the vegetable items on the menu, which costs $12 for two people, $23 for three, and $27 for four—all the dishes are priced separately as well. You sample from the following items on the platter: alicha ($5 separately), which is a subtly peppered vegetable fricassée with carrots, cabbage, potatoes, peppers, garlic, and spices; alicha ater ($5), a chickpea stew with onion and spices; hamli ($4), or spinach stew; kintishara ($4), or mushroom stew; and tumtumo ($5), or lentils with onion, tomato, and garlic, something like a daal. Omnivores can choose sighine ($7.50), which is beef cubes long-braised in tomato, onion, and spicy Ethiopian ghee; or tbisie ($8), a chicken version of the same. If your tastebuds just can't take all that blazing heat, request the milder stuff and they'll oblige. For drinks, try the Ethiopian beer, which isn't bad ($3.75), honey wine ($3.50), or steamed milk flavored with Kahlua or Amaretto ($3.50).

You can't beat this value, especially if you're a wallet-starved vegetarian with a hunger on you that's three times the size of your budget. Five dollars to spend on dinner will buy you plenty in here, which no doubt explains why it's always busy.

Cha Cha Cha

Think Santería altars and Screamin' Jay Hawkins meets Mexican tapas and Jamaican jerk chicken, with sangria highs. Philip Bellbert's Cha Cha Cha was the very first spot to dish Caribbean and Latino fast food for Generation X-ers and "Next-ers", who share small plates over a jug of spiked-up wine in an ultra-kitschy voodoo setting. Sheer novelty in the decor lends it an edge and it's been cramming in the multitudes ever since it opened. But only the food is fast, and since it's strictly walk-in and casual, you're not going to get a table immediately unless it's earlier in the evening, or a weekday.

Cost $7–20	
Address 1801 Haight St at Shrader	
☎ 415/386-7670	
Open Mon–Thurs & Sun 11am–4.30pm & 5–11pm, Fri & Sat 5–11.30pm	
Transportation 7, 33, 37	
Accepts MasterCard, Visa	

First, settle for a brunch plate of platanos con frijoles ($6.25), ripened and cross-sliced plantains fried in butter and artistically presented in drizzles of crema on a thick puddle of refried black beans; as Latino breakfasts go, this one is hard to get wrong, if unbeatably fattening. Quesadillas ($6.50) are another Central American staple, a crescent of folded maize tortilla that contains anything from barbecued chicken to pork, with abundant salsa, guacamole, and more of that sour cream. Fried potatoes ($4.25), dished up fast in a chile pasilla aioli that burns the tongue, make a swift tapas snack, as do sautéed mushrooms ($5.25) marinated in sherry, olive oil, and garlic. Cajun shrimp ($8.25) in spices, beer, and cream are addictively fiery, while fried calamari ($6.50) sings in a puckery lime aioli. Jerk chicken ($6) is one of the more filling choices; it's marinated and baked with rasins, lots of garlic, Scotch Bonnet peppers, and tomatoes, and served on a bed of rice. Dishes like these, from the small plates menu, magically leap a dollar or so dearer by evening, when a larger and more serious comida menu swings into place alongside. Among the more ribsticking Latino supper choices are Cuban steak with garlicked yucca ($14.50), pork loin in adobe criollo ($13.25), and some fish of the day platters.

Cha Cha Cha regulars who love the food, but not the wait, usually head across town to the Mission, where a new branch at McCarthy's old-time bar harbors party rooms and has more space.

Crêpes on Cole

Carl at Cole is a fairly residential neighborhood, away from the hurly-burly of the Haight proper. But this sunny Upper Haight corner is a tranquil spot, one where local students congregate on account of its nearness to medical schools, campuses, and lots of student housing, not to mention the N Streetcar. So the sidewalk tables of Crêpes on Cole are fully occupied on balmy days, and it stays open late enough for a quick bite on your way home. Of course, there are zillions of pancake cafes just like this one all over town, but luckily for the happy villagers of hilly Cole Valley, this one gets it right.

Cost $4–10

Address 100 Carl St at Cole
☎415/664-1800
Open Mon–Thurs & Sun
7am–11pm, Fri & Sat
7am–midnight
Transportation 37, N
Accepts MasterCard, Visa

Check the chalkboard over the counter for the latest lineup of daily specials and crêpe fillings here. They make a finer, lacier style of crêpe that comes extra thin and delicate here, and at a lower price than most too. The fillings start with the Mediterranean ($3.95), a plain, if always welcome, extra-sharp Cheddar with onions and ratatouille vegetables, nicely grilled and diced. The banana, chocolate, and walnuts dessert crêpe ($4.95) is a bestseller, and comes walloped with a massive mound of whipped cream. The basil crêpe ($3.95) is another favourite, featuring Greek feta cheese and basil, with onions and more melted Cheddar to finish. Crêpes aren't the only attraction at the busy spot, however, and a chalkboard over the counter lists a raft of side dishes, from hefty portions of sautéed potatoes to omelets, mountainous salads, and a few thick sandwiches; prices start at $5.

Thanks to those low, low prices—and the $2 pints of Guinness during the Happy Hour—there's hardly a soul over forty in here. Don't expect too much in the way of service; it exists alright, and it's friendly, but this is still the Haight, after all, and coffees, teas, and Italian sodas are brought to you at the same tempo that you will want to adopt if you come by for a crêpe fix. This quiet neighbourhood place is pleasant and inexpensive, just don't compare it to the more expensive crêpe joints in town, least of all to the mighty Ti Couz, in the Mission.

Eos Restaurant & Wine Bar

🍴 Dropping by to sample some of Arnold Eric Wong's sheer inventiveness on the Eos menu is something any San Franciscan or food-loving visitor will savor, especially if you haven't remembered to book a table in the restaurant. The wine bar is as cozy a space as the main dining room next door is exciting and industrial, and its menu provides easy access to some of the city's highest-concept food, plus one of

Cost $15–60
Address 901 Cole St at Carl
☎ 415/566-3063
Open Mon–Thurs 5.30–9.30pm, Fri & Sat 5.30–10pm, Sun 5–9.30pm
Transportation 6, 37, 43, N
Accepts All major credit cards except Diners

San Francisco's outstanding wine lists. Furthermore, you can get here easily by bus or streetcar, which is a real treat compared to the horrors of parking in Cole Valley. The full dining experience can come with a daunting price tag, and absolutely requires booking well in advance, but there's little wait to dine at the bar.

Wong's food has always called itself "fusion," but that barely describes its mix of delicate East and hearty West; his dishes aren't so much a melange as a playful commentary on both influences. For appetizers, try the scrumptious little goat cheese and shiitake mushroom parcels ($8), which come tied with tiny vegetable cords and dressed with a ginger vinaigrette. The world may feel it's "done" teetering towers of tuna tartare ($12), but Wong's is seared albacore, with lemongrass, daikon sprout, and white-miso dip on the side, and streets ahead of the competition. Bread salad with Thai spice ($9) comes with green papaya, berries, and mango, which glint like rubies, emeralds, and garnets in a conical glass saladière—beat that! Main dishes always include salmon, perhaps with a fermented black bean sauce and gingered oil dressing ($22). Five-spice oxtail ($24) is a truly Hunan-derived dish of delicate shreds of juicy meat served with pickled ginger, daikon radishes, and carrots. Grilled pork chops ($18) are chutneyed and gingered to a fare-thee-well—in fact, Eos is to ginger what Brazil is to samba.

For dessert, "bananamisu" of caramelized bananas ($7) keeps everyone happy, but there's also kaffir lime crème brûlée ($7), and if you decide to share a mousse bombe of valrhona chocolate cardamom mousse with hazelnut cookies and espresso ice cream, it'll arrive in a glass fishbowl with lots of spoons. No one will turn down a taste.

Grandeho Kameyko

Away from the hustle and bustle of the Haight, this quiet little sushi hideaway supplies the Cole Valley set with its raw fish. It's an unusually cute little vest pocket of minimal, blond-wood seating where you have the choice of a tiny table or a high chair at the bar. The bits of blue canopy, shoji screens, and fine ceramics are the sole accents. The counter is the domain of chef Yoshihiko Fujita, the highly respected high priest of the oceans who used to work at Kyo-Ya, at the Sheraton Palace. He deftly performs the raw fish cure as you lean on the counter top, warm sake at your elbow.

Cost $10–30

Address 943 Cole St at Carl
☎ 415/673-6828
Open Mon–Wed
11am–10.30pm, Thurs & Fri
11am–11pm, Sat noon–11pm
Transportation 43, N
Accepts MasterCard, Visa

Much in the way of positive press has focused on the special inventions of chef Fujita, and his expertise in the intricacies of tempura and teriyaki preparation. You can, of course, choose the sushi, and the smoked salmon ($4.75) and deep-fried softshell crab ($4.75) are standouts. Alternatively, go for the all-inclusive bento box lunch ($14.50), which combines two portions of delightfully presented chicken and salmon teriyaki with one of shrimp tempura, little mouthfuls of joy shown off by exemplary battering. It also comes with that heretical invention, the California roll, plus sashimi, oyster, red snapper, gingered pork, marinated beef, and sesame chicken, all served with steamed rice, miso soup, and salad. The lunch combination specials are also good, from the fresh tuna, hamachi, sake, maguro, whitefish, and tekka maki ($10.50), to the even better cooked version, which includes unagi, ani, tamago, and kani ($9.95).

There's only one complaint, which is that when you are proffered any little small extra, a sauce of sunomono cucumber, say, or a little piece of extra sashimi, you could hardly be blamed for assuming it is part of the deal. But no, you pay extra; it's Grandeho's way of surviving as a rather upscale and refined sushi bar in the Haight, a part of town where folks try to freewheel through life on a shoestring. Grandeho has another branch on Fisherman's Wharf, at 2721 Hyde St at Beach.

Kate's Kitchen

🍴 The typical Kate's Kitchen devotee is a young and adventurous world traveler, just back from the fermented yak milks of Tuva and buttered teas of the Himalayas, and jonesing for a giant stack of ginger-peach or cornmeal-banana-walnut pancakes with maple butter. At least, that describes the happy campers filling up Kate's homey little Lower Haight

Cost $8–15

Address 471 Haight St at Fillmore
☎ 415/626-3984
Open Daily 8am–3pm
Transportation 6, 7, 22, 66, 71
Accepts Cash only

hangout, with its wipe-down check cloths, humongous portions, and line stretching out the door. Word seems to have reached the backpacking community: even in the remotest reaches of Cambodia or Mongolia, they seem to know about Kate's. It's where returning natives head first, and it keeps them going for another thousand miles.

Kate's has more than a little whiff of the South about it, which is another reason returning home-birds come here to assuage their nostalgia. Kate's pancakes are crispy above and puffy below, but always golden and topped with fruit, and yes, the ginger-peach ($5.75) and the banana-walnut ($5.75) will get your vote. Kate's hush puppies ($3.75) come with maple or honey butter, while Cheddar Green cheese-and-onion biscuits come with juicy gravy, and bacon is a fat back-cut, nice and smoky. The most popular Southern soul food specialties include a dish called Flanched Farney Garney ($4.25), a kind of Creole eggs Benedict. French Toast Orgy ($7.95), another Southern offering, won last year's "Best Nonsexual Orgy" award in the *SF Bay Guardian* "Best of the Bay" awards. It turns out to be a dissolute and shameless riot of fruits and nuts partying in confusion atop a righteous portion of French toast that you could probably fix a roof with or use as a stepladder.

Be warned that Kate's is a tight squeeze at the best of times, and the bathroom is through the kitchen. Certainly, gourmets would do better elsewhere, and it gets pretty busy at the weekends, when a longish wait is in order. But give yourself a morning off and take yourself here for a long, drawn out brunch over the newspaper—especially if you're just back from abroad and need to reacquaint yourself with the pleasures of home. Then you can spend the rest of the day strolling up Haight Street to Golden Gate Park and back again.

Magnolia Pub and Brewery

Sometimes all you want in life is a burger with a pint, and that's when Magnolia fulfils its function. The young and restless can pound up and down Haight Street checking out the piercings and tattoos, but at Magnolia you can just settle back in a booth and order straight-forward, good-quality grub. It's handily situated in the heart of the Haight, with the boutiques just doors away, and not far from the Park, either. And it's known

Cost $10–15
Address 1398 Haight St at Masonic
☎ 415/864-7468
Open Mon–Fri noon–1am, Sat 10am–midnight
Transportation 6, 7, 33, 37, 43, 66, 71
Accepts MasterCard, Visa

for the best burger in the 'hood. Grab a booth next to a window and order one of a dozen homemade brews on tap–its English-style ale and "Cole Porter," Spud Boy," and "Stout of Circumstance" are hot favorites.

Burgers ($9.25) come on a rather doughy focaccia-style bappy bun, with chunky fries and bits of Magnolia salad plus tomato on the side. You can order them rarer-than-rare to almost cremated, and irresistibly topped with savagely blue cheese or bitingly mature Cheddar. Unlike the burger, the fries are not the best in town—they're not twice-fried— but if you want them as a side dish (from $2.75 separately) you can have them with cheese, garlic, onion, or chile toppings, and in small or large servings. If you're not a meat-eater there's the house salad, as well as a Caesar ($7.25) that replaces the usual dressing with a beer-frothed mayo—this is, after all, a brewery. More mysteries of a Haight kind occur in the calamari salad with an aioli of soy, sesame, and chile. Pan-fried ahi tuna ($14) is served with pasta or mashed potatoes, but stick to what Magnolia does best: pub grub and foaming pints that are made in-house and come in all colors. There's a happy hour from 4pm to 7pm and after 10pm.

The decor is more diner-like than pub-like, and service is loose to the point of being occasionally absentee. Parking is impossible, but then any-where around this neck of the woods is terrible for parking. Other popular Haight bars—Martin Mack's, the Bodhran, Kezar's—serve a full bar menu too, but Magnolia has its Stout of Circumstance, and it has those burgers too. For that reason alone it earns its keep.

Memphis Minnie's Smokehouse Bar-B-Que

The Haight is still a Mecca for young backpackers who seek mind-altering experiences rather than spare ribs, and San Francisco is not as meat-loving as, say, Texas. Despite those drawbacks, Memphis Minnie's has convinced the hungry of Lower Haight that they have a large hole in their stomachs that only spare ribs, smoked brisket, pork barbecue, and corn-crusted catfish can fill. With its screaming scarlet and yellow decor, and jukebox of throbbing B.B. King and other old blues masters, Minnie's has transformed this sliver of the Haight into Bubba-style bliss. Bare tables accommodate a score of diners up to their armpits in ribs and sauce, and the takeout trade is brisk. Something of an old, Southern-style sense of harmony pervades, as folks feast together on massive mounds of slow-smoked meat.

> **Cost** $7–15
>
> **Address** 576 Haight St at Fillmore
> ☎ 415/647-7427
> **Open** Tues–Sun 11am–10pm
> **Transportation** 6, 7, 22, 71
> **Accepts** All major credit cards

Minnie's is owned by Bob Cantor, the hospitable pigtailed guy under the blackboard advertising the $8.95 Rib Tips Special who says "Yeah, I'm from the South all right—South Brooklyn!" He moved Minnie's here from the Outer Mission, and now dreams of a honky-tonk piano for live music. Bob epitomizes down-home patience and eagerness to please, and he's hands-on at the grill all day, forever explaining why his hickory-smoked "Texas red sauce" has 21 spices and two sugars, and why his "Piggy Pork" South Carolina mustard sauce has the kick of a mule (extra mustard, extra cayenne pepper). The Southern Star pork-beef combo sandwich ($7.50) contains 15-hour-marinated and smoked "pull pork" that pulls apart, plus a tower of beef brisket, both inside a crusty bun with just enough inner doughiness to soak up juices. Lately, catfish has made great inroads into the San Francisco palate—Memphis Minnie's double-dipped cornmeal-crusted fried catfish ($7.95) is not yet outselling ribs ($7.95) or pork ($7.95), but it soon may.

Do not leave without trying the long-simmered collard and mustard greens ($2.50). Bob divulges the recipe: spicy multi-mix, brown sugar, lashings of pepper, and vinegar, simmered all day and half a night. This is American soul food, simple and good.

The Pork Store Cafe

At this Upper Haight greasy spoon, the name does not in fact really say it all, because vegetarian-friendly and vegan dishes co-exist with meat–this is the Haight, after all. The Pork Store is informal to the point of being a literal hole in the wall: half a dozen tables, a counter for owner-chef Nadia, old posters and a faded photograph of the place's glory days as an actual pork store. But for

Cost $5–15

Address 1451 Haight St at Ashbury
℡ 415/864-6981
Open Daily 8am–3pm
Transportation Muni 6, 7, 33, 37, 43, 71
Accepts All major credit cards except Diners

brunch, breakfast, or lunch there are few more popular landmarks, and you can count on a ribsticker of a repast for a bargain price. There's a line out of the door at weekends.

If Nadia is grilling at the counter, ask her for the specials of the day. Occasionally, she knocks up vivid and authentic Southern fare, like liver and onions ($7.50), made with beef and pork liver, or chicken breasts marinated in honey and vinegar ($5.45). But her trademark dish is the ever-popular Nadia's Piggy Combo ($7.95), to give her pork chop platter its full name, in which a couple of chops come splayed around a mini-mountain of mashed potatoes with steamed spinach and Southern biscuits, and soaked in a sensational mustard and sugar gravy. A chicken version also exists ($7.95), as do ordinary burgers ($5.95) and unfussy steaks ($7.95). Nadia can also whip up veggie dishes such as tofu scramble ($4.95), aimed at Haight Street vegan types who come in for a quickie before topping off lunch with the brewer's yeast and garlic-flavored popcorn at the Red Vic Movie House. Portions are enormous. If you want to fill yourself up at a still more modest price, go for the giant, plate-sized pancakes ($5), which come in piping hot stacks, with fruit both on top and in the batter, plus a tennis-ball-sized lump of fresh butter.

From time to time locals worry that the Pork Store might be taken over and changed, or somehow turned into one of the chain stores that seem to be taking over this famous bohemian crossroads, where so much took place in the 1960s and 1970s. Don't hold your breath, but do try the Pork Store before something untoward happens, like yet another Ben and Jerry's.

Thep Phanom Thai Cuisine

Once upon a time this was a corner shop in a downtrodden neighborhood. For the past fifteen years, however, Thep Phanom's square, sunny dining room has spread joy and aromas along the block. Bedecked with Victorian and Thai bric-a-brac, it's presided over by one of those vast Thai murals, where small angels from Thai mythology fly around bringing good vibes to hungry diners in paradise. Thep Phanom means "angels," so that must be why Phonchai and Patsame Wongsengam's place is always packed. Or maybe it's because world-recognized chefs like Delfina's Craig Stoll call it "the best Thai food in the universe."

Cost $20–40

Address 400 Waller St at Fillmore
☎ 415/431-2526
Open Daily 5.30–10.30pm
Transportation 6, 7, 22, 66, 71, N
Accepts All major credit cards

A central table deals with the inevitable birthdays, and beaming waiters bring cakes and belt "Happy Birthday" with un-Thai-like gusto. Smaller tables line the edges of the room, and there's a corner nook with a bar table where people wait with drinks and snacks. Thai salads of minced chicken, shrimp, and cashews ($7.95), or beef and green papaya ($9.95), are carnivals for the tastebuds. It's always worth checking the fish catch: deep-fried whole tilapia or seasonal catfish (both $13.95) come arched in ecstasy, their scales decorously crisped in a spicy-sour ginger sauce—though it must be said tilapia stands up to the ordeal less robustly. The paksa vehoh ($10.95) translates as "birds of paradise," and is twin quails marinated in garlic and pepper, then fried and clad in a superb spicy and sour sauce. The fanciful names of some Thep creations are classical allusions: the Shy Lady ($11.95), for example, refers to the modesty of Thai beauties, yet turns out to be stuffed jumbo prawns with crab, pan-fried in egg batter on sautéed cabbage!

The wine list makes surprising reading: prices are pleasantly low, and there are food-enhancing flowery Gewurztraminers (from $24). An herbaceous Frog's Leap Sauvignon Blanc is $7 a glass, and so are a dozen or so nicely chosen Chardonnays. The final check is also pleasant. That said, it helps to be in love or addicted to people-watching, since you can't hear what anyone at your own table is saying; communication is mainly through soulful glances or squeals. All the more reason to concentrate on the food, at the city's best Thai.

South

SoMa & South Beach

p.233

Potrero Hill & Bernal Heights

p.255

The Mission

p.275

The Castro & Noe Valley

p.309

The Sunset & West Portal

p.335

SoMa & South Beach

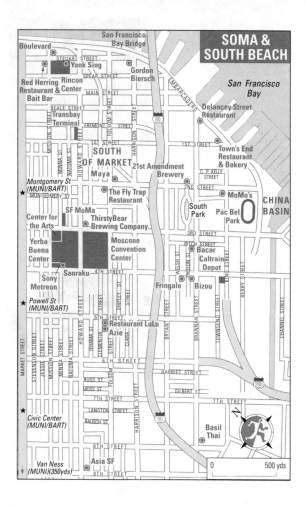

SOMA & SOUTH BEACH

San Francisco Bay Bridge

Boulevard

STEUART STREET

Yank Sing

Gordon Biersch

SPEAR STREET

Red Herring Restaurant & Bait Bar

Rincon Center

MAIN STREET

EMBARCADERO

San Francisco Bay

BEALE STREET

Transbay Terminal

FREMONT STREET

FOLSOM STREET

Delancey Street Restaurant

MISSION ST

HOWARD ST

NATOMA ST

1ST STREET

HARRISON STREET

80

SOUTH OF MARKET

21st Amendment Brewery

Maya

1ST STREET

Town's End Restaurant & Bakery

C. P. KELLY STREET

Montgomery St (MUNI/BART)

MONTGOMERY ST

The Fly Trap Restaurant

2ND STREET

MoMo's

CHINA BASIN

SF MoMa

ThirstyBear Brewing Company

South Park

Pac Bel Park

Center for the Arts

Yerba Buena Center

Moscone Convention Center

3RD STREET

RITCH STREET

Bacar

Sony Metreon

Sanraku

4TH STREET

WELSH ST

SHIPLEY ST

Caltrain Depot

BERRY STREET

KING STREET

CHANNEL STREET

Powell St (MUNI/BART)

Fringale

Bizou

BRYAN STREET

BRANNAN STREET

TOWNSEND STREET

5TH STREET

TEHAMA ST

SHIPLEY ST

CLEMENTINA

CLARA ST

Restaurant LuLu

Azie

MARKET STREET

STEVENSON STREET

JESSIE STREET

MISSION STREET

MINNA STREET

NATOMA STREET

HOWARD STREET

FOLSOM

6TH STREET

HARRIET STREET

BUSS ST

MOSS ST

GILBERT ST

280

7TH STREET

LANGTON STREET

RAUSCH ST

HARRISON STREET

7TH STREET

Civic Center (MUNI/BART)

80

Basil Thai

N

8TH STREET

Van Ness (MUNI)(350yds)

Asia SF

9TH STREET

0   500 yds

21st Amendment Brewery

South Beach is still nudging its way into an ever-shrinking Bay, despite the dotcom collapse, and PacBell Park is hopping throughout baseball season, so 21st Amendment's future seems assured. It's also secure, of course, because of the 21st Amendment to the US Constitution, which repealed Prohibition. More immediately, its future success is a given because of the $2.50 home-brewed pints, and the amazingly generous "happy hours" (2.30–6pm). On game nights the bar is packed solid with a mixture of suits and hardcore fans in Giants caps, all bellying up to a rather attractive wooden bar surrounded by windows. The 21st Amendment pulls its own fans in from blocks away, but if you don't happen to be heading to the stadium you might want to think twice about trying to get here on a game night.

Cost $12–30
Address 563 2nd St at Brannan
℡ 415/369-0900
Open Mon–Fri 11.30am–midnight, Sat & Sun noon–1am
Transportation 15, 42, N
Accepts MasterCard, Visa

This being colorful San Francisco, the lunch menu pitches a tiger shrimp and curried couscous plate ($12.50) as well as more usual bar fare, like burgers. Light snacks include something called sweet potato straws ($3.95), which are a Caribbean version of fries, as well as proper "hearty" fries ($3.95), and marinated, house-cured olives ($3). Caribbean-trained chef Eddy Blyden kicks off dinner with "21 A signature sweet potato soup" ($6.50), which is rich and warming, and comes with an inspirational walnut and blue cheese topping. Salads include arugula with baby spinach, pears, and Parmesan ($6.50). All the burgers (from $9) use top-quality Niman Ranch beef; there's one with Creole sauce, which is appropriate, since Blyden is a veteran of Creole cuisine. There's even a veggie burger ($7.95) with Swiss cheese, red onion, and southern barbecue sauce. Dinner dishes (from $11–15.95) add fish, pasta, hearty stews, steaks, chicken, and chops to all of the above.

Don't forget the hidden dining area behind the bar. Alternatively, take yourself upstairs to the loft of this echoing barn, where you'll be left in peace and quiet with a pint of light South Park Blonde or a bitey Anniversary Ale—until they play the anthem and the first pitch gets thrown in, that is. Better yet, wait until the Giants are away. When they're in town, all barstools are spoken for.

PAN-ASIAN

AsiaSF

🍴 Everyone's welcome at this SoMa hot spot where dressing for dinner doesn't involve dressing much at all. Or not for the diva "waitresses," anyway—though this is way too humble a word for the magnificent creatures in tottering heels who deign to bring food to your table. These queenly figures are also liable to leap onto the Chinese-red catwalk under the pulsing strobe lights, and sing along with Sister Sledge or Donna Summer, before condescending to return to their adoring fans—and diners.

Cost $25–65

Address 201 9th St at Howard
☎ 415/281-3818
Open Daily 5–10pm
Transportation 12, 19, 14, 42, BART Civic Center
Accepts All major credit cards except Diners

Decor is bamboo and shoji screens, while the menu is hiply pan-Asian with Latino tweaks, as in Asia-dillas ($8.75), a soft taco sandwich of tea-smoked duck with cilantro and sun-dried cherries, plus crème fraîche. Porcupines ($9) are scallops, shrimp, and water chestnuts, all rolled in bundles of cellophane noodles and deep-fried; it's an irresistible mix of crunch and munch, and comes with sweet-sour plum sauce. Firecrackers ($8.75) are fresh salmon spring rolls and mushroom spring rolls, dished up with a pickled ginger and Chinese mustard sauce. Among the main courses, "Baby Got Back" ribs ($15.50) arrive with delicately julienned carrots, while blackened tuna sashimi ($16.50) and the ahiburger ($11.50) come marinated in ginger. Grilled halibut ($17.50) is steamed in black bean and ginger with Asian broccoli, shiitakes, and snow peas over rice, while grilled shrimp and herbed salad ($12.95) teases the taste-buds with Chinese cabbage, cilantro, Thai basil, toasted coconut, and chopped peanuts in Thai chile vinaigrette. For a truly decadent dessert, try the brandy-flambéed and phyllo-wrapped baby banana split in macadamia nut brittle, served with chocolate and caramel on coconut and vanilla scoops ($12.50). All these dishes are available on the three-course Ménage à Trois menu ($29.95).

As for the beverages, this is a chance to sip the most extravagant cocktails in town. Pink Limo is for "those who believe in love and having a good time," while Bacardi with cranberry and lemon also comes with "a splash of storm." If you enjoyed Robin Williams and Nathan Lane in the movie *The Bird Cage*, this is the night out for you.

Azie

To say that SoMa's glittering high-tech heyday related to the year 2001 in roughly the same way that spit does to a stovetop might be overstating the case. Although lights have gone out all over SoMa, they still blaze at this block of Folsom any night of the week, and those stretch limos haven't all been garaged. Azie is a temple of transcendental calm, even though it's a sibling to LuLu's, the legendary hopping hot spot next door. The fascinating menu features cross-genre food, but with a uniquely fusion sensibility.

Cost $25–75

Address 826 Folsom St at 5th
☎ 415/538-0918
Open Mon–Wed 5.30–10pm, Thurs 5.30–10.30pm, Fri & Sat 5–11.30pm, Sun 5–10pm
Transportation 12, 27, BART Powell St
Accepts All major credit cards except Diners

FUSION

Azie is both an imposing and escapist spot to bring a guest. Cass Calder Smith's high-concept interior arranges booths with playful blinds and curtains around a central pavilion. Glamorous hostesses serve flashy cocktails, like Mandarin Cosmopolitans, and there's a partying soundtrack in the background. The live DJ is less in evidence than he was, however, and some of manager Judy Denton's flights of fancy are now a little closer to earth than they were. Azie no longer serves special caviars, for instance, but the famous "Nine Bites" appetizer ($18) is still there: thrillingly presented on a series of delicate, gorgeously translucent plates of every hue, it includes exquisite items such as a miniature sweet-sour gingered soup, a Quilcene oyster wearing a tiny hat of caviar, a slither of carpaccio of Thai-spiced beef, a dollop of raw mahi mahi, and sushi of rare and exotic provenance. The tasting menu is no more, but you can still get Azie's legendary one-day duck salad ($20), tossed with barbecued tropical fruit, and the lobster ($20) is still divinely delicious. A typical faux-sushi platter ($13) is a sandwich of fresher-than-fresh tuna topped with a wasabe dressing and rice. Granita ($20) comes with a series of tapioca, caramel, and mint sauces.

Presentation is still uppermost, but Azie's "attitude" seems to have been dropped along with the prices, which have shrunk to a reasonable twentysomething for main dishes, with a $29.95 tasting menu of three daily-changing courses. The fun and fabulous element is still here, however, and Azie seems to be going the right way about surviving as a sophisticated fantasy.

Bacar

CALIFORNIAN

🍴 Bacar is one of the city's epic stages, a fantasyland of beauty and bliss that's a law unto itself. A triple-deck of bars, an entire wall of wine, and Generation "Next" hipness blazes from its huge windowed facade by night. Not that it hasn't been a bumpy ride: the million-bucks-over-budget conversion of this warehouse was timed for the dotcom heyday, but got held up. As NASDAQ took its celebrated swan dive, Bacar

Cost	$20–75

Address 448 Brannan St at 3rd
🚇 415/904-4100
Open Mon–Sat 5.30pm–1am, Sun 4.30–11pm
Transportation 15, 30, 45, N
Accepts All major credit cards except Diners

(from the Latin for wine goblet) was struggling to find its feet. For all that, chef Arnold Eric Wong's restaurant is worth the wait, and the hype.

The three-course lunch special ($19) begins with one of the greatest winter soups ever invented: a double dose of roast chestnut and Jerusalem artichoke that's rich, warming, and delicious. Caesar salad ($8.50) may sound banal, yet it's very possible to get it wrong; this one is half a crisp romaine heart crowned with giant Parmesan flakes, and has a citric bite, an anchovy tang, and a smooth coating—you want to eat another on the spot. The other starters are equally come-hither, from smoked Idaho trout ($11) to spinach salad ($9). For a munch on the run, a natural beefburger on focaccia ($9) leaves the mesquite grill with red onion rings and pickles plus a southwestern whiff, while smoke-tinged pizzas emerge sensationally from the wood oven; choices range from Portobellini, with onion and gruyère ($12), to Serrano ham with asparagus and Manchego cheese ($12). Among main courses, pan-roasted mahi mahi ($15) comes on a little bed of quinoa, and is encrusted with roasted plantains—all very lipsmacking. Skirt of beef ($24) arrives with ratatouille amid a wanton tangle of onion rings, accessorized with raisin, almond, and spices.

Of several great desserts, the raisin sorbet in a five-petal sugar cookie ($5), and the too-intense—but great—Valrhona chocolate and Armagnac pot de crème with almond cookies ($5) will blow you away. No, the $19 lunches and $29 dinners will not always be available, but the dishes will be, and they offer some of the most interesting new food around. What's more, you can park on the street.

Basil Thai

THAI

"We're forward, we're very Thai, and we're here!" proclaims Basil's menu, which ought to advertise Basil Thai's vaunted "Thaicentricity", and hint that in this city of a few hundred Thai restaurants, this one marches to a different beat. Basil outstrips SoMa for cool—it even throws Momokawa sake tastings. The purple flapping canopy outside, the clubby bar with midnight-blue shelving and a glowing wall of glass bricks, and the vintage prints and comfy French cafe chairs are all the work of a Thai architectural student, Todd Sirimongkolvit. Like the glamorous staffers, the menu has picked up masses of Western influences, but remains Thai at core.

Cost $6–35

Address 1175 Folsom St at 8th
ⓣ 415/552-8999
Open Mon–Thurs
11.30am–2.45pm & 5–10pm,
Fri 11.30am–2.45pm &
5–10.30pm, Sat 5–10.30pm,
Sun 5–10pm
Transportation 12, 19
Accepts All major credit cards
except Diners

Purists complain that the dishes are moving away from their Thai roots and using more Western ingredients. But even if you don't find their fiery marinated calamari ($6) on every Bangkok street corner, at least not with sweetly sour tamarind vinaigrette, that's hardly a fault. The kao pode tod ($6), or corn and bean cake fritters with cucumber and the same tamarind dipping sauce, may be unusual in Thailand, but you'll probably love them anyway. But there's plenty of tradition here too, from green papaya salad ($6.75) and the ubiquitous larb gai ($7.50), which comes with an intense toasted rice flavor, to yum shian hai ($6), or delicious clear noodle rolls in chile and lime. A subtle fusion influence is discernible in the wok work: golden bean cakes ($8.75) are sautéed with wine and chile; and mussels inferno ($11.50) are wok-steamed in chile and lemongrass, and acquire a luscious coating of cream from the sauce. Skirt steak ($11.50) gets a peanut-coconut comforter, while barbecued pork ($11) is skewered on bamboo with pineapple. Fried ice cream, with its melting inside and burnt crisp exterior, is one dessert (all $6) to catch, as is the Thai coffee granita with cream; but the most exotic of all is the water chestnut with tapioca and coconut-fruit ice cream.

It's hard to argue that any of this doesn't work—either the edible fantasies or the exquisite decor. Happily, Basil has garnered large numbers of rave reviews in its few years of business, and the crowds won't stop coming.

Bizou

Laura Keller borrowed the name from the French slang for "kiss." When she opened, back in the mid-1990s, she painted the outside putty yellow then plastered the name in bold lettering that reminds you of those Provençal bar advertisements for Pastis on bottles and ashtrays. Bizou may be plain, but it somehow manages to look really French, right down to the window boxes. Inside, the high-ceilinged room with its dark wood and mirrored bar is alive with warmth and conviviality. Keller's food is both Californian and French, with local ingredients and flashes of native brilliance. Sunny service is a given here, on the button but never fussy.

Cost $30–60

Address 598 4th St at Brannan
☎ 415/543-2222
Open Sun–Wed 5.30–10pm, Thurs–Sat 5.30–10.30pm
Transportation 15, 30, 45, N
Accepts MasterCard, Visa

Batter-fried green beans with a dipping sauce ($6.75) is one of the biggest hits here—people dream of them. When Dungeness crab is in season, however, start with the crabcakes ($7.75). Large-flaked and minimally interfered with, they're lightly and simply held together with diced peppers and a smear of egg—almost a crab salad patty. Asian pear, Gorgonzola, and frisée salad with walnuts ($9.50) is familiar yet delicate, with the right balance of sweet, sour, crunchy, creamy, bitter, and tangy; it'll spoil you for other salads for a while. The tender scallops with seasonal vegetables and rosemary ($23) is excellent, but of all Keller's trademark dishes, beef cheeks Sainte Menehoud ($18.50) wins the prize. Long-simmered, and served under a generous coverlet of horseradish with a tuft of watercress, they're decadently luscious; they also alter seasonally, and come springtime they're wearing a mustard sauce and new potatoes. Desserts are also superb: you'll want to frame the panna cotta ($7) with a muted thyme-raspberry coulis; while the vacherin ($7) of minimal meringue and Rubenesque ice cream is redeemed by gorgeous toasted almonds and bittersweet chocolate sauce. A crisp, unpretentious 1998 Chablis ($40) is a compromise to suit every dish.

When SoMa was hip-hopping with dotcoms, Bizou was at the heart of the happening scene. Then, with the downfall of the start-ups, the glitz and glamour evanesced. But you'll see no fall-off here, and Bizou remains a Bay Area fixture. It's helped by easy street parking.

Boize Boulevard

If you want to criticize San Francisco's number one dining destination, go right ahead. Prices are sky-high and service sometimes glacially polite, while the atmosphere in the belle époque surroundings of the Audifredd Building gets so rarified that you feel like Bruce Willis meeting his wife over dinner in "The Sixth Sense": forgotten. But if you can get over all that, you'll remember Boulevard's hauntingly wonderful food forever. Chef Nancy Oakes used to run a great Sunset District diner called L'Avenue, but she unveiled this *fin-de-siècle* shrine to nouvelle-Cal cuisine after teaming up with restaurant designer Pat Kuleto.

Cost $30–80

Address 1 Mission St at Steuart
☎ 415/543-6084
Open Mon–Wed 11.30am–2pm & 5.30–10pm, Thurs & Fri 11.30am–2pm & 5.30–10.30pm, Sat 5.30–10.30pm, Sun 5.30–10pm
Transportation Market St lines, N, BART Embarcadero
Accepts All major credit cards except Diners

Oakes may not have been first to create the teetering tower of tartare approach to raw fish starters, but she was an early pioneer of New-Cal carpaccios. The wild king or coho salmon ($14) and ahi tuna in wasabe-cucumber soy ($14) thrust vertically towards heaven; dressings vary according to season, but they come with orange and lemon, abundant fennel (Oakes is all about abundance), and kicky fennel crisps. Seafood salads (from $15) come with citrus-ruby grapefruit or tangerine; such a sweet, green, crunchy, combo of ingredients might be called a Boulevard trademark. Bay Area fish are plentiful and their simplicity is preserved in a lightly grilled and subtly presented sand dab or petrale dishes (around $30). Sonoma Liberty duck breast à la Provençale ($26) comes stuffed with Lucques olives and German butterball potatoes. Wood-roasted and grilled lamb chops ($29.75) lounge sensuously upon a simmered onion bed with gratin and greens. A Napoleon of potato cakes ($18) is a mound of crispy latkes layered with fluffy amber-hued mash and surrounded by a butternut squash and wild mushrooms in truffle glaze—an odd dish but it works. If you can envision a dessert version of this theme of textural contrasts, it's angel-food coffee cake with coffee ice cream and rum ($8.75).

Oakes' food is well worth the expense. She remains the one to beat among local chefs, the icon others emulate for her generous way with plain ingredients—a kind of Alice Waters with more effusion and less philosophy. Book well ahead: this restaurant is one of the classics, maybe *the* classic.

Cosmopolitan Cafe

Out-of-towners often find themselves at a loose end in this area, thanks to the proximity of so many hotels. But until Steven Levine came along, the Rincon Center had a reputation as a kind of Bermuda Triangle for the unwary restaurant entrepreneur. Formerly of Sonoma's Freestyle, Levine has turned around this once-doomed space adroitly. There's a central bar, a visible kitchen, a balconied upstairs, and a menu that offers all Levine's trademarks. It brings in devoted regulars, and this is now a well-established hot spot.

Cost $15–50

Address Rincon Center, 121 Spear St between Howard and Mission
☎415/543-4001
Open Mon–Fri 11.15am–10.30pm, Sat 5.30–10.30pm
Transportation Market Street lines, 1, F, BART Embarcadero
Accepts All major credit cards

Levine glories in the reputation of being first chef in town to launch appetizer plates that feature the same star ingredient in a trio of different versions. For instance, a holy trinity of asparagus, wrapped in tenderest tempura with a dab of sweet hot mustard and ponzu sauce, in aioli, or else as creamy potage, or else a crab in three shockingly tasty and varying bites—cake, phyllo-ed, bisque—and all of it just going to prove that enough isn't as good as a feast, a feast is generally much, much better. The sautéed goat cheese gnocchi are also worth crossing town for, their divine puffiness brought down to earth with morel mushrooms plus endamame and a peppery pesto with crunchy walnut pieces ($8 at lunch, $16 for dinner entree). The grilled Niman pork chop is another stunner, inch thick and besieged by clouds of jalapeno-spiced Yukon gold mashed potato, diced chioggia beets, and watercress slaw ($19.50), and there's something equally imaginative yet satisfyingly homey about the semolina-encrusted crabcakes ($23.50), the lavishly peppered ahi tuna ($21), and the roast chicken and flank steak entrees: all seriously generous in portions. Wine? The Murphy Goode Sauvignon Blanc comes in a convenient and reasonable $10 half-bottle and takes care of most non-steak needs.

As for dessert, the Tahitian vanilla malt shake with warm chocolate chunk cookies ($7) has become a legend in many a diner's lunchtime…and for those who aren't man (or woman) enough to take the calories and crave a cocktail, there's always Berry Cosmopolitan, a rosily flushed glass aswim with fruit and a-tingle with fumes ($7).

Delancey Street Restaurant

Coming to this pleasant waterfront spot, with its glorious close-up view of the Bay Bridge, has long been a feel-good thing to do, thanks to Mimi Silbert, the widow of late Delancey Street Foundation crusader John Maher. In a short but heroic life, Maher did much to rehabilitate the homeless, including those with drug and alcohol addictions and sometime-occupants of the city's jails.

Cost	$10–30
Address	600 Embarcadero at Brannan
☎	415/512-5179
Open	Tues–Fri 11am–11pm, Sat & Sun 10am–11pm
Transportation	42, N
Accepts	All major credit cards except Diners

CALIFORNIAN

Unfortunately, he died young, but Mimi energetically continues the live/work complex he founded, where the down and out learn how to start over again. Ten years ago she launched this remarkable restaurant, which trains some of the Foundation's residents in restaurant management, including cooking and serving meals. Some of the city's most distinguished chefs pitch in by planning the menu of homey fare with multi-ethnic flavors. Delancey Street shines with fresh flowers, fruit, light and cheer, and has tables outside. It's almost always busy, and reservations are a must for Sunday brunch.

Sometimes the food's a bit erratic, and the service has occasional gaps, but patrons don't mind because the food fosters benign feelings. In fact, the trainee waiters are perhaps the best thing about Delancey—friendly to a fault but never smarmy. For dinner, a long, eclectic list of starters includes potato latkes ($5.95), spanakopita ($4.95), Hawaiian-style maki rolls ($5.95), and very tasty quesadillas ($3.25) containing either cheese and veggies, or seafood. Lavishly presented lamb and beef dishes include rare beef au jus ($13.95), crown roast ($13.95), and rib-eye steaks ($13.95). But you're pretty well home and dry with any of the rotisserie dishes. Chocoholics should make a beeline straight to the Snickers pie ($4.95), which is Mimi's own invention. It's a non-traditional cheese-cake—with a baked Graham-cracker and butter base—filled with a very rich and cakey chocolate fudge, topped with Snickers bars, and finished with cream cheese and entirely superfluous chocolate-cream drizzles. It's a dieter's nightmare that defies you to resist.

Delancey Street is a fine restaurant and an even better idea; San Franciscans are proud it has caught on in other cities. Unusually, they offer high tea—with a selection of 44 teas—at the Crossroads cafe and bookstore, down the alley behind, at 699 Delancey Street.

CALIFORNIAN

The Fly Trap Restaurant

Is there such a thing as a local Bay Area cuisine? Well, there's certainly such a thing as nineteenth-century Gold Rush food, simple dishes that miners looked for whenever they came to town. By tradition, they even enjoyed one of them—Hangtown Fry—when facing the gallows. Most of San Francisco's ancient specialties survive in ancient restaurants like Sam's Grill or the Old Clam House, but they can also be sampled at this attractive, retro spot, where the name is far older than its digs on Folsom Street. With its long bar and handsome, clubby feel, and with chef Glen Tinsley's exuberant, no-nonsense food, the Fly Trap is popular with out-of-towners, so you'll need to book ahead.

Cost $15–50

Address 606 Folsom St at 2nd

☏ 415/243-0580

Open Mon–Thurs 11.30am–9pm, Fri 11.30am–9.30pm, Sat 5–9.30pm

Transportation 12, 15, BART Montgomery St

Accepts All major credit cards except Diners

Start with a bowl of steamed manila clams ($7.75), or a spicy dish of Prince Edward Island mussels ($7.75) served with sausage chunks and tomato purée. Soups are homey and warming: the corn chowder ($3.50) has nice chunky pieces, and there's a delicious pumpkin soup with goat cheese topping ($3.50). Celery Victor ($7.50) is one of Tinsley's signatures, a real old-fashioned starter of poached celery in vinaigrette with hard-boiled eggs and anchovies crisscrossed on top. The Bay Area's number one fish is petrale ($15.75); this mild-fleshed sole is given a bit of zip with Parmesan crumb topping, lemon, and lots of capers, while salmon ($16.50) is finished with asparagus, roast fingerlings, a tuft of watercress, and beurre blanc. Hangtown Fry ($13.25) is essentially an oyster omelet with a ragged heap of fries. Other popular choices include veal liver with bacon, onions, and garlic mashed potatoes ($16), a hearty coq au vin ($16.25), and rib-eye steak ($17.75). Desserts ($6) include apple crisps, or mocha custard in a small crock.

The lack of refrigeration and reliance on local ingredients back in the mid-nineteenth century may have limited the menu in old San Francisco kitchens. But the Fly Trap is a good place to get a sense of how simple and fresh those ingredients really were. As for the odd name—leave that to the long explanation on the menu; no flies buzz around Fly Trap now.

Fringale

While San Francisco restaurants always favour yellow walls, from palest butter and lemon sorbet to sunshine or maize, Fringale's are a soft gold that lightens the mood, swells the room, and helps make Gerald Hirigoyen's restaurant into a holy grail for foodies. Chef Hirigoyen's own path has been golden, too, and Fringale has enjoyed a glow since it opened, way back before the here-today-dotgone-tomorrow era, when SoMa was still off the beaten track. Now it is surrounded by high-flying competition, but it remains the toniest of bistros, and is always on top ten lists.

Cost $18–65
Address 570 4th St at Brannan
☎ 415/543-0573
Open Mon–Fri 11.30am–3pm & 5.30–10.30pm, Sat 5.30–10.30pm
Transportation 9, 15, 45, BART Powell St
Accepts All major credit cards except Diners

The clientele is mostly San Franciscans treating visitors or looking after favorite relations. Diners may feel a bit deafened and elbowed at peak time, but the mood is upbeat. Hirigoyen's food is French-Basque with new-Basque splashes, from cherries in red wine soup—spiced with port, vanilla, star anise, and citrus—to his famous pork tenderloin confit and chicken with couscous. Some say he is preaching a new Basque cuisine, with old and new eclectic classics. Bass on a fava bean blanket with fennel and leeks in aioli and tapenade ($18), or braised osso buco done "comme il faut" ($18), are two worthy examples. And there are simple appetizers like mushroom ravioli ($10). Hirigoyen's signature pork tenderloin confit ($18) is usually—or should be—juicy and rich in sweet milk solids. It goes brilliantly with the cabbage, apple marmalade, and onion confit, though on occasions it has seemed dry. Duck confit ($19) comes in a warm mess of tasty green lentils and is succulent. Some accompaniments are great, some erratic. For dessert, lemon roll with whipped cream and pistachios ($6), and coffee and Armagnac parfait ($6), are both sweet and alcoholic.

Service is always excellent, and there's a high buzz at all times. The only flies in this ointment are the cramped seating and the recent hikes in the prices—especially the wines—at a point when other places are dropping theirs. But no doubt you could argue that they had long been charitably low.

BAR MENU

Gordon Biersch

This landmark brewpub, begun by brew-master Dan Gordon and his partner Dean Biersch, is popular for German lager-style craft brews that run the gamut from Blond Bock and Pilsner to Golden Export, Märzen and Dunkel. But Gordon Biersch is as much about its scene as its beer. It's a chaotic and seething social Valhalla for fratboys, jocks and the few surviving dotcommers, and part of a rapidly growing chain. The *Washington Post* recently gave the

Cost $10–30
Address 2 Harrison St at Embarcadero
☎ 415/243-8246
Open Mon & Sun 11.30am–11pm, Tues–Thurs 11.30am–midnight, Fri & Sat 11.30am–1am
Transportation 42, N
Accepts All major credit cards except Diners

newest Gordon Biersch branch in Washington, D.C. a rotten review for fries. Perhaps they didn't follow the recipe assiduously, because a *New York Times* baseball correspondent at Pac Bell Park stadium spent more column inches on the fries than on a four-run Giants rally.

The chat is unintelligible, but that doesn't matter because the beer is hoppy and the parsley-sprinkled garlic fries ($4.50) divinely tasty. They're made in the proper way: skillet-fried in the correct mix of olive oil and vegetable oil, with lashings of coarse-chopped garlic and kosher salt, plus liberal sprinklings of fresh chopped parsley. Beyond fries, finger foods start with artichokes in aioli ($5.95), beer-broiled prawns ($6.95), barbecued ribs in Märzen sauce ($7.95), smoky Portobello mushroom skewers with polenta and salsa ($5.25), and chicken wings ($7.95). It's a little more than mere tailgate Super Bowl fare. Main dishes are also invasively beery here and there, and start with trusty wood-fired pizzas ($7.95–9.95) sporting recherché toppings such as shrimp and goat cheese. They continue with herbed rotisserie chicken ($13.95) and the equally popular hangar steak with horseradish smashed potatoes in beer-mustard gravy ($15.95); all the gravy and even some of the mayo is beer-enriched. Cheesecake ($5.95), with fresh berry purée, but no beer, leads desserts. But who's going to get that far?

Gordon Biersch's fries even won the concession for feeding gourmet junk food to the masses who sit on the open-air bleachers in Pac Bell Park, just down the Embarcadero. So it's not just *New York Times* correspondents who can enjoy them, and baseball-lovers can now keep happy for hours on a wholesome diet of lager and fries.

Maya

Let's face it: not everybody will cry "Let's go Mexican!" when invited to pick an upscale night out, no matter how fond they may be of fish tacos. But Maya shares about as much with your average taqueria or tamale parlor as Bouvelard does with Burger King. In this haven South of Market, Richard Sandoval and chef de cuisine Adolfo Larreynaga illustrate the complex and rich diversity of Mexican food. The setting is restrained and mutedly sumptuous, with deep, burnt-orange walls accented with cleverly lit Mayan masks, and service that's always correct, and never stuffy. Unlike nearby haunts, Maya provides a soothing environment, with lots of space for private conversations.

Cost $15–50

Address 303 2nd St at Folsom
☎ 415/543-2928
Open Mon–Thurs
11.30am–2pm & 5–10pm, Fri
11.30am–2pm & 5–11pm, Sat
5–11pm, Sun 4–9pm
Transportation 10, 12, 15
Accepts All major credit cards except Diners

MEXICAN

They call their free mini-quesadilla appetizers "botanas," and pass them out with the tequila cocktails, just as they used to in Mexican or Spanish places in the good old days. Fish tacos are different from the usual too; their tacos de atun ($10.50) enfold neat squares of that-day-fresh, luridly red, barely-seared tuna, and are topped with sesame seed salsa and pomegranate sauce. They're delightful, and so is the creamy roasted corn soup ($7.95), served—like many items on the menu—with a huitlacoche dumpling swimming in the middle. Mahi mahi ceviche is tomato-heavy, but delicious ($9), as are corn quesadillas stuffed with Oaxacan cheese and zucchini blossoms ($7.95). After that fine start, the entrees go one better, starting with a cordera en mole de rosas ($21.95), which is grilled lamb sirloin with roasted chard, baby heirloom beets, and a rose-petal mole. This may just be the finest place for a mole in the city, so check out the mole poblano ($18.50), a chicken breast with plantains and cilantro rice. A pyramid of grilled skirt steak is served in a black bean purée ($18.95), while a conventional roast salmon comes with a chayote gratin ($21.50).

Too bad the desserts can't keep up, although there's a *muy rico* chocolate pastel de tres leches cake ($6.50), covered in fresh fruit and homemade ice cream. But why not go for an after-dinner tequila or mescal instead?

AMERICAN

MoMo's

When Pac Bell Park opened a few years ago, with a tremendous shout of millennial joy, the citizens of San Francisco were stuck with the problem of where to eat before or after a Giants baseball game. Pac Bell Park's own parsley-garlic fries and endamame sushi stalls are by no means inestimable, but relatively few eateries have opened nearby. MoMo's, however, is an obvious choice for ball fans. Indeed, it's almost the only choice, unless you prefer brewpubs or diners. Clubbily middle-of-the-road in service and decor, it's casual: you can wear whatever you like, and it might be a good idea not to be averse to baseball caps and beer bellies in shorts. The owner is genial English emigrant Peter Osborne, former maitre d' at the Washington Square Bar & Grill, where he ran the bar with author Frank McCourt's brother Michael.

Cost $25–50
Address 760 2nd St at Willie Mays Plaza
☎ 415/227-8660
Open Mon–Thurs 11.30am–10pm, Fri 11.30am–11pm, Sat 10.30am–11pm, Sun 10.30am–10pm
Transportation 15, N
Accepts All major credit cards except Diners

Trying to find anything experimental on the menu would be a stretch. MoMo's steak ($18.95), which weighs at least a kilo, is served on thickened pan-reduction gravy. Scalloped gratin potatoes only demonstrate how hard they are to prepare for multitudes, so go with the fries ($4.25) or reliable old onion rings ($4.25). Fish is expensive, ranging from the high teens up to $23.95 for a handsome wild king-salmon roast. Some of the meat entrees, however, like the barbecued baby-back ribs ($18.95), cost less than the fish, which is a puzzler in this city. Do wealthier people prefer fish? If you're here for lunch, or not in the mood for a heavy dinner, opt for Caesar salad ($8.50), which has enough lemon, anchovy, and Parmesan tang to please the most astringent palate. For dessert, raspberry crisp ($6.50) or cheesecake ($6.50) are pleasant enough.

Baseball fans, like soccer fans elsewhere in the world, tend to be plain folks with ten-year-old kids in tow. But here in San Francisco, if you offer fans a choice they'd just as soon choose sushi as a hamburger—maybe even their kids might choose the sushi, for that matter. So it takes more than just a two-pound steak or two-inch chop to please a baseball fan in San Francisco; it can also take parking, and MoMo's has valet parking.

Red Herring Restaurant and Bait Bar

Red Herring fills a definite need. It's the sort of place where a single person visiting town on business can feel comfortable, especially if they want to enjoy a baseball game in a bar while eating something and chatting with other roadweary strangers. Stylish and low-key, but affable for a hotel bar, it's close to downtown, and nicely decked out with brick, Tiffany-style lamps, a long and luscious wooden bar, friendly staff, and a show-off fireplace for roasting steaks and chickens. With its views of San Francisco Bay, the Bait Bar is also a perfect place to enjoy a plate of crabcakes and a cocktail.

Cost $25–50

Address 155 Steuart St at Mission
☎ 415/495-6500
Open Mon–Wed 11.30am–3pm & 5.30–10pm, Thurs & Fri 11.30am–3pm & 5.30pm–midnight, Sat 5.30pm–midnight
Transportation Market St lines, N, BART Embarcadero
Accepts All major credit cards

Portions are small, but Red Herring has a number of redeeming points, which begin with pleasant service at a lavishly stocked drinks bar, and fresh oysters and ceviches at the Raw and Not Bar. The Bait Bar menu shows attractive variety, too. Among the starters, crabcakes ($10.50) are a well-seasoned duo, if on the minute side, and come garnished with strawberry-papaya salsa and chipotle aioli. The Clam Digger chowder ($6.95) with Yukon gold potatoes and bacon is a good warmer-upper. Things get more high-fallutin' with the fire-braised mussels ($9.75), doused in tomatoes, basil, garlic, and jalapeno, while the baby lobster in mango cones with avocado and spicy tobiko caviar, or flying fish roe ($12.50), is downright pretentious. Neither can be faulted, but if you want to stick closer to turf, the cheeseburger ($9.95), made with high-quality Niman Ranch beef and "fully dressed in French fries," is filling. Hungrier still? Forgo that Bait Bar menu for the full dinner menu of hefty steaks, pork loin, and roast chicken. Dinner entrees start in the high teens and top out at Red's rib-eye steak with onion rings ($23.95), a travelling salesman's classic.

The wine list includes bottles such as Bonny Doon's Pacific Rim Riesling ($29), as well as South American varietals; glasses run from $5.50 for Chilean Malbecs. Too often, American bars are lonely or sad; that's not the case here, where anyone can fall into conversation with anyone.

Restaurant LuLu

After Reed Hearon and then Jody Denton—both legends in their lunchtime with too many skillets on the fire—left Restaurant LuLu, this legendary pleasure dome acquired new chef Robert Murphy and worked to hang onto its clientele of roiling young fun-seekers. They come in pursuit of LuLu's exciting vibe, as well as its fabulous wine list, weird but hip decor, fun cocktails and rotisserie food, plus those signature roast

Cost $15–55
Address 816 Folsom St at 4th
☎ 415/495-5775
Open Mon–Thurs & Sun 11.30am–10.30pm, Fri & Sat 11.30am–11.30pm
Transportation 12, 30, 45, 76, BART Powell St
Accepts All major credit cards except Diners

mussels, which were at the vanguard of the "small plates" tapas movement. For a while it appeared that success had gone to LuLu's head: the small plates were as good as ever but prices began crawling skywards, especially for wine, and patrons found the service strangely 'tudey, as they say in San Francisco—meaning it comes with attitude.

So it's nice to report that things have settled down again. And oh, those mussels! Now copied by all of LuLu's rivals—just like LuLu's roast beet salad and fritto misto— they're an example of how one simple but ideal dish can straddle either starter or main course categories, and make a menu. They're fresh, local, priced at $11.95, and a party out on the town can share them. The fruits de mer menu ($23.25) is another feast of love, starring oysters, clams, and prawns; it's not cheap, but there are five types of oyster to pick from. Oysters can also be ordered separately ($2.25 each). Denton's roast beet salad with walnuts and ricotta is a LuLu classic; it comes on an antipasti sampler of three ($13.50), along with a country terrine of olives, duck-liver mousse, and mushrooms, and a leek, goat-cheese, and bacon tart. That famous fritto misto ($11.95) comes with artichokes, fennel, and lemon with aioli. For flavour, wood-oven roasted Portobello mushrooms with polenta ($9.75) comes a close second. Butternut squash gnocchi with sage brown butter ($12.95) is something to get wild about, while the oak-fired rotisserie chicken ($14.95) is a must.

One of the unexpected results of the 2001 dotcom slump was that service mellowed overnight. No more are customers subjected to outrageous 'tude from the GQ models who used to glide amongst them, bearing mile-long wine menus and *noli me tangere* glares. Nowadays you'll practically be seduced by the chummy servers.

Sanraku

It's easy to get some of the best food in town at San Francisco's ballpark. So why is it usually so hard to get good food—any food—inside the city's giant movie-theater multiplexes? Is it because the schlockbusters and thrill-rides attract the young and the penniless? Whatever the reason, moviegoers will be pleased and relieved to find a restaurant they can afford here at the enormous, fif-teen-screen Metreon. Alongside the bou-tiques, game stations, climbing wall and children's play area, Sanraku is a useful option for those who want to eat decent food as well as catch a film.

Cost $8–25

Address 1st floor, Metreon Building, 101 4th St at Mission
☎415/369-6166
Transportation Market St lines, 30, 45, BART Montgomery St
Open Daily 11am–10pm
Accepts All major credit cards except Diners

JAPANESE

The Metreon Sanraku centers on chef Hiro Hattori's long menu of sushi, sashimi, teriyaki, tempura, udon, and donburi, but it also has some fusion dishes. How about a sautéed rib-eye and vegetable roll ($5.75), which comes with ginger glaze and a salad? Or spiced tuna tartare ($6.95) served with mayo in an avocado, which is for all the world like an old-style avocado appetizer? Or a delicious softshell crab with aioli ($7.95)? Chicken curry ($9.25) comes with rice, and it's sort of a shock to find it here, even if curries are popular in Japan. Main dishes include tonkatsu, a pork tenderloin cutlet that's very much like a Midwestern version. Broiled mackerel comes with a wonderfully peppery grated daikon radish ($8.75), or ginger-miso sauce ($9.25). There are any number of good combination bargains and bento box specials, but per-haps the best meal here is the sesame chicken ($9.25), which is a chicken breast marinated in teriyaki then deep fried, and comes with a few bits and pieces of cucumber.

The space on Metreon's ground floor, with its pleasant view of Yerba Buena Gardens, is calming. The owner is also the chef at Sanraku Four Seasons (see p.35), but you'll soon realize that Metreon's Sanraku could hardly be more different from its Sutter Street namesake, which runs a very high-minded menu, and even performs elaborate keiseki meals for special occasions.

ThirstyBear Brewing Company

Taking its name from an escaped Russian circus bear that stole a man's pint, ThirstyBear was the pioneer of the tapas and brewhouse movements, and it's still one of the best. The interior has been carved out of a warehouse, with brick walls left exposed. When they first launched their celebrated fish cheeks tapas dish, one wisecracking beer fan asked a Spanish waitress what had happened to the rest of the fish? "Oh, he have no face now, so nobody love him any more!" she replied. You may want to

Cost S5–25
Address 661 Howard St at 3rd
☎ 415/974-0905
Open Mon–Thurs 11.30am–10.30pm, Fri 11.30am–midnight, Sat noon–midnight
Transportation 14, 15, BART Montgomery St
Accepts All major credit cards except Diners

never eat another cheek after this, but frankly it's a vow you'll soon break—the kokotxas Donostiarra are a Basque classic that nobody resists for long.

Cod or halibut cheeks ($6.75) are first choices: the white slices of fish are marinated then pan-fried in olive oil, sherry, and garlic, and finished with parsley, chile, and lemon. Pan con tomate ($3.95) is big slices of rustic bread rubbed with garlic, tomato, and olive oil, perfect for plugging a raging hunger immediately. Tart, hard, and crumbly Manchego cheese ($4.75) is another great choice, as is the plate of ham with olives ($6.75). Another stalwart is tortilla española ($4.75), the classic Spanish egg and potato omelet, served cold. A number of tasty potato tapas, from patatas al ajillo ($3.95) to papas bravas ($4.75), come out of ThirstyBear's frenzied kitchen. The setas a la plancha ($6.75) are shy little woodland mushrooms, pan-fried. Morcilla and other types of native Spanish sausage come on a mixed chorizo plate ($5.75), while gambas a la plancha ($6.50) are fat crisp-edged prawns, served with their heads on. Escalivada ($6.50) is a dish of roasted vegetables, with onions, peppers, and eggplant slices, all surrounding a roast tomato. Paella ($16) can also be found on the menu, in variations ranging from a seafood version to one made with Serrano ham, sausage, and chicken.

ThirstyBear's co-owner is Princess Ragnhild A. Lorentzen—better known as Raggi—who turns out to be 66th in line to the British throne. You may be less surprised to learn that ThirstyBear is a good (if noisy) spot for a pint after visiting the Museum of Modern Art next door.

Town's End Restaurant and Bakery

Down on San Francisco's southern waterfront and right across from the bay, Town's End would have been in the water a few decades ago. The new neighborhood is still on a bit of an economic rollercoaster, thanks to the dotcom boom and bust, but South Beach has been filling up rapidly since Pac Bell Park arrived, bringing plenty of Giants fans in the baseball season. So for the geeks who are clinging on in readiness for the

Cost	$10–25

Address 2 Townsend St
☎ 415/512-0749
Open Tues–Fri
7.30am–2.30pm, Tues–Thurs
5–9pm, Fri & Sat 5–10pm, Sat
& Sun 8am–2.30pm
Transportation 80, N
Accepts All major credit cards
except Diners

next dotcom boom, Town's End is an absolute godsend when they're desperate for a soy latte with an extra kick of espresso, and a ciabatta all toasty warm from the oven.

There's plenty of room for pleasant outdoor brunching, while inside has enough in the way of modest extra touches to make it a pleasing choice at any time. Don't expect anything exciting; just expect it to be really terrific. Fresh baked goods start with Town's End's rocking good Parmesan breadsticks, which arrive at your table more or less as you do, and are followed by a mixed breadbasket of rolls and pastries, bringing anything from sourdough and cheesy scones to little buns and rye. Brunch is a mixture of these, accompanied by a few frittatas and tortilla dishes. The artichoke frittata ($10.25) and Italian mushroom tortilla ($10.25) are both made with very fresh vegetables, pastrami, and eggs, and there's a credible eggs Benedict ($10.25). The hardworking and popular couple who run this place take a special pride in the pastas, among which the smoked chicken risotto ($11.75) comes with different kinds of porcini and crimini mushrooms. They also deliver a mean polenta grilled with a sauté of mushrooms in Madeira ($11.25), and any of the fetuccine and ravioli dishes are creditable dinner options too. For afters, lots varieties of crêpes ($7), a bread pudding ($5.75), and wonderfully filling waffles await.

The Sunday brunch scene in here is really something else and seems to have sucked in trade from all over town. Even when there isn't a match on, the crowd chews and chows like there's no tomorrow.

Yank Sing

San Franciscans have had a dim sum habit for years. At weekends, dim sum "parlors" are filled with happy families sitting at round tables and eating these rustic, Southern Cantonese "touch the heart" snacks, which are served from passing trolleys. Yank Sing was founded by Alice Chen, an influential business-woman whose downtown dim sum par-lors replaced old-style business lunch venues, becoming the calm, civilized places to nail deals over cups of tea. In other words, dim sum is a kind of social glue that helps keep San Francisco's wheels turning. Yank Sing's old place was on Battery Street, but the Rincon Center—an art deco former post office with WPA murals, an impressive central cascade and glass cases displaying archeological finds—is an ideal downtown niche for Yank Sing's enormous staff and fleets of steaming dim sum trolleys.

Cost $10–25

Address Rincon Center Atrium, 101 Spear St at Mission
☏ 415/957-9300
Open Mon–Fri 11am–3pm, Sat & Sun 10am–4pm
Transportation Market St lines, N, BART Embarcadero
Accepts All major credit cards except Diners

Service and setting are faultless, and there's a reassuring sense of every-thing being in order, with a constantly refilled glass teapot of jasmine tea to wash down the dozens of choices. Those little saucers really stack up once you get going. Smoky duck in sweet-and-sour sauce ($5) comes by the slice. Vegetarian choices include chun guen ($2.75), or spring rolls with pea-vines and mushroom, and cheung fen (from $2.75), or rice noodle rolls filled with sprouts and thread noodles. Noh mei gei ($4.50) are sticky rice dumplings in lotus leaves and something of an acquired taste, while jin dui zei ($2.75) are crispy rice flour balls. Sweet dim sum, like the daan tad ($3.75), or egg tarts, also pass by your table. Yank Sing's simple wu gok ($2.75), or taro dumpling, comes in a vegetarian version here and vies neck and neck with Jasmine Tea Garden's version for "best in town".

The wu gok and the duck are both exquisitely made and presented, and are likely to become favorites. But then everything is as near to per-fect as possible here at this white-cloth sanctuary of immaculate, reliable and reasonably priced dim sum. Yank Sing has another branch at 49 Stevenson Street, just off Market Street, near the Montgomery Street BART station.

Potrero Hill & Bernal Heights

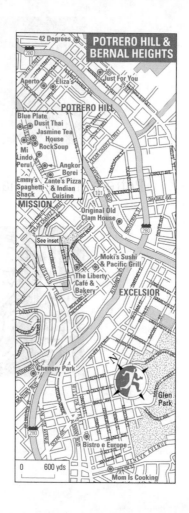

POTRERO HILL & BERNAL HEIGHTS

42 Degrees

Aperto Eliza's Just For You

POTRERO HILL

Blue Plate
Dusit Thai
Jasmine Tea House
RockSoup
Mi Lindo Peru!
Angkor Borei
Emmy's Spaghetti Shack
Zante's Pizza & Indian Cuisine

MISSION

Original Old Clam House

See inset

Moki's Sushi & Pacific Grill

The Liberty Café & Bakery

EXCELSIOR

Chenery Park

Glen Park

Bistro e Europe

0   600 yds

Mom Is Cooking

42 Degrees

How 42 Degrees has managed to remain quite this hot and lively—at a remote location in an industrial wasteland—for more than five years is one of life's great mysteries. On the edge of Potrero Hill, in the neighborhood poetically known as Dogpatch, this shelter of live jazz and industrial chic was converted from a former Esprit outhouse. The

Cost $10–50

Address 499 Illinois St
☎ 415/777-5558
Open Wed–Sat 6–10pm
Transportation 15, 22
Accepts All major credit cards except Diners

location has become less remote since 42 Degrees opened, since this is where many old port buildings were converted into tech-head warrens during the dotcom boom. 42 Degrees fits right into that techie planet, with its cavernous, dim interior and long upper balcony overlooking the water. Romantic lighting takes the edge off the block walls and metal trim, while outdoor tables are popular in the summer.

The food may seem secondary to the jazz, but in fact you can get a nicely made hamburger ($9). Of the many other house options, try the mozzarella and basil salad ($9), the Portobello mushroom sandwich ($9), or cod brandade ($9). The short menu always includes a terrific piece of fish like sockeye salmon or striped sea bass, priced in the high twenties (there are good wholesalers nearby), and a similarly priced meat dish such as lamb shank. Roast rabbit ($23) has a good chance of knocking your socks off, as does the roast veal bones with marrow and toast points ($22). Desserts (around $8) include biscotti and mousses. Cappuccinos are excellent here, and there's a long, distinguished wine list, as well as some impressive shelves of rare Scotch whiskies.

There's no doubt about it, owner Jimmy Moffatt's food is what makes 42 Degrees a "destination" place—though the romantic ambience helps too. In case you're wondering why main dishes are almost ten dollars more than at some upscale downtown places, it's because of the occasional live entertainment and general air of hipster 'tude. In case you were wondering, 42 degrees owes its name to the latitudes of Barcelona, Rome, and Istanbul—San Francisco itself being just over 38 degrees!

Angkor Borei

CAMBODIAN

It's not an entirely unsung treasure, but Angkor Borei is a find that is likely to startle visitors into wondering why Khmer cuisine is not better known. Out here on a limb, among burrito bars and taquerias in the Bernal Heights foothills, this modest neighborhood restaurant has been thriving for years with a cult following. The decor falls somewhere between classical Khmer and tired kitsch: pinkish tablecloths are covered by glass and starched napkins; costumed servers come with ornamental rice tureens of heavenly saffron-flecked jasmine rice; and Khmer paintings adorn the walls. Angkor Borei prepares certain dishes better than anywhere else in San Francisco, and the refined presentation and service can't be faulted.

Cost $10–25
Address 3471 Mission St between 30th and Cortland ⓉⓉ 415/550-8417 Open Mon–Sat 11am–10.30pm, Sun 4–10.30pm Transportation 14, 26, 49, 67, BART 24th St Accepts MasterCard, Visa

First and foremost, Angkor Borei's version of the ubiquitous green papaya salad ($4.95) beats everyone else's hands down; every chiffonéed component is distinct. Spinach leaves ($4.95) turns out to be a platter of leaves, bean sprouts, nuts, noodles, cucumber, basil, chile, and carrot, all artfully positioned in a mandala; you stuff your own leaf, rolling it into an untidy, fat cigar, then dip it into a lime and coconut sauce. The vegetarian crêpe ($5.95) is a lacy, crunchy, plate-sized rice pancake so big that the waiter has to chop it into two with shears, letting the herbs, nuts, and sprouts spill out. Not everybody will fall passionately in love with Ah-mohk ($9), a delicate fish and coconut-milk mousse served in a banana leaf basket, but few would dispute its exquisite appearance and unusual subtlety. Curries are not just plain hot, they're brightly layered and textured and luscious and hot. There's chicken curry with red chile and coconut ($8.95), beef with ground peanuts in coconut ($8.95), or spicy green curry, which comes with shrimp ($8.95), duck ($9.95), or fish ($9.95). Sticky rice and mango ($2.50), or fried bananas ($2.50), make up dessert. You'll be content with Tsingao beer or tea.

How did this quiet artistry appear in such an unlikely spot and at such low prices? Only the tragedy of Cambodian history can explain it. Owners have come and gone, but the cooks stay. At its best, Angkor Borei is a humble godsend.

Aperto

Aperto exudes neighborhood night-out bonhomie. To eat at this Potrero Hill bistro, among yuppy-but-friendly locals, is to glory in San Franciscan life itself, because it's an example of what the city does best. You wait by the door over Campari or Kir—sometimes for half an hour, because come 6pm on a weekend the locals crowd in, and you can't make reservations. Service is affable and tables are so cramped that you get to check out your neighbors and what they think of their food; nobody minds, you'll know them intimately by the end of the night!

Cost $10–30

Address 1434 18th St at Connecticut
☎ 415/252-1625
Open Mon–Fri 11.30am–2.30pm & 5.30–10pm, Sat 11am–2.30pm & 5.30–10pm, Sun 10am–2.30pm & 5–9pm
Transportation 19, 22, 48
Accepts All major credit cards except Diners

When it's good, the food is very good, in an honest and simple way. A blackboard lists the dishes of the day, which are dictated by the season.

Americans rarely eat Brussels sprouts, or didn't until a recent craze for braising them as an appetizer gripped town, transforming how people thought of them from stodgy greens to pieces of oral bliss. In season, appetizers might include tiny, delicious, dot-sized buds of sprouts ($4.50), steamed for five minutes until al dente, then flash-fried in butter and braised a little with cracked pepper. Homemade bruschetta ($3.40) is a constant at Aperto's, and it's served with house pomodoro sauce. Crabcakes ($8.75) are unusually meaty and delectable. Pastas are daily specials whipped up with whatever is at hand: there might be that sweet-tasting universal favorite, butternut squash ravioli in sage butter ($9.25). It's not hard to work out why this is the city's most requested pasta dish: butter and sage with butternut make an addictive sweet-salty combination, flavors that work together so well you wonder why anyone ever tries others. Fish of the day generally include tuna or sea bass, and you may be fortunate enough to have it served with chanterelles ($15.75). A narrow wine list is particularly strong on woody Chardonnays, priced from around $7 per glass.

Places like Aperto live by the gospel of using whatever grew or swam nearest to home, without adding any fancy extras. Luckily for San Franciscans, the city is rich in this kind of neighborhood hangout, where young chefs are cooking their boots off, and doing so with unflagging energy and brio.

Bistro e Europe

(🍴) If there's a more unlikely restaurant than Julia Pacek's little place, it must be exotic indeed. Sitting on a drab corner in the outlying Excelsior District, Bistro e Europe inhabits a narrow former diner. Inside, however, wild canvases of fiery flamenco queens hover over a hodgepodge of seats and small tables—don't be surprised if you find a tsambal player entertaining his Russian comrades with Chopin waltzes. Julia and her consort will emerge from the kitchen, warm, animated, and full of gruesome tales of Vlad the Impaler. They'll explain the menu between chunks of a life story only marginally less dramatic than Vlad's. Interludes in refugee camp kitchens on the Austro-Hungarian borders have left their stamp on Julia's goulashes and langos (delicious Hungarian fried bread), while her Transylvanian Roma roots show up in lavishly garlicked specials.

Cost $15–40

Address 4901 Mission St near Geneva Ave
(☎) 415/469-5637
Open Tues–Sun 5.30–10pm
Transportation 14, 15, 29, 43
Accepts Cash only

For starters, a simple beet salad ($4.50) or chilled cherry soup ($5.50) are good mouth cleansers. Among the mains, the house specialty is burek ($14.50), a labor-intensive Romany strudel filled with spinach and cabbage. Sopka ($13.50), or mushroom crêpe, is filled with peppers and porcini, with tomato and cucumber on the side. Roma steak ($15) is hearty and plain, and comes with plenty of peppers and polenta, while the Romany feast ($16) brings a potpourri of vegetables around a slab of hot-peppered steak. Another hot-blooded feast dish, chicken paprikash ($15.50), is tender paprika-sauced white chicken with peppers, potato, and either spätzle or polenta. To follow, Julia enthusiastically flambées crêpe Suzette ($5.50), which is served with cherries and cream. All dishes can be washed down with bottles of perfectly drinkable Bull's Blood, a Hungarian red wine, or fine Tokays (from $15 per bottle), but you'll love the gutsy Romanian Murfathar ($15).

The fare is filling but homey, the kind of meal you imagine Jonathan Harker gratefully tucking into at his Transylvanian village inn before heading to Dracula's castle. The food may even seem secondary to the entertainment (there's gypsy, folk, or klezmer music from Thursday to Sunday), and the flambéing may even ignite more than just the food, but it never fazes the management. In fact, it's hard to imagine anything denting the atmosphere in here.

Blue Plate

(i) "Blue-plate specials" were an institution of the Depression: wholesome, all-American meatloaf or ham and
corn-bread dishes that were priced under
a dollar and served, on blue china plates,
at joints called Mom's or Bill's; "Never eat
at a place called Mom's" is an old
American saying from this era. This twen-
ty-first-century Blue Plate is too self-con-
sciously hip to call itself Mom's or Bill's,
but you'll find solidly American fare of the

Cost $15–35

Address 3218 Mission St at
29th
(T) 415/282-6777
Open Tues–Thurs 6–10pm, Fri
& Sat 6–11pm
Transportation 14, 26, 49, J,
BART 24th St
Accepts All major credit cards
except Diners

AMERICAN

kind you generally have to go home for, only with quirks. Aside from the
prices, Blue Plate is like home in other ways too: its blue plates don't
match and many have an air of coming from Thriftown or the Salvation
Army. There's a sort of thrown-together folksiness about the tins used for
vases, the huge wall art and the table decorations, as though the owners
have cruised the Mission junkshops.

Starters salads may include arugula with apple, Gorgonzola, and pecans
($7), or rosemary scallop skewers with blood orange salad ($6). When
the food hits a high note, it dawns on you that it's exactly what this
town has been missing: well-thought-out, upscale chuckwagon food of
steaks and chops and fish fillets, just like your Mom's only bigger, juicier,
and better. Mains are priced between $13 and $18. Greens and mashed
potatoes are a large part of the attraction: this is comfort food flavored in
interesting ways, with celery root here or a dash of chile there to create
unique touches. This could be the only place you'll ever eat nettle
ravioli, though admittedly it doesn't sound like a Blue Plate special. You
can't always order it at night, either, because the menu changes daily—
and wildly. Desserts are cobblers such as peach or plum served a la
mode, with ice cream ($5).

Wines come by the glass ($6–7), and include an Argentinian Malbec
plus some light Sancerres and Proseccos. Beer includes fancy brews like
Chimay. If you find Blue Plate a bit hit and miss, you're not alone; but
there's a very creative soul out there in the open kitchen, so it's definitely worth the gamble. Sometimes the food here is goosebump good.

Chenery Park

AMERICAN/CREOLE

When Chenery Park first opened in Glen Park, the old Outer Mission neighborhood finally got its chance to eat Southern comfort food. Having long thrived on Salvadoran pupusas, Mexican tacos and takeout pizzas, locals were suddenly encountering panko-encrusted catfish, gumbo, and ribs. As a whole, San Francisco is short on authentic and generously seasoned Southern soul food, but you can find it here at Chenery Park, albeit in rather upscale surroundings and

Cost $15–30

Address 683 Chenery St at Diamond
☎ 415/337-8537
Open Mon–Thurs & Sun 5.30–9.30pm, Fri & Sat 5.30–10pm
Transportation 23, 26, 35, 44, J, BART Glen Park
Accepts All major credit cards except Diners

at heightened (yet still reasonable) prices. The split-level space is converted from a former pizzeria, and with its dramatic beams and staircase against tall windows, it feels like a showroom. It can also be noisy, though pockets of space pop up for privacy and conversation.

The evolving menu spins new twists on old Southern reliables. The undeniably authentic seafood gumbo ($15) boasts all the right ingredients and more, including catfish, fresh shrimp, and scallops, set against those Creole undernotes of thyme, oregano, and cayenne. In season, a mixed salad ($8) bursts with delicate frisée, plus persimmons, pistachios, and pomegranate in pear vinaigrette. Pumpkin, squash, or wild mushroom risottos ($12) are as creamy as you could hope. Chenery's catfish ($15) is another favorite, thanks to its crunchy skin, though out of season it's taken off the menu in favor of lamb and duck dishes. Similarly, nightly specials ($14–20) vary according to season, and may feature American favorites such as baby back ribs with mandarin marmalade, "chicken and fixins," or homemade meatloaf with blue cheese smashed pot. For dessert, the Thomas Kemper root beer float ($5) is popular, while warm gingerbread or chocolate cake ($6) comes with caramel sauce and pumpkin ice cream.

Service is another plus, as is the good wine list, which includes several drinkable Cabernets (from $7 per glass). As a rather upscale restaurant in a newish location, Chenery Park is trying hard to win local and neighboring hearts. Now it needs get over that "Glen Park" tag and woo outsiders too. Signs are that it has been busting a gut, and it deserves its success.

Dusit Thai

(🍴) So many little Thai places on the corner compete for the hearts and stomachs of San Franciscans that they sometimes seem interchangeable. So when you find one that Thai San Franciscans keep coming back to, it's worth taking note. *Dusit* means "paradise" in Thai, but truth to tell, Dusit looks fairly earthbound at first sight, with its brown batik tablecloths under glass and fanned napkins. But then, the servers,

Cost $10–25

Address 3221 Mission St at Valencia
☎ 415/826-4639
Open Mon & Wed–Fri 11am–2.30pm & 5–10pm, Sat & Sun 5–10pm
Transportation 14, 26, 49
Accepts MasterCard, Visa

who wear Thai dress, are welcoming and warmhearted, and are responsible in no small part for the faithfulness of the clientele. From time to time, locals have even had phone calls from the cook and owner, saying "Come by, we just got in a great leg of lamb today." With any other restaurant you would find a prompt like that annoying. But around these parts, when Dusit's chef announces a feast the locals simply grab their house keys and plunge downhill.

Even Dusit's rice ($1) seems to be tastier than elsewhere: perfumed, plump, and speckled with golden saffron, it arrives in an ornamental, domed rice tureen. The chicken salad ($6.25) is a perfectly balanced mix of minced chicken, chile, lime, shredded carrot, mint, and basil and feeds two as a main dish or one as a starter. Dusit's tofu and ginger soup ($4.25) is always restorative and warming. The duck dishes are much admired, as is the seafood; among the red, yellow, and green curries, the subtlety of the yellow seafood curry ($5.95) is striking. Moreover, if Dusit really has managed to lay hands on a leg of lamb ($11.95), seize it with both fists and don't let anyone share. A sticky rice and mango dessert ($2) makes a pleasant finisher. You can get the usual Thai beer or a bottle of rather standard wine (from $18) here, or bring your own, but don't miss out on the refreshing Thai iced tea or coffee.

Dusit survives not only the competition from several nearby Thai places, but also the rivalry of some fine Cambodian and Mandarin restaurants. It practices budgetary restraint, too, never raising its prices during the boom years. And who needs fancy surroundings with reliable food like this?

CHINESE

Eliza's

Upscale, inventive but bargain-priced Mandarin food served in a civilized environment in a restaurant that just happens to be on the corner: that sums up the trend in new neighborhood Chinese restaurants in San Francisco. Eliza's was one of the first examples, and it remains the best. In case you've heard otherwise, Eliza's is not, in fact, any relation to the popular Eric's and Alice's in Noe Valley, although both feature exotic carved screens, Buddhist statues, paintings, fancy glassware, giant palms and cane furniture. They may be kissing cousins in stylishness, but Eliza's is the lovelier to look at, with its rare Asian orchids and collectibles. A Vietnamese-Chinese couple, whose culinary specialties are Hunan and Mandarin cuisine, run the restaurant, and it was their daughter who lent it her name.

Cost $7–25
Address 1457 18th St at Connecticut
☎ 415/648-9999
Open Mon–Fri 11am–3pm, 5–9.45pm, Sat 11am–9.45pm, Sun noon–9.45pm
Transportation 19, 22, 53
Accepts MasterCard, Visa

Service is spanking quick and the clientele, for the most part, local. For all the advertised specialties, the food reinvents Chinese-Californian dishes as much as Hunan or Mandarin, and it comes on an inventive and very low-priced menu. Lunch specials, which change daily and begin with the house egg-drop soup on Tuesdays, are excellent deals at $6 inclusive, while bargain appetizers include delicately crispy vegetarian egg rolls ($2.50). A platter of assorted rolls, dumplings, and potstickers ($6.95) comes with richly sticky hoisin sauce, and is way enough of a meal in itself. A favorite house dish is the garlicked eggplant ($3.50), while the house mu shu ($7.50), served with crunchy cabbage and lacy little pancakes, and the crab Rangoon ($6.50) are close rivals for attention. All the wonderful whole fish dishes (around $10) are poached in five-spice sauces, while Hunan lamb ($8) is another major five-spice production number. Both are special occasion dishes ordered by proud hosts entertaining important out-of-towners, or by locals enjoying a birthday.

Eliza's seems to be having a good influence on other Chinese restaurants, as its classy interior and creative approach to the standard Mandarin menu seem to be catching on in other parts of the city. It really earns its large local following, and gets a wider audience from lunching dotcom-ers or business types on foraging trips from nearby convention centers.

Emmy's Spaghetti Shack

When Emmy's opened, in a former burrito dive at the foot of Bernal Heights, it gave the impression of being run by enthusiastic amateurs who had just been pinkslipped in the dotcom collapse. The mood is casual and there's a rudely cheerful vibe. Diners are locals who look like the owner's buddies, and the food is simple, fresh Cal-Italian. A big bar takes over half the room in Emmy's skinny and cheerfully primitive interior, and one table holds a DJ and turntable. It's a busy, popular joint, and you may wait half an hour for a table (they don't take reservations), watching staff rub dishes off the chalkboard menu and praying that they don't erase the risotto.

Cost	$5–20
Address	18 Virginia Ave at Mission
☎	415/206-2086
Open	Mon–Thurs & Sun 5pm–midnight, Fri & Sat 5pm–2am
Transportation	14, 26, 49, J
Accepts	MasterCard, Visa

ITALIAN

Salads ($3) or soup ($4) are fresh but tend to run out early. Luckily, Emmy's always has spaghetti and meatballs, and plenty of garlicky baguettes—the latter come automatically. Table water also comes unbidden in jugs, aswim with lemon slices. That spaghetti ($5) is the old-fashioned and heartwarming type, a blessed memory of the tomato and starch that you scarfed down as a kid and still nurture a soft spot for. Meatballs ($9) are herbed with oregano and parsley, and come with a pomodoro sauce that is trippily seasoned with spice and topped off with fresh Parmesan. Emmy's stirs an unbeatable risotto, too: the porcini risotto ($7.50) is made on a creamed and wined stock, with flakes of nicely aged Parmesan. The chef had obviously stroked it for a good 25 minutes or more—attention to detail that doesn't go unnoticed with this dish. The rest of the menu stays just as simple and low-priced as the spaghetti: fish of the day, chicken, nothing over $11. Apple cobbler ($2.50) makes a homey dessert.

Like the menu, the wine list is scrawled on a blackboard. Californian red Zinfandels start at $18.50, while good Riojas start at a slightly higher price. Emmy's has an endearing habit of icing their malt drinks in a bubbly bucket, but then they have a lot of endearing qualities—like staying open until 2am and having DJs on Friday and Saturday nights. No wonder it took off like a meteor.

CHINESE

Jasmine Tea House

(Y) When Robert Feng Hui and Frank Xu's place opened up on one of the grittier Mission blocks, beyond the end of Valencia Street, locals were initially wary. Its predecessor had been the cheap and cheerful Royal Kitchen, a funky local favorite, so there was resistance to this "fancy" newcomer. But Jasmine has since trounced any doubts by dishing up crisp, cleanly executed Mandarin cuisine that's imaginative and often exciting. The

Cost $5–25

Address 3243 Mission St at Valencia
(T) 415/826-6288
Open Mon–Fri 10.30am–10pm, Sat & Sun 10.30am–11pm
Transportation 14, 26, 49, BART 24th St
Accepts All major credit cards

ambiance took a giant leap skyward too, and Jasmine manages to be both decorous and laid-back. A plate window lets in light, restrained Chinese prints and traditional china have replaced the kitsch, and jokey waiters welcome regulars.

Dim sum is served all day, and doubles for appetizers by night. Unusual offerings such as green chive cakes ($3.95) and feather-light crab puffs ($3.95) match the best taro puffs, or wu gok ($3.95) around. A combination plate ($4.95) is enough to share among two or three, and offers those dainty crab puffs along with crunchy vegetarian egg rolls ($3.25), delectable potstickers ($3.95), and chicken wings ($5.25). On the Chef's Special night menu, ginger chicken ($8.95) in an unusually spicy sauce is outstanding, as is a whopping plate of tender Peking Duck ($10.95), and sautéed frog legs ($9.95). Distinguished dishes all, they're remarkable in this modest price range. Braised, pencil-thin water eels ($8.95) are stir-fried with julienned zucchini in a garlicky chile sauce, and make for a real discovery, though diners of feverish imagination may find it too Indiana Jones for comfort, and those who can't take spice should also desist. Subtly tea-tinged and smoky, in a delicate five-spice sauce that emphasizes star anise, it's Frank's Oolong duck ($10.95) that makes newcomers realize they are in the presence of gifted cooks. This is a competent kitchen that has the guts to go for unusual combinations.

Yes, the Jasmine Tea House is marginally dearer than the old Royal Kitchen, but lunch versions of the main dishes come at a bargain price of $5, and it's well worth a trip even at night. Drinks include rare rice wine imports. Try some: it tastes strong and sweet at first, and richly endows the food with oomph.

Just For You

Lastly Café and Bakery

For over fifteen years the women who ran Just For You dished out the hearty breakfasts that Gold Miners survived on from a counter-wide little dot of a place on top of Potrero Hill. They struck their loyal following as hardy pioneers in their own right. Folks waited outside patiently for one of their half-dozen or so seats, where you sat so near the cooking you could smell all the good ingredients. In 2001, however, the chef-owners found themselves across the other side of the hill to the part of town known as Dogpatch (at the end of 3rd Street's dockyard hinterland) in search of more elbowroom and less waiting time. Now they have premises around four or five times bigger and some actual tables to sit at, plus a gay paint job on the steel shutters outside. Luckily, the food is exactly the same.

Cost	$8–25

Address 732 22nd Street at 3rd
☎415/647-3033
Open Daily 7am–3pm
Transportation 15, 22, 48
Accepts Cash only

AMERICAN/MEXICAN

At brunch, the star is no-nonsense American home cooking, with piping hot plates of straightforward eggs and grills, French toast, hot cakes, huevos rancheros, and even grits. There are stacks of perfect pancakes, or eggs served scrambled with chile and cheese on toast, or with hash browns or fried potatoes. All these dishes cost less than five dollars. Terrific grits ($3.50) come with butter and syrup, and there's even an all-stops-out traditional Hangtown Fry ($7.50), with bacon, Louisiana link sausages, and oysters with eggs. Wondrously tasty crabcakes ($6.50) hint at a Creole cookout on the Bayou with a hint of cayenne and Tabasco. Huevos rancheros ($4.50) come with homemade salsa and potatoes. During breakfast and brunch, bowls of healthy oatmeal and Californian granola are dished with home-baked bread, and scones and muffins are made every morning. Owner Ariane is still on the job here, but no longer opens in the evenings.

Just For You almost never gets a mention in the food columns and never advertises. It's a puzzle why it does not get more publicity, but perhaps that's because it never has to look for it—the food speaks for itself.

Liberty Cafe and Bakery

Ever since Liberty Cafe's first opened in 1995, a small knot of hopefuls has gathered outside, waiting for their gravy-rich, flaky-crusted, creamed chicken potpie—and the banana cream pie has its fanatical adherents too. The cafe is white-clothed, plank-floored, and seats thirty or so, but what might be plain and poky is somehow cozy. Almost a lone pioneer when Cathie Guntli first launched it, the cafe lent a gentrified tone to this little hilltop, and it has since been joined by other places. It's hard to believe that a decade ago there were still bars on the windows of the liquor stores; now the same places on Cortland sell wines and organic produce.

Cost $15–50

Address 401 Cortland Ave at Wool
ⓣ 415/695-8777
Open Tues–Fri 5.30–9pm, Sat & Sun 10am–2pm & 5.30–9.30pm
Transportation 24, 67
Accepts MasterCard, Visa

Former chef Randy Windham's menu emphasized homey American fare, including the famous potpie, but under Cynthia Shea the menu has acquired cosmopolitan notes, satisfying the curiosity and expectations of the regulars. Daily soups ($5.50) include vegetable in season, and a thick fava bean with chervil that could teach other places a thing or two. That golden-crusted chicken pie ($10 for lunch, $13.50 for dinner) now comes in a fava bean, carrot, pea, and tomato version ($11), aimed at vegetarians, who are numerous in these parts. But the short and seasonal changing menu also includes a darkly juicy duck leg confit ($14.50) with avocado, grapefruit, and endive to counteract its sweetness. A well-considered penne a la carbonara ($10.50) has perfect bite, and a skirt steak comes with spring vegetable bruschetta ($16). On no account let their dessert pies slip you by if you have a sweet tooth—the banana cream pie ($5.95) is the stuff of dreams.

The cafe doesn't accept reservations and the wait is usually half an hour at weekends. Once, you passed the time at the Wild Side West bar next door; now, there's an annex at the rear with a little bakery and bar where hopefuls wait, glass and appetizer in hand. Croissants and coffee are available here during the daytime, or you can check out the daily menu if you want to sample something but can't handle the idea of waiting for a table.

Mi Lindo Peru!

While all Latin American cooking is distinct and different, Peruvian food is truly varied, thanks to the diverse terrain. Potato-enriched and homey, it roams from Andean freeze-dried potatoes to the fish of cold Pacific currents, and includes steaks with fried eggs, shellfish, and sugary desserts. Ask a Peruvian what he or she misses most from home, however, and they will probably reply that it's beef hearts on skewers, or potatoes done in the way that only Peruvians can do them.

Cost $5–30
Address 3226 Mission St at Valencia
☎ 415/642-4897
Open Daily 11am–11pm
Transportation 14, 26, 49, BART 24th St
Accepts MasterCard, Visa

Ceviches—fish or shellfish marinated in fresh-squeezed limejuice with chopped cilantro and red chile—originated in Peru. The idea is that the acid of the lime macerates and breaks down the flesh and thus "cooks" the fish. The house ceviche here is calamari and snapper ($5.50), and it comes with plenty of chile and in a generous portion. For vegetarians, or those who find ceviche a bit intimidating, potatoes prepared in the Huancayo manner ($4.50) make a perfect appetizer: they're boiled, sliced, tossed in onions, then dressed in a very pungent, creamy cheese sauce. Anticuchos ($4.50) is the Peruvian name for the marinated beef-heart skewers, and here they are served like shish kebabs, juicy, well grilled, and with hot sauce on the side. If that seems a little too hearty, try the causa de camarones ($6.75), which is a potato and shrimp starter; the caldo de gallina ($6), which is a chicken soup; or fried stuffed peppers ($4.50), a fast-food snack sold everywhere in the markets of Lima. Andeans like their steaks a la chorillera ($8.75), which means battered with onions and peppers, adding a dollop of a palate-rousing Habanera chile sauce. Also breadcrumbed is the pork loin, or Milanesa de carne ($9.50). Peruvian desserts can be labor-intensive and fancy; here a simple custard flan ($2) tastes pleasantly neutral after the fiery main courses.

Although Peru's cuisine is still under-appreciated, a rising Peruvian headcount in the Bay Area is changing that rapidly. Now that Gladys and Carlos Miyihara and their compatriots are thriving at "My lovely Peru!" (as the name of their little place translates), Andeans can be sure of finding a cure for their homesickness.

JAPANESE/PAN-ASIAN

Moki's Sushi & Pacific Grill

Moki's gets crowded with Bernal Heights locals seeking out their "PacRim" mix-and-match 21st-century diet of nagiri, tempura, curry, coconut-coated tofu, and lime dipping sauce, especially on Mondays, when many other places are closed. If this restaurant didn't exist, the clientele would have to forsake this Latino-flavored Bayside hood to find their pan-Asian fusion fix. A former neigh-borhood corner shop, Moki's is Japanese-Hawaiian owned, and has been painted in South Seas papaya and teal hues, and decorated with Hawaiian flourishes and raki stoneware. Small tables jostle stools at the sushi counter where you can watch (non-Japanese) hands hard at work, flashing their knives to flutter out and fan the tips of daikon and crab-meat. Service is casual and so is the ambiance.

Cost $15–35
Address 830 Cortland St at Folsom
☎ 415/970-9336
Open Mon–Fri 5–10pm, Sat & Sun 8am–2pm
Transportation 24, 67
Accepts All major credit cards

Imaginative combinations make the samurai sushi ($8.95) worth sampling: smoked salmon, avocado, cream cheese, and feather-light tempura shrimp tails plus pickled ginger sounds busy and strange, yet tastes divinely creamy. Aji ($4.75), or mackerel sashimi, consist of two huge, rosy pillows of fresher-than-fresh flesh, as naked in all their glory as nature itself, lying upon beds of sticky rice. Green papaya salads ($3.95) are ten a penny in this city, but Moki's refreshing palate-cleanser hits an expert balance of papaya, carrot, and red pepper filaments in cilantro, lime, chile, and fish sauce. Pacific three seaweed salad in sesame oil ($8.50) is unconvincing, however: a small ration of nori comes with something like weedy kelp, and is plumped out with little neon-green jelloid sticks. Dishes of the day may include offerings as diverse as Thai green curry ($11.25), flatiron steak ($12.50), and lemongrass opah ($14.95), the latter made with opakapaka, a dense, lean Hawaiian snapper. Dessert pies ($6.25) number strawberry, blueberry, and Fiji apple, but they're all over-sweetened and over-fussy. Warm sake and nihon-cha, or green tea, are better to wash it all down, along with Sapporo.

Moki's has its niche with an eclectic, quirky menu that is as catholic as it gets. This is Anglo sushi for *gaijin* rather than for Japanese, and the Californian ingredients make whimsical bedfellows for the more classical offerings. Sharing side dishes and appetizers is the best way to go in here.

Mom Is Cooking

When a local newspaper first wrote up Mom Is Cooking, it became an overnight cult favorite, growing like a burriteria on steroids, and it soon overspilled its hole-in-the-wall out in the Mission's outlying Excelsior District. Ten years on, it remains the neighborhood Mexican diner to beat, complete with its unlovely extension of naugahyde seating, formica, linoleum tiles, and strip lighting, plus a yard behind for warmer days. As long as Abigail Murillo, the "Mom" of the casa, is still cooking in the kitchen, you'll find plain and honest burritos and bocadillos, made on the spot, and nobody's going to mind what her place looks like, or even the occasional wait for tables and service.

The first item to try is boquitos de nogales ($4.50), little mouthfuls of chopped-up cactus paddles fried in batter and served along with a plate of accompaniments like guacamole, cream, refried beans, and salsa. The menu has all the usual tacos, quesadillas, and tamales, plus empanadas (around $7), fajitas (around $9), and chimichangas (around $8). Fillings range from several different kinds of roast pork to chicken, sausage, brains, and menudo (tripe). Mom's homemade mole ($3 with rice, or $1 extra on top of anything) gets the biggest raves of all. This sauce is made with crushed sesame, peanuts, almonds, coriander, and other spices, arduously ground up with chile and dark chocolate; it gives a powerful flavor of Oaxacan cooking. Mole poblano ($7.95) is made with chicken or turkey. The Mexican lunch or brunch of huevos rancheros ($6.25) is a standard, along with chilaquiles ($4.25), a dish of fried-up tortilla scraps with scrambled eggs. There are scaled-down children's versions on the menu, too. The only drawback is that Mom's blond bouffant hairdo isn't always seen in the kitchen these days.

Aside from the food, a real draw is the homemade Margaritas, which are made with ice cubes (not pulsed into a smoothie) and one of the hundred or more rare Jalisco tequilas that line Mom's shelves. You can easily withstand a half-hour wait or so with the help of one huge ceramic jugful (from $10) and perhaps a bowl of chips with salsa ($2.50).

Cost $6–20

Address 1166 Geneva Ave at Naples
☎ 415/586-7000
Open Daily 10am–10pm
Transportation 9X, 14, 43, 52
Accepts Cash only

MEXICAN

SEAFOOD

Original Old Clam House

Traditionalists searching for original San Francisco clam chowder always swear by this crusty old blue-collar joint, with its wooden stalls, antique jukebox—someone does remember the Sixties here—and vintage Jaguar suspended over the bar. The menu has scarcely changed in 140-odd years, save for the addition of some pastas and that crazy new cioppino. The Clam House itself dates back to 1861's Silver Rush, so it is younger than the venerable Tadich Grill by only a few years. The mere fact it survives out in Bayshore's tarmac wilderness seems miraculous, but the Farmer's Market and DIY stores nearby must help.

Cost $10–35

Address 299 Bayshore Boulevard at Oakdale
☎ 415/826-4880
Open Mon–Thurs 11.30am–9.30pm, Fri & Sat 11.30am–10pm, Sun noon–9.30pm
Transportation 9, 23
Accepts All major credit cards except Diners

The atmosphere is one of good ol' boy bonhomie, and despite a couple of steak dishes this place really is all about shellfish. Lazy man's cioppino ($19.95) is hefty, creamy, and well seasoned, and bobs with clams, calamari, prawns, scallops, diced snapper, shrimp, mussels, and crab's legs; it's served with garlic sourdough bread ($3.50 sold separately). A whopper of a hot crab sandwich ($11.95) arrives with Hollandaise, but also something that seems suspiciously like Cheese Whiz spilling out; other sandwiches include hot shrimp ($10.95) and cold crab ($10.95). There's deep-fried everything, from oysters ($12.95) to calamari in Giorgio sauce ($12.95). Crab Louie ($13.95) is a classic, but pleasantly crunchy mouthfuls of popcorn shrimp ($7.95) may be less well known. The many clam dishes range from plain steamed clams au nature ($14.95), to cherrystone clams Bordelaise ($14), plus two classical clam chowders ($4.95), and a deeply traditional clambake special ($18.95), which comes with an ear of corn.

You have to imagine the Clam House in 1861, before landfill ate a third of the Bay, when the restaurant was directly on the water. In this part of town, you rolled your pants up to the knee, took a spade out, and *voilà*—clams! Is nostalgia reason enough to eat at this historic landmark? Well, there's no fear of parking blues along Bayshore. And there's always the deep-fried calamari in Giorgio sauce...

Rock Soup

Set behind an arched sandstone façade, Rock Soup occupies a former bank vault. Stewpots are now housed behind the high oak counter, and there's live music around the grand piano where the deposit section used to be. The menu features likeable home cooking, from chicken potpie to meatloaf and turkey gumbo, at low prices. The slightly Dungeons and Dragons ambiance is a distinct plus. Lofty walls glow in a deep marmalade orange, spot-lit here and there with glass sconces, with a huge, golden Tiffany bowl high overhead. Little wooden tables face the counter, affording close-ups of the hardworking young staff at work on their risottos and salads. A very child-friendly vibe brings in young families from the neighborhood, as well as solitaires and big parties. You might start to dream about having your own simpatico bar-bistro—it would be like this, you muse.

Cost $10–25

Address 3299 Mission St at 29th

℡ 415/641-7687

Open Tues–Thurs 11am–2.30pm & 5.30–10pm, Fri 11am–2.30pm & 5.30–11pm, Sat 5.30–11pm, Sun 9.30am–2.30pm

Transportation 14, 24, 26, 49, J

Accepts MasterCard, Visa

Created from scratch and served with homemade buttermilk biscuits, soups of the day might include crab soup, pozole, bisque, and a baked potato and roast butternut squash broth ($3.50 cup, $4.95 bowl), which is creamily authentic and satisfying. Always available are meatloaf ($8.95) and Brunswick stew ($8.95), which is a kind of upside-down shepherd's pie. The beef-pork meatloaf sandwich ($7.95) gets a big cheer for its bacon-juiced, extra-tasty filling, and extra-punchy flavor, in quite a light-grained meatloaf, though the accompanying mashed potatoes can be unreliable—some have tasted as though they came from a box. If requested, grilled lamp chops ($11.95) will be served rare, and with rosemary-tinged pan juices on top of arugula with couscous. An ice cream pie comes with a minute ginger crust and scant fudge sauce ($3.95), but a Hershey bar cake ($3.95) usually does better.

Draft micro-brews include a light Flemish Hoegaarden ($4.25), while wines offer a creditable David Bruce Petit Syrah ($7.75 glass, $31 bottle), if you're celebrating. There's Terrazas Malbec ($4.75/$19) or Los Vascos Cabernet ($4.50/$18) for less important occasions. Bernal Heights is spoiled for choice—Rock Soup is one of a string of fun options along this strip.

Zante's Pizza and Indian Cuisine

Is tandoori pizza just the latest in Californian food fads, or an idea whose time has truly come? In the spirit of research, mount an expedition to the Bernal Heights frontier to investigate Zante's award-winning Indian pizza, a marriage of exceptionally chewy, nan-like pizza dough with garam masala-based toppings. Spinach, eggplant, cauliflower, lamb, chicken, and prawn pizzas are all so heavy with garlic, ginger, and chile that soon your tastebuds will sing like football fans. Like the avocado ice cream at the nearby Mitchell's ice-cream parlor, the match sounds ideal, but your mouth just doesn't quite know if it likes the taste or not.

Cost $5–20
Address 3489 Mission St at Cortland
⊤ 415/821-3949
Open Daily 11.30am–10.30pm
Transportation 14, 24, 26, 49
Accepts All major credit cards except Diners

But you'll adjust to the combination within seconds. Surprisingly, it is both spicy and digestible, perhaps because the nan-bread crust makes a spongy foil to the spices, and the cheese is a bland mozzarella. At $13 for the not-so-small smallest pizza and $18 for the eight-serving wagon-wheel, it's not going to hang you high and out to dry, either. Zante's owner Dalvinder Multani worked at a New York City pizzeria after leaving the Punjab. After moving to the Mission district, he started Zante's, one of the city's earlier Indian restaurants to get tandoori lamb ghoshts right. Heartening rotis and nan breads, and crispy, spicy samosas (all under $2) fill the appetizer list, while mains (from $7) include the usual vindaloo, biriyani, korma, masala, and paneer dishes. Lunchtime specials ($5.50–8.95) that combine nan bread, daal, raita, and pilao make a good deal. These Indian dishes are all acceptable enough, but Zante's is really about the tandoori pizza.

Where other Indian restaurants in San Francisco have tended to go off over time, Zante's is miraculously getting better—even the service, which could have used it. When the ravages of age are miraculously disguised by candlelight, its decor even seems borderline romantic. The consistency of the food is praised all over Bernal Heights, and $3 corkage is well worth paying to open a good bottle. To think that ten years ago Zante's was little more than a reminder of how hard it was to find good Indian food in San Francisco!

The Mission

THE MISSION

Andalu

In Madrid they serve hot chocolate and donuts for breakfast. So how *loco* do you have to be to serve it as an appetizer? Well, crazy enough to open the ninety-first restaurant along the Valencia—Guerrero corridor, where launching yet another Mission tapas joint in a former taqueria makes you nothing less than an up-against-the-odds El Cid. Despite the difficulties, chef Ben de Vries has a good vibe going, and there's often a wait at this playpen for the young and the restless. His adventurous menu offers two dozen tapas dishes and three dozen wines, and hipsters have lined up to eat at the glowing, high-topped tables below swirling murals.

Cost $6–25

Address 3198 16th St at Guerrero
☎ 415/621-2211
Open Mon–Thurs 5.30–11pm, Fri & Sat 5.30–11.30pm
Transportation 22, 26, 33, 14, J, BART 16th St
Accepts MasterCard, Visa

A couple of year ago, fish tacos ($6) became the snack of choice for everybody out on the town. Andalu's are a fancy riff on a basic fish-inside-tortillas recipe in which marinated ahi tuna is spiked with chiles, lime, and salsa; it's *muy sabroso*. Crab-avocado tempura ($7) is dressed with daikon and fennel, a pleasant creamy-crisp mouthful. To let you know that fondue's back, Fuji apples and Asian pear slices are served with candlelit fondue pots of Cambazola blue-cheese sauce ($8). A rabbit and chanterelles potpie ($11) and wafer-thin steak rubbed in green peppercorn sauce with onion rings ($11) are both main dish compositions, although in minute portions. Far and away the best dessert is the dulce de leche sundae of caramel ice cream with cherries, nuts, and candied fruit, though gingerbread in rum sauce makes a distant second. No dish is over $12, but then you'll need several if you're hungry.

Perhaps what you need after a long tough night of clubbing are those too-early-for-breakfast chocolate and churros ($6), the favourite reviver of Madrid clubsters. Chef Ben used to be the guiding star of Ristorante Ecco in South Park but its closure catapulted him into this festive spot, in the busy restaurant scene of the Mission. The effect is some more late-night uplift for the good-times beat along 16th and Valencia Street.

The Mission

Bissap Baobob

When Bissap Baobob opened, during the dotcom madness, it wasn't the first Senegalese joint in town, but overnight it turned into the hottest hangout on the lower neck of the Mission. Back in those long-gone days, people needed new ways to feel cool and get high, and word on the street was that this was where to come for fun drinks—and they're still fun. Gingered tamarind and hibiscus Margaritas come in a riot of tropical stripe and hue, as exuberant as the Yoruba charms on the rattan walls, and the pink and orange strobes set to a thumping Highlife soundtrack. Since spilling around the corner onto the Mission, Baobob has added more food and more live music.

Cost	$12–30

Address 2323 Mission St between 19th and 20th
℡ 415/826-9287
Transportation 14, 33, 49, BART 16th St
Open Tues–Sun 6–11pm, bar open to 2am
Accepts All major credit cards except AmEx

The menu is familiar yet unfamiliar, because the same African ingredients overlap with the Hispanic plantains and yams available in every Mission grocery store. Service is unhurried and never hassled. The $4.50 drinks must subsidize the food, because Baobob is as bargain-priced as it gets. This must be the only eatery in town with dishes for under a dollar—75 cents for a couscous order! Senegalese chefs know their North African food, so along with couscous, you'll find delicious pastelles, those nuttily herbed savory pastries. They come in a fish version here, for a knockdown $4.50. Plantain chips ($3.25) come with a lime-garlic dip. Teriyaki-soy tofu kebab ($5.75), Baobob's own African-fusion creation, is a wonderful idea. Mafe ($7) is the rich and nourishing Malian stew of plentiful sweet potatoes, yams, onions, and carrots, while the fish of the day ($7) is grilled with caramelized onions, and tossed into mustardy, lemony, garlicky, Yassa sauce. Juicy lamb stew ($10.25) and chicken also come with Yassa ($8.25). A seafood stew ($10.50) uses tchou shrimp and tomatoes, while n'bole of spinach and roast peanuts ($9.50) will please veg-heads. If a lone dried-out couscous proves disappointing, it will be the only off-note here.

Bissap Baobob is calmer now that the tech Gold Rush is over, and the nerve-wracking cool quotient has plunged. It's now safe to come in looking as unhip as you like, braving the DJs and turntables. But don't dare forget those magnificently gingered cocktails.

Butterfly Restaurant & Jazz Bar

If you're in the mood for bold fusion flavors, a little cool jazz, and a hot, hip nightspot all in one, this converted auto-repair shop is the place. No longer will you be in danger of being swamped by dotcom-ers—they've all gone, making this a good place to gather with friends to drink and dine at the bar, or commandeer a table off to the side, or sit on one of the high chairs sipping cocktails at a cozy table for two, soaking in the Mission ambiance and the soothing rhythms of the music. Architecturally, butterfly (they're annoyingly keen on that lower case "b") combines a warehouse look and feel. Brick walls and exposed wooden beams are set off by glass and metal, there's a koi pond and a softly tinkling fountain, abstract art fills the nooks behind the grand piano, and it all adds to the funky, warm feel of the place.

Cost $15–30

Address 1710 Mission St at Duboce
℡ 415/864-8999
Open Tues–Thurs & Sun 6–11pm, Fri & Sat 6pm–midnight
Transportation BART 16th St
Accepts All major credit cards

FUSION

Chef Robert Lam combines French influences with Asian ingredients and techniques. Begin with Bloody Mary oyster shooters ($2) and sesame-coated endamame ($3). Complaints about portion sizes appear to have been heard, and prices have been almost halved in the past year. Duck confit spring rolls ($8) come with Chinese mustard and honey dipping sauce. Ahi tempura rolls ($10) are served with crunchy salmon row, soft Thai black rice, and a crisp cucumber salad with ginger and wasabe sauce. Crispy fried whole fish of the day (from $15) is often sold out by 10pm. If you're out of luck, a ponzu-grilled hanger steak with Portobello mushrooms, spring peas, and Cabernet jus de veau ($17), is sensational. There's a small but good wine selection. For dessert, the house specialty is the mango and mascarpone turnovers ($5), served with mixed berry compote and passion fruit sorbet.

Since the original owners opened the partnership up to executive kitchen staff, the service is better than ever, too. Many restaurants went belly-up in this neck of the woods after the dotcom bomb, but this one seems to have survival skills, and it's lively even on quieter nights.

ETHIOPIAN

Cafe Ethiopia

As a favorite college student hang-out, Cafe Ethiopia is always humming with people hunched over laptops or chewing pencil ends. And there's a whiff of the seraglio about its backroom, which is curtained off behind a strip of 1970s-style beads and macramé. Mission District denizens like to kill time here over tiny coffees, sprawling on old sofas and cushions and, from time to time, getting up to fetch a few portions of fiery Ethiopian stew. They find it easy to adapt to a student lifestyle that involves using no eating utensils.

Cost $5–10
Address 878 Valencia St
☎ 415/285-2728
Open Mon–Thurs & Sun 10am–10pm, Fri & Sat 10am–10.30pm
Transportation 14, 26, 49, BART 24th St
Accepts MasterCard, Visa

Traditional injera bread replaces them, of course. Made from the African corn called "teff," its distinctive, flannel-like texture matches an inoffensive flavor, and you'll soon become clever at shoveling food with it. Luckily, the warmhearted couple who run Cafe Ethiopia never tire of demonstrating how to do so, or explaining the head-clearing virtues of their fiery berbere seasoning. Vegetarians do particularly well at the cafe with the kantisharas ($7), which are berbere-spiced vegetable and lentil stews, rendered bearably tame by alternating mouthfuls with bites of injera. The cafe is strong on salads too, and their fit-fit fit-fit (meaning "mixed together") is like an Ethiopian version of a Tuscan bread salad, an herbed veggie wonderland of injera chunks and diced tomatoes, onions, and peppers of all persuasions. No, it's not easy to eat with your injera, but the cafe issues forks on request. Kitfo ($7), or Ethiopian steak tartare, has interesting spices along with plenty more berbere. The cafe's version of tibsie dorho ($7), or chicken stew, is so long-simmered that the meat practically melts straight into your injera. Gored gored ($7) is the beef version of the same stew, and it's outstanding value—but then more or less everything costs either $7 or just over.

Cafe Ethiopia does very little in the dessert line, but that's neither here nor there when you consider that delicious coffee ($2), which is as thick and cardamomed as a thimble of caffeinated Turkish velvet. Students take note: if you're watching your budget, this is the very best value along Valencia Street.

Il Cantuccio

Occupying the hallowed spot that seems to be reserved for rustic Italian cooking in the otherwise Hispanic Mission, Il Cantuccio looks incongruous in this location just a block or so west of the taquerias. With enough designer lettering, plate glass, and pretty table settings and lampshades to make you fumble for your credit card, its classy exterior and interior suggest a budget that far outpaces salsa and burritos. Inside, however, the very pally staff are at pains to make you feel as though you were visiting your Italian grandmother's kitchen.

Cost $10–30

Address 3228 16th St between Dolores and Guerrero
℡ 415/861-3899
Open Mon–Wed 5.30–9.30pm, Thurs–Sun 5.30–10pm
Transportation 22, 26, 33, BART 16th St
Accepts MasterCard, Visa

ITALIAN

Meals certainly start well here, with bowls of piperade and tapenade ready for dipping chunks of complementary focaccia. Two especially popular (and bargain-priced) classic starters are carpaccio di manzo ($6), or beef slices with arugula, and carpaccio di salmone ($6), which comes with plentiful pine nuts. A Caprese salad ($6) brings lots of fresh mozzarella and fresh basil with slices of Roma tomato drizzled with fine olive oil. Il Cantuccio does a lot of pizza these days (they also do deliveries), and on top of the usual Margherita ($9.50) and sausage with mushroom ($9.50) varieties, you can try a couple of interestingly yuppified pizza toppings, such as arugula and Gorgonzola ($9.50). All the pastas are fresh, and some are downright great. Opt for the ravioli mezzelune all zucca di sugo ($11.50), which is pumpkin in brown sage butter—yes, butternut squash pumpkin always seems to come with brown sage butter in this town. Ravioli al granchio ($12.75) is stuffed with crab and ricotta in a brandied pomodoro that has an ambrosial touch of cream; it's enough to make anyone swoon. People watching their cholesterol are more likely to go for the penne tossed in garlic ($8.50) or the capellini puttanesca ($9.50). Straightforward salmon, lamb, and chicken classics are reasonably priced at around $15.

More great pizzas and pastas can be scarfed nearby—Pauline's Pizza at Valencia and 14th leaps to mind. But because Il Cantuccio has had to downscale its prices to fight off trendy opposition, it's a pleasant surprise, as well as a bargain.

The Mission

Charanga

A large, spare barn of a place with one long brick wall decorated with raffia shopping baskets, Charanga spills over nightly with hungry hordes, shouting to make themselves heard above the relentless salsa beat. This is the funkier stretch of the Mission, the old *rinconcito latino* that dates to the Spanish era, and which is now gentrifying itself from the bottom up. The varieties of Hispanic food around the Mission run the gamut from Salvadorean pupusas to Nicaraguan nacatamales. But nowadays the hip gatherings come down to Charanga for Cuban-Caribbean rhythms and tapas.

Cost $10–25

Address 2351 Mission St between 19th and 20th
☏ 415/282-1813
Open Tues & Wed
5.30–10pm, Thurs–Sat
5.30–11pm
Transportation 14, 26, 33, 49, BART 16th St
Accepts All major credit cards except AmEx

Bring a big gang of friends with you to quaff the sangria ($3.75 per glass, $13 for a 5-glass mini-pitcher) and party down, Havana style. A dozen or so choices begin with organic spinach salad of onions, fennel, pears, walnuts, goat cheese, and tarragon-lemon vinaigrette ($6.50), which is simple enough but felicitously matched with deep-fried maduros, or sweet plantains. Patatas a la brava ($4.50) come with peppery tomato salsa, while fried yucca wedges in smoky chipotle aioli ($5.50) pack a dark and smoldering kick. Ceviche ($4.50) is made with red snapper and served with marquitas, or plantain chips. Chalupas de salmon "Quepena" ($9) is a tortilla layered with puréed black beans, salmon, and cabbage. You may prefer to lose the tortilla, but you'll refuse to share a single crumb of the flambéed shrimp and squid with coconut rice in ginger sauce ($9.50), or the chicken with rice, raisins, and vivid black and green olives ($9.50). Picadillo Cubano con platanos ($9.50), or minced beef with plantains, olives, and raisins, is a staple of Cuban cuisine that's found across the Hispanic Caribbean and even in Brazil; feel reassured—Cubans have tested Charanga's picadillo and pronounced it the real thing. Blackberry mango crisp cobbler ($6) is the best dessert, and yes, they encourage you to share.

Service is exceptionally amiable, with a discernibly gay- and lesbian-friendly vibe. All in all, this is a fair bet for a big party of night-crawlers. Friends, salsa at ear-splitting decibels, enough sangria to float your boat—how can any band of merrymakers go wrong?

Delfina

High marks go to Craig Stoll and Anne Spencer's hyped and hard-to-get-into darling of the Mission. All other felicities aside, even the acoustics can be praised—now that they've been improved by baffling. The decor is exceedingly plain, with a couple of abstract canvases adorning the walls, plus something that looks like plastic quilting wound around the top as a frieze, but somehow it's cool. There's no linen,

Cost $25–60

Address 3621 18th St at Guerrero
📞 415/552-4055
Open Mon–Thurs & Sun 5.30–10pm, Fri & Sat 5.30–11pm
Transportation 22, 26, 33, J, BART 16th St
Accepts MasterCard, Visa

ITALIAN

but the small, aluminium tables are frequently cleaned, and the longish bar has seating. The emphasis is all on food.

Nobody could fault the swift, intelligent service, which really works that floor. The sausage appetizer ($8.50) is a good way to begin. And what a sausage! Bouncy, bendy, fennel-flecked pork is flavoured with pepper and chile flakes, plus discreet ginger, pickle juice, and beet-stained onions. The fish in the brandade of salt cod ($8.50) is baked with potatoes, cream, and lots of caramelized onions, dished in a small ramekin and served with caraway-seeded lavosh; it's an imaginatively dressed, if small, classic. To follow, locally caught Bolinas halibut roasted in fig leaves with lemon-tarragon butter ($17.25) is inspired; the tarragon adds anise depth, with enough citric tang to pick up the lean white flesh of the fish. Pappardelle sugo ($13) is pasta with a hint of brown sugar picking up the porky sweetness. Grilled local king salmon with fresh cranberry beans and salsa verde ($17) comes just seared, with a hint of mint in the salsa smear and fruitiness in the Tom Thumb tomatoes and garden beans. Profiteroles ($7.95) are done the way Americans like them: crispy, crunchy dough balls are filled with homemade espresso ice cream, and covered with toasted almonds and a plain black chocolate sauce.

The wine list is eclectic but well chosen. Cold Heaven Viognier from Paso Robles ($8.25 per glass) is bright and white with a citrus afterbite, while Floating Mountain Sauvignon Blanc, from New Zealand's Waipara region, is aromatic with lots of pear ($6.50). Delfina may be over-hyped, but all in all it's living up to its publicity, which is a pleasant surprise in itself.

Esperpento Tapas Restaurant

If you're in the Mission and missing Madrid or Seville, Esperpento is one solution—among many—and it's not unreasonably priced. This crowded, informal hangout tapped straight into the craze for tapas when it opened in the early 1990s, and ten years on, it retains its energy, along with a festive red and yellow interior that's full of coming-at-you sights and sounds, as well as trademark jugs of sangria. Tables loaded with ravers spill over onto the sidewalk and strolling mariachi bands—even an occasional flamenco dancer—come by on Fridays and Saturdays. Happily, the food is as lively as the decor.

Cost S15–25
Address 3295 22nd St at Valencia
☎ 415/282-8867
Open Mon–Thurs 11am–3pm & 5–10pm, Fri 11am–3pm & 5–11pm, Sat 11am–11pm, Sun noon–10pm
Transportation 14, 26, 48, BART 24th St
Accepts MasterCard, Visa

A jug of sangria ($15) fills around five glasses. Fifty or more tapas choices start at around $4 per plate and include some familiar potato dishes, such as papas bravas ($3.50). There's also a classic tortilla de papas, worthy of the counter of a real Spanish bar, which is served in a number of varieties, including hot braised peppers, asparagus, and spinach ($5.50). A calamari ceviche is one of the most sustaining and tasty choices, as is the mussels in wine and pepper vinaigrette, and a dish of fried chicken livers ($4.50) which tastes like pâté. Don't forget ropa vieja ($4), literally "old clothes," which is long-simmered beef that's pull-apart tender. If you don't think tapas are going to fill you, try a paella marinera ($26 for two people, $78 for six). It's chock full of prawns, clams, and calamari, and you can easily share this filling fare around the table.

The Mission has dozens of tapas restaurants these days, so it's worth pointing out some of Esperpento's advantages, such as the lower prices and fun sidewalk scene. Points like these make it enduringly popular, so big parties should make reservations ahead. European visitors can be nonplussed at how tough it is to find somewhere that lets them smoke, and Esperpento's sidewalk tables make a rare solution in this city—although whether neighboring diners will take kindly to the smoke is another question.

Foreign Cinema

Foreign Cinema aims to be about movies as much as food. This is the place that dares to give that dinner-and-a-movie concept an extra spell of *verismo*, Via Veneto-style. Housed around a high-walled patio open to the sky, the ambiance is one of industrial chic. Owner John Varnedoe lowered a giant statue of Jesus by helicopter when he opened this place with an inaugural screening of

Cost $20–35
Address 2534 Mission St
☎ 415/648-7600
Open Tues–Sat 6–11pm
Transportation 14, 49, BART 24th St
Accepts All major credit cards except Diners

Fellini's *La Dolce Vita*—a gesture that gladdened cinema-lovers' hearts. Since Varnedoe also owns the fabled on-again, off-again music bar and bistro Bruno's, over the road—a running melodrama in itself—it must have taken nerves of steel to launch an adventure like this one.

Films continue to flicker on the patio walls, but the fare is cheaper and less pretentious than it once was. Incoming chefs John Clark and Gayle Pirie have been imported from Zuni to be the new team, and super-chefs like Alice Waters line up to try their roast chicken and granitas. The new menu is homey Italian rather than haute French—hold the foie gras, said the zeitgeist—and prices have been eased down to match. Rather than the snails and frogs' legs of yore, starters now kick off with heart-warming zuppas ($7), fresh tomato and basil salads ($8), and chunky crostini ($7), made with Foreign Cinema's trademark breads and focaccia. Recession-proof comfort food, that's the message. Main courses feature familiar pork loin and chicken dishes, as well as classics such as a filet steak au poivre vert with purée of fava beans, greens, and caramelized carrots and zucchini, pegged at a restrained $19. Fruit crumbles and soufflés follow, with an ever-welcome bread pudding ($5) and those pineapple or seasonal fruit granitas ($5).

So, cutting frills hasn't cut the atmosphere, and fanatic cinemagoers can now enjoy their Fellini and food for less. The truth is people have always come here to eat rather than to watch the flickering images projected against the concrete walls. Long-term fans of Bruno's and Foreign Cinema may miss those crazy earlier days, but they'll stay the course, because Vanadoe's mini-miracle is a glorious adornment to the ever-lively Mission.

VEGAN

Herbivore: The Earthly Grill

Vegetarian places grow like weeds in San Francisco, but vegan restaurants are fewer and farther between, which is the main reason that Herbivore has its following among the evolved and forward-thinking young of the Mission District. There's even an oxygen bar next door, with a special, half-price oxygen deal during the Tuesday happy hour—what a bargain appetizer to have before popping in here! Herbivore's light golden walls, bowls of fresh pomegranates and apples, poppy-red-stained wooden furniture and patio seating make for a calming environment, though service can be casual. This is one of only a handful of places in town that can ensure that the food has absolutely no animal products, but non-vegans will generally find something to enjoy, too.

Cost	$9–25
Address	983 Valencia St at 21st
☎	415/826-5657
Open	Mon–Thurs & Sun 11am–10pm, Fri & Sat 11am–11pm
Transportation	14, 26, J, BART 24th St
Accepts	MasterCard, Visa

The menu is a veritable United Nations of food favorites, from pad thai, falafel and tacos to shish kebab and lasagne, as though the owners were trying to ensure the global impact of their vegan gospel. Vegetables and herbs are used as creatively as you'd expect in a variety of herby salsas and pestos. Various Japanese-style noodle starters ($6.25–7.50) change regularly, but may include one of pesto and sun-dried tomatoes, another with curried coconut sauce, or a third with zippy coriander and horseradish. Bruschetta with the same sun-dried tomato spread, or alternatively with garlic aioli and corn in red pepper and lemon, makes another good choice, as does a mixed grilled vegetables plate ($6.50). Among the main dishes, lasagna with porcini mushrooms ($7.95) comes with a non-fat, not-real-cheese dressing, which just about gets by on the forest-floor taste of the porcini.

The cheese at Herbivore gives rise to debates about its desirability. Notoriously, non-fat cheese has little to recommend it other than a lack of animal milk solids. When fat falls below a certain percentage, say ten percent, food simply ceases to taste the way it used to, and some of Herbivore's cheese dishes may strike you as not worthy of a non-vegan's time. But this is a pleasant place to meet someone and while away the time, and it's certainly a boon for vegans.

Hung Yen Restaurant

Lost in nowhere-land behind what used to be called "Intermission," this phenomenally cheap Vietnamese pho palace is housed in a former taqueria originally assembled from a Nissan hut. Plonked down among the artists' lofts and warehouses, year by year it seemed to acquire another palm, another piece of plastic awning, then a bigger side section outdoors. Now it has mysteriously blossomed into a feasible place for a sunny brunch or modest celebration, and it all comes down—in local opinion, anyway—to the hot and spicy pho soup. This is not inverted snobbery—many San Franciscans swear that it has curative powers that border on the paranormal.

Cost $5–15

Address 3100 18th St at Harrison
☎ 415/621-8531
Open Daily 11am–11pm
Transportation 12, 27, 33
Accepts MasterCard, Visa

VIETNAMESE

Whether you're coming down with something or not, a trip to get this soup is a good investment in your health. Hot and sour pho soup ($5.40) is aromatic with Thai basil and lemongrass and swims with chile spices. Deep within the bowl bob slices of onion, beef, mint, noodles, and more, and you can add peppers, greens, and sprouts, in classic pho style. Somehow, it adds up to a meal and a half, and it's sinus-clearing and mood-altering to boot; if you lived on two bowls of this a day, you'd surely be a healthier and happier person. Portions are large here, prices rock-bottom cheap, and if it's a fine day you can sit in the partial shade of the makeshift outdoor terrazzo. On cold winter nights, you can perch at a little formica seat inside to keep warm. The usual imperial and spring rolls ($4.25) are excellent and come quickly, along with addictive Vietnamese dipping sauces. Other appetizers include bean cakes ($5.40), which also come with a curry ($6.40) as a main dish, and there are also some standard main-course dishes like sweet-and-sour pork ($6), or barbecued pork over rice ($6.50), and variations on chicken with bean sprouts over noodles ($6.50). Vietnamese coffee ($2) or Tsingao tops it off.

Service is the very best kind: brusquely goodnatured and speedy. Public transport means a long walk in any direction, but anyone with wheels should try a detour for that legendary soup.

The Mission

Le Krewe

(icon) Maybe the company and friendly service help, but Le Krewe does do that Creole voodoo well. Situated in the cursed spot where 3Ring and Val 21 sickened and died, it is run by former P.J.'s Oysterbed staffers, and specializes in New Orleans seafood—with a fusion spell or two. Taking its name from the New Orleans brotherhoods that march in Mardi Gras, it sports in-your-face sweet pepper colors of red, yellow, and green, with the addition of a funky faux tree, a French Quarter-style oyster bar, and bluesy Neville and Allman Brothers sounds. There's even a black magic shop across the road.

Cost $15–35

Address 995 Valencia St at 21st
(T) 415/643-0995
Open Tues–Thurs & Sun 5.30–10pm, Fri & Sat 5.30–11pm; brunch Sat & Sun 10am–3pm
Transportation 14, 26, 49, BART 24th St
Accepts All major credit cards except Diners

If the menu isn't a string of unbroken successes, neither is it traditionally Creole—they even dish up Cajun-Asian "Let the good times roll!" spring rolls ($5.95). Nor are fried green tomatoes ($5.50) strictly Cajun-Creole in their pretty basil and red pepper coulis. Popcorn shrimp ($6.50) is soggy, but comes with well-crisped okra and with a lime-edged mustard sauce that lingers; it's a lavish portion, too. The Mumbo Jumbo Gumbo ($4 small, $6 large) has the right stuff: it's dark, viscous and cayenne-fiery with a thyme underlay. The crawfish étoufée ($6.50) is a rich compilation of sweet flesh and spiced sauce on a light roux, while N'Awlins po' boys ($7) spill over with oysters, catfish, or shrimp. Jambalaya with andouille chicken and shrimp ($8) is a little dull, but (whenever available as a special) the wine-braised beef brisket with peppery mustard greens and ketchup "lightning" ($8) merits a flash. You'll also want to try the grilled alligator tail with green papaya salad ($8)—how "fusion" is that? Fall back on plantation fried chicken ($8) if it's all too much. Beignets ($6) are tough and wizened, albeit honey-soaked, while bread pudding ($6) hits a deep bourbon stop.

Of the ninety-odd restaurants along the Valencia restaurant strip, Krewe is the only one doing that Cajun-Creole gris-gris magic. Oh, and you don't have to raise your top and flash anyone for Mardi Gras beads; just ask.

The Liberties

If haute Irish pub cuisine exists, Eugene Power is partly responsible—he certainly leads the cooks at the roaring bars of this town. Eugene introduced Myles O'Reilly's stunning raw bar at O'Reilly's of North Beach—a courageous move, since American bars generally keep to fries and chicken wings. When he opened his own place in this former bar on a parking-challenged corner of Guerrero, he called it after the oldest part of Dublin, the Liberties. Not all boozers want to be gourmet choosers, but Eugene upgraded his menu from burgers and sandwiches to salmon and venison potpies, and served homemade Hollandaise with his fries. The times have now convinced him to carry on with the staples, however, and he has now abandoned the wild game au jus and venison potpies for less costly fare.

Cost $12–20

Address 998 Guerrero St at 22nd
℡ 415/282-6789
Open Daily 11am–midnight
Transportation 26, 48, 49, 67, J, BART 24th St
Accepts All major credit cards

Not that Eugene's Cal-Hibernian take on food was ever pretentious. It is straightforward and anything but folksy. His Irish carbonara ($11.50), marries penne to Irish bacon, parsley, and cheese, and it is deeply satisfying. His fish and chips ($9.50) are arguably the best in town, and he has brought the potato cake back into prominence, so you could reasonably call the no-nonsense menu "Irish." The salmon boxty ($7.95) are potato fishcakes, and resemble Yiddish latkes or what the French call criques—but whatever you call them, they're a great brunch dish, and also come in a hopped-up version with roast peppers. Beg for his secret recipe, and Eugene insists it comes down to refrigeration—leave the mashed potatoes for a day, and the starch apparently stiffens. The rest of his menu introduces soups ($4), ever-popular beef and mushroom potpies ($10.50), very fat burgers with fries ($10.50), and fillet of salmon with mashed potatoes and vegetables ($13.95), along with roast Cornish hens ($12.50).

A dining nook at the front and a small room at the back accommodate parties, while the huge and handsome bar counter with its carved wood is handy for solo diners or twosomes. Eugene has now taken over the Phoenix on Valencia, too, but clearly this is still where his heart lies.

Lorca Spanish Bar & Restaurant

(🍴) This place is friendly: a Spanish waiter greets parties like they're old friends, even if it's after 10pm, the place has emptied and the group includes a teething baby. Window tables are thrillingly reminiscent of the set of "The Cook, The Thief, His Wife and Her Lover," crisp linen contrasting with deep Rioja walls. The entire experience of Lorca is like a magic carpet to Seville, and if that voyeuristic window onto 24th Street makes diners self-conscious by night, it

Cost $8–25
Address 3200 24th St at South Van Ness
☎ 415/550-7510
Open Mon–Sun 7am–midnight
Transportation 12, 14, 48, 49, BART 24th St
Accepts All major credit cards except Diners

also provides for fine people watching over breakfast and lunch. And then there's the music—what other Spanish restaurant has the sheer breadth of imagination to follow Mongolian throat-singing tapes with a live guitarist singing and whistling "two-tone" songs simultaneously?

Swig your way through a pitcher of rather potent sangria (from $15) while you hoover down every tapas ($4–7.50) that appears magically from the kitchen. Crispy calamari with anchovy aioli and lemon is tongue tingling, while pimientos de piquillo ($9) stuffed with bacalao and sweet pea purée is mouth-watering (but not eye-watering). Fresh prawns come smothered in garlic, and a classical patatas bravas is well spiced. The tapas are enough to keep you going, but if you're ravenous go for the pièce de résistance from chef David Rodriguez: fillet of bass with creamed spinach, caramelized onions, pinole, and raisins ($18). It's piping hot when it comes, and puffs of aromatic steam rise from the striped layers, torta-style. Exquisite presentations sometimes conceal a certain lack of excitement, but not in this dish, which has a vitality born of careful preparation and fine ingredients. Alternatively there's baked chicken with a brochette of mixed vegetables ($14). Desserts (all $5) offer a fine flan, an acceptable cheesecake and sponge cake in strawberry jam and ice cream. Among the wines are some vintage Riojas.

The waiters display admirable tolerance and ease. You can easily linger over a meal here, and you're never rushed, even as closing time approaches. When the bill eventually arrives, you'll find it more than reasonable.

Luna Park

"Exactly why is Luna Park so magnetic?" people ask, whenever they pass the boys and girls swarming around one of Valencia's busiest doorways. This part of town is the hipster section—cool bars, cool bookstores and cool boutiques, with the Roxie movie house on the corner—and Luna's amiable charm is not so hard to work out once you're inside. It feels very young: this is the stately pleasure dome you'd imagine Bjork would run if Bjork had gone to an American summer camp and later decided to open her own hipster hangout on a whim. Luna Park's madcap design includes an assembly of *objets trouvés* dangling across exposed brick above a cluster of old, gray-green church pews, and the gigantic, throbbing bar comes complete with a very social cocktail scene.

Chef Joe Jack and A.J. Gilbert's "most excellent" menu features fondue or barbecue pots that help make an evening here curiously childlike fun. Much of the food brings on instant feelings of nostalgia, but it often comes with a modern twist. Fondue ($6.50) is made with delicious local goat cheese and served with grilled toast and apple slices. Starters include a handful of everything-but-the-sink salads in mammoth portions—the romaine with nuts and Gorgonzola is a standout. A big plate of mussels comes with French fries of crispy distinction, and there's a splendidly thick and juicy hamburger ($14) those same fries. Pastas include dishes such as rigatoni with sausage ($7.75), and there are playful pizzas (up to $12). A Pot on Fire ($13.95) turns out to be beef brisket in simmered vegetables, and there's always a fish of the day.

Desserts are exceptionally inventive, and aimed straight below the belt of any ten-year-old child—ten-year-olds of all ages, in fact. The most enjoyable must be marshmallow s'mores ($5.50), which are lickable squares of brownie, marshmallow, and chocolate that you paste together on a fork then melt into a swoony mess over the fondue flame, though the San Francisco Chronicle pronounces the pecan-bourbon chocolate cake ($6.50) "one of the best". Decibels just keep on rising here, but the welcome is toasty warm. Come at lunchtime if you hate waiting, and come hungry.

El Nuevo Frutilandia

In a neatly repainted Mission diner that's been around forever, the Frutilandia serves tropical tapas and drinks that nobody else used to do, and now everyone wants. Amazingly, this modest charmer has morphed from Cuban dive to pan-Caribbean tapas bar, seemingly overnight. Plonk yourself down at the counter or at one of the tiny tables to chat with the friendly woman owner who dishes Cuban and Puerto-Rican fare on the spot. A backtrack of Jesus Alemañy and the Afro-Cuban All Stars helps the ambiance along. But Puerto-Rican newspapers sit near the door, and the food is as much Caribbean as Cuban, you'll note.

Cost $8–15

Address 3077 24th St
between Folsom and Treat
℡ 415/648-2958
Open Tues–Fri 11.30am–3pm
& 5–9.30pm, Sat & Sun
noon–10pm
Transportation 12, 14, 48, 49,
BART 24th St
Accepts MasterCard, Visa

Calamares ($7.95), fried up simply with salt and lemon, make a good appetizer for helping down a Cuban beer like a Hatuey, as do the crispy alcapurrias ($1.50), or meat-stuffed yucca fritters. There's usually a soup, such as black bean ($5), and a salad such as the zingy ceviche de pargo ($5.25), or carp ceviche. An appetizer platter ($7.25) of deep-fried green plantains with a tamale-style dumpling, some banana chips, and more stuffed yucca fritters makes a good introduction to Puerto-Rican food, and two could share it for lunch. Plantains fried with beans and rice with cream ($5.25) is a ubiquitous dish in the Latino Mission, and they do plantains well here. Main dishes begin with chicken stew with tropical vegetables ($7.75) and continue with picadillo a la Habana vieja ($7.95), a braised beef stew, and mofongo ($7.50), or garlicky mashed plantain and pork. At lunchtime, especially on hot days, regulars opt for the refreshing guayabana and tamarindo tropical shakes (around $2.50), although a few wines and excellent Mexican beers like Modelo are also served.

Sometimes the Frutilandia could use more help: its warmhearted chef-owners cook affordable, bright food with vivid flavours, but on weekend nights they occasionally get swamped. This used to be a dodgy corner of 24th Street, but not anymore—the surrounding shops are panaderias and "mexicatessens," making this a gloriously aromatic *rinconcito latino*. Come here in the morning, when the street smells of Mexican fresh-baked bread, and you'll join the ranks of brunching Mission-aries.

Pakwan

(🍴) One thing everyone agrees on: the rowdy environment and service at this place are flat-out offputting. But everyone also agrees that the aromatic tandoori food is so amazingly good and comes so quickly that it mitigates that first impression—and recently, Pakwan made a surprisingly successful attempt to smarten up the formerly bare-bones joint up a little. These days you may catch smiles on the counter-hands, a welcome sight. The owners also improved the acoustics by draping silken fabric across the ceiling, adding old utensils like sieves to the walls. Somehow this muffles the noise and adds color. Pakwan is the best Indian at this end of town, bar none. It draws a young and wallet-challenged crowd, and the low, low prices explain the high volume.

Cost $4–15

Address 3180 16th St at Guerrero
☎ 415/255-2440
Open Daily 11.30am–3pm & 4.30–11pm
Transportation 22, 26, 33, J, BART 16th St
Accepts Cash only

Sinus-blasting tandoori choices on a short, pungent menu are the thing here. You take a number from the aforementioned counter-hand, then head for a seat under the big top. Start with the crisp and golden nan bread ($1), then choose from any of the lamb or chicken kebabs, curries and kormas ($3.99–6.99), adding pakoras or samosas (from $1.50). Generally speaking, the high volume and turnover in this madhouse ensure that everything's fresher than fresh. An unbeatable chicken masala ($6.99) in a thick blanket of smooth yogurt and coconut-creamed dressing is spiked with cardamom, fenugreek, and chile. The other great favorites on Pakwan's menu are the vegetarian dishes, such as the curried chickpea stew ($4.50), vegetables in spices ($4.50), or bhartha pakwan ($5.50), a justly celebrated specialty of the house that brings eggplant together with a yogurt and tomato sauce.

Students on a budget would feel right at home in this place. They don't serve beer, but you can bring your own, and wine too. Don't come if you can't stand noise or searing spices—or the heat of the kitchen, for that matter. But if you like piping hot, eye-tearing Indian, or Pakistani food, and can put up with the busy atmosphere, Pakwan is unbeatable value.

Pancho Villa Taqueria

It's not clear exactly who invented the Mission District's first meal of choice, the burrito. Most people believe it was born here, around San Francisco's oldest streets, but the truth of the matter is that its birthplace probably lies in Sonora. Whatever its origins, nothing can beat the burrito as cheap, healthy fast food—unless it's the taco or quesadilla. Of all the Mission's taquerias, Pancho Villa is probably the most reliable and popular, and it's always got a line, though luckily it's a fast-moving one. The tiled interior is bleak, with glaring overhead lighting, plastic tables, and no frills whatsoever—and it's not at all Americanized in the clearing-up department either.

Cost $6–20
Address 3071 16th St at Barlett
☏ 415/864-8840
Open Daily 8am–10pm
Transportation 14, 22, 26, 49, 53, BART 16th St
Accepts Cash only

But their burritos and soft tacos are dependably big, good, and cheap—probably the fattest and fastest in town. They start at around $7, and come with a choice of beans, plus picante sauce and fixings like four different kinds of salsa, fresh radishes, guacamole, lettuce, and cream, which usually adds another 85 cents or so. You don't need Spanish in here, but you do need to eyeball the menu and say what you want as soon as it's your turn at the counter. Choose from beef chicken, sausage, tongue, or one of the different kinds of pork; decide what kind of tortilla to wrap it in ("de harina" means flour, but there's also tomato, chile, or wheat); make up your mind if you want hot, mild, tomatillo, or fire-roasted salsa; and then select your beans, whether black, red, or refried. The estimable Huachinango fish taco ($3.45), made with snapper, is a standout, and you can go for broke on a couple of surf 'n' turf quesadilla combos ($16.80), with steak, cheese, and prawns, plus the works. Good Mexican beer such as Dos Equis is available.

You can eat in-house, but Pancho Villa is mostly about the food—scores of Mission places have better atmosphere. Try: San Jose Taqueria, 2830 Mission St, which has highly sought-after tripe and roast pork burritos; Can-Cun, 2288 Mission St, which rides high on vegetarian; or El Farolito, 2779 Mission St, which for quesadillas runs neck and neck with El Tonayense's roving vans.

Puerto Alegre Restaurant

Of all the 383 Mission eateries and the 90 possible spots along the Valencia strip that lie in wait for a group of hell-raisers bent on partying down, Puerto Alegre is a sure bet. It's beloved as much for its crazy, zoo-like atmosphere and the sky-high decibels of its music as for its food, although the gut-punchy Margaritas have a large part to play, too. It's possible that the venerable La Rondalla, at 18th St and Valencia—with its dead buzzard, mariachi academy and crazy Christmas decorations—has more in the way of oddities and atmospherics, but Puerto Alegre boasts both the killer Margaritas and the Oaxacan menu that keeps them coming back for more. The clientele is entirely gringo, and Puerto Alegre serves gringo versions of Mexican fare, but it pulls in the regulars all the same.

MEXICAN

Cost $5–25

Address 546 Valencia St at 16th
☎415/255-8201
Open Mon 11am–10pm, Tues 5–11pm, Wed–Sun 11am–11pm
Transportation 22, 26, BART 16th St
Accepts All major credit cards except AmEx

The stellar reputation of the Puerto Alegre Margarita derives in part from the reasonable cost of a pitcher ($10), which is about the cheapest in town. The price tag rises to $15 for pitchers of this ever-popular tequila and lime cocktail in different fruit permutations. Pitchers come slushy with ice or with salt—but try one plain on the rocks for the real kick. Nibbles include big bowls of chips ($4.95) and nachos with cheese ($4.95). The burritos, tacos, and quesadillas start at just over $4 for chicken or pork or cheese and chile with beans and rice. Various combination plates include a quesadilla and chicken enchilada ($6.95), and a steak with onions, beans, and rice ($7.95). But frankly, the food can be disappointing, and you may find yourself wondering why you remembered it as being so much better the last time you came—until the considerable charms of those cheap Margaritas help you figure it out, that is.

Be warned: you'll have to wait if you haven't made a booking, but a bowl of chips and salsa at the bar will keep you happy for the duration. There are nights when you have to wait at least half an hour, so if it's someone's birthday be sure to call ahead.

Ramblas

🍴 Yet another tapas bar on the Valencia corridor? Where Lorca, Andalu and several others have also opened, and when competition from Timo's and Esperpento is already strong? This ear-splitting hipster hangout is decked out in sympathetic deep reds and mustards, with occasional wood columns, a mosaic or two, some striking photographs of Cuban faces, one or two inlaid antique doors made into glass-topped tables, and a wall of interesting prints and paintings. The noise level is deafening. Yes, there's sangria in jugs, and a reasonable wine list of Riojas, but the real reason Ramblas is winning the young and thirsty to its side is because the ThirstyBear Brewing Company, the avatar of San Francisco tapas bars, runs it, and supplies its boastworthy list of Belgian and craft-brewed beers.

Cost $7–35
Address 557 Valencia St at 16th
☎ 415/565-0207
Open Mon–Thurs & Sun 5–11pm, Fri & Sat 5pm–1am
Transportation 14, 22, 26, 49, BART 16th St
Accepts All major credit cards except Diners

If the sangria is a little bit too sweet and fruity—and what exotic tropical fruit exactly *is* that unidentifiable taste?—it comes in an enormous pitcher ($20), so you'll soon feel better about the food, which is on the stingy side, portions-wise, even for tapas snacks. The list starts with familiar classics like the papas bravas ($4.75), which are dished up nicely on a large earthenware platter in a heavily red-peppered and spiced tomato salsa; they aren't the best you'll find on the strip, though they're certainly good. The morcilla ($5.25), or Barcelona black sausage, the fresh sardines ($5.25), the calamares in garlic ($6.25), and the membrillo or quince jam ($5.50), served with the local cheeses of Barcelona, are all interesting choices, and the Serrano ham ($6.75) is plentiful. Salmon carpaccio ($5.75) is homemade, but tends to be rather dry, while the potato tortilla ($7.75), a bar staple that lives at room temperature under a bell jar on every Spanish counter, arrives somewhat bland and undistinguished, lacking some thyme or diced pepper, perhaps.

But the wait staff are sympathetic, and you'll fall in love with the service, the tables, the atmosphere and the general look of the place—especially those old photographs of Havana.

Ristorante Mereb

One word and one dish wraps up Eritrean, Ethiopian, and Somalian cooking beautifully: injera. This bread fulfils the same role as tortillas do in Mexican food, and no meal comes without this convenient, dinner-plate-sized disk of floppy, flannel-like dough. It's perfect for parceling around messy stews, ideal for sopping up the juices, and a great counterfoil for the tearing heat of berbere spices. At first chew, you wonder if injera couldn't be a bit tastier, but later on its functionality dawns on you and you'll find yourself craving more. A recent influx of Ethiopians has made San Franciscans more familiar with the cuisine of this part of Africa, and this corner restaurant, pristine in its clean, plate-glass, and wood decor, is the highest-profile of several Ethiopian eateries.

Cost $10–25
Address 598 Guerrero St at 18th
☎ 415/863-3031
Open Tues–Sun 5–10pm
Transportation 22, 26, 33, J, BART 18th St
Accepts MasterCard, Visa

Choose from a simple menu of three main meat dishes plus a selection of side dishes, or from six vegetarian options (all $6.95) that can be either side dishes or mains. Almost all of them smoulder with African berbere spices. Vegetarian dishes include the hellaciously hot hamli, the spicy kantisha and the more subtle ades alicha, all of which are variations on rich vegetable casseroles of sweet potatoes and grain, and they all cost the same ($9.95). For carnivores, tsebi derho ($8.95), a stew of marinated chicken chunks, is simmered with fit-fit, a chopped mix of diced tomatoes, peppers, and extra spices; while a lamb stew of juicy chunks simmered in a red-pepper sauce called zigni ($11.95), is juicy and nourishing, with lots of background complexity in the seasoning. Beer, for preference a really choppy lager, makes the best accompaniment, but Mereb does also serve a variety of wines by the bottle (from $18). Coffee comes in tiny thimbles of black purée that resemble the coffee you'd expect to find in a Turkish seraglio—try it!

Service is spanking and the prices reasonable. Mereb is a former grocery redecorated in stylish simplicity, and lacks the funky ambiance of many other Ethiopian places. A very much more elegant vibe is present here, and the airy and immaculate space at first feels a little at odds with the earthiness of the cuisine.

MEXICAN

Roosevelt Tamale Parlor

Tamales are festive little parcels of steamed maize flour with a core of chicken, beef, or cheese and chile, all snugly wrapped up in a husk and tightly tied. Tamale-making is a reason for a fiesta around Christmas time, and you can get the masa harina, lard, and other ingredients to make them anywhere on this end of 24th Street. But they take two days to make from scratch, so it's easier to eat them here, at a place where they've been making them for over eighty

Cost	$5–15
Address	2817 24th St at Bryant
☎	415/550-9213
Open	Tues–Sat 10am–9.45pm, Sun 10am–8.45pm
Transportation	48, BART 24th St
Accepts	Cash only

years. Renamed during the New Deal, Tamales Roosevelt (as it's popularly known) has been run by the same family for the past thirty years. Its cramped, dim interior with Seventies-style formica tables and faux-Spanish colonial touches has not changed in at least a quarter of a century.

Tamales ($6.50) usually have an outer layer of greaseproof paper knotted firmly with string that you have to cut, to reveal another layer of cornhusk. Here, however, they're unwrapped and sit atop rice and a choice of red or black beans, refried or boiled. For this knockdown price, you get two tamales in a choice of cheese and chile, pork, chicken, or beef with rice and beans, with optional extras like a dark brown mole sauce. You can also combine one with an enchilada and a taco on a $9 combination plate. Estimable enchiladas (around $6 separately) and burrito specials ($7) fill out the menu, along with "special treats" such as beefsteak ranchero with rice ($10). Large portions and low prices is why Roosevelt's thrives. There are those who come for the tacos rather than the tamales, and it must be said that it can be a tough choice.

The Mission's tamale-tasting public has many choices, starting with a woman from Merida who sells homemade ones from a bucket at the 24th Street BART station, at a dollar each. Failing that, tamale fanciers mention La Perla, Mexicatessen, Costa del Sol, and El Paisa. But Roosevelt Tamales is as fine an introduction to this wonderful dish—and to a wonderful neighborhood—as you'll find anywhere.

Saigon Saigon

Saigon Saigon offers exquisite Vietnamese food in an immaculate if spartan setting for low prices, and there's no sign of the cell phone and palm pilot crowd that infests places further up Valencia. It's also a paradigm for how fast all things fashionable change in this transient town. When it opened, way back in the last century, this restaurant felt hipper than hip, and looked offputtingly expensive. With almost a decade under its belt,

Cost $4–15

Address 1132 Valencia St at 23rd
☎ 415/206-9635
Open Daily 11.30am–2.30pm & 5.30–10pm
Transportation 14, 26, 49, BART 24th St
Accepts MasterCard, Visa

VIETNAMESE

it has morphed into a useful but déclassé local hangout: its clean, original mix of traditional and new has been mimicked everywhere and yet its prices have hardly gone up. No longer a trendsetting scene, it's a refuge from trendiness instead.

Lunch specials ($4.25) are a terrific deal of four courses, including salad, and generous enough for you to take some home for supper. Later on, traditional starters begin with Vietnamese banh cuon ($4.50), rolls wrapped in translucently thin rice-paper and filled with pork, tofu, or shrimp, with mint and cellophane noodles as topping. Two good salads are the Thai-style larb ($4.25), which is a beef salad with papaya, and the chilled green papaya salad ($4.25), which comes with carrot, a chile-lime dressing, and a tangy herbal trinity of mint, basil, and cilantro. Hot-and-sour soup ($5) is fiery and well considered. Fried softshell crabs are available in season, and the price varies accordingly. Among dinner entrees, the duck salad ($7.95) is a winner, and very modestly priced, as is the delectable salmon in coconut ($7.95). Lemongrass chicken ($6.50) is faultless, and the red curried eggplant ($6.50) more than generous. Most folks opt for the fried banana dessert ($2.95), a flambéed wonder that comes with baby coconut ice cream.

So Saigon Saigon has mysteriously made the transition from frighteningly chic to affordable and friendly. Most Mission-aries are not about to complain—especially those who get hungry of a Monday, as this is that rare and useful thing, a restaurant that opens right through the week.

Ti Couz

From the moment it opened, in the early 1990s, Ti Couz seethed with crêpe-lovers overflowing all over the pavement. It's been expanding ever since, and now boasts some sidewalk cafe tables. All over town, other crêpe places emulate Ti Couz, but they don't do it nearly as well, or at such reasonable prices. If there were any practical way to snag a table ahead of time, people would

Cost S6–20

Address 3108 16th St at Valencia
✆ 415/252-7373
Open Daily 11am–midnight
Transportation 14, 22, 26, 33, 49, BART 16th St
Accepts MasterCard, Visa

probably pay through the nose to do just that. Amazingly, Ti Couz doesn't suffer from all this popularity, and their crêpes seem even more desirable than the best cheese-filled pancake you might buy from a French street stall.

Ti Couz is Breton for "my house" and the specialty of the *couz* is traditional, Breton, savory buckwheat crêpes ($4.50–7), not the usual dessert variety available elsewhere—although they serve those, too. They come with a wide variety of fillings, including combinations such as caramelized onions with mushrooms, cheese and almonds, shrimp and crab, and the old reliable tomato, basil, and cheese. These fill twelve-inch square, chunky crêpes, whose sides are then pressed over. Ratatouille makes another wonderful filling, as do saumon fumé, saucisson, and spinach with toasted pecans and Roquefort. One crêpe will suffice at lunch, but for dinner you might want to add soupe à l'oignon ($3.50) as a starter; it has thick croutons and surprising intensity. Salads ($3.75–9.95) are made from organic greens and come in a range of sizes. For dessert, sweeter pancakes are offered, with another wide variety of fillings. Fans of Nutella need look no further for their hazelnut-chocolate fix, as Nutella dessert pancakes are top sellers; the delice version ($5) comes with banana ice cream. Alternatively, try fruit-and-hint-o'kerosene flambéed crêpe Suzette ($5).

Five different kinds of cider are served, including Woodchuck and the usual weak Breton Clos Normandy cider, plus a few wines by the glass. They also serve French non-alcoholic drinks like citron pressé, in darling little china bowls. This success story is simple. San Franciscans like to feel French for under $20 per head; for the pleasure of meeting a tiny bit of Brittany, they'll wait.

Timo's

Ever since Colombian chefs Carlos and Theresa Corredor took over the "alternative" Crystal bar at this corner and turned it into the Mission's first tapas joint, it has been a hit. Timo's interior is a packed bar bubbling with Fauvist oranges and blue hues. Extra minty, stiff mojitos are served up by the Irish barman, the sangria rocks, and the wine list is rich in Riojas. An odd confluence of people winds up here, cramming the tables and overwhelming the benches in the long backroom. What they have in common is a passion for garlic, sangria, and talk. What more could you want? Well, parking, and maybe another slice of creamy tortilla, golden and pepper-flecked outside and near-runny inside.

Cost $8–35

Address 842 Valencia St at 19th
☎ 415/647-0558
Open Mon–Thurs & Sun 5.30–10.30pm, Fri & Sat 5.30–11pm, Sun 5–10pm
Transportation 14, 26, 33, 49
Accepts All major credit cards except Diners

SPANISH

The tortilla ($4.75) is something of a Spanish tradition, although here they call it tortilla española to ensure the Mission crowd doesn't expect a flattened burrito. Several other dishes pay homage to the potato, including papas y hongos, here re-christened Potato Decadence ($7.75), which is a gratin of Yukon Gold scallops with wild mushrooms. Along with a carafe of berry, citrus, and peach-sweetened red or white sangria ($14), try ajiaco ($8.50), a Colombian three-potato soup with capers, corn, cilantro, and cream; or garlic soup with poached egg gratinada ($6.75). Champiñones a la plancha ($4.75) are mushrooms in garlic and parsley, while juicy gambas al ajillo ($8.75) are prawns sautéed in wine. Mushroom quesadillas ($5.75) bubble with cheese, cilantro, and chiles. The tender duck confit cassoulet ($11.75) is simmered with white beans and pork pieces and then sprinkled with crumbs. Mejillones en escabeche ($8.75) are mussels grilled with paprika and wine, while sweet-sauced spinach ($4.75) comes Catalan-style with pinenuts, raisins, and apricots. Fish (from $11.50) is spice-rubbed salmon, tuna, or monkfish.

Carlos is an eclectic cook as well as a tapas pioneer. Since the arrival of Timo's, the Mission has burst into tapas all over, but this is one of the few to take reservations. Drivers will find parking tedious; so difficult, in fact, that some park in the median. Tapas lovers may risk this discreet weekend solution, but it can't exactly be recommended.

The Mission

Tokyo Go Go

San Francisco is such a heaven for sushi lovers that even in the mainly Latino Mission district you're spoiled for choice. Choose upscale sushi, downscale sushi, sushi in a funky decor, even Country and Western sushi. But the reason Tokyo Go Go pulls crowds is because it marries the weird glamor of retro seating and lime and tangerine circles of color in its decor to an izakaya cocktail bar theme, complete with Japanese lounge seating, dangling globe lights of varying sizes, tall tables, and counter stools that rise and fall. The owner, Ken Lowe, also runs the equally fun Ace Wasabi, in the Marina.

Cost $15–35

Address 3174 16th St at Guerrero
☎ 415/864-2288
Open Tues–Thurs 5.30–10.30pm, Fri & Sat 5.30–11pm, Sun 5–11pm
Transportation 22, 26, BART 24th St
Accepts MasterCard, Visa

The food is as playful as the decor. It's a judicious mix of traditional sushi and chef Kiyoshi Hayakawa's not-so-traditional inventions. Set on futuristic-looking, glazed cobalt-blue plates—in triangular, round or square shapes—the sushi, sashimi, and temaki look so beautiful that you want to take photographs. Some of the chef's far-out flights of fancy may confuse Japanese traditionalists: anyone for salmon, cucumber, sun-dried tomatoes, and capers in Tuscan temaki ($4)? Try it anyway, and then order the "duck duck" ($9.75), a plate of spinach tossed with chunks of duck breast dressed in zesty ume, with fried duck slivers wrapped around rice balls, nori, and crackling; it's delicious, and enough for two to share. Tuna nigiri, or maguro ($3.95), and eel, or unagi ($3.95), come in ample chunks, as does marinated sake ($3.50), and yellowtail, or hamachi ($3.95). Creative maki include an ever-popular spider roll ($9.75) made with fried softshell crab, avocado, and lettuce. Flying Kamikaze ($10.50) is tuna on an asparagus and tuna roll in ponzu sauce. Satays are another wildly eclectic bunch: try the large, rare shrimp in vinegar ($7.95), the tofu in garlic-miso ($3.25), or chicken with teriyaki ($3.75). For dessert, banana banzai ($6), a brilliant concoction, is banana tempura on ice cream in phyllo.

Zippy cocktails (from $6) like Hawaiian Aloha, Mandarin Cosmo, Geisha Girl, and Cold Fusion complete the rakish kick of pearly nigiri in martini glasses, as do unusual Scotch whiskies like Macallan 18-year-old and Highland Park 12-year-old.

La Traviata

(🍴) Tucked into a downtrodden block of the Mission District, this half-hidden trattoria aims to ambush you. Step into their cramped lobby and you're faced with big photos of a costumed Pavarotti as Alfredo and Beverly Sills as Violetta, matched inside by photos of other stars giving Verdi their top Cs to a soundtrack of operatic arias. With all these grandiose trappings, La Traviata deserves to be somewhere near the

Cost $10–35
Address 2854 Mission St at 25th
☎ 415/282-0500
Open Tues–Sun 4.30–10.30pm
Transportation 14, 26, 48, 49, BART 24th St
Accepts All major credit cards

ITALIAN

Opera House. Its interior lies somewhere between cozy and claustrophobic, with wood-paneled walls and tables wedged closely against one another, all surrounded by operatic memorabilia. The owners are Albanians with a big appetite for Verdi, but their fare is strictly Italian, with an emphasis on Calabrian regional specialties. La Traviata has been here forever—during the 1989 earthquake this was one of the few places to stay open, sustaining legions of stranded foreign journalists—so they've been doing something right.

Portions are Pavarotti-sized. The soups are inspired and change daily; you may find chard and tomato ($4.25), which is especially rich. The antipasti always include several salads, often with a tomato and mozzarella plate ($6.50). Gnocchi ($10) are homemade, and to be treasured: although they are supposed to be mere first courses, you'll find every gnocchi dish heaped high enough for two. Pastas (from $16) such as linguine with speck and wild mushrooms fill all available gaps, while creamed risottos ($16) with wine, clams, shrimp, and more are ideal for shellfish lovers. The desserts are conventional tiramisus ($4.50), but don't worry, you'd have trouble finding room. The wine list is short, with bottles priced from $18, but it's enough to make any fat lady sing.

La Traviata has a decidedly old-fashioned, comforting feel, and perhaps it deserves a slightly less dog-eared block. It's ideal for an occasion like a cozy get-together with relatives, or just for someone living near this neck of the woods who feels the urge to eat decent Italian food. It'll certainly fill you up if you're starving, so remember the Albanians near 25th and Mission.

Truly Mediterranean

(🍴) Whenever debates fire up on the topic ‚of the very best homemade falafel in the city, Truly Mediterranean wins hands down. It's a fixture of San Francisco life—and it really *does* make the best falafel sandwich. It certainly furnishes the indispensable fuel to keep you going through any movie at the Roxie cinema next door, or even to last out the ludicrously funny, five-hour Oscars send-up party that's hosted there. But with just two tiny tables and a counter, you could hardly call it a restaurant, and besides, there's never any room to sit down; it's simply too crowded—the line winds down the block.

Cost $5–10
Address 3109 16th St at Valencia
☎ 415/252-7482
Open Mon-Sat 11am–midnight, Sun 11am–10pm
Transportation 22, 26, 33, BART 16th St
Accepts Cash only

More or less everybody orders the same thing here: the shawarma ($5.25), which is an over-spilling, toppling, jumbo bundle of two falafel balls in a bulging lavash, stuffed with grilled eggplant and drowned in a grainy, lemon-herbed tahini sauce, with a well-parsleyed portion of carrot, diced tomato, and romaine salad, plus a healthy dash of Tabasco; sometimes there are more vegetables lurking in there, too—it's a lucky dip. The whole is encased in silver foil, but be careful with your fillings. The entire elaborate parcel will give you the strength to carry on all day long—in fact, it's so generous in size that most people can only eat half at once. Falafel balls can also be ordered on their own ($3.50), and there are kebabs ($6.25) too, such as a marinated skewer of spiced lamb with a souvlaki-style minted yogurt sauce and onions.

Full marks then, unless you actually want eat sitting down. In that case you'll do better to head for Truly Mediterranean's other branch, in the Haight, at 1724 Haight St, or else plump for Ali Baba's Cave or Amira, around the corner on Valencia, where you'll be able to get your Mission district Middle-Eastern fix while you lounge around in cushioned comfort, and watch belly-dancers as a bonus. The city may be spoiled for shawarma joints, but Truly Med is the best for sheer takeout value.

Walzwerk

Isabell and Christiane work hard to champion the snubbed potential of East German fare at this plain brathaus on the Mission's edge. It's unfair to make jokes about it, they say. Walzwerk means "industrial mill," by the way, and there are several nearby. The aesthetic is minimalist to the point of bare, and shared wooden tables are set with assorted cutlery and crockery. But the service is really friendly and the food, especially the herring, is unbeatable when the fraüleins are in the kitchen.

Cost $10–30

Address 381 South Van Ness Ave at 14th
☎ 415/551-7181
Open Tues–Sat 5.30–10.30pm
Transportation 12, 16, 22, 26
Accepts All major credit cards

The beer is foaming and zesty, especially the golden-tinted Berline Heisse ($4 a pint), which you can have with a shot of syrup to counterbalance the aftertaste. There's a soup of the day ($5), perhaps a simple beet soup, but otherwise the cooking is what you'd hope for from a Valkyrie earth goddess: pickled herring salad with potatoes; bratwurst with potatoes; pork chops with potatoes; potato pancakes. First, the herring ($7), two fillets don't in fact just come with potatoes, but also with potato salad and beets. The bratwurst ($11) is the real imported kind, and comes with pickles and salad. Pork chops ($13) come with red cabbage in vinegar with juniper berries and caraway, just as they should. The chicken main dish ($12) comes stuffed with apple and with vinegar-cured cabbage, while fish of the day (from $12) often comes with, yes, potatoes—but this time sautéed—and may be bass, halibut, snapper, or salmon. This short menu changes daily, and the prices vary, but never by very much. Try their flourless chocolate cake ($5), if it's available (it's not always); it makes diners shout for insulin.

Walzwerk serves a meal that's inexpensive for its excellence, and you can park easily. And it's hardly an "industrial mill." So if you like to hoist a foaming beer stein and try a few words on the mainly German-speaking diners, and you like your potatoes served as German potato cakes along with hearty sausages, and your herrings pickled and served with a potato salad, then drop by. Walzwerk is a tribute to German cuisine.

Watergate

FUSION

(icon) Watergate feels a bit out of place for Valencia Street, as though it got lost on the way to Nob Hill. No doubt deluxe restraint was what the designers aimed for when they laid on extra-dark paneling and Ethan Allen showroom furniture—you keep looking around for duck decoys and scented candles. But diners get over that feeling the moment they meet the amiable staff and regulars—Mission locals in hipster black to a woman—and the food here dispels any lingering qualms. It's splurge-worthy "tall" food, and created quite a sensation when it opened back in the late 1990s. For a while it was difficult to get a table without booking ahead and sounding determined, but all that has changed since the dot-com slump, and Watergate have added purse-friendly enticements such as the prix fixe tasting menu.

Cost $20–40
Address 1152 Valencia St
(T) 415/648-6000
Open Mon–Thurs & Sun 5.30–10pm, Fri & Sat 5.30–11pm
Transportation 14, 26, 48, 49, BART 24th St
Accepts All major credit cards except Diners

You may first meet the tall food in the dazzling salmon or ahi tuna tartares ($8.50), which have delicate Asian accents in their presentation. Tartares are a San Francisco craze, part of the raw fish cult that overtook the city after the sushi boom, and these ones are pieces of fresh, delicious artistry that do you nothing but good: fat pieces of fish are stuffed into an intriguing architectural scaffolding of crispy crackers, buttressed stiffly amidships with julienned potato and wasabe butter, and textured with crunch and crackle between. They are just one highlight among several extravagant marine appetizers and raw bar specialties that include Dungeness crabcakes with daikon radish ($7), and warm lobster martini with cilantro, orange, and Champagne sauce ($12). Main-course fish dishes are well executed but boring by comparison. Not that Watergate's "grandes assiettes" (all $17) are in any way bad: lamb noisettes, calf kidneys, and whopping steaks all come copiously dressed in fresh vegetables and gratins of peerless tastiness. You can also choose from them on the prix fixe menu ($25), which is terrific value.

Watergate's dessert soufflés and crisps (from $6) are equally successful, and there's a neat little wine list with great local varietals on it. Failing that, fragrant Oolong and Poochong teas, specially imported, wrap up the meal.

Woodward's Garden

A dinky vest-pocket of a bistro underneath a concrete overpass at the funkier end of Mission, Woodward's Garden takes its name from the fairy-like nineteenth-century garden and conservatory that once stood on this spot. Some fans think that this romantic lost history, and the urban concrete that now surrounds Woodward's, makes the chefs exert themselves harder by way of compensation. Perhaps they're right. It certainly helps to be in love here, since if you don't book one of a dozen miniature tables you'll be practically sitting on your companion's lap at the bar, while the ex-Postrio and ex-Greens owners rattle the pots not more than two feet away.

Cost $30–60

Address 1700 Mission St at 14th
☎ 415/621-7122
Open Tues–Sun, seatings at 6.30pm, 8pm & 8.30pm
Transportation Market St lines, BART 16th St
Accepts MasterCard, Visa

Since there's nowhere to keep anything, it's no surprise that they change the menu daily here. Salads are a major success of the house, and feature everything from Chiogga beets to tiny greens, with different fruits and nuts in season thrown in. Appetizers are object lessons in how to use fresh produce. Figs with goat cheese ($12), and a spiced, nutted, and crunchier-than-usual crabcake ($8.75) are dazzling. As a matter of fact, they do really like to top dishes with nuts or fruit here—even the salmon en croûte ($21.50) has a crust of pine-nut topping in place of the usual choux or brioche dough; come here during wild salmon season, from late spring to late summer, and you'll see. Risottos and ravioli (around $18) come in rare and interesting variations. Entrees come in at around the $20–25 mark: the beef is top quality Niman Ranch, while a two-inch pork chop crowds a round moat of garlicky mashed potatoes. Desserts (from around $5) are imaginative too, and usually feature fresh fruit crumbles and crisps, though there may be a cheese plate such as semi-soft goat cheese with caramelized pecans ($8).

Since the recent expansion brought up the available seating up to 52—double what it used to be—a change in the ambiance has struck anxiety into some customers' hearts, but it's still welcoming. Book a couple of weeks ahead, and try not to make it a Valentine's Night, when all bets are off.

The Castro & Noe Valley

THE CASTRO & NOE VALLEY

N

500 yds
0

NOE VALLEY

TWIN PEAKS

THE CASTRO

Alice's Restaurant
Eric's Restaurant
Fattoush
Chloe's Café
Lovejoy's Tea Room
Savor
Le Zinc
Miss Millie's
Noi
Firefly
Anchor Oyster Bar & Seafood Market
Bacco Ristorante Italiano
Firewood Café
LaMooné
Tita's Hale 'Aina
Ma Tante Sumi
Castro Theater
Leticia's
Yokoso Nippon Sushi
Mission Dolores
Dolores Park
Chow
Home
Mecca
La Méditerranée 2223 Market Street

GUERRERO STREET
DOLORES STREET
CHURCH STREET
SANCHEZ STREET
NOE STREET
CASTRO STREET
DIAMOND STREET
CLIPPER STREET
MARKET STREET

2223 Restaurant & Bar

It's a common enough dilemma in the Castro: you have visitors and you want to take them somewhere, but not intimidating and not costing an arm and a leg. That's why if 2223 didn't exist you'd probably have to invent it. Like the venerable Cafe Flore, nearby, it's a place in which to see and be seen. The vibe is casually hip but so artlessly artsy that it's a diverting choice for just sitting over brunch. But it's also a restaurant proper, and comes with some useful extra virtues such as Melinda Randolph and David Gray's cooking, which is decidedly oriented towards comfort food.

Cost $15–30

Address 2223 Market St at Noe
℡ 415/431-0692
Open Mon–Thurs & Sun 5.30–10pm, Fri & Sat 5.30–11pm
Transportation 22, 23, 35, F, J, K, L, M
Accepts All major credit cards except Diners

Most brunchers go for "two eggs as you like them" on toasted sourdough ($6.50) with the house sausage and fries ($7.95). They're pure breakfast classics and probably the best choice for brunch, although the corned beef hash with two poached eggs ($8.95) is another one, and so is the roast banana French toast with coconut-rum butter and chocolate shavings ($7.95). But 2223's most interesting brunch dish is a newish invention that takes elements from classic Mexican and Salvadorean breakfasts, and comes up with what they call chorizo scramble with warm corn tortillas ($8.50). There's also a very lively eggs Benedict ($9.95) that comes with an unusually tangy Hollandaise and a fine homemade scone. By evening, the menu shifts into an array of house salads (from $5.95) such as romaine ($6.95) or spinach ($6.50), and pizzas that include toppings like French pear and Gorgonzola ($9.50), or potato, artichoke, and garlic ($9.50). Main dishes always include classics such as salmon or chops, or perhaps an Angus New York steak with truffled crème-fraîche potatoes ($22). There's usually a risotto combination of some kind, such as spring vegetables ($12.50).

Add the profiteroles ($6.75) and it's downright philanthropic. Come alone to drink in the art, the pretty waiters, and exchange glances over eggs and espresso, or perhaps make it a rendezvous for brunch or a cocktail before or after a movie date.

Alice's Restaurant

Like its older brother Eric's, around the corner, or Eliza's, over the way on Potrero Hill, Alice's is first and foremost a comfortable and reliable neighborhood Chinese restaurant. Its setting, however, is more elegant than average, graced with a carved screen, decorative glassware, oriental china, and enough orchids in the window to pick up a flower show prize. The food, too, is prepared and presented with extra style and attention, though it's essentially a standard menu of hot, sweet, salty, spicy, and aromatic Mandarin and Hunan food. But Noe Valley is always looking to kick it up a notch, so Alice's also has a few extras in the way of Californicated ingredients. It can surprise with flashes of panache, and the whole effect is topped off with particularly pleasant service.

Cost $10–25
Address 1599 Sanchez St near 29th
☎ 415/282-8999
Open Mon–Thurs 11am–9.15pm, Fri & Sat 11am–10pm, Sun noon–9.15pm
Transportation 24, J
Accepts MasterCard, Visa

Since some of the dishes—notably the spicy and aromatic orange beef and coconut prawns ($6.95), and the popular mango chicken ($6.95)—are similar to those at Eric's and Eliza's, locals inevitably compare the three. Alice's mango chicken comes with red cabbage, diced bell peppers, and cilantro in a sweet-sour sauce, and Alice's version of wonton soup ($3.75) uses seafood-stuffed wontons rather than pork, and is served with a dollop of sour cream in the middle, borscht-style. The curried basil prawns ($6.95) are Thai-influenced and delicious, while the prawns in pine nuts and peas ($7.75) are another fusion combination that's not exactly Chinese. In other words, someone in the kitchen is inventing their own new cuisine here, taking the basics and classics as their starting point, but using Californian ingredients and pan-Asian elements, and tossing in items like sour cream that are alien to Mandarin food.

While Alice's is more or less as cheap as Eric's, it's not as loud and hectic—if not exactly silent—and you'll be able to chat. The menu is familiar enough to make ordering easy, but with a few great touches that mark it as borderline gourmet. Choose Eric's for a group or a family occasion, but pick Alice's if you're out on a date or just want a more tranquil environment.

Anchor Oyster Bar and Seafood Market

You may wonder why the little Anchor Oyster Bar on Castro Street isn't better known. It's been here forever, the food couldn't be fresher—the oysters are certainly fresh—and the staff are extra friendly. Yes, it's crowded at weekends, and since it's the size of a small grocery shop it's never anything but full. Yet the Anchor is a well-kept and well-loved secret among people in the neighborhood. Not only can you slurp half a dozen oysters on the shell over a glass of well-chilled Chardonnay, but you can buy the daily catch at the fresh fish counter in the back and take it home. Oysters, crabs, mussels, clams, and lobsters from two coasts and three continents swim their way into the Anchor from places as exotic and as far-flung as New Zealand, Maine, Canada, and Chile.

Cost $15–35

Address 579 Castro St at 18th
☏ 415/431-3990
Open Mon–Fri 11.30am–10pm, Sat noon–10pm, Sun 4.30–9.30pm
Transportation 24, 33, 35, 37, F, K, L, M
Accepts MasterCard, Visa

If lunch is what you need, the clam chowder ($4.95) fills an empty stomach fast, and it's perfect for dipping buttery sourdough bread into; it's made with chunky celery and potatoes on a creamed clam stock. Sandwiches are hefty; if anything, the shrimp-crab salad sandwich with melted cheese ($10) is almost too rich. Evening appetizers start with more oysters: the oyster shooter ($10) is plopped straight into a stiff Bloody Mary complete with a squirt of Worcestershire sauce, a whiff of Tabasco, and a lemon spritz. Among the other items frequently requested by Anchor regulars are the shrimp Louis salad in Thousand Island dressing ($16.95), or the crab salad ($19.95), which is beautifully presented and laid out on a traditional butterball lettuce with no fussy frisée or arugula frills.

There are only good things to say about Anchor and its food, though do note that it's quite upscale in price. The dress code isn't particularly upscale, however, and neither is the decor, with its minimalist steel tables, wipe-down bar stools and long counter. Stick your elbows on that formica top and grab yourself a quick and briny lunch in merry company.

Bacco Ristorante Italiano

ITALIAN

When this side-street Tuscan sub-palazzo opened several years ago, its terracotta walls, Etruscan-style frescoes, come-hither windows and roomy dining arena thrilled the locals. At last, an upscale Italian in Noe! Back in the mid-1990s, the food seemed sophisticated: it may have been the first time molded roast peppers, eggplant, and goat cheese were put together in a striped tricolor vegetable terrine in the colors of the Italian flag—in this neighborhood at least. Bacco serves Northern Italian fare, specializing in gutsy Tuscan-tinged risottos and homemade pastas that change daily, with flashes of inspiration here and there. It's relatively affordable, which makes it perfect for a nice celebration night out.

Cost $10–35
Address 737 Diamond St at 24th
☎ 415/282-4969
Open Mon–Sat 5.30–10pm, Sun 5–9.30pm
Transportation 24, 35, 48
Accepts MasterCard, Visa

Needless to say, they do a salmon carpaccio, but their version is a homemade gravlax ($8.50), served on the same bed of fennel on which it was cured—a practical presentation. A plate of darkly glinting squid-ink risotto comes with a terrific asiago and Parmesan topping ($16.95). Bacco is so fond of its risottos it has a special employee for stirring them and nothing else! Sadly, the tricolor pepper terrine is no longer on the menu, but try any of the pastas, which are freshly made in-house and rarely disappoint. Ravioli (from $11.25) comes in a pomodoro sauce, stuffed with everything from butternut squash to grilled eggplant or four cheeses, while the terrific penne ($11.25) are paired with a peppery puttanesca sauce and seasonal vegetables. A giant calzone stuffed with vegetables ($11.50) is so substantial that it's obviously intended as a main course for vegetarians. Lamb chops ($17) are certainly tender, but chef-owner Vicenzo Cucco's Italian roots are starting to cross-pollinate. Hawaiian ono ($18) recently appeared on something akin to a pomodoro sauce, while the grilled vegetable medleys are acquiring that merry disregard for propriety that characterizes Californian cookery—asparagus with red peppers, artichokes with anything to hand.

But it is the celebrated sweets of the house that you should save a little room for. They do all the usual stickies, including pot de crèmes and tiramisu, but the most fabulously decadent specialty is the white chocolate-sauced cannoli with added crème fraîche ($6.50).

AMERICAN

Chloe's Cafe

For years, Noe Valley people have been waking up on Saturdays with one thought on their minds: breakfast at Chloe's. It's the holy grail of the Church Street brunch brigade. Minute rather than bijou, and more cramped than cozy, it's hectic beyond belief. There's no parking, and prices are not especially cheap, but it's never, ever going to close. It's always so busy that you have to squeeze in by 11am for a weekday lunch date, or simply wait. On weekend mornings, crowds billow around the door, hovering over the half-dozen seats outside, writing names down on a big yellow pad, sticking their heads around the door to harass the one over-worked waitress, and looking hangdog.

Cost $10–15

Address 1399 Church St at 26th
℡ 415/648-4116
Open Daily 8am–3.30pm
Transportation J
Accepts Cash only

There's a good chance of that waitress being speedy and highly efficient, however, and it won't be long before you're settled in with a just-that-minute-squeezed orange juice ($1.25) or grapefruit juice ($1.50). Bacon, lettuce, and tomato sandwiches are a staple of American diners, but an exceptional version is hard to find. Chloe's BLT ($6.25), however, is particularly good, and many regulars come here just for that combination of crispy, frilly-edged back bacon (and yes, it's real Canadian bacon), avocado at its firm best, pristine, red-leafed lettuce, and tomatoes with taste, all held together by crispy rosemary toast. If that doesn't tempt, try the eggs on rosemary or wholewheat-walnut toast, as omelets and breads (around $5–7) are great here. Grilled sandwich options include Jarlsberg cheese and tomato on wheat-walnut bread, and dilled egg and Jarlsberg on buttered rosemary toast, both of which are really good. The only other item to rival the BLT is pain perdu-style French toast made from their own homemade cinnamon croissants ($5.95), and light yet filling banana-pecan pancakes ($5.95), both well worth the wait in themselves.

For consistently top-quality ingredients like these, the prices really aren't too high. Plus, there's a good-natured atmosphere, particularly given the potentially stressful high volume. Any error is corrected happily and quickly, and the service is every bit as good as the food. In other words, lucky Noe Valley.

Chow

(icon) Someone has been trying hard in Chow's kitchen ever since it opened to cheers in the mid-1990s, and it hasn't skipped a beat since. At Tony Gulisano's place, the mood is informal and upbeat, and the service is right on the mark. It's cozily cramped inside, with counter stools at the bar, and a couple of tables appear outside on clement days. The fare is ordinary, Italian-style comfort food, and the hearty portions and gener-

Cost $10–30
Address 215 Church St at Market
(phone) 415/552-2469
Open Mon–Thurs & Sun 11am–11pm, Fri & Sat 11am–midnight
Transportation Market St lines, J, F
Accepts MasterCard, Visa

ally high quality make it about the best value in the city. A great big chalkboard lists the sandwich specials, and menu choices change more or less daily. If it suffers an occasional lapse, Chow never loses the overall match.

Mussels ($7) arrive more or less unadorned except in their own perfume and juices, and they're perfect that way. Chow's wood-baked pizza is a dependable favorite that comes in varieties that change daily; fennel sausage and arugula pizza ($8.50) is an unusual appetizer that's almost big enough for a main course. A frisée lettuce salad ($4.50) of apricots, walnuts, nectarines, cherries, and Gorgonzola in fruity vinaigrette is irresistible. Pastas (from $6.95) are new takes on old themes, using fresh produce. Meat dishes such as roast chicken breast ($10.95) can be less reliable, but they're redeemed by the Himalaya of potato, cranberry sauce, and snap peas served alongside. Since the eclectic chef Laurence Jossel (formerly of Kokkari and Chez Nous) climbed on board, the menu has acquired fancier fusion notes, from polenta with Gorgonzola and mushrooms ($8.50) to noodles with tofu and pesto ($6.95), or couscous with duck confit ($8.95). Ginger pumpkin ice cream in caramel sauce, ($4.50) is a dessert to die for, though most people order the robust, meltingly rich chocolate cake ($4.50). What more does anyone need to know? Beer-lovers will rejoice that several good Belgian beers are available, and a few wines are priced by the glass—though there's no corkage charge if you bring your own bottle.

Locals always remark how good it is to know that you can always fall back on Chow, and now Gulisano has opened another branch in the Inner Sunset, at Irving and 9th Avenue, there's a choice.

Eric's Restaurant

(🍴) When you're tired and hungry and on your way home after a long day, there's always Eric's and Alice's. Of the two, Eric's has been here longer and is slightly more traditionally Chinese. That's the way Noe Valley feels about this place, with its big windows in a high-ceilinged and airy corner dining room, and its kitchen aromas, loud chatter and clattering background. It's a popular local spot for get-togethers and ear-bending sessions between neighbors and buddies. Best of all, Eric's is fairly low-priced, and it's ideal for sharing a bunch of dishes between four or five people, especially as it proffers a long list of veggie variations.

Cost $5–20

Address 1500 Church St at 27th
☎ 415/282-0919
Open Mon–Thurs 11am–9.15pm, Fri & Sat 11am–10pm
Transportation 24, J
Accepts MasterCard, Visa

It's not such a good idea for a first date, however, as numerous sorry diners have learned, and not only because shreds of egg roll ($3.50) are liable to lodge between your teeth, and potstickers ($4.25) will spill down your collar when you bite into their stuffed depths. Not that you'll complain, though it may put off your companion; the main drawback for dates is that it's rather noisy. The menu offers familiar Hunan and Mandarin standards, and they'll alter the degree of "hot" and "spicy" on request. The delicious Drums of Heaven ($3.50) is crispy fried chicken that has been marinated crimson-red, and is served with slices of lemon. Eric's wonton soup ($4.25 cup, $5.95 bowl) contains pork and shrimp dumplings in a chicken broth floating with snap peas and mushrooms. Ocean party soup ($4.25/$5.95) is aswim with little scallops and shrimps, and dotted with snow peas. Eric's also does Californian-Chinese fusion dishes, such as the mango prawn special ($8.95) in sweet-and-sour sauce, which also comes in beef and chicken ($7.50) and mushroom and prawn ($10.25) versions. Walnut prawns ($8.95) is another fine invention, while a salmon special ($9.25) is nicely herbed with loads of basil and reminiscent of Thai cuisine.

Vegetarians get lots of choices here, including Buddha's Delight ($6.50), a chile-hot veggie stir-fry whose contents vary from day to day according to what's in season. Eric's also serves a standard lunch portion of all these dishes for a daily flat price ($4.75). That's some deal!

Fattoush

The soft spot that San Franciscans nurse for Fattoush goes back to an earlier restaurant, YaYa's, near Golden Gate Park, which specialized in Mesopotamian food. It was co-chefed by Iraqi-born Manal Al-Shafi, who convinced the city that pomegranates, dates, honey, raisins, cashews, roses, almonds, pine nuts, and lamb go together like love and marriage, or maybe like the Tigris and the Euphrates. A couple of years ago, Manal's friend Abed Amas found an old

Cost $15–35

Address 1361 Church St at 25th
☎ 415/641-0678
Open Tues–Thurs 11.30am–9.30pm, Fri 11.30am–10pm, Sat 9am–10pm, Sun 9am–9pm
Transportation 48, J
Accepts All major credit cards

Noe Valley diner and transformed it with colored-glass panels, iron candelabras, and tables made of glass-mosaic and salvaged wood. He opened Fattoush as a showcase for Manal whose recipes come from Syria, Iraq, Palestine, and Morocco.

Middle Eastern spices like sumac, cardamom, and cumin smolder deep within Fattoush's sauces, and intensify the tangy vinaigrette on the Lebanese–Syrian toast and cucumber salad ($5.95) that lent Fattoush its name. Tossed with Italian parsley, onion, tomatoes, eggplant, and cucumber, it's the house signature salad. Chunky, marinated lamb kebabs on saffron rice ($11.95) is a hit, as is the grilled cauliflower with lamb shanks ($13.95). Indeed, cauliflower is so unexpectedly delicious—as much for its sultan-seducing silky texture as for its taste—that it's served separately ($7), in the same spicy sumac sauce, along with toasted herb-and-seed-speckled rounds of flat bread. A sultan's feast ($11.95) is a special package deal of extra dishes, and includes Fattoush's trademark Palestinian mansaf of lamb chunks in aged, mint-flecked yogurt, and comes with dried apricots, almonds, pistachios, pine nuts, rice, and perfect bulgur or kasha on the side. Delicate Moroccan phyllo pies ($11) of layered, nutted minced beef come with sweetened date syrup in tahini paste. Among the desserts, baklava ($5.25) is a layered honey, pistachio, and grated coconut phyllo pastry, topped with date syrup and clotted cream—a dish to genie up Omar Khayyám and the Arabian nights.

The wine list includes the heady, violet-nosed Blockheadia ($6 per glass), among others. The half-covered patio to the rear is in demand for brunching on omelets and pancakes at weekends, when the sultry sensuality of the evening menu gives way to filling alfresco fare.

Firefly

If you find yourself in Noe Valley with a guest to treat to a special evening out, Firefly is a good choice. It showcases chef-owner Brad Levy's personal statement food, which features often-provocative "fusion" cuisine — at times, "confusion" is also apt. It comes at a price, and you'll need to reserve ahead. Firefly's two little rooms, one with a bar, are full to bursting on weeknights, since Firefly has an enviable reputation both as a local favorite and as a destination place. The decor is homey, with blue and white plates and fig-colored panelling.

Cost $15–40

Address 4288 24th St at Douglass
☎ 415/821-7652
Open Mon–Wed 5.30–9.30pm, Fri & Sat 5.30–10pm, Sun 5.30–9pm
Transportation 35, 48
Accepts All major credit cards except Diners

CALIFORNIAN

The menu is small, with no more than six choices in each course. All bear Levy's trademark eclectic influences, even if they sometimes miss the mark. Soup of the day may be five-onion soup with gruyère toast ($6.75); it's made with a number of onion varieties, and not a bad idea. Another starter might be roast Brussels sprouts drenched with truffle oil ($6.50). Some unusual potato side dishes are served alongside main-course dishes: purple mashed potatoes look like Cézanne but rarely taste priceless; potato "hair" is crisped strands of potato angel-hair—it's a decorative oddity that doesn't actually liberate the taste of potatoes. Sea scallops—about eight big ones—come with more potato "hair" (in this case, strands on top of mashed spuds). The duck confit ($17.50) wins kudos for both presentation and the gentle treatment of the juices. Several vegetarian main dishes are imaginative, but not always convincing. Wild mushroom and cannellini cassoulet ($17.50) is an overwhelming scoop of mixture (not in a ramekin) surrounded by mashed blue-purple potatoes. Vegetable pho ($13) is a massive bowl of veggie broth surrounded by heaps of whatever is in the garden. Tommaso's pozole ($13) is a variation of the Mexican hominy dish, with "bounteous" veggies. Desserts include pineapple crêpe with mango sorbet ($6).

Although Firefly is usually very busy, service is always excellent—one reason that it's worth a visit, despite the occasionally over-experimental, hit or miss nature of the food. And the affable staff will happily bring out the ruby port for a special request!

ITALIAN

Firewood Cafe

Once upon a time, dining in the Castro District meant burgers or pizza, period. Then Ma Tante Sumi opened on 18th Street, and little by little the neighborhood started showing some culinary variety. Firewood Cafe, just across the street from Sumi's, doesn't aspire to culinary heights, but it has a certain flair, and it's justifiably popular. This is one of the few places in the area where the indecisive can find everything from a whole roasted chicken to pizza, pasta, and impressive salads. In fact, vegetarians will be pleased to find enough grilled or chilled vegetable dishes to more than hold their own at a table of carnivorous friends.

Cost $6–15
Address 4248 18th St at Diamond
☎ 415/252-0999
Open Mon–Thurs 11am–10.30pm, Fri & Sat 11am–11pm, Sun 11am–10pm
Transportation 24, 33, K, L, M, F
Accepts MasterCard, Visa

A wood-burning pizza oven turns out deliciously thin specimens worthy of Naples. The mushroom pizza ($8.50) is topped with shiitake, oyster, and crimini mushrooms, plus good tomato sauce, and is big enough for two. You order at the counter, after passing the oven and a tantalizing display of freshly prepared vegetable dishes, which can be ordered individually ($2.95) or on a platter of four ($8.50) that's more than enough for one person. The caramelized onions, dolmas, and roasted red peppers are always delicious, as are the beets. Gargantuan Caesar and garden salads (both $6.50) are among the best in the vicinity, and would make almost a full meal for two. Pastas tend to be over-sauced, but there's something satisfying about the gloppy penne in white wine cream sauce ($7.75). You'll find a nicely roasted chicken (half $7.25, whole $13.50), served either stuffed with citrus fruits or roasted with sage, rosemary, and garlic, and at lunch they'll throw in a free soda. There are also a few decent California or Italian wines by the glass, and local bottled beers.

The Castro is nothing if not a see-and-be-seen neighborhood, especially if you happen to be a gay man, and Firewood is one place where you'll never feel alone. In the front room, you can either pull up a chair at the big windows facing 18th Street, or at the long table, where everyone dines family-style. There are also more intimate booths and tables at the back. Another branch is found downtown, in the Metreon Center.

Home

🍴 Talk about a heavy clue as to the change of name—a new sign at the door reads "Welcome Home!" Formerly an upscale restaurant called John Frank, this place has now gone straighter—more Norman Rockwell, more conservative—and following remodelling, it has reopened as Home. The location is borderline Castro, and the clientele is mixed, attracting couples of all persuasions, solitaries, first-daters, and even families. The owners have gone to great lengths to fix the acoustics and give the place a homier hum, and there's now a low-priced menu and a more casual look. A brunching patio is now called the "Back Porch," with smokers allowed, room for parties, outdoor heating, and a fireplace for cheering up foggy nights. The new makeover is a successful effort to roll with recent economic punches, and to imitate the no-nonsense, low-key value of Chow, over the road.

Cost	$10–25

Address 2100 Market St at Church

☎ 415/503-0333

Transportation Market Street lines, 22, 37, F

Open Mon–Thurs & Sun 5.30–10pm, Fri & Sat 5.30–11pm

Accepts All major credit cards except Diners

AMERICAN

Was there a psychological need for comfort food after September 11? It seems so. John Hurley, Stu Gordon, and Lance Dean Velasquez's menu was not the only one to start offering wholesome, fat-friendly and good-value "homey" fare like roast chicken, macaroni cheese, and meatloaf. Roast chicken and mashed potatoes ($12.95) hits the spot, even if it's somewhat bland and is occasionally over-seasoned. Mahi mahi ($13) is also a little bit on the innocent side. Pasta dishes, however, burst with fresh produce like mushrooms and Tom Thumb tomatoes, and include classics such as macaroni cheese ($6). While this should keep vegetarians happy, the pot roast special ($13) is meltingly, persuasively tender. Order fries with anything you get, since they far outperform the usual sticks of stodge. Home excels with potatoes, and the gnocchi are excellent too. The dessert menu offers various chocolate and cake efforts, including a frozen chocolate pudding sandwich ($5) served "with a shot of milk"—just like an Oreo cookie snack your mother might leave you on the kitchen table as an after-school snack.

By 8pm on a weeknight the place is packed. It's not hard to see why, as this place is right at the Church Street Muni stop.

LaMooné

FUSION

(🍴) When the passion for fusion hit San Francisco, this little pan-Asian concept bistro—named after "ramune," a popular, Japanese, blue-glass-bottled lemonade—opened in North Beach. But owners Tomi Grooney and Rob Low quickly realized that the Castro District was better suited to their fusion cuisine, so they moved to this dinky upstairs haven. Ramune bottles are luminous

Cost $10–40
Address 4072 18th St at Castro
☎ 415/355-1999
Open Daily 5.30–11pm
Transportation 24, 33, 35, F, K, L, M
Accepts All major credit cards except AmEx

blue, so lapis-lazuli blue glass is inlaid in the tables, and aqua-blue velvet cushions match the twinkling fairy-lights. Jazz fans get the Dave Parker Trio on Thursday nights and every weeknight has a happy hour from 5.30 to 8pm—one-dollar sakes and a list of pan-Asian appetizers will make it more like two and a half happy hours, but who's quibbling?

LaMooné doubles as a congenial cocktail bar, sheltering six small, blueish tables, six bar stools, lots of music, and communal finger food for messy sharing. You can sit around sipping cocktails, listening to Parker and nibbling from pupu platters of Hawaiian appetizers (all $5) such as won ton chips with tropical (mango and cilantro) salsa, eggplant cobblers in lamb marinara, vegetarian kakiage vegetable fritters in ponzu sauce, and prawn and calamari cigars with Japanese herbs and dipping sauce; they're sized for sharing between two to five people. A special "Feed me!" tasting buffet ($40) features portions of everything on the day's menu for sharing, ranging from Vietnamese shrimp-filled rice-paper rolls with nuoc cham ($6.50 served separately), to pear salad with avocado and walnuts ($11.50), roast mussels with coconut curry cream and green onions ($10.50), and Filipino pork adobo ($10). There's also a Maki Plate ($17), which turns out to mean a big plate of tofu, salmon, or tuna sashimi.

"Dishes to slurp, swirl and share," is the motto here. Cocktails are variations on classics, made with sake, like LaMooné Shine ($6.50), which is whisky with sake, saffron, and hibiscus on the rocks, or Sake-Kazi ($7.50), a vodka-sake lemon and lime shake. Alternatively, try the refreshing LaMooné soda ($2.50), the ramune of the restaurant's name. Since each serving is enough for a group, this is all good, affordable festive food. It makes a good date spot too, though it can get plenty busy.

Leticia's

You've got an evening ahead or behind you at the Singalong Sound of Music or the Asian and Pan-Pacific Gay and Lesbian Movie Festival, and you need a moderately rollicking spot for a bite and a drink, where you can hear yourselves think and decompress in comfort. That pretty much describes Leticia's, a comparatively innocent time warp set in a time warp—a Seventies Mexican diner housed in a really old-fashioned Irish bar where the room-long counter and the naugahyde banquettes are reminiscent of a Fifties saloon. All of this can be nostalgic if you're hungry and thirsty enough, and prompt service and excellent Margaritas help the impression along.

Cost $8–30

Address 2247 Market St at Sanchez
℗ 415/521-0442
Open Mon–Fri 11am–10.30pm, Sat 11am–11pm, Sun 11am–10pm
Transportation 24, F, J, N
Accepts MasterCard, Visa

MEXICAN

The Margaritas arrive in front of you in a nicely chilled pitcher accompanied by homemade chips and salsa ($7.50) before you can bless yourself. As beginnings go, that one is hard to beat. That said, Leticia's menu is not quite up to the standard of the promising start. It's about on the level of a good Mexican burrito joint in the Mission, but presented generously in a comfortable setting for a few dollars more, which is reasonable enough if that's what you need. If you like seafood, this is a heartening menu, and the calamari with tartar sauce ($8.50) is tasty. Crab nachos ($11.95) are amply and colorfully arrayed upon a large platter with refried beans, jalapeno, and Mexican cheese. A fiesta platter of guacamole and quesadillas with taquitos ($13.95) might be a wiser starter for those who can't stand the combination, however, and it brings enough for three or four mouths. As quesadillas go, Leticia's does one with grilled chicken or sausage version ($8.95) that's a dilly, as well as a non-traditional Acapulco Tostada ($14.25). Traditional Mexican sopapillas ($4.95), which is a kind of square fritter, and banana vallarta ($4.95) follow.

Leticia's may not be haute cuisine, but it's likely to earn its slightly cheesy niche in any gringo's heart, and you'll probably find yourself back there for more at regular intervals.

Lovejoy's Tea Room

When writer Jessica Mitford lived in Oakland, across the Bay, she was occasionally asked by journalists if she ever missed her native England, or simply a nice cup of tea. Shaking her head vehemently and snorting "Gosh, no!" Mitford sometimes added, "Well, occasionally I find myself thinking, 'Oh *God,* how I'd love a sausage roll!'" For a cuppa and a feathery-light sausage roll, she could

Cost $8–15	
Address 1351 Church St at Clipper	
☎ 415/648-5895	
Open Daily 11am–5.30pm	
Transportation J	
Accepts All major credit cards except Diners	

have come straight to this little tea shoppe, stuffed with sofas, precious Cotswold Toby jugs, porcelain and antimacassars, all of which are for sale.

There's a $7.50 minimum for credit card transactions here, and that happens to be exactly what you're charged for Devonshire Cream Tea. That means a china pot of black Taylor's blend, plus a darling little cakestand bearing aloft two homemade scones, a dish of clotted cream (excellent, flown in from Devon), another of homemade strawberry jam (even better), and a doll's-size tea strainer. Surrounding these are canteloupe and orange slices, a fig and two strawberries, pertly arranged upon antique porcelain. Lovejoy's also serves Light Tea ($9.95), which adds a sandwich to that ladylike total, or High Tea ($12.95), the same with an added two sandwiches plus coleslaw and shortbread. Queen's Tea ($16.95) arrives on a grander tray replete with a plate of crumpets, lemon curd, and sandwiches ranging from Lady Bracknell-style cucumber to Finnan Haddie, salmon mousse or pear and Stilton, all wafer-thin. Along with various plates of homemade scones, crumpets, and shortbread, the homesick or anglophile can get British specialties such as Cornish pasties ($7.50), familiar in California since Cornish miners brought them here in the Gold Rush, shepherd's pie ($7.50), and chicken potpie ($7.50).

But loose Darjeeling in a real pot is the main draw, along with Yorkshire Gold, Oolong, and Dragonwell green tea too. You can get ginger beer ($1.95) and Ribena ($1.95), though sadly there's no Lucozade, red lemonade, or Marmite (for that try White Caps Cafe). Even Agatha Christie would raise a pinky over porcelain in this haunt of ladies who take tea, rather than lunch.

Ma Tante Sumi

For many years, people had things other than food in mind when visiting the Castro. So when it opened more than a decade ago, Ma Tante Sumi was a rare outpost of fine dining in a culinary wasteland. It's nice to see that this cozy little spot, with its vaguely South Seas decor, has settled in for the long run, even now that it has formidable competition. It's a mystery why it isn't more "discovered," but that means you can usually squeeze into a table at short notice, even though making reservations might be wiser.

Cost **$15–35**

Address 4243 18th St
℡415/626-7864
Open Mon–Thurs & Sun
5.30–10pm, Fri & Sat
5.30–11pm
Transportation 24, 33, 35, 37, F
Accepts All major credit cards
except AmEx

Current chef Brenda Buenviaje continues the Asian-Californian fusion theme that was pioneered here, and somehow manages to keep the genre fresh. Appetizers always include the unexpected, like an airily light chèvre soufflé salad ($7.25), its tiny soufflé perched atop a pretty plate of grilled asparagus, red and gold beets, and greens. In season, a marvelous heirloom tomato salad ($8) glistens with shiso vinaigrette, mizuna greens, blue cheese, and pine nuts. A sushi-inspired appetizer like salmon tartare ($8) and a simpler salad ($8), for the less intrepid, round out choices. An appetizer cheese plate ($11) is inexplicably priced, considering that a dessert cheese plate costs five dollars less. Main courses always include a roasted half-chicken in spicy hoisin glaze ($16), served with sticky rice pilaf, baby carrots, and sweet peas—tasty but sometimes a little too salty. The tender veal cheeks Bourguignon ($16) are accompanied by steamed potato-leek dumplings and thin green beans, pretentiously listed as haricots verts. High marks go to the pan-roasted duck breast with apricot-ginger sauce ($18.50) and whatever fish happens to be of the day, usually grilled king salmon or Hawaiian specialties like Ono (both $18.50). Desserts aren't Sumi's selling point, but homemade fruit sorbets ($5.50) are light and refreshing after a spicy meal. A crème brûlée trio ($5.75) of vanilla, dark chocolate, and lemon verbena makes a nice change from the usual.

The wine list is short but adequate on whites, and weighted, interestingly enough, toward Gewurztraminers; Pinot Noirs dominate the reds, which are mostly Californian and priced around $30. Service is occasionally chaotic but always friendly.

Mecca

🍴 Mecca's exterior is oddly reminiscent of the nearby Old Mint, an unrelieved slab of industrial gray. But inside, it lives up to all the charisma of its name as San Francisco's most exciting supper club. If you're looking for post-midnight action with a cocktail and a plate to keep you going, it's down to Martoonie's (great piano but no food) Twin Peaks (nostalgic, but no food), and the Zodiac Club (better for drink than food these days). Or there's Mecca, where live jazz and entertainers like Mamie Van Gorgeous beckon you to the sumptuous, oval, copper bar with offers of "fun and fabulousness".

Cost $15–60
Address 2029 Market St at Dolores
☎ 415/621-7000
Open Mon–Wed 5–11pm, Thurs–Sat 5pm–midnight
Transportation 24, F, J, N
Accepts All major credit cards except Diners

It's hard to imagine anyone not succumbing to all this *La Cage aux Folles* extravagance. But hit any hold-outs with an Estonian vodka Tall Blond Martini ($10) or the lethal Mecca Drop ($7.50), made with blue Caraçao. Mecca's chef is Mike Fenelly, who leads a bar menu with oysters on the half-shell with a citrus-soy ponzu sauce ($2.25 apiece), and osetra caviar ($68 an ounce). These are high-end downtown prices, but what would you expect? Barbecued oysters with pancetta ($14) is a likelier casse-croûte, as is a Mecca Caesar salad ($9), rather pretentiously described as containing "Anaheim brioche croutons". The crab claws (seasonal price, around $15) are from those big, meaty stone crabs, flown in from Florida. Pizzas are excellent appetite-stoppers, with toppings like oven-dried "100 tomato" sauce, basil, and mozzarella ($12), or smoked chicken with roast tomatillo and goat cheese ($12). Beyond this useful little bar menu come the serious entrees of chicken, tuna, chops, and so on, all a little uppity in price, around the high teens or twenties. Chilean sea bass has just been added to the world's endangered species list so it may be time to take it off the menu here—and at $24 it won't be a huge sacrifice.

Crème brûlée, profiteroles, and key lime pie all cost $7.50, and there are some great Navarro late-harvest Rieslings and Napa dolces ($7.75 per glass) to go with them from a stunning wine list. Best of all, small tables are kept for drop-in passers-by, and the dress code runs from tuxedo to jeans.

La Méditerranée

🍴 So it's time for a quick break from all that cruising, and you want to stick those aching dogs under a table for a quick beer and sandwich? The Castro is full of cheap fast-food joints of every possible level of grease and ethnic flavor, from terrific burritos to what must be the cheapest burgers in town. But if you want somewhere more interesting to sit, La Méditerranée offers a few cramped seats in a minute room, where you can nibble Middle Eastern appetizers or mezes off colorful pottery as you sit beneath the artsy light fittings.

Cost $8–15

Address 288 Noe St at Market
☎ 415/431-7210
Open Mon–Thurs
11am–10pm, Fri & Sat
11am–11pm, Sun
10am–9.30pm
Transportation 24, F, J, N
Accepts MasterCard, Visa

SEAFOOD

This place is not related to Truly Mediterranean, farther into the Mission, but it does have much the same menu of falafel, tabbouleh salad, hummus, and babaganoush, with the addition of some perches to sit on and a few extra salads and phyllo pies. The sampler plate ($7.50) gives little tasters of most of the dishes above, and plugs a modest lunch-sized gap adequately. A more unusual and filling offering is the phyllo pastry platter ($8.50), which brings many different kinds of pies, from the Moroccan spiced chicken and the Balkan spinach to cheese curds; a slice of each is accompanied by roast veggies and a leg of chicken. Different kinds of simple salad include a Greek-style feta side-salad ($2.50). Baklavas come with coffee ($3.75). Wash this down with the house beer ($7), which is an interesting and rare kind of Armenian brew, or the standard house red wine (from $3.35 per glass, with retsina at $3.75), and you'll have the strength to get up and go again. If this is literally all you need, La Méditerranée is perfect, but be warned: it can get busy, and you're liable to find yourself falling over the Pottery Barn bags in the middle of all the traffic.

La Méditerranée also caters to parties and conventions, so large trays of food come and go as well. There are other branches, too, at 2210 Fillmore Street, in the Upper Fillmore (☎ 415/931-2956), and on College Avenue, in Berkeley (☎ 510/540-7773).

Miss Millie's

Miss Millie's is so cutely retro that you'll wonder if you've wandered onto a Frank Capra movie set. A visit starts with a gorgeous aroma and a guess-your-weight machine at the door—you'll need it after breakfast here! The lemon ricotta pancakes are so famous around this part of San Francisco that people crawl from under the covers to line up and wait for them Saturday

Cost $10–25
Address 4123 24th St at Castro
☎ 415/285-5598
Open Tues–Fri 6–10pm, Sat & Sun 9am–2pm & 6–10pm
Transportation 24, 35, 48
Accepts MasterCard, Visa

mornings. The rest of the deal is equally beguiling. High, cozy booths are trellised with ivy, and old antique plates and 1930s aprons bedeck the walls. On a fine day, try the tented backyard, with its cafe tables, but steel yourself for long waits for weekend brunch, for which no reservations are taken.

Along with those famous lemon ricotta pancakes ($8.75) comes a homemade blueberry syrup, not forgetting the homemade cinnamon rolls ($2.90) and scones ($2.90), French toast made from baguette slices with bananas ($9.75), maple syrup (real, of course), and vanilla mango pain perdu ($9.75). You'll also find delicious waffles, among which the gingerbread with fresh fruit in season ($9.25) is the most popular option, and some inventive egg dishes ($9.75), such as skillet-scrambled egg and tortilla chilaquiles, omelet, and curried tofu egg scramble. Don't forget the mimosas, of which the cherry and the raspberry ($7.25) are the prizes. Miss Millie's isn't especially inexpensive, but it's all worth it, even the wait. Reservations are taken for dinner, and since the restaurant began as a vegetarian hangout, the menu still has a few healthy alternatives. Dinner entrees (around $15) change all the time, but you may find roast vegetable stews, pan-fried chifoletti, or potato gnocchi, as well as fish of the day and a golden and juicily succulent roast chicken. Calamari ceviche ($9) makes a great starter.

Coming by night is a nice idea, in fact, because the patio is candlelit in dry weather, and makes a romantic spot for dinner. By day, it's useful for kids or parties. Let's just hope success doesn't spoil Miss Millie's. It's been around for so long that from time to time locals may complain the quality is dipping, although less demanding regulars don't seem to have noticed.

Noi

(🍴) Castro and Noe Valley old-timers who had long hankered after their long-beloved red-sauce trattoria, Little Italy, were plunged into gloom when that authentic cobble of old Calabria evanesced, leaving only a scent of garlic. But new boy on the block Diego Ragazzo has now rewarded local loyalty with his casual new Italian trattoria, which offers lots of Little Italy's good points—an old-time feel, the cozy 'hood clientele, moderate prices—plus some new ones of his own. Noi means "we" in Italian, and the Noe Noi succeeds in filling Little Italy's gap, and more. The decor is fresh, with daffodil-washed walls, and Ragazzo's dishes are authentically made from scratch.

Cost $15–25

Address 4109 24th St between Castro and Diamond
☎ 415/642-4664
Open Mon–Thurs & Sun 5.30–10.30pm
Transportation 24, 35, 48
Accepts MasterCard, Visa

ITALIAN

Starters include a grilled-cheese-in-a-skillet dish made with scamorza and wild mushrooms ($6.50). There are excellent soups, including a rich one of pasta and beans ($5) and a lentil soup made on good ham stock with real bits of tasso ham ($5). A good old-fashioned prosciutto and melon plate reminds you of why Italians like this dish as a starter: it's a mouth-freshener as well as appetite-whetter ($7.50). The veal saltim-bocca is a delicate piece of flattened beef in an even more delicate sauce of wine, Parmigiano, and seasoning ($15). Entrees include a fish of the day, also around $15; if it's on, grab the mahi mahi ($17), which lounges resplendently upon a salvia-tinged puttanesca, and seize anything made with fresh mussels, which are regulars on the menu. For dessert, a home-made chocolate tart is far better than the other choices on the menu ($5), and it comes with a nice nip of Limoncello, the sweet lemon liquor.

An ample wine list is dominated by Chianti, or you can bring your own for a nominal corkage fee—another good reason to come here, since there are excellent wine shops in this neck of the woods. Though Little Italy's red-checked tablecloths are history, locals agree that Noi is a worthy successor. There's even something of the Little Italy nip still in the air here too, just with food that's a little better.

Savor

Locals love this place for casual meetings and day-long breakfasts, and for taking a mimosa or homemade lemonade (with free refills) and crêpe break in the little patio at the back—even on bad weather days, it's sheltered enough. While its popularity means that there's an occasional longueur in service, it's also laid-back and informal. If you're around the Castro end of 24th Street and looking for somewhere to greet an old friend and dish the dish over scrambled eggs and cappuccino, Savor makes a fine choice. But it's also appealing at night, when the real, working fireplace and tapestried walls give it a cozier glow. Indeed, the new, young King of Jordan ate here while passing through town.

Cost $7–20	
Address 3913 24th St at Sanchez	
☎ 415/282-0344	
Open Daily 8am–10pm	
Transportation 24, 48, J	
Accepts MasterCard, Visa	

Eggs and crêpes are served all day and evening long, together with sandwiches and salads. Any-which-way pancakes (from $6.50), filled with anything from meat to sweet, make the brunch or lunch of choice here, and you can pick from some truly unusual fillings such as oyster mushrooms with peanuts in ginger sauce, tofu skin ($6.75), or grilled eggplant with ricotta ($7.95). They come with potato wedges or salad on the side. A ratatouille and Parmesan crêpe is called, for obvious reasons, "the Parma" ($6.25). Omelets and frittatas ($4.75–7.50) enshrine a similar range of fillings—black bean, salsa, avocado, and sour cream omelet ($7.25) anybody? New Orleans crabcakes ($9.95) arrive with peppers and the same, zinging Hollandaise as eggs Benedict. In the evening, the menu acquires nightly changing dinner specials and some fancy touches. Appetizers (all $7.95) may include items such as a ceviche, gazpacho, or steamed mussels, while entree choices may feature dishes such as pecan-crusted fresh trout with mango chutney and roast potato wedges ($14.95), juicy pork chop with garlicky mashed potatoes ($15.95), or house fettucine with shrimp ($14.95). A short but gallant wine list does its best to help the mood, along with some reasonable beers.

Since Noe Valley is the notorious haunt of stroller-pushing yuppy moms, Savor provides a special $1.95 children's portion of most dishes. In this way, they are particularly kind to the afflicted parent in this most non-parent-oriented of cities.

Tita's Hale 'Aina

Tita's Hale 'Aina—Tita's for short—is a converted shopfront restaurant on the outskirts of the Castro District, far enough away from the boisterous bar strip, yet still definitely part of this world-renowned neighborhood. You'll find no hula dolls at Tita's "home place," as the name translates, but you will find spam dishes on the breakfast menu, and no jokes please: Hawaiians defend their relish for spam with the same ardor as poi.

Cost $8–25

Address 3870 17th St between Sanchez and Noe
☎ 415/626-2477
Open Mon–Fri 11am–10pm, Sat 9am–10pm, Sun 9am–3pm
Transportation K, L, M, F
Accepts MasterCard, Visa

New arrivals are greeted with the soulful strains of Hawaiian slide-guitar music on the restaurant's sound system, and who can help but admire the beautifully framed vintage photos of Hawaiian dancers that hang on the room's petal-pink walls? Fresh irises adorn tidy little tables and there's an alluring, all-enveloping smell of cooking. The only drawback? Tita's has no alcohol license.

Tita is an island-born chef-owner who serves Portuguese-tinged cooking, since Portuguese emigration influenced the islands' cuisine. Her Hawaiian waiter, Do Ho, delivers a hearty "aloha" with a pupu platter of canapés, such as Tita's golden and crunchy malasadas ($2.95), Hawaiian donuts that make an oddly dessert-like start. Portuguese bean soup ($7.95), a hearty mix of ham hocks and Portuguese sausage in a thick tomato, cabbage, and bean stew, is is a more conventional starter and a real tonic against the fog. The more traditional Hawaiian da lomi lomi ($8.75) is a lovely bowl of freshly chopped salmon with tomatoes and chives; on Fridays, salmon is also served steamed with ti leaves and ginger ($9.95). Even more authentic is a steaming platter of long-simmered Kalua pig ($7.50), accompanied by adobo, khal bi, and macaroni salad, and da loco moku ($8.25), rice topped with eggs and a beef patty, and smothered in shiitake mushrooms. Teriyaki meatloaf ($7.50) is a house specialty, a perfectly basted chunk with rice and macaroni salad.

Homey and delicious, Tita's golden, crunchy malasadas ($3.25) are yeasty Hawaiian donuts, but diners who find a spot for rum and raisin bread pudding ($3.95), or Tita's Delite ($3.95)—coconut mousse pie with chocolate-macadamia pastry—will not complain. Best of all, Tita's charges no corkage for your own wine. What a cure for the blues!

SUSHI

Yokoso Nippon Sushi

Popularly known as "No-Name Sushi," Yokoso Nippon is set away down the block from the Market Street bustle, and lacks any obvious self-promotion other than a rather timid sign belatedly stuck on the window. It's a humble sushi joint that seats barely thirty. While it's far from being the smallest in the city, it's undoubtedly the busiest, and very possibly the cheapest too.

Cost $10–25

Address 314 Church St near Market
ⓣ No phone
Open Mon–Sat noon–10pm
Transportation 22, 37, F, J, K, L, M
Accepts Cash only

Customers line up outside at all kinds of hours. Inside, a first glance at the loaded and sagging tables and ungroomed decor might make an aghast newcomer wonder what the appeal is. Incredibly low prices are certainly part of it, and "No-Name" is a boon to the impoverished students who congregate here in hordes.

Sushi choices are more extensive than you might expect, and surprisingly good, too. Portions of tuna, salmon, mackerel, and roast eel (unagi) sushi for fish-lovers, or cucumber, avocado, and asparagus vegetarian sushi are prettily presented on wooden blocks with ginger, wasabe, and a sour-sweet ponzu sauce. So are umeboshi, plum, and natto-fermented soybean sushi. All arrive in portions of three that are far larger than at most other sushi places, and they start at a very reasonable $2.50 or $3.00. Even the combination plates of three come to just under $10. In fact, no matter how young and hungry you are, you would be hard put to eat more than ten dollars of sushi here, which is a proud boast in its own way. Toasted rice, green nichon-cha and other teas are on tap, but you can also bring your own wine or beer—a handy liquor store is just a few doors away on the corner—which endears this place even more to the happy young diners who throng here nightly.

Perhaps only Miyabi, over the road, We Be Sushi, Country Station Sushi Cafe, and Sushi Boom come anywhere close to rivaling No-Name for value; this is a town where people regularly drop $50 per head for their raw fish fix, after all. There are other pluses, too: it's close to the heart of the Castro district and convenient for transit lines, and the service is tolerant and unobtrusive, making for a good-natured, family-run atmosphere.

Le Zinc

🍴 Le Zinc reminds you that there's more to "authentic" French bistros than the now-ubiquitous steak frites. It's not on the menu here anyway, but virtually every other proper bistro specialty appears, from cassoulet to mousse au chocolat, and the execution is usually flawless. The menu is definitely right-of-center, yet with enough creative touches to make it seem hip. "Zinc" is slang for the kind of old bistro this is meant to recall, and Le Zinc has the requisite zinc-topped bar; too bad you can't sit at it, but there's simply no room for stools. Space is at a premium throughout, unfortunately. At least the friendly French waiters will steer you to the best dishes.

Cost $20–50

Address 4063 24th St between Castro and Noe
☎ 415/647-9400
Open Mon–Fri 7am–2.30pm & 5.30–10pm, Sat & Sun 10am–2pm & 5.30–10pm
Transportation 24, 48
Accepts All major credit cards except Diners

Appetizers, including classic foie gras and toast ($14), hearty soups like butternut squash ($6.50) and pleasant if too oily sautéed spinach and wild mushrooms ($10) start things off well enough, but the main courses shine. Boeuf Bourguignon ($19) is impeccably authentic and almost shockingly flavorful; the beef melts off your fork and the splendid sauce is straight out of Beaune. The waiter won't sneer if you order a red Graves instead of a Burgundy, which is just as well since there are (strangely) no French Pinots on an otherwise French-dominated wine list. Cod ($19) is rarely seen in fillet form in California, but here it's exquisitely fresh, perfectly pan-roasted, and served in a gorgeous walnut-cream sauce; only the accompanying fettucine hints at overkill. Vegetarians can enjoy a pretty main course of roasted seasonal vegetables ($17). There are also large platters of seafood, with prices ranging from $20 to $50. Save room for desserts (all $7). A serious chocolate mousse is artfully stacked amid layers of meringue, and makes a more satisfying choice than the tiny circle of chocolate cake with crème anglaise. But the prize goes to the fruit gratin, an assortment of diced fruit and fresh berries swimming in a lovely crème anglaise, lightly browned on top and concealing a surprise square of elegant pound cake. Spiked with Grand Marnier, this is a Catherine Deneuve among desserts.

Reserve ahead for dinner and keep Le Zinc in mind for lunch or weekend brunch—or even, surprisingly, for breakfast.

The Sunset & West Portal

THE SUNSET & WEST PORTAL

Park Chow
Avenue 9
PJ's Oysterbed
House on Ninth
Ebisu
PPQ Vietnamese Cuisine
Yum-Yum Fish
Marnee Thai
Lotus
Thanh Long
Vanida
Ristorante Marcello
Rick's
Café for all Seasons
Old Krakow Polish Art Restaurant
Fresca
Spiazzo Caffè
Fuji

WARREN DRIVE
WOODSIDE AVE
LAGUNA HONDA BLVD
9TH AVE
11TH AVE
PACHECO ST
RIVERA ST
14TH AVE
17TH AVE
19TH AVE
21ST AVE
23RD AVE
25TH AVE
27TH AVE
29TH AVE
31ST AVE
33RD AVE
35TH AVE
SUNSET BLVD
39TH AVE
41ST AVE
43RD AVE
45TH AVE
47TH AVE
GREAT HIGHWAY
LOWER ROAD
SUNSET
SUNSET BLVD

IRVING STREET
JUDAH STREET
KIRKHAM STREET
LAWTON STREET
MORAGA STREET
NORIEGA STREET
PACHECO ST
FUNSTON AVE
14TH AVE STREET
15TH AVE
LINCOLN WAY
JUDAH ST
PORTOLA DRIVE
TARAVAL ST
ULLOA ST
VICENTE ST
WAWONA STREET
SANTIAGO ST
TILLO ST

N

PACIFIC OCEAN

0   500 yds

Avenue 9

(🍴) "Somewhat cramped" is one way to describe Avenue 9, but another might be "cozy and toasty"—it's perfect for the singleton who wants to chat up the chefs at the counter or prop a paperback against a menu. As well as the open kitchen counter, Jeff and Mara Rosen's Sunset bistro has a handful of tables set against tangerine walls, where couples can tuck into the idiosyncratic cooking undisturbed. The menu changes often, and reveals glimpses of Jeff's past at PJ's Oysterbed. The hip and friendly chefs will flip something for everyone, from burgers and latkes to fanciful spins on Asian classics and very haute French.

Cost $15–30
Address 1243 9th Ave at Irving
☏ 415/664-6999
Open Mon–Thurs 11am–3.30pm & 5.30–10pm, Fri 11am–3.30pm & 5.30–11pm, Sat 10am–3pm & 5.30–11pm, Sun 10am–3pm
Transportation N
Accepts All major credit cards except Diners

You'll quickly get yourself a reliable Niman Ranch burger ($7.50), if that's all you want for lunch, and you could add a shock of thick-cut and heavily garlicked sautéed fries ($4), and top them with that totally irresistible Maytag blue cheese dressing. A delicious potato latke ($8) comes topped with alderwood-smoked lox, chives, pea-sprouts, and pickled onion, as well as the more usual sour cream. You can also enjoy that smoky salmon in the crispy salmon and shrimp cakes with a spicy remoulade ($8). Feeling feisty? Try pan-fried veal sweetbreads with a stack of pear hotcakes and honey jus ($10), or a buttermilk battered oyster on focaccia with bacon and aioli ($8). Battered Maryland blue softshell crab ($12) is served with that green goddess, English pea cake (they're big on English peas), plus pea shoots (pea shoots too), morels, and more green-pea stuff you probably haven't met before. Sonoma leg of lamb confit ($15) is a pièce de résistance, and comes with a big wedge of corn spoon bread, field greens with blackberries, almonds, and goat cheese. Warm gingerbread dessert ($5) is a must-have for later. "Wine dinners" with wine tastings are regulars here, and brunches are also worthwhile for the eggs Benedict ($7–9) and lemon ricotta pancakes ($7).

So if you're feeling adventurous, cozy up to that counter and ask what's on the specials for the day. Once again, San Franciscans find themselves blessed with a neighborhood bistro which comes with a pair of local kitchen geniuses.

Cafe For All Seasons

Ladies who lunch in West Portal come in all shapes and sizes and ages, complete with strollers or mobile phones or laptops, and they have a surprisingly wide range of restaurant choices to match. But if it's a quick sandwich or pasta they're after, it comes down to Cafe For All Seasons or Spiazzo Caffè, across the road. Both of them are low-maintenance, cheerful, comforting spots with friendly service, full of the clatter of everyday life, and they both function as mini town halls where people bump into each other with their arms full of shopping bags or infants. Cafe For All Seasons dishes salads, pastas, and homey fare, with a gonzo weekend brunch as well as the burgers and pastas. You're quite likely to wait at peak times.

Cost $10–25
Address 150 West Portal Ave at Vicente
☎ 415/665-0900
Open Mon–Thurs 11.30am–2.30pm & 5.30–9.30pm, Fri 11.30am–2.30pm & 5–9pm, Sat 10am–2.30pm & 5–9pm, Sun 10am–2.30pm
Transportation K, L, M
Accepts All major credit cards except Diners

All that said, the Cafe's owner has something of a reputation as an enterprising kitchen warrior. Donna Katzl studied with James Beard, no less, so it comes as not too much of a surprise to meet a truite de rivière grillé au frites ($11.95 at lunch, $12.95 at dinner), a really fine grilled trout that comes with some of the best French fries in the neighborhood. The pork tenderloin piccata sandwich ($9.95) is a chunky lunch offering, while the famous hamburger ($12.95) is another healthy chunk in a hearty focaccia-style bun, and comes with all the fixings. The Cafe is also known for good cuts of really sizzling steak, such as a T-bone ($16.50), which comes with gorgeously garlicked mashed potatoes and sweated spinach—or whatever's in season. Polenta comes grilled with mushrooms and a tart asiago ($9.95). At dinner, the calamari ($8.95) and a carpaccio ($10.95) make popular choices from the appetizer list. The Caesar ($6.95) is a serious Caesar here, and comes with little extras like homemade toasted croutons.

Whatever you do, don't miss the apple pie ($5.95), which comes with a caramel sauce that's a little like dulce de leche in that it's tooth-hurting sweet; other desserts include classics such as bread pudding. Reasonable Californian and French wines, with some good Sauvignon Blancs, finish the options. Lucky West Portal!

Ebisu

🍴 Most San Franciscans are convinced that Ebisu makes the best sushi in the city. This is so widely believed that on Friday and Saturday nights the traditional floor-level seating at the back is crammed with lolling twentysomethings popping raw fish in each other's mouths, while more of them mill around hoping to find a seat at the bar. Others wait outside half the night. Crazy? Well, it *is* very good sushi.

Cost $15–30
Address 1283 9th Ave at Irving
☎415/566-1770
Open Mon–Wed 11.30am–2pm & 5–10pm, Thurs & Fri 11.30am–2pm & 5pm–midnight, Sat 11.30am–midnight, Sun 11.30am–10pm
Transportation 6, 44, N
Accepts All major credit cards except Diners

JAPANESE

Sansei sushi chef Kevin is the reigning star at this sushi shrine. As well as serving the usual—but uncommonly good—masago (smelt roe), hokki (surf clam), unagi (water eel), and all types of roe, such as tobiko, Kevin scrawls extra specials of the day on a board at the end of the counter, and invents fanciful originals to add to them, like "Pink Cadillac" and "the Dragon." Specials may include monk liver—monkfish, that is, not a Trappist's—which reminds you of the finest, most melting pâté; if it's available, you're also likely to find abalone. Not everyone manages to acquire a taste for the grainy, slurpy-custard texture of sea urchins, but Kevin's uni deserve a standing ovation with all your tastebuds cheering in unison. His most popular creation, however, is rainbow sushi, a much-imitated variety plate of yellowtail, mackerel, and salmon that curves in a luscious arch and is topped with roe; you almost want to varnish it and hang it on the wall. Perhaps the only topper to that is the 49-er of salmon and avocado, named for the red and gold colors of the city's football team; it's as bolstered as a footballer's shoulder and comes gussied up with cellophane-thin Meyer lemon frills. Sushi plates are mostly pegged at around $3.50 to $6.50, so you can bliss yourself out without breaking the bank; sashimi plates start at around $11.

Oregon and Washington Cabernets and Chardonnays dominate wines; beer includes North Californian boutique ales that go better with sushi, though nothing is more seductive than warmed sukkori sake, as Ebisu's sake-savvy staff might agree.

Fresca

If you had to put your finger on the moment when West Portal metamorphosed from a plodding strip of random tat and fast food joints into a happily humming village, it might be around the time that Fresca spiced up its menu, dropping tacos in favor of ethnic Peruvian dishes. This busy spot now gets lots of business, perhaps because it also serves pan-Latino fare for Californian tastebuds, with plenty of seafood, lots of potatoes, and a couple of recherché Andean pork specialties. Not unlike a comfortable kitchen extension, it sports a folksy tiled floor and sandy-pink walls.

Cost $10–25

Address 24 West Portal Ave at Ulloa
☎415/759-8087
Open Daily 11am–10pm
Transportation L
Accepts All major credit cards except Diners

Sopa de tortilla ($5.50) is irreproachably healing chicken soup with fried tortilla strips. Chef Julio Calvo-Perez pays homage to the noble Andean tuber with causa a la limeña ($7.25), or pork- and onion-filled yellow (or blue) potato cakes. Papas a la huancaina ($6.95) is potatoes in olive- and turmeric-spiked cheese sauce, while papas rellenas ($7.95) are meat-stuffed, deep-fried spuds with salad. Crabcakes ($8.50) come with something called remoulade Fresca, which is a chile crema. For main course, all manner of upscale fish dishes are listed in season, priced from the low to mid-teens. Chupe is a gutsy chowder with lots of protein bobbing about in it, and Fresca's chupe de mariscos ($14) has clams, mussels, squid, and every other shellfish, plus a poached egg. Adding an egg as a finishing touch is a Peruvian trick that's also used in bisteck a la pobre ($16.95), or breaded steak with one plonked on top. Potatoes take on a different character in the loma or pork dishes. Carapulcra ($10.25) is the robust national pork and potato stew, made with nutty, crunchy *papa seca*, or dried potato. If you like it, have a go at cau cau ($9.50), a deep bowl of fiery, peppered tripe with spiced potatoes and mint. Even a wary child would adore Fresca's quesadilla ($5.50), a melting cheese-filled tortilla that's simple and tasty. For dessert there's sugar-sprinkled alfajores ($1.50) or the ubiquitous flan ($2.95).

Fresca covers all the bases: Peruvian or pan-Latino, there's something for everyone, plus a short wine list and a big $20 pitcher of fruity sangria to round it off.

Fuji

A corner place on West Portal's main village street, Fuji fulfils the quest for a lunch find that's convenient and affordable. Lunchtime fare is emphatically pitched at Sunset workers with little time to spare, who dash in to pick up a quick bento box. By night it becomes slightly more relaxed and interesting, even borderline romantic—despite a rickety, blue-painted interior—thanks to gracious service and decent teriyaki, udon, and tempura specials. All are more than generously priced.

Cost $5–20
Address 301 West Portal Ave at 14th
☎ 415/564-6360
Open Mon–Thurs 11.30am–10pm, Fri 5–10.30pm, Sat noon–10.30pm, Sun 5–9.30pm
Transportation 17, K, M
Accepts MasterCard, Visa

California rolls ($4.50) are a peculiarly Californian invention—perhaps they should have crab and avocado sushi on the state flag? You'll sing the praises of Fuji's, even though they're generally made with surimi (that candy-pink cylindrical roll you meet at sushi joints), rather than real Dungeness or Alaskan crab. But they taste "real", and the surimi explains why six plump and tasty rolls cost so little here. In any case, for an extra dollar you can have the Special California rolls, which use delicious real Dungeness crab meat. Fuji also makes the more fanciful "49er" combinations popularized by those fusion-crazy California sushi heretics, using the colors of salmon and roe to imitate football team colors. The caliente, or fried fish with chile is tasty enough, but would make sushi purists blush pink and blue; and they would call Fuji's Twin Peaks roll of raw beef, crab, tobiko, and green onion an abomination. Other sushi favorites include unakyu ($5.50), or eel and cucumber—a happy marriage of fish and crunch—and the extra-spicy tuna ($4.95). Teriyaki lunch offerings include chicken and beef tenderized in mirin and ginger with soy sauce; if you like to mix and match, you can have a California roll with chicken teriyaki ($7.95), and it will also come with featherlight, batter-dipped tempura variations.

Fuji's is not really a simple sushi bar, or a quick-slurp udon noodle joint, or even a teriyaki spot. It fits any size of appetite or any kind of occasion with a menu of both meals and snacks, and fulfils a modest but useful slot in West Portal village life.

House on Ninth

House on Ninth proclaims its offbeat message loudly, with its doll's house front window that looks as if it was tipped on its corner, and an air of incorrigible hipness of being within. Behind that window is a room of high-ceilinged, high-concept chic that houses a high-end fusion menu that's all about marrying California and Asian cuisines in inventive ways. This might not sound so extraordinary except that the original House, which is still going on Grant Avenue in

Cost $25–40
Address 1269 9th Ave at Irving
☏ 415/682-3898
Open Tues–Fri 11.30am–3pm & 5.30–10pm, Sat & Sun 5.30–10pm
Transportation 6, 43, N
Accepts All major credit cards except Diners

North Beach, was a real fusion pioneer. Ex-accountant, Larry Tse and his chef/wife Angela have bigger premises here in the heart of the Sunset, just off Golden Gate Park. They've been here for a few years, too, pre-dating this block's arrival as a foodie paradise.

The Tses serve highly personalized concept food, and are famous for their interesting seafood combinations. Some dishes are so essential to House's menu that people come back for them specially. Number one is Larry's deep-fried salmon roll ($6) with hot Chinese mustard dip. Then there's the take-me-now garlic-encrusted chicken wings ($9) with another special dip, this one more complex and made with buttermilk—a great combination since the sauce is a cooling contrast to the searingly hot chile that has been rubbed on the wings. The five-spice calamari ($9) is also superb. Among the main courses, seared Chilean sea bass ($18) is another trademark recipe; it comes with braised green beans and jasmine rice. Rack of lamb ($19), the meat itself from either Australia or New Zealand, is done perfectly here, dotted with chopped Korean red peppers and served with potatoes and greens—the works.

The creamy tapioca dessert ($6) is a luscious dream, topped with chilled whipped cream and sweetened mango purée by way of inspired contrast. In fact, hang onto an inch or two of room for sweets; in their own scaled-down way, they enshrine House's Californian-Asian philosophy in miniature, and you'll be glad you tried them. The original House can be found in North Beach, at 1230 Grant Avenue (☏ 415/986-8612).

Lotus

FUSION

When the young partners who run this new corner place first opened their doors, they were pitching a cutting-edge fusion menu, inspired by the innovations they'd seen at places like House. Will and Joe have family connections among the bakeries and restaurants along Noriega, and Willy has a background in design. In this homey neighborhood, their innovative decor—glass walls on two sides, soft lighting from crumpled-tissue and tortoiseshell lighting fixtures, minimalist tables and settings—seemed quite out of place. But word of mouth has built up a local following, and their young chef Aaron Cooper (formerly at Hawthorne Lane) has tweaked the menu to make it less "fusion" and more "something for everyone".

Cost $10–25

Address 1395 Noriega St at 21st
☎ 415/661-0303
Open Tues–Sun
5.30–10.30pm
Transportation 28, 48, 66
Accepts All major credit cards except Diners

Among the starters, crab-lovers will drool over the fluffy crab rolls ($6), and everyone will applaud the arugula and pear ravioli ($6), which are magically subtle and softly scented parcels in brown butter and pine nuts; this is one to go back for again and again. Chicken satay ($6) is flavored with tamarind and smoked in chile, but not so spicy that a six-year-old might not finish it. Coconut-crusted calamari in mint sauce ($7) is equally delectable; you'll find yourself mopping up the crumbs. Main dishes include a seared sterling bass ($19), which arrives in a saffron-coconut broth over garlicky mashed potatoes. Crab ravioli ($11), and a tender duck breast with mustard and honey ($13), properly cooked rather than dried out, are other fine choices. Among the side dishes, okra ($5), grilled simply with garlic and lemon, is surprisingly delicious. Tempura asparagus ($6) have a little dried mustard in the feathery batter. There are tempting desserts such as banana ecstasy ($4.95) of fresh mango and banana over homemade vanilla ice cream.

Among the wines, a dependable Rosemount Shiraz ($19) from Down Under is reasonably marked up. From beginning to end it's difficult to find fault with anything here. Lotus takes the local restaurant scene up a few notches and makes yet another good reason to visit "the Avenues."

Marnee Thai

With over two hundred Thai restaurants sprinkled throughout the 49 square miles of San Francisco, it's hardly surprising that competition throws up some truly great places. The Sunset has an ongoing debate about the respective merits of its various Thai places; Marnee Thai is costlier than Thai Spice, on the next block, but in any case both are pleasant spots to spend an evening. Year after year, Marnee's chef-owner Chaimatt Siriyarn wins awards for his clean, distinctive, and sizzling inventions. His wife Muaymee—known to Outer Sunset regulars as May—is the keeper of Marnee's door, and full of suggestions once you're seated. Tatami mat walls, flowers, cane, candles, and Thai artwork make for a soothing, hut-like feel inside, even when it's overflowing with noisy diners.

Cost $10–25

Address 2225 Irving St at 23rd
☎ 415/665-9500
Open Daily 11.30am–10pm
Transportation 71, N
Accepts All major credit cards except Diners

One of Marnee's most requested dishes is koong sarong ($6.50), or prawns wrapped in bacon and a rice paper crêpe, then fried and served with a sweet-sour red dip. Another regular is tom yum kung ($6.95) or fragrantly lemongrass-scented spicy-sour prawn soup, and Chaimatt's version is all you could wish. But perhaps the dish you'll find yourself ordering again and again is kang kar ree ($8.25), a delicate lemon-yellow curried chicken with basil, chile, and coconut; or possibly the fierier spicy duck in chile with spinach greens ($8.25). Angel wings ($6.95) is another dish that keeps the regulars coming for their deep-fried chicken wings sautéed with chile and basil. When mangoes are available and fresh, you get the much-coveted mango with sticky rice ($4.50) for dessert; if not, it's usually flaming bananas ($4.50).

Chaimatt won the Thai national award for Best Pad Thai, though he was pipped for Best Thai by Thep Phanom more recently; he's also the only Thai chef with an MBA. Perhaps its all that carved wood, but Thai Spice, at 2123 Irving St and 1720 Polk St, gains an advantage for its lower prices and romantic temple decor. On the other hand, Chaimatt scores for Marnee with his koong sarong, kang kar ree, and angel wings. Are Sunset residents spoiled for choice? You bet.

Old Krakow Polish Art Restaurant

On a foggy night in West Portal—and this is one of the foggiest bits of Fog City—a diner's thoughts will often stray to this bit of old Poland. Even if your grandmother didn't hail from the parts of Europe where stuffed cabbage and dumplings were staples, you'll appreciate this Old World showcase. It must be the only Polish place in town, and it's a mystery why it's not better known. The inside has pastel walls hung with Polish paintings, and there are comfortable booths and tables. The Polish waiters are the kind that make you almost expect a kiss on the hand.

Cost $7–25

Address 385 West Portal Ave at 15th
☎ 415/564-4848
Open Mon–Thurs 5–10pm, Fri–Sun noon–10pm
Transportation 17, K, M
Accepts MasterCard, Visa

POLISH

Old Krakow's borscht is made with beef stock and comes with meaty dumplings—a Polish variation. You can try a small cup ($3.75) if you're not ready for an entire bowl ($7). Alternatively, try garlic, mushroom, or sourdough soup ($3.75 cup, $7.95 bowl), or an interesting, hearty beef tripe soup ($4.50/$7.95). Appetizers include a plate of Polish-style marinated wild mushrooms ($7.95), which are mixed with domestic mushrooms but delightfully vinegared, and a classic beef tartare ($8.95) served with the works, including sliced onions, pickles, egg yolk, and marinated wild mushrooms, with homemade rye bread on the side; it's a popular choice. Needless to say, salads include a fresh beet plate ($4.95), but there's also a cucumber, sour cream, and dill salad ($3.95), which is nice but small, and an everything-that-grows Polish Chef's salad ($12.95). Old Krakow has a special affinity for the forest-floor flavors of wild mushrooms, so home in on the mushroom crêpes: three sautéed mushroom-stuffed crêpes ($10.95) or sweetened cheese-filled crêpes ($10.95) make homey meals in themselves. Silesian potato dumplings, or pirogy ($11.95), also come smothered in that earthy mushroom sauce and go nicely with a side order of garlicky, homemade kielbasa ($5.50) or sauerkraut ($3).

Old Krakow is filled with women friends deconstructing world events over a glass of Polish house red wine ($7), and sweethearts feeding each other the delicious strudel ($6). You'll want to huddle in here with them when the mist off Twin Peaks is like the wind off the steppes and you can almost hear the hooves of Cossacks around the corner.

Park Chow

When Tony Gulisano of the Castro's Chow took over the pleasant spot that was a former Macedonian hangout called Stoyanof's, he was doing the Inner Sunset a favor. Although the predecessors are fondly remembered, Park Chow's mix of upbeat atmosphere and low prices for homey food have made it a worthy replacement, especially for weekend brunches. The heated sidewalk tables, plant-plastered back deck and very cozy interior—complete with exposed beams, lots of wood, long counter, and welcoming fireplace in the front section—make it all homey; too homey, alas, the joint is always jumping. Philanthropic Gulisano gets the casual menu, friendly service, and the prices just right; it's no wonder Park Chow is just as busy as his older branch.

Cost $8–25

Address 1240 9th Ave at Lincoln
℗ 415/665-9912
Open Mon–Thurs 11am–10pm, Fri 11am–11pm, Sat & Sun 10am–11pm
Transportation 44, 71, N
Accepts MasterCard, Visa

The food is roughly the same comfort food as at the original Chow, a sort of melee of homey Italian trattoria and American diner with some Asian touches, occasional misfires, and particularly generous portions. Roast mussels ($6.50) are the appetizer of choice here, arriving in a numerous posse upon a skillet lined with rock salt, butter, and parsley. Cheese-filled focaccia ($5.75) is another zinger, with three kinds of cheese inside the crunchy crust. The wood-baked pizzas are another favorite, and the thin-crusted, tender and lavishly topped lamb pizza ($7.50) is a kind of Chow signature dish. It's one of the more expensive pizzas on a short, constantly changing list. Park Chow also scores on herbed roast chicken with heaps of mashed potato ($9.95) and on the regular hamburger ($7.95), which comes lathered with sweet, caramelized onions upon a halved and scooped baguette with good fries—a candidate for "best burger in town". Desserts include the homemade pies ($3.95) for which the first Chow was famous, along with a renowned ginger cake with pumpkin ice cream and caramel sauce ($4.50).

The wine list is short but as friendly in price as everything else. Finally, don't forget the European beers on tap; the Czech Urquell is a standout. Weekend brunches and lunch specials are an institution here. You may have to storm your way past the phalanx of regulars who eat here day and night, but try the counter.

PJ's Oyster Bed

(🍴) Granted, it's not totally authentic in every detail, but nobody does Creole and Cajun cooking better than PJ's Oyster Bed. But then not many other places try to rival this place for New Orleans seafood anyway, and weather aside, it's not a stretch to imagine this jolly spot full of revelers in the French Quarter. It has been a showcase for oys-

Cost $8–35

Address 737 Irving St at 9th
☎ 415/566-7775
Open Mon–Fri 5–10pm, Sat &
Sun 4–10pm
Transportation 6, 66, 71, N
Accepts All major credit cards

ters, shellfish roasts, gumbo, and corn-encrusted catfish for well over a decade. If you can't put up with a wait, reserve ahead of time; the space is pleasant enough but tables are at a premium.

At lunchtime, however, things are quieter, and a shrimp po'boy ($7.95) makes a fair casse-croûte. To kick off at dinner, PJ's does a Hemingway-style Mojito made with two rums, light and dark, plus a spritz of pineapple. It goes well with a basket of cornbread and sourdough, and oysters on the half-shell ($2 each, or $4 barbecue-style—downtown prices here). Perhaps you'll be better off going straight to the sensational "shell feast roast" ($22), an enormous frying pan heaped profusely with mussels upon scallops upon calamari and crab and prawns—if it crawls, creeps or swims it's probably here, cayenned and Tabascoed into a fiery afterworld. Don't let this take up all the room, because there's fat, fricas-séed alligator tail ($18) for those who've never tasted it. Blackened or corn-encrusted catfish ($19) contrasts crunch with tender flesh, while the andouille jambalaya ($17) hides more chicken than sausage. Save a spot for one of PJ's pies, in particular the pecan and praline pie with ice cream ($6).

Granted, this is very hearty fair, and it comes in a festive atmosphere that's just right for special guests, but Emeril and Paul Proudhomme won't be quaking in their shoes—even Justin Wilson is safe, in fact. Some locals have been mumbling about the threat of PJ's resting on its laurels, but loyal regulars are still booking well in advance—this place is always packed. Others just angle for a bar stool, or put down their names before heading across the road to wait at the venerable Yancy's bar.

PPQ Vietnamese Cuisine

The scene in PPQ on a Saturday would arouse anyone's curiosity about pho, the national dish of Vietnam. This is a community crossroads, with people coming and going, and lots of strollers parked in front of the door. PPQ stands for Pho Phu Quoc, which means "pho diner" in Vietnamese, and pho, of course, is a big bowl of beef broth with noodles. It comes with a platter of condiments to season the broth to your liking, from crunchy sprouts and lime, to basil, cilantro, and chile. PPQ sports a few calligraphic texts on the walls above the constantly wiped sea of formica tables, but that's it for decor. It's functional and bare bones in here, with high decibels of chatter.

Cost $5–10

Address 1816 Irving St at 19th
☏ 415/661-8869
Open Daily 10.30am–11pm
Transportation 28, 29, 71, N
Accepts MasterCard, Visa

Good pho ($4.95) derives from strong, unadulterated beef stock like PPQ's. It simmers in various versions: you can enjoy it clear (and grease-free) or with slices of beef, meatballs, and tripe. With the broth come heaps of bean sprouts, chopped mint, basil, cilantro, and crushed nuts, plus slices of lime and bits of ginger, with chile oil alongside. But this is only one of PPQ's meal options. Their cha gio ($5.95), or pork-stuffed imperial spring rolls, arrive fried in the crispiest rice paper, while the green papaya and shrimp salad ($6.50) is a generously zesty meal. They also serve up a slew of vermicelli dishes, while charbroiled pork dishes are another specialty; the meat is shredded and used like sandwich filling in banh mi at lunchtime, or on a bed of slithery vermicelli ($5.95) as a dinner entree. Desserts (from $2.50) consist of tapioca and rice-based dishes, and there's excellent Vietnamese coffee.

Amid the ebb and flow of the Outer Sunset's ethnic communities, this pho palace is a beacon for Vietnamese immigrants, not least because of the quality of its certified Angus beef and the lack of MSG in the cooking. Anyone queasy about the usual price of beef can relax; two bowls daily would make up a nutritious diet for less than ten dollars. If you're looking for a quick snack, however, don't come at busy times like Saturday lunch. Another branch can be found at 2332 Clement St (☏ 415/386-8266).

Rick's

AMERICAN

One of the more startling surprises of Rick's, out west in Parkside, is its formidable captain's-poop interior of polished brass, teak portholes, and forest-green walls. But Richard Oku's place is full of surprises. Where else can you order toasted ravioli with a dip? Where else will you find fish poke from the land of the poi and the pupu platter, or a luau

Cost $10–50
Address 1940 Taraval St at 30th
☎ 415/731-8900
Transportation 66, L
Open Daily 4.30–10pm
Accepts MasterCard, Visa

with roast suckling piglet every first Monday of the month? Or weekend-long hula parties with live music and happy hours? After a stint at Union Square's venerable Gold Spike, Oku now runs Rick's with his partner Victoria, who once worked at the late, lamented Washington Square Bar & Grill. Here at his own place, Oku fuses the dishes of his Hawaiian roots with what he calls "comfort food."

Comfort food is probably the only way to describe dishes like Rick's tapioca pudding, though it may drag you back to schooldays. But there's more or less something for everybody here, starting with Danell's hot crab dip ($9.50), served with brioche toast points, or that fish poke ($10.95), which is a seaweed-cured tuna ceviche. Spinach soup is subtly creamed ($6). Other starters are fishy finger foods like prawns, calamari, and mussels, but for the total marine blow-out, keep space for Rick's goliah ($18.95), an authentic Hawaiian fish stew that's a bouillabaisse and a half. Meat eaters have the old-school choices: there's something called Jurassic Classic ($19.75), which turns out to be Angus steak in green peppercorn sauce with trimmings, while veal chops in a creamy mushroom sauce ($15.50) are praiseworthy, and so is the bargain-priced pot roast ($9.95). Vegetarians can fall back on eggplant Parmigiano ($11.95) and linguine arrabiata ($8.50).

Weeknights feature rotating all-in meal deals, such as meatloaf on Mondays and petrale on Fridays, and are priced from $18.95, including soup, salad, and dessert. For dessert ($2.75 separately), there's that tapioca pudding, or a sweet cheese pie. The fair prices extend to Rick's wine list—you won't be the first to notice that a 1993 Fetzer Eagle Peak ($15) is not a bad offer. Rick's has a fun-loving retinue, but it's as much for the music and mood as for the food.

ITALIAN

Ristorante Marcello

The Bay Area has no shortage of transplanted East Coasters, and they'll feel right at home in the cozy confines of Marcello's. This Outer Sunset fixture is reminiscent of an Italian restaurant of a certain age from South Philadelphia or New York's Little Italy. Old-school Italian dining rooms of this sort are rarer over here on the West Coast, so it's appropriate that this one is way out at the far end of the Sunset District, which in so many ways resembles a town on the Jersey Shore. Like many San Franciscan Italians, the owners trace their roots to Lucca, in Tuscany. The clientele tends to the mature, and dresses for the occasion even if this isn't a particularly formal place. You're likely to hear Italian spoken at neighboring tables.

Cost	$10–35
Address	2100 Taraval St at 31st
☎	415/665-1430
Open	Tues–Sat 5–10.30pm, Sun 4–10pm
Transportation	L
Accepts	MasterCard, Visa

Comparisons start with the long, white bar as you enter, its stone backdrop stacked high with the sort of bottles used for making Manhattans, Old Fashioneds, and other pre-1950 drinks. The menu has something for everyone. Classical Tuscan meat, chicken, and fish dishes are priced a la carte (from $13.50), but you can also get them on dinner menus ($16.25–19.25) that include soup or salad, a sensibly downsized pasta, and tea or coffee. It's a deal that's hard to resist, even if the iceberg salad is drenched in a dressing that tastes bottled. Veal with porcini mushrooms is made with top-quality scaloppine, and covered in a gloppy, brownish sauce that is, happily, much more flavorful than it looks. Grilled swordfish with rosemary is literally just that—satisfyingly unfussy, and paired with sautéed greens. Pastas are priced at just over ten dollars, and even if you're having one of the non-pasta dinners, it's likely to be accompanied by perfect penne with Bolognese sauce; they'll gladly substitute a non-meat sauce if you ask.

If you must have dessert ($5–7), there's a fun, if inauthentic tiramisu, weirdly slathered in chocolate syrup. The wine list is dominated by good Italian choices at very fair prices, such as a 1995 Machiavelli Chianti Classico Riserva ($28). Marcello's is about authenticity, but of a certain kind. It will leave visitors from New Jersey pining for the old Italian joints of home.

Spiazzo Caffè

West Portal Avenue seems like a pleasant and useful version of small-town Main Street, but it also supports a San Francisco-like diversity of restaurants and cuisines. Spiazzo has been here for several years, yet its smart, salmon-colored interior and brisk, friendly service always seem refreshing. If the menu seldom breaks new ground, it's

Cost	$10–35

Address 33 West Portal Ave near Ulloa
☎ 415/664-9511
Open Daily 11am–10.30pm
Transportation 17, 48, K, L, M
Accepts All major credit cards

also scrupulously loyal to its Italian roots, as West Portal's considerable expatriate Italian community will agree. You're liable to find some native speakers at the next table, and while Spiazzo isn't known to many non-West Portal residents, it's easy to get here by streetcar.

If you appreciate the simplicity of Tuscan cuisine, start with mixed grilled vegetables ($4.95). It's a pretty melange of radicchio, eggplant, zucchini, and endive, marinated in balsamic vinegar and olive oil and prepared on the same wood-burning grill they use to make the eight different pizzas ($8–10), each of which is big enough to serve two nicely. There's always a risotto special ($13.95), frequently of mixed wild mushrooms, which makes a good main course though they'll gladly divide it into two bowls so you can share it as an appetizer; the consistency could be creamier but it's bursting with flavor. A dozen pastas form the bulk of the menu, from a very creamy penne with salmon ($9.95), which is not for the weight-conscious, to the tasty ravioli naturale ($9.95), which is saffron-infused pasta stuffed with an inventive combination of swiss chard, watercress, and Parmesan cheese, with fresh tomato sauce. Meat will be simple and good: if you're really starving, order the mixed grill ($13.95) of lamb chops, chicken, and sausage with potatoes and vegetables; the chicken breast ($9.95) with diced artichoke hearts, capers, and a pleasant if unremarkable white wine and lemon sauce is a somewhat lighter alternative.

The wine list is well rounded and moderately priced, with Chiantis starting at $16 a bottle. There are also several wines by the glass and that too-rare alternative, half-bottles, including a nice 1997 Barbera ($14). If you have room for dessert (around $5)—which is unlikely—skip the blah tiramisu and opt for one of the three ice cream cakes.

Thanh Long

🍴 Generally, people don't look for dining this far out toward Ocean Beach, other than the sunset-hour watering holes of the Cliff House and Beach Chalet. But for over thirty years Thanh Long has drawn shellfish-lovers from all over for huge crab feeds. The original parent to Polk Street's classy Crustacean, it offers the kind of messy gustatory experience that makes you wonder why you'd look farther, though you'll risk a wait.

Cost $10–50

Address 4101 Judah St at 46th
☎ 415/665-1146
Open Tues–Thurs & Sun 4.30–10pm, Fri & Sat 4.30–10.30pm
Transportation 18, N
Accepts MasterCard, Visa

Luckily, Thanh Long—Vietnamese for "Green Dragon"—has a bar serving cocktails like...Green Dragon (midori and vodka plus a grenadine spritz), so nurse one ($6) while you angle for a free table.

Appetizers, such as the salmon plate, are mainly fish, but you can also opt for starter portions of salads and crab-filled pasta, as well as Thanh Lonh's not-so-secret ace in the hole, their to-die-for garlic noodles ($7.95), which are buttery and pungent. A veggie stir-fry ($11) is on offer, as is a spice-rubbed chicken ($15). But let's not beat about the bay! Dungeness crab is what people come here for, and it's silly to order anything else. The pièce de résistance is a whopper of a roast Dungeness billy crab ($35) served with your personal bib and utensils plus butter. Roll up your sleeves, choose your weapon and get stuck in. For the lactose intolerant, other versions are drunken crab, in wine and shallots, or tamarind sauce. Splitting a crab between two people is practical as well as a good bonding exercise; this is labor-intensive work, remember, and it saves it from getting cold.

Thanh Long sits on sand dunes, almost at the Pacific's edge. After the creation of Golden Gate Park in the 1870s, what was then called "the Lots" began to acquire some anchoring turf, thanks to Scots gardener John McClaren. Later came racecourses, farms, a gunpowder factory, and "wedding cakes floating on sand" as a recent mayor described the Sunset Avenues housing. Alongside the South African vegetarian restaurant Joubert's, Thanh Long is an oasis out here that's well worth the trek.

Vanida

Yet another Thai? With nearly four hundred Thai places in San Francisco, every street seems to have its own favorite, and each new candidate has to plead a special case to make the grade. Parkside, however, in the farthest Outer Sunset, was once a dining desert—relative to the rest of the city, at least. There's still not a huge choice here—unless you like corner pho or Chinese diners, Hawaiian luau or old-style Italian places—but this friendly Thai local stands out for being actually filled with Thai people. They're not there by mistake: Vanida is indeed a trooper, and especially useful for vegetarians. The decor is of spotless white table-cloths and plants, and it's pretty in an unassuming way.

Cost $6–15	

Address 3050 Taraval at 41st
☎ 415/564-6766
Transportation L
Open Mon–Thurs
11.30am–9.30pm, Fri & Sat
11.30am–10pm
Accepts All major credit cards
except AMEX

THAI

The menu titillates vegetarians with a sparky list of interesting appetizers, starting with pra ram ($5.95), which is deep-fried tofu with a crunchy, pungent peanut dip, and a dish of cubed taro root tubers deep-fried in wonton wrappers ($5.50). Best of all is the simple and fresh miang kum ($5.50), a platter heaped with roast coconut flakes, sliced limes, fine-diced red onion, minced ginger, cashews, and other nuts; you parcel the ingredients into spinach leaves and dip the whole thing into a sweet-fiery dipping sauce. Vegetarians may be in luck, but for omnivores there are great chicken, pork, and beef dishes too. The koa nar ped ($5.95) is crispy duck on a bed of noodles, while gaeng karee ($5.75) is a milder chicken curry on rice, spiced with turmeric, cumin, and chile. Moo prig ($5.95) is a rustic pork curry with vegetables, while nuer kang ($5.95) is marinated beef cubes with liberal cilantro and cucumber for garnish. Beer and Thai coffee or tea round the feast off.

Best of all, nothing costs over seven dollars here—they even throw in free dessert of flambéed bananas, or mangoes and sticky rice. Not that Vanida needs to give desserts away to lure in the locals. Not only is it a bargain, but it's a real find too, and there's no trouble parking around here. What more do you need to say to a San Franciscan?

Yum-Yum Fish

If Clement Street is New Chinatown, then Irving Street is "New" New Chinatown, where cheek-by-jowl Thai and Viet restaurants, Korean barbecue places and sushi shops waft aromas around these blocks south of Golden Gate Park. Of a Saturday morning, local families parade up and down, doing their food shopping and stopping off at pho parlors or dim sum palaces. Among the oriental emporia are sweet shops that sell the Rowntree's Blackcurrant Pastilles, McVitie's Digestives, and Fisherman's Friend lozenges that some Asians developed a mysterious taste for during the Commonwealth period. Meanwhile, the donuts, smoked pork, and pho smells will lure you on to the next food stall. Smaller than its nearby rivals, May Wah or Irving Seafood, but thriving nonetheless, is Yum-Yum Fish.

Cost $5–25

Address 2181 Irving Ave at 23rd
☎ 415/566-6433
Open Daily 9.30am–6.30pm
Transportation 71, N
Accepts Cash only

Displayed in the front window and in their refrigerated cabinet is Yum-Yum's catch of fresh, locally caught salmon, tuna, sand dabs, petrale, and crustaceans. Oysters (from 70 cents) are local Tomales Bay or Hog Island. Local mussels and clams and calamari are also available here in season, while at the same time some rather crowded-looking sushi lovers are sitting inside, chowing down on the astounding sushi deals available from the counter at the back. Bargains include fifteen pieces of tuna, yellowtail, albacore, octopus, salmon, and salmon roe for $12.50, or more impressive still, seventy pieces of sushi for $53. Beat that! Jumbo steamed Dungeness crabs ($14.75) in season are fresher than at most places. Pick one of these babies up, find the cracker and some butter and lemon, sit down at one of the three very cramped tables just inside the door, and have a messy good time right here. Alternatively, you can take it home and have a solitary orgy on your own kitchen table.

Those who question the quality of San Francisco's local crustaceans should note that shellfish that's cooked as quickly as possibly after leaving the water is the healthiest. What you try to avoid is those tanks where they have an extended, post-oceanic life. Yum-Yum, a branch of 3rd Street's Nikko, which supplies city sushi bars, has a spanking turnover, which is a good sign.

The Bay Area & Outlying Districts

East Bay
p.357

North Bay & Marin
p.381

South Bay & the Peninsula
p.397

East Bay

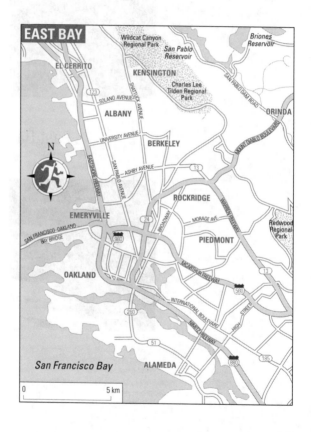

Asena Restaurant

Sometimes a place can come second and still be a winner. Proud winner of second place in the Contra Costa Times "Best French" category, Asena also got a nomination for its outdoor and patio dining and live music. Alameda could do with a few more mid-range places like Asena, in fact. It's an island where eating out is dominated by a handful of high-end restaurants and lots of fast food places, so a casually "nice" spot with relatively affordable prices fills a serious gap. There's a firm local following, especially at weekends.

Cost $15–45

Address 2508 Santa Clara Ave at Broadway, Alameda
☏510/521-4100
Open Mon–Thurs 11.30am–3.30pm & 4.30–9.30pm, Fri 11.30am–3.30pm & 5–10pm, Sat 5–10pm
Transportation AC transit
Accepts All major credit cards except Diners

Good pizzas have interesting toppings such as pear and blue cheese ($9), and are fine lunch options here, along with the salads and sandwiches. The evening meal is a prix fixe type, and comes with a choice of soup or salad for $13 to $16, depending on the choice of main course. The accompanying salads are quite elegant, and are made with really crisp and fresh romaine leaves dressed in a vinaigrette that boasts candied pecans and a tinge of pomegranate molasses—something fruity and wonderfully sweet, anyway. Paellas ($30, for two people) are a big draw here, and among the lightest and tastiest in the Bay Area. All too often, paellas get bogged down in their own overcooked and under-seasoned weight, but this one is subtle yet tasty, thanks to the real saffron strands that spike up the rice grains. A roast chicken breast ($15) is stuffed with apple slices and gets little kicky additions of biscuit on the side. Breaded pork tenderloin is stuffed with artichoke hearts ($15), spinach comes in sherry pink peppercorn cream sauce ($13), and a grilled marinated lamb sirloin has a Burgundy and rosemary demi-glace ($15).

One drawback is the noise level of the room, which on a really busy night can make it hard to have a conversation. A few really loud diners can quickly up the volume by several ratchets—everyone reacts by talking even louder and soon the sound climbs beyond comfort level. But then on other nights that vibrant atmosphere is a sure sign of Asena's charm and popularity.

THE BAY AREA & OUTLYING DISTRICTS CALIFORNIAN

Banzai Garlic Cafe

Along with Asena, Banzai is one of a few really good places to eat in the island city of Alameda, a sleepy refuge from urban San Francisco and Oakland. Getting here may mean crossing at least one bridge and one body of water, and reservations are necessary—despite which you may still wait, so leave plenty of time for dinner. Rumors of future expansion into the theater next door have been confirmed. It's a shimmering dream that may arrive some day, but meanwhile, Banzai is so...well, bonsai, that it seats only twenty, including those at the bar. It breeds immediate chumminess and a lot of patience among the patrons. Dinner can take as long as three hours from the time you enter to the time you finish coffee! "Da joint is small, hard to work, *good luck!*" warns the menu.

Cost $7–35
Address 2319 Central Ave, Alameda
☎ 510/864-7222
Open Mon 11.30am–3pm, Tues–Fri 11.30am–3pm & 5–11pm, Sat & Sun 5–11pm
Transportation AC Transit W-WA
Accepts All major credit cards

Everything on chef Mario Garcia's menu is maximally garlicky and, notwithstanding the occasional misstep, most of the food is prepared simply and well. Service is casual and extremely friendly, with quirkiness and Tuesday lobster nights as hallmarks. The menu notes that "this is a very very high class low class joint!" In the mid-afternoon hours, they serve quirky appetizers such as a plate of spicy endamame beans ($5) that may be too hot for some tastebuds, or a salad with creamy garlic dressing ($4). Both the Hawaiian pan-seared ahi tuna ($18), and fresh pork-loin chop ($17) are outstanding, and come in a package deal with salad and potatoes, or noodles with side vegetables. You can choose two side dishes, and you'll love the fabulously garlicky noodles ($7). Desserts are hit or miss: the key lime cheesecake ($6) looks good, but one diner reported that theirs was served frozen at the center.

So Banzai can be erratic, but in a good and friendly way. They claim to have fed the last four US presidents, yet Mario's menu is still down-homey enough to offer a free ride home to anyone who imbibes a little too much. It's a given that all dining is destination dining on this island, but in this case you might well think it's worth the journey.

Bay Wolf Restaurant

The food here is Michael Wild and Larry Goldman's take on all of the Mediterranean, blending the flavors of Tuscany, Provence, and the Basque country—and it's unbeatable. Inside the sweet old Victorian building, two flatteringly lit rooms take in a modicum of diners. The lunch menu is small and comes loaded with local fruit and vegetables; evening menus change monthly and focus on a new country or region each time. Locally raised duck is always a feature, however.

Cost $25–60
Address 3853 Piedmont Ave at Rio Vista, Oakland
☎ 510/655-6004
Open Mon–Fri 11.30am–2pm & 6–9.30pm, Sat & Sun 5.30–9.30pm
Transportation AC Transit 1–6 or 59, 60 to Piedmont
Accepts All major credit cards except Diners

At lunch, potato and celery root soup with leeks ($5.75) is deeply homey, with a peppery edge and an oniony sour note offset by the familiar spuddiness. A bursting salad Niçoise ($10.50) is made with large flakes of just-roasted tuna and lots of fresh anchovies and eggs, plus potatoes that have been well soaked in a spiked vinaigrette. Barbecued pork salad ($10.75) is tossed in slices of blood orange with green rice and spinach, a great mix of sweet and sour, and hard and soft textures. Butternut ravioli with ricotta ($11.50) come in a sage, almond, and Meyer lemon sauce, a far more adventurously edgy blending than this staple usually gets, dependent on the crunch and slightly burned tinge of the almonds. Dinner menus may include a duck breast and citrus salad with anise-marinated beets and ginger vinaigrette ($8.75), a dish people will cross the Bay Bridge for. The Bay Wolf cassoulet ($19) is famous for its very garlicky sausage and smoked pork, and the mirepoix vegetables. Goat cheese-stuffed peppers ($15.75) are festively dressed in black beans and mango salsa, and served with spicy green rice.

A brioche-based dessert always seems to be on the menu, such as the brioche with brandied cherry compote ($6.50), but there may also be a mixed citrus marmalade tart with kumquats and tangerine sauce ($6.50), and blood orange sherbet with lemon cooler ($6). Book ahead! Bay Wolf is a destination mecca for the foodies of the nation, as well as for locals. It keeps a room for parties, and its verandah is an agreeable spot to sit outside and try a cheeky little California varietal, or a small vineyard label.

THE BAY AREA & OUTLYING DISTRICTS VIETNAMESE

Le Cheval

(‖₁‖) In among the Art Deco buildings of downtown Oakland, Le Cheval boasts a huge horse in the entrance, making its point about the name. Inside are high ceilings and parquet floors, and this is the prettier of the two Oakland branches, though it offers the same dishes at the same rock-bottom prices. The service is spanking to the point of being brusque, which helps move along the waiting lines, the noise is incessant, and

Cost $7–25
Address 1007 Clay St at 10th, Oakland
☏ 510/763-8495
Open Mon–Sat 11am–3pm & 5–9pm, Sun 5–9pm
Transportation BART Oakland City Center
Accepts All major credit cards except Diners

you don't need to book. The top-quality Chinese and Vietnamese cuisine makes this a place to know about. Evidently the locals agree—it's always bustling and busy.

Le Cheval provides several versions of pho ($4.75), the traditional beef broth of Vietnam, with its gorgeously aromatic lemongrass and whiffs of bird chile-scented heat, and its accompaniments of mint and basil. Try their special watercress salad (around $5), with a tossed medley of whatever fruit is in season. Sautéed pea sprouts in garlic ($6.95) are simmered in onions and Le Cheval's own secret sauce. Crispy and refreshing shrimp rolls ($3.50) are eaten in lettuce rolled up with fresh sprigs of cilantro, translucent cellophane noodles, and mint, and come with the special nuoc cham dipping sauce. Imperial rolls ($3.40) are the cold version, filled again with the noodles, and wonderfully minted in flavor. Of the bigger dishes, a beef kebab ($7.55) on skewers is marinated in lemongrass and sweetened with a coating of hoisin plum sauce. Prawn kebab ($7.55) comes on the same skewers and is crunchy fresh, and served with additional dipping sauce. Bo lac luc ($8.55), or cubed lemongrass beef in a lightly curried sauce, is another well-executed variation on the classics. In season, Le Cheval does a big production-number roast crab (from $25) that folks will cross the bridge to try, and not just because of the tab.

Even their very traditional desserts of mango and sticky rice don't let you down with their simple freshness. As well as wine and beer, they serve lemon ice tea or freshmade lemonade by the glass ($1.50). The other branch is at 344 20th Street, Oakland (☏ 510/763-3610).

Chez Panisse Cafe

Chez Panisse is it: the holy grail of Californian cuisine. When its founder and high priestess Alice Waters began here over thirty years ago, Sixties' idealism was still effervescing in Berkeley, and the credo of fresh and seasonal greens, bought from the farmer on the day they were picked, was part of the revolution. Waters became the visionary who tried to get Bill Clinton to plant organic vegetable gardens at the White House; she's still the icon that other cooks look to for the shining path, and her restaurant has launched two genera-

Cost $25–60

Address 1517 Shattuck Ave, Berkeley
☎510/548-5525
Open Mon–Thurs 11.30am–3pm & 5–10.30pm, Fri & Sat 11.30am–4pm & 5–11.30pm
Transportation BART Berkeley City Center, AC Transit Shattuck Street lines
Accepts All major credit cards except Diners

tions of great chefs. Unfortunately, the hushed downstairs dining room falls outside most people's price range. Happily, however, Alice's cooking still holds sway in the much less expensive upstairs cafe, with its elegant polished redwood interior, abundant flowers, and wraparound eye-level mirrors that are so tempting for celebrity watching. They even take reservations. Servers never take notes and tell you the menu verbally without intoning the terrible "tonight's specials" mantra.

The Cafe provides a mini-introduction to its grander parent downstairs and makes the whole deal fun. It has a prix fixe menu of three courses ($24.50) which changes daily. It might include a salad, then penne with asparagus and pancetta, followed by lemon and orange sherbet, and kumquat ice cream. A la carte, you may come across a brilliant plate of ahi tuna tartare ($13) with provocative olives and mint. Salads are jewel boxes that may include orange and avocado ($8.25) or chicory with anchovy, lemon, and egg ($7.75). Ceviches come with squid, chard, chicories, and Tuscan grilled bread ($13). Risottos are daily features: one triumph stars black trumpet mushrooms ($16). Skirt steak ($23) gets conventional cauliflower with a Gentleman's Relish of anchovy salsa.

All this is the work of the cafe, rather than the Chez Panisse shrine that is so heavily over-publicized by the glossies. Those who expect fancy, complex presentation in a hushed and posh setting are invariably disillusioned by Chez Panisse, but let the fresh ingredients speak for themselves, just as Alice always intended, and you'll see her point.

Citron

🍴 Just as Albany and upper Shattuck pride themselves on Solano Avenue, Rockridge is rejoicing in this happening little restaurant strip along College Avenue. Citron wins a special mention because of chef Chris Rossi's determinedly authentic French cooking, which emphasizes provincial classics and, at its best, delivers the best. The outside is simple, with a black-tiled frontage under a small red canopy, while the inside combines buttery walls with old vintage photos and flowers. A heated outdoor terrace at the back makes for a pleasant evening.

Cost £24–50
Address 5484 College Ave at Lawton and Taft, Rockridge
☎ 510/653-5484
Open Mon 5.30–9pm, Tues–Thurs 5.30–9.30pm, Fri & Sat 5–10pm, Sun 5–9pm
Transportation BART Rockridge, AC Transit 17
Accepts All major credit cards

Although it's expensive, Citron offers several prix fixe menus (from $24, available from Sunday to Wednesday) that change weekly, while the narrow a la carte menu of eleven dishes switches every three weeks or so. A favorite seafood appetizer is the fruits de mer vol-au-vent ($11), which is just a few mouthfuls of lobster and shiitake in pastry, but delicately seasoned. A classical vichyssoise ($7) is reminiscent of France: homey and simply good. Main dishes on the prix fixe might include halibut seared with pancetta and broccoli, or duck confit on escarole served with pinole ravioli. A la carte, the succulent prime rib ($26) comes with very creamy gratin Dauphinois, and roasted rabbit ($24) is served on a luscious bed of polenta. Birds such as squab, poussin, and quail (from $28 a la carte) are often found on the menu, and have a faithful following. Don't leave without trying the panna cotta ($7.50), which comes in a little puddle of cherry preserves and cannot be faulted, or the rhubarb tart in raspberry coulis ($7.50), or the equally delicious goat cheese cheesecake ($7.50), a fascinating concept whose time has decidedly come.

That three-course prix fixe is a pretty amazing bargain. Citron may not initially seem like the upscale establishment it really is, but it outstrips several rivals for the title of the East Bay's topnotch French restaurant—just boggle at that winelist. There's free parking at the nearby BART station after six in the evening. Keep Citron's back patio in mind for your next anniversary or birthday or special outing.

La Furia Chalaca

This homey Peruvian restaurant is one of the zillion ethnic dining choices in and around Jack London Square, which is getting to be a festive spot for an evening out, thanks in part to the varied street entertainment. La Furia gets off to a good start. Its chef-owner Carlos Anton has done a fine decorating job, enshrining pre-Columbian artefacts on the shelves around the wall-alcoves with special lighting. He has even made the very large bathroom into a "featured destination," with its handsome tiling, flowers, and Incan relics. In addition, soulful singer José Manuel is at hand to deliver the *canciónes antiguas* — which range from Guantanamera to El Condor Pasa, neither of which is particularly Peruvian, but still, it shows effort. A very prompt and deferential waiter immediately supplies corn kernels and plantain chips.

Cost $15–25
Address 310 Broadway at Jack London Square, Oakland ☎510/451-4206
Open Mon & Thurs–Sun 11am–10pm, Wed 6–10pm
Transportation AC Transit 58, 59, ferry to Jack London Square
Accepts All major credit cards except Diners

"Chalaca" refers to the native specialties of Callao, a seaport that considers itself the birthplace of the cevicheria, the Peruvian fish shacks that peddle the seafood salad known worldwide as ceviche. La Furia's rendition ($8.50 for lunch, $13 for dinner) is fresh, tasty, and entirely acceptable, even if it's a quite standard mix of shellfish in a lemon-based marinade. Chicharrones a su gusto ($9.30/$14) are a snack of pork rind deep-fried in lard, very indigenous to Andean countries and much missed by expatriate Peruvians, but you might find sopa de pollo ($6) an easier start, or the ensalada russa ($6). Adobo de chancho ($9.30/$14) is another Peruvian specialty, a fiery pork stew with sweet potatoes and chiles. A more interesting and enjoyable specialty are jaleas ($9.30/$14), a kind of quick-fried fish cake that's really quite delicious. The papas a la huancaina ($9) and papa rellena ($9) can be a little dried out, but the anticuchos or skewered beef hearts ($9) are the real thing.

They have good beers from Peru, including Cusqueña, from Cuzco, and another from Callao, which is noted for its beers. There's a kids' menu too, with quesadillas ($3) and Inca Cola ($3). La Furia Chalaca is certainly a pleasant addition to the increasingly interesting precinct of Jack London Square.

Hahn's Hibachi

Hahn's Hibachi is a small Asian barbecue chain with several branches around the Bay Area, all of them hugely popular with families. They exude glorious aromas and exciting sizzles, despite a heavy emphasis on plastic at the tables. There are more seriously authentic Korean places to eat traditional hibachi barbecue, but Hahn's following for barbecued pork and other marinated meats is growing, probably because it's so kid-friendly. The Oakland branch is the best place to sample several of their other dishes too, especially the flaming bananas. It helps that the restaurant is situated in the rapidly growing restaurant scene around Jack London Square, which is now all bustle and cheer after a few dismal introductory years.

Cost $6–25
Address 63 Jack London Square, Franklin St at Embarcadero, Oakland
☎510/628-0717
Open Mon–Sat 11am–10pm, Sun 11am–9.30pm
Transportation AC Transit 58, 59, ferry to Jack London Square
Accepts MasterCard, Visa

You'll find an interesting variety of the very Korean dish of kim chee here, because this branch draws in the local Korean community. But you don't need to know anything more about it to dive straight into their barbecue mounds. Just opt for pork, chicken, ribs, shrimp, or beef, and watch it arrive in a sizzling skillet, covered with the Hahn trademark spicy-sweet sauce, with prices ranging from $6.95 for the chicken to $14 for Long Life vegetables—"scientifically tested by our psychologist and executive staff," says the menu. Included in the price are side dishes of rice, cucumber salad in sesame-vinegar dressing, generous bowls of udon noodles, and kimchee, which is spicy-sour pickled cabbage. Other dishes to try include the bibimpap ($7.50) of rice topped with meat and a fried egg, or kebabs ($8.50). The vegetable tempura ($5.50) and vegetarian potstickers ($5.50) are only nominally satisfying choices for vegetarians, but Hahn's isn't a very sensible choice for vegetarians to begin with.

As for that flaming banana dessert ($5.50), like the meat, it arrives in a sizzling skillet, but this time the servers flambé it tableside, always a thrill for the young. Hahn's also has branches in San Francisco's Haight, Marina, Noe Valley, and Sunset districts, and on Polk Street, which is the first and smallest. All have minimal decor but make up for it in the way of hearty plates that groan with barbecue.

Inn Kensington

If you hear East Bay folks talking about dining "Inn Kensington", you may be taken aback at first. It's a puzzler, until you realize they mean this quintessentially East Bay bistro just under the El Cerrito hills. It has a stunning view and it's quite affordable—a genuine "little treasure." Owned by Hong Tran, Inn Kensington is essentially a converted shop next to a drug store cum sub-post office, with Mozart on the sound track, Chagall prints, linen napiery, and friendly servers, plus a general ambiance of conviviality.

Cost $7–25

Address 293 Arlington Ave at Amherst, Kensington
☎ 510/527-5919
Open Mon & Tues
7am–2.30pm, Wed-Fri
7am–2.30pm & 5.30–9pm, Sat
5.30–9pm, Sun 8am–3pm
Transportation BART El Cerrito Plaza, then Kensington shuttle
Accepts Cash only

Weekday lunches are the thing as well as weekend brunches, say faithful Kensingtonites who frequent the place. You may take their recommendation and choose the house salad ($4.95) of seasonal mixed greens in a lemon vinaigrette. The Caesar ($6.75) makes a respectable lunch, and another dollar adds shredded grilled chicken breast. Roasted beet salad ($6.95) is this year's fashion favorite in spiffier establishments, and this version is prettily studded with sliced Granny Smiths, dried cranberries, red onion rings, and roasted walnuts, plus arugula with balsamic vinaigrette. A beef satay appetizer ($6.95) is loaded skewers of marinated skirt beef with a very crunchy peanut dipping sauce and a generous helping of cucumber, onion, and tomato salad. Melon with prosciutto ($6.95) is the Italian classic, but this time served on arugula with a lemon vinaigrette. The kids get their own burgers ($6.50) or pappardelle noodles and meatballs ($6.50), while Mom and Pop can choose a combination supper ($9.50) of Inn Kensington burger or grilled chickenburger served with extra cheese and aioli, plus roasted red creamer potatoes, and a choice of soup or salad. All the main dishes are great value: chicken breast ($11.25) is pan-roasted, topped with red pepper and grilled eggplant, and served with saffron-parsley couscous.

Not only does Hong Tran change the menus monthly but he also mails and emails the new menus to regulars, the mark of a community fixture. It really works: by night there's an influx of families getting together after the day, and at weekends it's a brunch magnet and come-all-ye.

Jesso's Seafood

This Friday night fish-fry joint on Telegraph is an excellent little place, even if it's sometimes noisier than the Superbowl. It's very clean and, more to the point, the oil used to fry the fish is noticeably cleaner than at many other old-style places. Jesso himself is a warm and friendly presence behind the counter, and there's a blackboard of today's fish above his head. A fascinating wall exhibits photos and football memorabilia—they're all Raiders fans in here—and a few tables outside wait for warmer days. The inside has a few small, formica tables and that's it.

Cost $10–25
Address 2817 Telegraph Ave at 29th, Berkeley
☎510/451-1561
Open Mon–Thurs 11am–9pm, Fri & Sat 11am–10pm, Sun noon–7pm
Transportation BART McArthur Boulevard
Accepts All major credit cards except Diners

Jesso's is a straight-down-the-line Cajun-style fish shack, offering dishes from catfish to fried chicken. Seafood gumbo ($4.95 cup, $9.95 bowl) has an honest dark roux base and doesn't cheat on large chunks of crab, Creole seasoning, okra, or time of preparation. Oysters and prawns are good starters: one of the better deals is the "5 Prawn 5 Oysters" special ($13), served with three hush puppies—puffy, golf-ball-sized corn muffins to the uninitiated—plus salad or fries. Fish specials for three people are served in lavishly sized "family buckets," and there's not a hint of superfluous grease; you'll also get twenty more of those hush puppies on the side. The buckets start at $30 for the snapper and go up to $37.95 for fillet of sole. Braised collard greens in smoky Jesso Sauce ($2.25 small, $3.50 large) come with very generous scoops of mashed yam. The Cajun fries can be bought separately ($2.25/$3.25) and are deliciously rubbed in those blackened Cajun spices. Massive torpedo-shaped sandwiches, or po'boys (from $6.50), will fill a gap, and there are several fried chicken combos (from $12.75) with prawns, oysters, or catfish, which come with salad, fries, and hush puppies. Drinks are milk, sodas or SoBe, a soymilk beverage ($1.50).

Very friendly folks run this place. Some items may be a little pricier than other Oakland places, but you won't go hungry, and the Cajun-Creole food is absolutely the real thing.

Lalime's

The residential, front-parlor looks of Lalime's derive from just that, as the restaurant grew out of a private home (actually, a white-painted "Craftsman"-era house) in the Westbrae area of North Berkeley, a dull-looking suburb not far from Gilman Street's shopping outlets. "Chez Panisse for locals," as Berkeleyites dub it, first opened two decades ago on Albany's Solano Avenue, and now there's an offshoot there, the Mexican-flavored Fonda Solana. Lalime's has acquired an enviable cult-following for its interesting food, as well as for its special, prix fixe theme dinners, food events star-ring celebrity chefs, wine tastings, and the like.

Cost $10–35
Address 1329 Gilman St between Peralta and Neilson, Berkeley
☎ 510/527-9838
Open Mon–Thurs 5.30–9.30pm, Fri & Sat 5.30–10pm, Sun 5–9pm
Transportation BART North Berkeley, AC Transit 9
Accepts All major credit cards

This is an eclectic menu with Middle Eastern moments—the owners are, in fact, part Armenian, and the main chef was, until recently, an Irishwoman from Cork. But new chef Steve Jaramillo has added Mexican classics, such as a vegetarian bean pozole, to the Mediterranean-influenced menu, and his frog's legs are now a staple item, alongside the familiar sweetbreads and foie gras found in the delicately sherried sweetbreads Matignon ($10.50). Moules Tunisian ($9.75) is mussels steamed in a harissa broth with grilled flatbread, while the Caesar ($7.75) comes with blue cheese dressing and roast chestnuts. Lalime's is justly famous for its zippy way with vegetables, and a duck breast ($19) makes the best main-course choice, with its roast shallots and dried cherries jus on parsnips. Chestnut-encrusted venison ($22.50) comes with an inspired blackcurrant sauce—an unusual bonus because currant bushes are prohibited in California (for FDA ordinance reasons to do with crop mites), so these had to be flown in. For dessert, they always feature a chocolate torte ($6.25), or you could try the Clockwork Orange tartlette ($6.25), which is a zesty, orange-flavored chocolate pie.

The wine list is a huge bonus, with some unusual European imports as well as interesting local offerings like the 1999 Navarro Gewürztraminer, Anderson Valley ($24), and a Ravenswood 1999 Cabernet ($32). Booking is required here, as locals know to their cost, and the only alternative is an off-putting wait.

East Bay: Albany

Mangia Mangia

Mangia Mangia is Albany's "straight-up Italian," one of several dependable spots for a pasta fix, and a stalwart in the firmament of many flavors available to Albany's foodies—the "Albanian Pavlovians," as journalist Herb Caen used to dub the members of this multiethnic East Bay community. A gust of olive oil and garlic hits you as soon as you walk in the door to meet a welcoming interior of ice cream colors; ranks of bottles divide the open kitchen from the tables. A green, white, and red theme is everywhere, and clever little touches in the pretty plates and seating match the artistic presentation of the fare. Lida and Sotaya Ghaemi unveiled this neighborhood trattoria in a former barbecue spot some years after emigrating here from Iran, and they've exercised their interior-decorating gifts to help the ambiance.

Cost $15–35

Address 755 San Pablo Ave near Washington, Albany
☎ 510/526-9700
Open Tues 5–9pm, Wed–Sat 11am–3pm & 5–10pm, Sun 5–9pm
Transportation BART El Cerrito Plaza, AC Transit Z
Accepts MasterCard, Visa

The Italian fare cooked by chef Richard Lucido is more than just by-the-book rustic. Antipasti are good here, in particular a plate of many snacks invented by Lucido. Christened antipasto Mangia ($6.75), it's a merry medley of vegetable confusion, a platter of mixed greens, eggplant, zucchini, and carrots with prosciutto and barbecued shrimp in a little pepper coulis, and a tart aioli on the side. Only in this part of California can you get eggplant, pepper, and carrots in season at the same time! The grilled polenta slices ($6.95) are also good, as are the prosciutto-wrapped zucchini sticks ($5.95), and a caprina goat cheese salad ($8.95) that blasts the tastebuds away. Rigatoni in a strong Bolognese sauce ($11.50) is very herby and tinged with extra meat and tomato, and there's a risotto Parmigiano. Main dishes include a richly sauced and succulent chicken in Marsala ($12.75) which comes with spinach and a little garnish of cheese. A tenderloin roast in milk solids with mashed potatoes ($13.75) is unbeatable as comfort food.

You might want to skip the desserts ($5) of tiramisu, gelati, and zabaglione, not because there's anything wrong with them, but because you've had them before and you'll be full. Albany has a fascinating roll-call of eateries, and this is a solid option.

Nizza La Bella

Albany's small-town charms are increasingly overlaid with a sheen of culinary glamor. One terrific eatery after another lines Solano, with more gems tucked away off San Pablo's drag. The allure lies in the combination of the sweetly 1950s main street and the availability of cuisines of many kinds, not forgetting delis and food shopping. Nizza La Bella is a Provençal stronghold, a little oasis with a heated sidewalk terrace and Beaujolais Nouveau dinners. The name means "the beautiful Nice" in Provençal argot, and Evelyne Solomon and Eleanor Triboletti's place is indeed beautiful, carefully and lovingly converted into a teensy francophile pocket within.

Cost $10–35
Address 825–27 San Pablo Ave at Solano, Albany
☎ 510/526-2552
Open Mon & Tues 5.30–10pm, Wed & Thurs 11am–3pm & 5.30–10pm, Fri 11am–3pm & 5.30–11pm, Sat 11am–3pm & 5.30–11pm, Sun 10am–3pm & 5.30–10pm
Transportation BART El Cerrito Plaza, AC Transit G
Accepts MasterCard, Visa

An enormous wood-fired oven is Solomon and Triboletti's ace in the hole, and since both have pedigrees in pizzas, that's another reason their southern French and northern Italian food is a local favorite. Pizzas (from $10) often star the Nice flavors of anchovies, olives, and onions, and feature on their weekend late-night menu after 10.30pm. A much-requested starter is the outstanding roast mussels ($9.50), served with wonderful fries and garlicky aioli on the side. If you're looking for Nice's most famous salad, the blend of fresh tuna, olives, and egg on romaine that we know as a Niçoise and they call salada missarda ($7.50), theirs has good fresh tuna chunks—the secret of a great one. Plump and fragrant light butternut ravioli ($12) come in the inevitable sage-butter sauce and are all you wish for. Another favorite is the petit steak ($16.50), a straightforward piece of fillet that's just so, and comes with pink peppercorn sauce and Triboletti's truly wonderful fries on the side. The beef stew ($15) is another hit; richly braised and tender, it comes with a glorious veggie medley.

Not everything is a five-star zinger, however. Fritto misto ($10.50) has been known to be heavily over-battered, and sheer volume and traffic in the kitchen may mean occasional slips in finish. But Nizza La Bella redeems any such shortcomings with its positive points, which include an outstanding wine list that offers many French and Italian wines by the half-bottle.

O Chame Restaurant Tea Room

🍴 Berkeley types like to take their time off along Gilman and 4th Streets, with their curiously seductive shopping outlets. This area has become a bustling retail center in recent years, but once you leave the street to enter O Chame's portico, you'll be in a calmer place. This restaurant has always charmed Berkeley with its special Japanese cuisines, courtesy of chef David Vardy, who studied in Taiwan and Japan. He formerly ran the Daruma Teashop, a glowing memory for many Berkeleyites of a certain age. Vardy brings reverence and artistry to this very classically Japanese environment, matching the ambiance with regional kansai and kaiseki cuisines. It's decorated in shoji screens and bamboo like an ancient Japanese tavern, with the addition of Mayumi Oda prints.

Cost $10–35

Address 1830 4th St, Berkeley
☏ 510/841-8783
Open Mon–Thurs 11am–3pm & 5–9pm, Fri & Sat 11am–3pm & 5–9.30pm
Transportation AC Transit 9, 51
Accepts All major credit cards except Diners

Start with one of the many unusual and difficult-to-find green teas on the shelves, then move on to the smallish menu of East-West starters. Taking a strictly authentic bent, it marries classical techniques to local ingredients and changes every day—with up and down results. The tofu dumpling with hiziki seaweed ($6), and the grilled shiitake mushrooms with lotus root ($6) are good. But udon or soba noodle dishes (from $11.50) are superb. They come in steaming, lovely bowls aswim with gorgeously aromatic doshi broth, with salmon, pork, trout, and chicken versions. The goyza ($8.50), or dumplings, come stuffed with carrot and tofu; green onion pancakes ($8.50) are filled with shiitake mushrooms. Western-themed choices for main dishes include a flatiron steak with collard greens, endamame, and Portobello mushrooms ($18.50). The kaiseki (from $23) is a stepped meal that consists of the serial arrival of several small plates, including sashimi and sushi, with small salads, bowls of pickles, and appetizers. It requires considerable time to get through, and should be arranged ahead.

Meals end with very simple little sweets, like a small square of green moshi ($4.50) or a tiny cup of custard ($4.50). The old teahouse atmosphere and simpatico vibe that so characterized Daruma Teashop survives, though old-timers say it used to be a lot more charming.

Oliveto Cafe

It's Oakland-on-the-Arno at Rockridge Market Hall's lynchpin, which bears the unusual distinction of being a former favorite haunt of both the late Eldridge Cleaver and author Jessica Mitford. Although they didn't care for each other, they both liked superchef (and Chez Panisse alumnus) Paul Bertolli's civilized Tuscan trattoria, a shrine of North Italian roasts that people cross the bridge to visit. The hushed and high-priced upstairs restaurant requires advance reservations and deep pockets. But don't despair, there's also a casual downstairs cafe where you can usually find a table.

Cost $15–35

Address 5655 College Ave at Shafter, Rockridge
℗ 510/547-5356
Open Cafe: Mon–Sat 11.30am–10pm, Sun noon–9pm
Transportation BART Rockridge, AC Transit 7, 17
Accepts All major credit cards except Diners

As one of the more happening spots in Oakland (or, more specifically, in Rockridge), the cafe is also a lot more reasonable than upstairs, and some would say it's more fun. At lunchtime, take a series of small plates from the counter, picking from spit-roasted pork or beef sandwiches ($5), or the great ricotta and roasted fennel tart ($5). You'll also enjoy the pizzas of the day (from $6), with toppings like new potato, Pecorino, and herbs. Heartier dinner dishes are equally humble but delicious, and include dishes such as potato and meatball polpettone ($14.50) that stick to your ribs, or potato gnocchi a la Romana ($13.50), in Parmesan and porcini sauce, which are a fabulously filling tribute to the potato. Tagliolini pasta with capers, olives, anchovies, chiles, and tuna ($14.50) make another generous and flavorful main course. A couple of chicken dishes and one fish of the day are always on the cafe dinner menu too. The tremendous desserts are an Oliveto's specialty, and those at the cafe are the same as the ones on the list upstairs: coconut ice cream in chocolate rum sauce ($5) is a knockout, as is the date and walnut tart with home-made spice persimmon ice cream ($6).

If you stay downstairs there'll be no panic about the prices, and you can still say you sampled Paul Bertolli's masterful cuisine—and you'll enjoy the people-watching, slightly cruising vibe too. Try a glass of the excellent Chianti Castello di Bossi ($9) and you'll be more than happy to fall in love with the peach cobbler over shortbread crust, or the death-by-bittersweet chocolate cake of your dreams.

East Bay: Berkeley

Oriental Restaurant

🍴 Every diner gets a frisson of glee when they find a truly "undiscovered" gem. In this neck of the woods, you might fail to get into Chez Panisse and then stumble into this unpretentious place, quite by accident. It's a terrific place with a long, low room painted day-glo green and lined with large, lurid photographic blowups of the dishes. The very friendly owner is a more reliable source of information, however, and happily stops whatever he's doing in order to explain items.

Cost $3.75–15

Address 1782 Shattuck
Avenue at Francisco, Berkeley
☏ 510/644–1005
Open Mon–Sat 11am–9.30pm
Transportation BART
Berkeley Downtown
Accepts Cash only

To start there's an exceptionally good salad of tofu and sprouts with snow peas, and a pancake of seafood in a crunchy golden rice crêpe (both $4.60). The seaweed and tofu soup ($2.45 cup, $3.95 bowl) is a special joy, the clean and clear stock picking up the ocean tang and lending it to the fresh chunks of tofu ($3.95). Their pho ($4.60) is another exemplary version, with shrimps and chicken and beef or seafood variations, as well as vegetable, tofu, or barbecued chicken. Very interesting clay pot specialties are on offer, from "fish cooked in a pot and served with rice" ($6.10) to "squids deep cooked in a pot and served with rice," ($6.10)— every main dish here comes in a "shrimps, chickens, beef, pork, or squids" variety, and they also do a lot of pompano dishes (that's another local fish, a puffball type). For vegetarians there are more than twenty choices, with items like curried vegetable tofu ($3.65), crispy tofu in spicy ginger sauce ($3.95), or tofu and black mushrooms ($3.95). Everything is served with white or brown rice, in two portion sizes for every item (the larger comes at a couple of dollars more).

Despite these prices—surely the cheapest for good Vietnamese fare in the entire Bay Area?—Oriental is up there with Tú Lan and many a higher priced establishment. If you're ordering food to take home you can pass the time with a delicious Vietnamese coffee ($1.85) until your food is ready.

Purple Plum

Sharon Anderson and Sherrie Sparks, owners of this Glenview district eatery, describe their food as "California soul kitchen." The pair grew up with Southern home food and African-American cooking, and they share duties, though Sparks does the front and Anderson the back of the house. Service is Southern-style hospitable: relaxed but efficient—sometimes too efficient if you want to linger. A lovely, high-ceilinged room is decorated with gargantuan wall murals of oversized beet, chard leaf, and purple plums, and the noise level is civilized, despite a full house, thanks to a rebaffled ceiling created by Sparks to keep noise down. Alumnae of Chez Panisse and Bay Wolf, the partners have the toniest of credentials. They bake as brilliantly as well as they cook—Sparks' old-fashioned, bap-like dinner rolls will bring you here on their own.

Cost $15–40

Address 4228 Park
Boulevard, Oakland
☎ 510/336-0990
Open Tues, Wed & Sun
5–9.30pm, Thurs–Sat 5–10pm
Transportation BART Lake
Merritt, AC transit 15
Accepts All major credit cards

The little menu offers three of everything but it's enough. Warm and soothing as eiderdowns and hot water bottles, the soups ($5) are superb; try the butternut, if it's on, and you'll get the idea. You have to sample the collard and curly kale greens ($3.75), which are a Low Country classic of Gullah cuisine; long simmered, sweetened, spiced, and braised in stock and mustard spices, they may be the best in the entire Bay Area. A main dish of braised short ribs ($15.50) comes with cubes of rich-sauced parsnips and baby Brussels spouts that are little dots of intense greeny flavor, as well as a polenta so creamy that you might think at first that it's mashed potato. A cider-brined pork chop ($14.50) is served with drop-dead delicious, vanilla-infused mashed sweet potatoes, and once again, those long-braised greens. A risotto ($10) comes as standard on the menu, and often features spring vegetables. But it's the homey Southern fare you came for, so why not try the perfect fried chicken with mashed potatoes and gravy ($11.50)?

Sparks shows her true colors in the best of German chocolate cakes—not too sweet, but enough to satisfy any sweet tooth. On a short but varied winelist, the Navarro Chenin Blanc ($5.75 glass, $24 bottle) is good value.

Restaurant Doña Tomás

As one of the only high-class Mexican restaurants in the Bay Area to get it totally right, Doña Tomás is a great many notches up from your standard taqueria. It's also a great culinary addition to Oakland and a totally trip-worthy night out for other Bay Area folks. The exterior is a smallish storefront that doesn't look exciting. But inside, it's got a full bar with the best Daiquiris, Mojitos, and Margaritas in the Western world, plus a long menu of authentic Mexican food.

Cost $15–30
Address 5004 Telegraph Ave, Oakland
☎510/450-0522
Open Tues–Thurs 5.30–9.30pm, Fri & Sat 5.30–10pm
Transportation BART Downtown Oakland
Accepts All major credit cards except Diners

Soups ($5.95) are regular favorites here, and include a chicken, lime, and cilantro soup. Bean soup is full of chile and garlic, nicely spiked with peppery heat and garnished with bits of bread and herbs. The cooking here is heavy on moles and shows a strong Oaxacan influence. Mole verde Oaxaqueño con pollo ($13.95) is the real thing, necessitating a grind of several different chiles (chilcuales negros, ancho, chipotle, mulatto, pasilla, poblano), four kinds of nuts (peanuts, almonds, pecans, walnuts), and three seeds (sesame, coriander, anise), plus cinnamon, cloves, and Mexican chocolate. The resulting mahogany-brown paste that coats the pieces of chicken thickly is intense and complicated, fiery in its depths and comforting. Enchiladas de carnitas ($15.75) are subtly spiked up a notch or two here with more chile. The bountiful pozole ($14.95), a hominy stew that hails from the Sonoran desert, is not always on the changing menu, but grab it when it is. Asada al guajillo ($15.95) is another authentic labor-intensive classic: it's roast pork loin in a tomatillo sauce made with the darkish red, dried guajillo chile. Lavish sundaes ($6.50) with four scoops of vanilla ice cream—made with cream and a real vanilla pod, and drizzled with chocolate and cajeta—are the sweet of choice.

The friendly folks who run the place could not be nicer or try harder to please; all in all, it's a very superior restaurant for what looks to be just a modest neighborhood spot. It's also a good place to learn about Oaxacan food and the amazing array of chiles of every level of fieriness and texture.

Rivoli Restaurant

Chef-owner Wendy Brucker met her husband Roscoe Skipper at San Francisco's Square One, and the two honeymooned on the Rue de Rivoli in Paris. Eight years ago they opened their own Rivoli, and they haven't skipped a night or missed a beat since. This prime venue was a pioneer on Albany's hot Solano Avenue restaurant strip, and despite the fact that it remains relatively unadvertised, it's always busy (book ahead) and deserves its growing reputation. The rear wall of the smallish restaurant is taken up by floor-to-ceiling windows that overlook a pretty, terraced garden; you're liable to see a racoon, rabbit, or even a fox foraging amid the greenery—this place may be small, but it's got character!

Cost $7–35

Address 1539 Solano Ave at Peralta, Albany
℗ 510/526-2542
Open Mon–Thurs 5.30–9.30pm, Fri 5.30–10pm, Sat 5–10pm, Sun 5–9pm
Transportation AC Transit 15, 43, 67
Accepts All major credit cards

Regulars return again and again, since the menu—following the Chez Panisse mantra—offers only what's seasonal, local, and organic, and it changes every three weeks. Soups emphasize the paradoxical, an example being roast eggplant and lentil soup with lime yogurt ($6.75), a titillating trade-off of the sweet and the tangy that's smoothly satisfying. But the trademark starter is a smallish plate of Portobello mushroom fritters ($6.95), deep-fried until they're very crisp, sprinkled with Parmesan and a caper-lemon aioli and served with arugula on the side; it's simple and wonderful. The excellent salmon tart ($7.50) uses home-cured salmon, but unfortunately it's not always available. Another great appetizer is house-smoked trout on cornmeal blini with beets, lemon, mâche, and crème fraîche ($7.50). Liberty duck cooked two ways ($17.50), with pear and cranberry, sweet potato soufflé, and brown buttered brussels sprouts, is another trademark dish. Along with the Niman Ranch sirloin steak in apple and horseradish ($19.50), or the lamb shanks with flageolet beans ($18.75), it's a reason for driving out here to sample this clean, well-executed classical fare.

Warm walnut and caramel tart with orange and date ice cream ($6.50) is a typical Rivoli dessert, divinely marrying the freshest of the nearby Valley fruits and produce. There's a great cheese plate ($7), with local goat and Jack cheese, and excellent walnut bread. Wines start at a very reasonable $5.50 per glass, and a sparkling Kir Royale is a welcome $7.50.

East Bay: Berkeley

Vik's Chaat Corner

Dining at its cheapest and tastiest thrives at this authentic snack house, where locals feast on Indian food for practically nothing. But Vik's is also a grocery, so whenever you crave a jar of lime pickle or pappadums to go with your chicken korma, this big old warehouse in a funkier part of West Berkeley is where to go. The premises don't look promisingly like a restaurant at first. You enter via a giant steel front, then wait in line, ordering from a written board over the glass counter of sticky Indian sweets, and twiddling your thumbs until your name comes up over the speaker. Seating is a row of plastic tables and the papers and forks are disposable—and disposed mainly onto the floor, for some reason. But none of this will matter when your food arrives.

Cost $5–15

Address 726 Allston Way, West Berkeley
☎ 510/644-4412
Open Tues–Fri 11am–6pm, Sat & Sun 11am–6.30pm
Transportation AC Transit 5, 71
Accepts MasterCard, Visa

The clientele is a mix of students and locals who stuff themselves on the usual range of biryanis and kormas, vindaloos and koftas, all of them outstanding even by the sky-high standards of the East Bay standards. All cost about two to three dollars less than anywhere else. The samosa chole ($3) is a dynamic three mouthfuls of feathery pastry stuffed with peas, potatoes, and carrots, and spiced to the max. Sag paneer ($3) is simmered spinach in homemade cheese and herbs, and a masala dosa ($4.50) uses a gentle blend of spices. All lunch specials start at $4 and change daily, as does the selection. Don't forget the chapatis and the many different variations on nan breads, samosas, and pooris (from $1), or the cardamom and cinnamon tea drinks, or the lusciously dreamy mango lassi ($2), a drink of liquid yogurt that you'll wish they would patent and pour on every street corner.

Detractors insist that Vik's is a basic cafeteria rather than an actual dining place—but the price is right. And if you bring a group to pick up a meal to share together, you can either head home with it and party down, or take off for Tilden Park and enjoy a picnic.

Yoshi's at Jack London Square

San Franciscans find crossing bridges alarming, even the Bay Bridge, but the Bay Area's premier destination for top-flight live jazz is an elegant, if somewhat antiseptic, nightclub fronting on Jack London Square on the far side of the Bay. Everybody knows about Yoshi's terrific roster of jazz and blues musicians and cooler-than-cool reputation, but fewer sing about its sashimi, sushi, and satays. The decor is a crowded mish-mash of sushi chic and cocktail-lounge modernity, with wall-to-wall windows overlooking the passing parade of the square. Jazz fans are plied with an impressive sushi, teriyaki, and yakitori menu in the club, while the sushi counter and tatami mats at the front seat folks who want to just sample the dishes on offer.

Cost $20–45

Address 510 Embarcadero West, Oakland
☎ 510/238-9200
Open Mon–Thurs 11.30am–2.30pm & 5.30–9.30pm, Fri 11.30am–2.30pm & 5.30–10pm, Sat noon–3pm & 5.30–10pm, Sun noon–3pm & 5.30–9.30pm
Transportation BART Lake Merritt then shuttle; ferry to Jack London Square
Accepts All major credit cards except Diners

You need only look at the pre-show bento boxes to realize that Yoshi's food equals its jazz in high-flying ambition, though there are those who feel that the music outstrips the food for value. Saba, or mackerel sushi ($4), and yellowtail, or hamachi nigiri ($5) are good choices, faultless and fresh, as are unagi, or eel ($5), and tuna, or maguro ($5). Those bento boxes ($15–25) include feathery tempura, sashimi and sushi, and some teriyaki as well as a couple of pickles and salad plates. Vegetarian versions ($20) come with pieces of avocado, eggplant, peas, and other vegetables. Yakitori skewers groan with shellfish: try the marinated prawns with a sweet-sour sauce ($9.50). Spider rolls ($6) blend softshell crab with fresh avocado, and sushi plates begin at $3.75. Yoshi's also does children's jazz matinees with special yakitori dishes.

Regular sake tastings feature Ko-Chi, Migata, and Hyogo Prefecture wines (from $5.75 per glass), and the Nigori ufiltered sake is sure to capture your attention. If you're coming from San Francisco, take the ferry, as it's definitely the romantic transportation of choice; but be warned, you'll probably want to return to the city via BART, since the late ferry docks at Fisherman's Wharf rather than the downtown Ferry Building.

North Bay & Marin

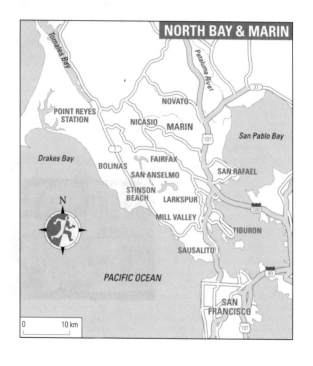

Bubba's Diner

Run by the former manager of Lark Creek Inn, Beth Casey, and serving diner food with zest and flourish, Bubba's is a favorite of folks returning from trips around Marin's coastline and Point Reyes National Seashore. Its cherry-red naugahyde booths, black and white floor tiles, and chalkboard of specials lend it diner-like cheer. One of its most beguiling charms is a colorful stack of old cookbooks on the counter, ranging from 1950s marketing brochures like "Cooking and Canning" to Julia Child's *Mastering The Art of French Provincial Cookery, Volume Two*.

Cost $10–20

Address 566 San Anselmo Ave at Tunstead Ave, San Anselmo
℗ 415/459-6862
Open Mon & Wed–Sun 8am–2pm & 5.30–9pm, Tues 5.30–9pm
Transportation Highway 101, Golden Gate transit
Accepts MasterCard, Visa

Who else has the chutzpah to serve great peanut butter and jelly sandwiches ($4.95), or a terrific grilled three cheeses sandwich ($6.95) with wonderful shoestring fries? But there are more ambitious sandwiches too, such as Bubba's well-loved grilled Portabella mushroom sandwich ($6.95), or a burger with jack, blue, or provolone cheese ($7.25), served with fries. Fried green tomatoes ($6.95) are a seasonal appetizer—served between August and November—and come with coffee-spiked "red-eye gravy" and salsa. A fried oyster sandwich ($11.25) comes with Jack cheese, bacon, fries, and a remoulade of celery-lemon mayo. Like the hot dogs ($4), it's justly popular. Breakfast and lunch dishes include homey corned beef hash with eggs any style and toast or biscuit ($10.25), as well as a range of sandwiches and salads. After 5.30pm, a specials menu kicks in, including the "blue plate" special, which brings some real comfort food, typically a meatloaf with mashed potatoes ($10.95), or a Saturday pot roast ($12.95). These old-fashioned plates are slightly nouveau in an "Old Cal cuisine" way; the Wednesday night fried chicken ($15), for instance, comes with those fried green tomatoes, along with shakes and chocolate cake. Another special might be a lickably sweet and juicy dish such as red snapper with dynamite summertime succotash ($17), a parsleyed and minted mix of lima beans and southern corn that perfectly offsets the fish.

Homemade pies like strawberry ($5.95) and chocolate layer cake with a creamy topping ($5) help to give Bubba's kid-appeal, and those fine fries and grilled cheese sandwiches make it a natural for families too.

Buckeye Roadhouse

When this lodge first opened in 1937, it was the newest concept in roadside dining, and the first to greet the first Model Ts and Packards from the just-opened Golden Gate Bridge with steaks, ribs, and other traditional dishes. Nostalgic and old-fashioned, the Buckeye survived many food fads, downturns, and periods of unmodishness. But people still duck in when tired of beating the traffic on the way down from the Wine Country or Muir Woods. The old lady has just been done over by the decorators yet again, this time emphasizing fashionable warm wood and Arts and Crafts deco touches, from the patio at the rear and the bar's circular stuffed banquettes to the stone fireplace and Tiffany glass.

Cost $10–35

Address 15 Shoreline Highway, Mill Valley
ⓣ 415/331-2600
Open Mon–Thurs 11.30am–10.30pm, Fri & Sat 11.30am–11pm, Sun 10.30am–10pm
Transportation Highway 101, Golden Gate transit
Accepts All major credit cards except AmEx

All the waiters are sweet, which is just as well since the food—formerly solid American fare—can be inconsistent, and is frequently overpriced. That said, it's a fun place to stop, and the barbecue meats and desserts are cholesterol-raising dreams. Excellent Zinfandel-braised, barbecued baby back ribs ($17.50) go well with warmed spinach salad, olives, feta, and bacon ($7.50) or pan-roasted artichokes with tarragon dip ($6.95), and in season they're served with maple-mashed sweet potatoes as part of the dish. Buckeye is a meat-eater's paradise, with a wide selection of steaks rising over the twenty-dollar mark; grilled dry-aged New York steak ($29.95) comes with Yukon potato-artichoke hash. The spicy pork sandwich ($11.50) can be too hot to eat, however, and hamburgers and cheeseburgers ($9.95) are sometimes overdone. Maine lobster Bisque linguine with cognac and lemon ($29.50) is excellent, but at these prices, you want consistency as well as a few high-end dishes.

The main room, with its fireplace and lovely, retro lodge-house ambiance, accounts for the high prices, but you can eat for less in the bar at the side, with its comfortable booths, or at the back patio. Choose from bar items like oysters bingo ($9), a Rockefeller variation, the hefty roast chicken in mashed potatoes ($11), or the S'mores dessert ($6.95), and grab a beer or glass of wine too.

Las Camelias Cocina Mexicana

🍴 Beautiful hacienda-style stucco and indigenous artwork, pretty windows and fresh flowers, plus the tastiest quesadillas this side of the border: who can beat Las Camelias? It's a spot for home-style Mexican cooking that's been recognized as one of the best in the Bay Area. Chef-owner Gabriel Fergoso formerly worked at Lark Creek Inn, then opened this place with his wife Carol, a sculptor whose work is on display. Taking recipes from his Jaliscan mother and grandmother, he created a menu of soups, stuffed poblanos, carnitas, and every other Mexican comfort food you might crave. Jalisco is the home of tequila, of course, and Fergoso uses plenty.

Cost $10–25

Address 912 Lincoln Ave between 3rd and 4th, San Rafael
ⓣ 415/453-5850
Open Mon–Thurs 11.30am–9.30pm, Fri & Sat 11.30am–10pm, Sun 3–9pm
Transportation Highway 101, Golden Gate transit
Accepts MasterCard, Visa

Start with homemade salsa—a signature, milder salsa—with homemade tortilla chips, which arrive on the house. Fergoso's soups, or caldillos, are outstanding bowls of health, and they're lovely to look at. Black bean soup, or sopa de frijol negro con chochoyones ($3.25 small bowl, $4.95 large), is a good choice; it's a vegetarian soup that takes three days to make. Refried beans are unusual (and unusually good) in that they're made with a long-simmered Great Northern White bean of the kind eaten during Lent in northern parts of Mexico; they're pale, richly suffused with seasoning and soothing on the tongue. Zincronizadas ($7.95–9.50) are quesadillas stuffed with different choyote and chile mixes, chicken with avocado, tomato, and bell pepper in a chipotle chile sauce being one variation. Roast poblano chiles are another traditional staple, but these ones are stuffed with a generously all-vegetable mix and come with a crema and guacamole accompaniment. Tamales ($7.95) hold little pockets of grilled chicken or vegetables at their hearts, tightly wrapped and steamed in their corn husks. A tequila-marinated poussin ($12.95) is Las Camelias' stop-the-traffic top dish.

Fergoso gets top marks for his daily flans and very *rico* chocolate cake ($3), too. Aside from one or two specials, all the dishes appear on combination one- two- or three-course menus ($9.95, $11.95 or $14.95), with rice and beans included. A pleasant house sangria is less cloyingly sweet than usual ($9 half-carafe, $18 carafe), and makes a good accompaniment to the meal.

Dipsea Cafe

Hikers, bikers, and joggers come here on their way to Mount Tamalpais and Muir Woods, so the Dipsea Cafe is always jammed with Sierra Club-types, passionately pursuing a hearty breakfast before pursuing the Great Outdoors. The cafe gets its name from the major hiking trail that leads from Mill Valley and Mount Tam to Stinson Beach via Muir Woods (and a pint of cider at the Pelican Inn). The trail begins with a series of 671 infamous steps that grind vertically skywards, so if this is where you're headed, you'll definitely need a stack of the Dipsea's beloved blueberry or buckwheat pancakes with real maple syrup, known to give even the most fainthearted the will to stagger on.

Cost $7–15
Address 200 Shoreline Highway, Mill Valley
☎ 415/381-0298
Open Mon–Fri 7am–3pm, Sat & Sun 7am–4pm
Transportation Highway 1
Accepts MasterCard, Visa

There's no better way to begin the long, killer Mount Tam solstice or equinox climbs, than coming early to sit by the fireplace or out on the deck, which overlooks Coyote Creek with its wading shorebirds. At brunch time the wait can be very long. The cafe is very child-friendly and casual, with pretty wall murals of farm animals, checked tablecloths, and a generally childlike mood in the blue and white fittings. The Dipsea Special ($9) is a nice way to start the day; it's a platter of egg, bacon, sausage, fries, and pancakes that will certainly stay with you to the top of the mountain. The buckwheat pancakes ($7) come with fresh berries, or you can opt instead for pear and poppy-seed pancakes ($6), filled with cranberry butter. Various egg dishes are on offer, starting with giant three-egg omelets ($7) or frittatas ($6) with mushrooms, spinach, zucchini, and some fries. Later in the day, as well as the usual flurry of sandwiches and hamburgers, you can choose one of several salads, including a great Niçoise ($10.95), or just keep on with brunch right up until 3pm.

The service is always speedy and warm, and there's a free parking lot across the road. Be warned that you can't bike up the Dipsea Trail, and since it takes a chunk of the day to hike you'll need someone to shuttle you back from the other end. Dipsea has also opened another branch in San Anselmo.

Guaymas

Need a jug of Margarita, a lump of bread to throw to the pelicans, and a 180-degree view of water with some city thrown in? With its spectacular view of Richardson Bay and San Francisco, and its convenient location next to the Tiburon ferry dock, Guaymas is a great place for sunshine and great Mexican food, especially on summer afternoons, when the city is frequently fogged in. Every July, another flock of Kerouac fans arrives in San Francisco with their hopes high, their sleeves short, and shorts shorter; then they freeze, and that's the moment that natives whip out the old Mark Twain saw about the coldest winter he ever spent being—yawn—summer in San Francisco. But if you want to put your feet up on a railing in the sunshine with a drink at one elbow and a quesadilla at the other, then this is it.

Cost $10–30	
Address 5 Main Street, Tiburon	
☎ 415/435-6300	
Open Mon–Thurs 11.30am–9.30pm, Fri & Sat 11.30am–10.30pm, Sun 10.30am–9.30pm	
Transportation Ferry to Tiburon	
Accepts All major credit cards	

Guaymas's Mexican grill and seafood cuisine is authentic enough for real Mexicans. The tortillas have a chewy cornmeal taste you never get with the factory-made variety, and they're served still warm and with three salsas on the side, instead of the usual chips. Do not fail to try the camarones de Guaymas ($12.95), or grilled shrimp, with their little blackened corners of tasty shell and the chipotle sauce on the side; and yes, you can suck the heads. Prawns also come grilled and served on rock salt ($10.05). Appetizers continue with miniature tamales ($5.95), which enshrine nuggets of chicken and pork inside their corn sweetness. Grilled plantains ($5.95) are kissed with a little crema, and the ceviches ($9.95), of which there are several, are sophisticated in seasoning. Among the main courses, Michoacan-style roast pork ($14.95) gets the thumbs up from Mexican visitors, and roasted duck in pumpkin-seed sauce ($16.95) is another favorite. Helpings are large, although so are the prices.

You can bike here from the city and take the ferry back—revelers leaving for the last boat have been seen in colorful condition. Small wonder the staff have seen it all, and sometimes get a little brusque. That ferry leaves from Fisherman's Wharf, Pier 41, but check ahead, especially for the time of that last ferry.

Lark Creek Inn

When Michigan farmer's son Bradley Ogden arrived in the little Marin County town of Larkspur to kick up some excitement with his first restaurant, he brought the corn from his farming roots and then added the local Dungeness crab, proclaiming it "one of God's gifts to humanity." The winter season gives Ogden a chance to flaunt this gift in all its rosy-clawed variations, from bisques to crabcakes to roasts, while the summer season is the cue for him to start cooking his corn chowders and corn risottos. At Lark Creek Inn, he's found a lovely spot to do it in; the main room is wood-planked and endowed with windows onto the garden, and there's also a pleasant sun porch.

Cost $15–75

Address 234 Magnolia Ave at Madrone, Larkspur
☎ 415/924-7766
Open Mon–Fri 11.30am–2pm & 5.30–10pm, Sat 5–10pm, Sun 10am–2pm & 5–9pm
Transportation Ferry to Larkspur
Accepts All major credit cards except Diners

The dining room has a brick oven where lambs, pigs, and loaves of bread are baked over oak. The menu features flatbread pizzas and "simply American" food, emphasizing fresh produce from nearby. One flatbread comes with arugula, pesto, onions, dry Jack cheese, and prosciutto ($9.95); another is onion and sausage ($9.95). A crabcake ($10.50) comes with mango-papaya salsa and lemon-pepper aioli. The farmer's market mini-menu ($24.50) is a three-course prix fixe intended to highlight what's in season, such as an organic carrot soup with spiced crème fraîche, then chestnut ravioli with chanterelles and onions, followed by candy cap mushroom brûlée. That would make a banquet fit for a vegetarian, or a non-vegetarian for that matter. Lots of great pan-fried fresh fish are always available here, and it's one of the very few places to serve California white sturgeon with apple hash, butternut squash, and bacon ($16.75). Sturgeon is a curious looking mild white fish that used to be eaten more, but here they've invented new ways to dress it in all its glory.

Set in a yellow and white Victorian house among lark-deprived but otherwise quite lovely laurels and redwoods, Ogden's inn has a creek that flows just beyond the back dining verandah, a fireplace, and a bar for casual dining without reservations. It has been here for over a decade and has won every possible accolade in that time.

Moylan's of Novato

When Brendan Moylan and Paddy Giffen met the great love of their lives and started home-brewing, they were young and giddy. After winning several gold medals at Great American Beer festivals, they were even giddier, so the idea of starting Moylan's of Novato did not seem initially ambitious. Barn-like, and sporting odd Tudor touches, this beer palace de luxe is filled to the gills with live Irish music at weekends and with families by day; in fact, it's not unlike the old Irish dancehall where Brendan's Da met his Ma, except that there's more beer and less dancing.

Cost $10–20

Address 15 Rowland Way, Novato
☎ 415/898-4677
Open Mon–Thurs & Sun 11.30am–midnight, Fri & Sat 11.30am–1am
Transportation Highway 101, Golden Gate transit
Accepts MasterCard, Visa

Once ensconced in your nook by one of the massive stone fireplaces and nursing your pint, you can safely tackle the Moylan bar menu, which can only be described as "haute pub." The list of salads is fancy even for a pub in Marin. How about a dynamite sesame chicken salad with hearts of romaine, and Savoy and Napa cabbages, made with green onions and roasted peanuts, tossed in a sesame-oil vinaigrette, and topped with rice noodles ($8.95)? Equally serious sandwiches ensue, from grilled beer sausage ($6.95) to a classic Reuben ($7.95). Fish and chips ($9.95) stars decently battered fish with reasonably crispy chips that wear way more garlic than this dish gets in its native land. There's a decent Irish stew ($10.95) that uses carrots, potatoes, onions, peas, and the correct kind of meat—although lamb is more gourmet than the best-end-of-neck mutton that Irish children used to be raised on. The children's cheeseburger ($7.95) could use slightly better fries and meat, but pizzas and hot dogs are child-friendly and cost under $5. If Mexican food seems tastier when you have a big old pint in your hand, try the bay shrimp quesadilla ($8.95) or the black and white bean chile ($4.95), made with shredded beef and served with Cheddar cheese.

But Moylan's is about the beer, and it certainly holds its own. From its doughty "Kiltlifter" Scotch and Paddy's Irish Red, to Moylan's Special Bitter and Ryan's Imperial Stout, there are eleven on tap, and all of them are made on the premises.

Ondine

If you're in a romantic mood and crave some serious pampering, consider taking the ferry to Sausalito to have dinner at this landmark restaurant. Ondine answers several needs, the first being a wraparound view of the Bay with Angel and Alcatraz Islands and the shining city in the distance. The next is the foodie-pleasing fusion food from John Caputo. Finally, Ondine is an ambitious piece of interior design that includes curving eggplant-colored banquettes, terracotta and burgundy walls, little translucent tables, and lots of mahogany details, plus Asian touches in the fabrics.

Cost $20–75

Address 558 Bridgeway at Princess Ave, Sausalito
℡ 415/331-1133
Open Mon–Thurs 5.30–10pm, Fri & Sat 5–10pm, Sun 10am–2pm & 5.30–10pm
Transportation Ferry to Sausalito
Accepts All major credit cards except Diners

Under incoming chef Caputo, it's trying to be more populist in its approach these days. Mind you, in Ondine's case this is relative. The wine list now has bottles that start in the mid-twenties, for example, and while the menu still has main courses that are over $30, it also offers several less expensive, appetizer-sized seafood options, such as a warm crawfish salad ($12), or smoked salmon sushi terrine with ikura caviar ($15). At a time when other places are giving fish roe the chop, Ondine still offers a caviar service, and this caviar, served with a brioche, crème fraîche, and red onion, will set you back $90 (Oestra) or $75 (Beluga). There are still elegant fusion touches to the menu, starting with the green papaya salad with chrysanthemum leaves, sweet ginger cream, and bits of Maine crab ($13). A fresh corn and crayfish chowder ($9) comes with a little dribble of tarragon. On the other hand, entrees seem to have become more mainstream, from the Maine lobster with black spaghettini and Asian vegetables ($32), to the rack of lamb ($22) and filet mignon ($28). Romance-hunters who have gotten this far will not shrink from the chocolate Grand Marnier soufflé.

Formerly a yacht club—there are still docking facilities for seafaring diners—Ondine has been born again after yet another makeover. This is most definitely an expensive night out—wine mark-ups are shocking—but Ondine has got the necessary pzazz.

Point Reyes Station House Cafe

On mellow Sundays when you're in the mood for a hike at Point Reyes National Seashore to look for elk or wild morels, or watch for whales, a host of long-established restaurants beckons. Local favorites include Tony's Oyster Bar, Vladimir's Czech restaurant, the Bovine Bakery, and the Cowgirl Creamery. But Pat Healy's cafe in the old railway station can claim a hotline to the local oyster beds, a pretty trellised garden, and the best potato pancakes this side of Dublin, as well as home-baked breads, corn breads, and buns, served piping hot. When Healy took over the old depot more than a quarter century ago, she gave it a mirrored bar, wooden booths, an old-fashioned counter next to the kitchen, and better yet, that fairylit garden, softly romantic on summer nights.

Cost $7–30

Address Main St, Point Reyes
☎ 415/663-1515
Open Mon–Thurs 8am–9pm,
Fri & Sat 8am–10pm
Transportation Highway 1
Accepts MasterCard, Visa

The moment you get here you should try the fruits of nearby Tomales Bay. All you need do is nudge the Hog Island oysters (around $12.50 a dozen), then knock them back with no more than a squeeze of lemon. Farmed oysters come barbecued ($12.50 a dozen). Mussels ($9.50) come very simply but freshly delivered in their own nectar, with a dash of wine and garlic and parsley. Plain ingredients also soar and sing in a plate of polenta with Gorgonzola chunks ($7), which is blended with a darkly earthy confit of local mushrooms. It's filling enough to be a main dish. Other dishes can be a bit under-seasoned, but not the regular meatloaf ($10.25), which comes in doorstop-sized portions, with Healy's trademark roasted garlic mashed potatoes. Regulars particularly love the smoked salmon and potato cakes ($12.50) because of those same garlicky potatoes under the poached eggs, plus some creamed spinach. Grilled chicken breast in basil cream with bow-tie pasta ($14), and seared halibut with sorrel ($16) are frequent dinner choices.

Is there a better brunch in the entire Bay Area? San Franciscans hardly ever get here in time, sadly, since it's over by around 3pm, but when they do it's the Platonic brunch ideal that lives on in their imaginations. You can't go wrong with any of the local fish either, or the pastries.

Rancho Nicasio

🍴 Lucas Valley Road, which connects Highway 101 to Olema and Tomales Bay on the coast, is a favorite California highway, and driving along it requires a stop at the live R&B and blues hangout at Rancho Nicasio. Cradled in Marin's golden hills above Samuel P. Taylor State Park, with its towering redwoods, Nicasio was built as a rancho by Spanish settlers in 1830, and still resembles a genuine frontier town—from a distance, anyway. Since it was taken over by Bob Brown and his wife, Texan blues

Cost $10–30
Address 1 Old Rancheria Rd, Town Square, Nicasio
☎ 415/662-2219
Open Mon–Thurs 11.30am–3pm & 5.30–9pm, Fri 5.30–10pm, Sat 11am–3pm & 5.30–10pm, Sun 11am–3pm & 5.30–9pm
Transportation Highway 1
Accepts All major credit cards

singer Angela Strehli, the old ranch house has been a magnet for music fans as a frequent live concert venue. It also hosts private parties and, not incidentally, serves good American fare under Bob's son Max.

The food has to please music fans and local families alike, so it's unfancy American diner and barbecue fare. You'll find no vertical food here—or vertical anything after the legendary concert nights! But they use fresh and very local ingredients, adding Max's own touches. You can slurp a dozen Hog Island oysters ($9.50), which couldn't come any fresher and are served with Max's hot-and-smoky sauce (45 cents extra). Baked garlicky oysters ($9.95) get a little asiago cheese topping and do the trick for those who cannot take oysters raw. Calamari ($7.95) comes with a creamy aioli of chopped capers. Popcorn shrimp ($8.95) are as crispy as they ought to be and come in a nice red-pepper aioli. Thick and meaty salmon cakes ($8.95) are served with a spicy chile remoulade on the side, while the grilled chicken breast sandwich ($8.95) comes with a thick topping of melted Vella Jack cheese from nearby Sonoma.

A fire burned down the old Nicasio Hotel decades ago, so Nicasio is not all authentically unchanged, since the current hotel is a replica. But the ranch is nonetheless a trip back in time, and getting here always involves a fabulously woodsy drive past the reservoirs and horse country of western Marin County. Other than San Juan Bautista, south of San Francisco, it would be hard think of anywhere else preserving quite this much Spanish colonial atmosphere.

The Rice Table

You could say that this is where the whole small-plate craze began. But when the late, great Leonie Hool first opened her restaurant, over a quarter century ago, the idea of introducing the elaborate Dutch Indonesian colonial cuisine, and in particular its rijsttafel or "rice table" tradition, must have seemed imprudently exotic. Undaunted, the Indonesian matriarch opened this little place in downtown San Rafael, self-published her own cookbook in order to explain what the dishes were about, stuck a few pretty batiked shirts upon the menfolk in her family, and made this into a destination dining experience that still persuades people to cross the bridge.

Cost $20–50

Address 1617 4th St at G St, San Rafael
☎ 415/456-1808
Open Wed–Sat 5.30–10pm, Sun 5–9pm
Transportation Ferry to Larkspur then shuttle
Accepts MasterCard, Visa

When Mrs Hool's son, Freddy, took over a few years ago, he stuck to the successful formula. This is labor-intensive, highly spiced fare that requires lots of artistry. The Rice Table ($20) is a special prix fixe banquet of four courses. You start with big, crunchy, shellfish-flavored chips, and then dipping sauces appear before you, including a fiery Jakartan peanut sauce and a green chile sauce. The bowl of lentils that follows reflects Indonesian cuisine's Indian influences, while the little spring rolls take their cues from Southeast Asia. They're mouthfuls of tiny clear noodles and shellfish with cilantro, deep-fried in thin dough and garnished with a salad of minutely julienned carrot, mint, and ground peanut. The satays all come with their own sauces, from pork in peanut to beef in soy, and the complex curries that follow are aromatic with coconut and mint. Then come pastry puffs and rice dishes. All of this is arrayed around your small table until you can't find room for more. Your job is to pick from all these, but since the side dishes are thrown in with the deal for no more, you wind up with the immense bounty of the Indonesian archipelago under your belt for a modest outlay.

Cardamom-spiked coffee and scented teas are another bonus, but the Indonesian or local beers make a better choice than the simple house wines. Freddy Hool points out that some of his regulars prefer taking the Larkspur ferry (there's a shuttle) to confronting the bridge traffic. Smart advice!

THE BAY AREA & OUTLYING DISTRICTS   BAR MENU

Ross Valley Brewing Company

🍴 If there's such a thing as upscale haute pub cuisine, this is what you find at Sven Revel and Larry Berlin's brewery in the affluent center of Fairfax, where young professionals congregate to eat Sven's gourmet fare and drink Larry's award-winning pints. The regulars at Ross Valley are the children of privilege, and are used to a higher class of fare than that available at most watering holes. If they have children themselves, they come here on Wednesday after-noons, when the kids get fed for free—as long as Mom and Pop are around too. The other regulars who come here are mountain-bikers on their way down from a long day on rocky roads.

Cost S10–30
Address 765A Center Boulevard, Fairfax
☎ 415/485-1005
Open Mon–Fri 4–10pm, Sat noon–11pm, Sun noon–10pm
Transportation Highway 101, ferry to Larkspur, Golden Gate transit
Accepts MasterCard, Visa

The Ross Valley kitchen really does make a point of rivaling the better restaurants in the area with its menu, a sometimes Latino-tinged and classy assortment of fresh fish and salads. The fresh fish sandwich of the day ($12.95) may be a whopping chunk of snapper on a house-baked bun, with good fries and a spicy remoulade. Empanadas ($6.50) are stuffed with chile-marinated chicken and come with chipotle-honey crème fraîche. The chef's seasonal steamed and grilled vegetable plate ($11.95) could be a gay motley of local squash and root vegetables tossed in a dressing. Herb-roasted Sonoma chicken ($15.95) comes with Yukon gold mashed potatoes and grilled Star Route Farm escarole and rose-mary jus; a pint of light, dry Kosch Golden Ale is recommended as a companion. For that homey feel there's the classic meatloaf ($13.95), which comes with the same potatoes in a wild mushroom gravy. It's not every pub that can come up with that kind of fare, and also add a honey lavender vinaigrette and pistachio goat cheese to its Star Route Farm greens salad ($7.25).

The idea of recommending one of their different brewskis to go along with the food is a new one, and some of the beers are definitely worth the trip on their own. One such is the very hoppy St Mark's Ale, made by Belgian Trappist monks. Consider downing a chilled pint of this with a plate of their empanadas...

Seafood Peddler

The food scene has long been thriving up in San Rafael, a small Marin town with lots of lures for foodies, from the County Farmers Market to cafes, cheese joints, delicatessens, and bakeries, plus several great eateries and a generally nostalgic 1950s-style glow. Marin foodies now have yet another stop on the waterfront with the Seafood Peddler, a seafood market and restaurant among the boats that brings in customers in search of oysters, mussels, lobsters, and crabs, which it then cooks and dishes up. The slightly hokey touches in the Peddler's marine theme exterior are belied by the buoyant nature of Eric Bradtmiller's food, which offers enough fresh shellfish to float your heart, without requiring a bloated wallet.

Cost $10–35

Address 100 Yacht Club Drive, near San Franciso Boulevard, San Rafael
☎ 415/460-6669
Open Mon–Thurs & Sun 3.30–9.30pm, Fri & Sat 3.30–10.30pm
Transportation Golden Gate transit
Accepts All major credit cards except Diners

Bradtmiller cooks up every kind of fish in every kind of way, many of them flown in from the East Coast or from Canada. Soups (all $5.50 per bowl) include velvety, very meaty bisques. Exiles will home in on the fresh-broiled Boston scrod ($9.95) from George's Bank with glee, and mop up the lemon-butter sauces and seasoned breadcrumbs happily. If you've seen "The Perfect Storm" you may not feel quite the same way about swordfish ($12.95) as you used to; in any case, these swordfish come from Point Judith and are served broiled, wood-grilled, or blackened. Try the blackened New Orleans spices version for a change; swordfish is a dark, short-grained fish that's fatty enough to take it. A very simple New Bedford sole ($9.95) is broiled in lemon butter or fried. For some reason they don't use local shellfish in their simply prepared mussels dish, but rather Prince Edward Island mussels from over the border in Canada, which are tomato-tinged and meaty.

Using Seafood's own local suppliers, Bradtmiller cooks up crabs in a number of different ways, starting with crab au naturel ($16.95), simply steamed and rosy-hued as the sunset on a plate, with just some lemon-spiked drawn butter and bits of slaw on the side. You can also order it roasted with lavishly garlicked lemon butter on the side ($26.75), which is perhaps the best choice.

North Bay & Marin: Larkspur

Yankee Pier

🍴 Lark Creek Inn chef Bradley Ogden has turned his energies to jump-starting this little sidekick further down Larkspur's town center. Housed in a quaint late-Victorian home, with outdoor patio tables, kids' crayons, and a little counter, it's meant to be a casual "fish shack," in his words, but "shack" hardly does justice to either the little house with its porch, or the seafood. A black-tiled counter and functional booths are found inside, and diners wear shorts and T-shirts often as not. The atmosphere is informal—there are no reservations, which usually means a wait—but there's nothing humble about his chef de cuisine Jack Mitchell's seafood.

Cost $10–30
Address 286 Magnolia Ave, Larkspur
☎ 415/924-7676
Open Mon & Tues 5–10pm, Wed & Thurs noon–2.30pm & 5–10pm, Fri & Sat noon–2.30pm & 5–11pm, Sun noon–2.30pm & 5–9pm
Transportation Ferry to Larkspur
Accepts MasterCard, Visa

There's certainly nothing wrong with his raw bar offering of malpeque or Hog Island oysters ($11.50 for six), or, come to that, with the fish and chips, served with malt vinegar and homemade tartar sauce, and only lacking a tabloid newspaper to wrap them in. Ogden's roast crab claws and cracked lobster claws ($3.95) come with simple butter or lemon, and the taste is unsullied and sweet and pure. Meanwhile Prince Edward Island mussels served in a combination with chorizo and Boston lager ($10.95) make a rather Belgian combination. Oyster pan-roast with griddle biscuits ($8.50) is another authentic Old World dish. In season there are flash-fried local fish such as sand dabs or petrale (around $14.50), served with chunks of lemon. All the side dishes ($3 each, or three for $8.75) are homey items like brown bag fries, butternut squash in sage brown butter, or cider whipped yams, plus a bunch of other items you wouldn't mind seeing on a Thanksgiving platter. Even the desserts are old-fashioned: try the warm Granny Smith apple crisp and lemon meringue pie ($5.50).

In uncertain times, many Americans have returned to familiar staples like these, not only because they feel good but because they tend to be less expensive than the fussy cooking of the 1990s. And the Yankee Pier is deliberately set up to attract families and local families. There isn't a single non-American wine on the short wine list, either, and all are available by the glass (from $5.75).

South Bay & the Peninsula

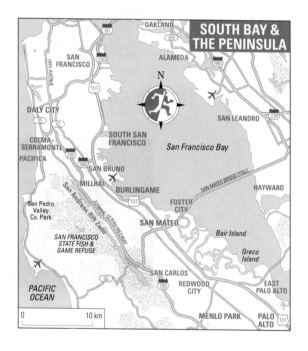

231 Ellsworth

An intangible air of hushed privilege hangs in an invisible microclimate around the entrance of 231 Ellsworth. Behind small and darkened windows, a finely stocked day cellar full of bottles stashed away in polished cherry-wood shelving is manned by one lonely barman. Beyond it, the vaulted and carefully lit holy of holies is set with small, elaborately draped tables that offer plenty of privacy within the wood-paneled walls. A mauve domed ceiling hangs above. This is one of the Bay Area's top twenty restaurants, carefully hatched by a group

Cost $30–75

Address 231 South Ellsworth Ave at 3rd, San Mateo
℡ 650/347-7231
Open Mon–Thurs
11.30am–2pm &
5.30–9.30pm, Fri
11.30am–2pm & 5.30–10pm,
Sat 5.30–10pm, Sun
5.30–9pm
Transportation Caltrain, SamTrans
Accepts All major credit cards

of local restaurateurs that include a Gordon Biersch director, a Sent Sovi partner, and young whiz-kid and superchef, William Collier.

At first you may feel as if such a place wouldn't admit you, or that the prices would land you in jail. But take a look at the menus posted in a glass box outside the curved, Art Nouveau front door and you'll see a prix fixe lunch menu for $20—the creations of William Collier are within your grasp! In the evening, the three-course prix fixe ($32) is available from Sunday to Wednesday. That lunch menu may feature that famous dish, twice-baked goat cheese soufflé with baby beets and arugula, or hearts of romaine salad in garlic-Parmesan vinaigrette with white Meyer-lemon marinated anchovies. This may be followed by a simple but glorious dish such as Atlantic skate wing in browned butter with braised greens and confit potatoes, or beef stew with wild mushrooms, onion ragout, and risotto. On the a la carte menu, duck and cherries ($28) features sliced breast and confit of duck leg; this twinning is replicated in dishes like roasted pork chop and braised pork cheeks ($28). This is young chef's cooking: heady and intoxicating, sometimes overwhelming, but what a bargain!

In no time you'll be snubbing an interesting St André cheese plate ($12) in favor of cajeta custard with bunuelos, cinnamon cream, and pepita brittle ($8). An astounding (it's reasonably priced!) fifty-page wine list comes with the territory, and so does a famous pastry chef, Alicia Smiley.

THE BAY AREA & OUTLYING DISTRICTS   CAL-MED

Bistro Elan

Palo Alto boasts a number of high-end haunts for Peninsula gourmets, and Bistro Elan, which came in with the Millennium, has already made its mark as a spot for Silicon Valley's movers and shakers. At the rear is a little outdoor patio that's perfect for a long, liquid lunch in the sunshine. The interior is simple but elegant, made over in chrome and hardwood with soft lamplight and comfy banquettes that offer privacy for chatting, with a chance to spot local celebs.

Cost $20–50
Address 448 California Ave at El Camino Real, Palo Alto
☎ 650/327-0284
Open Tues–Sat 11.30am–2pm & 5.30–10pm
Transportation Caltrain or SamTrans
Accepts All major credit cards

Far from being pure "bistro," the cuisine is as haute as the atmosphere. They do "amuses" here, as locals call the French *amuse-gueule* idea of an appetizer for the appetizers. A typical one is bresaola, or Italian-style sun-dried beef, of which there's enough for it to be a real appetizer. Next, a starter of sautéed Sonoma foie gras on toasted brioche ($16) comes with an orange and arugula salad in hazelnut oil; it's way-over-the-top delicious, but comes in a serving much too small for anyone other than ladies who lunch, who may find it too fattening. Chilled cucumber soup with yogurt and dill ($6.75) is light and refreshing on a hot Peninsula day, while mussels in a tomato and mushroom broth ($7.75) makes a fragrant starter. A main dish of duck confit with risotto, sautéed black figs, and red onions ($19) is delicate and delicious. The duck is crispy-skinned and somehow absolved of any fat, the risotto is creamy yet still holds authentic bite at the heart of the grain, and the black figs, though redundant, look pretty. Roasted whole Mediterranean branzino with summer vegetables and tomato confit ($22) is a light and perfect whole bass. Pan-seared Niman Ranch pepper steak ($25) comes the way Mother Nature meant it to taste, accompanied by Brobdinagian heirloom tomatoes and French fries.

For dessert, coconut custard ($5) comes with diced mango and sesame cookies, while a cream cheese tartlet ($5) comes with berries; both are divine. A few bigger tables make sense for family blowouts or professional lunch meetings—this is a place where connections and deals can get made.

Bodeguita del Medio

The Bodeguita del Medio takes its name from Ernest Hemingway's favorite bar in downtown Havana, and in honor of the Cuban connection it has a cigar smoking "divan" at the back of the house. The earth may not move for him any more, but Hemingway is all over this yuppity little California Avenue joint— along with Bill Clinton. Bubba liked to get his mojito fix of rum-spiked julep here, when he visited Chelsea down on "the Farm," as locals call Stanford University. A small blond-wood bar for cocktails rules in front, while the dining room behind is all pale yellow walls and soft light from above. The friendly and warm servers are a great asset.

Cost $15–40

Address 463 California Ave, Palo Alto

☎ 650/326-7762

Open Mon–Thurs 11.30am–3pm & 5–9.30pm, Fri & Sat 11.30am–3pm & 5–10pm

Transportation Caltrain, SamTrans

Accepts All major credit cards except Diners

Torpedo-shaped Cuban sandwiches with barbecued pork are served at lunchtime, along with plantains, empanadas, and other snacks. They all cost around $7, and are actually Latino rather than strictly Cuban mouthfuls. Evening appetizers begin with oyster shots ($2.75), which are a fresh Tomales Bay oyster in a glass of Habanero pepper-spiked Cuban rum. Don't resist the Cuban croquetas ($7.50), or deep-fried potato rissoles, though they could be bigger; try them with ensalata bodeguita ($7), which dishes up papaya, mango, and avocado with radiccio. Cuban surf and turf, or tierra y mar ($21), is an abundance of marinated skirt steak with coconut-crusted tiger prawns, making a crunchy contrast in each bite. You'll be bowled over by the grilled lobster tail in a key-lime drawn butter sauce ($22.50), although you may be unlucky enough to find yourself deprived of an adequate portion. As for the yucca-encrusted mahi mahi ($23), it's flat-out sensational. Yucca meal crisps the skin of the tender Hawaiian fish, which is accompanied by those purpley-blue potatoes and golden beets that usually look more colorful than they taste.

Dessert might be a pleasant custardy flan ($5) or possibly a chocolate mousse ($5). No word on if the former president visited the humidor to pluck a cigar to take to the "cigar divan" at the rear. Cubans complaining about the lack of true Havana cigars can muse about his visit as they puff away.

Buca di Beppo

You walk into this jammed neighborhood spot—or, even more weirdly, line up for a table—through the kitchen, where the very young and bouncy kitchen staff enjoy ribbing the patrons. Buca di Beppo is known for this zany style of doing things, along with wacko decorations like Christmas lights and giant tomato tins. This is one of Vinny Testa's Midwestern chain, modeled on the family-style "red sauce" neighborhood restaurants of every American's

Cost	$8–25

Address 643 Emerson Ave at Forest, Palo Alto
℡ 650/329-0665
Open Mon–Thurs 5–10pm, Fri 5–11pm, Sat 4–11pm, Sun noon–9pm
Transportation Caltrain, SamTrans
Accepts All major credit cards except Diners

youth. Several rooms upstairs wear "Eyetalian" clutter, including the uneven results of many photo ops with His Holiness the Pope. The noisy crowd at big tables varies from families out for a birthday dinner where the kids can spill their drinks, to Stanford geeks. Occasionally the entire 49ers football team can be spotted concentrating on heavy carbohydrate-loading at a long table.

Service can only be described as "take it or leave it," but it's mostly efficient, so you do take it. This is a carbo palace de luxe, so the food is pasta, pizza, and more pasta, with a few grilled dishes. Portions come in two sizes, "uno" and "due." If you order "due," be sure to have a hungry eating companion, since "due" is more like "cinque." A good, but not great, spaghetti marinara ($7.95/$13.95) or penne San Sereno with spinach, onions, capers, and red peppers ($8.95/$15.95) make brave takeover bids for your entire body. Quattro formaggi ravioli ($8.95/$15.95) is a good choice, as marinara and Bolognese sauces suffer from a reddish sameness. Caesar salad ($4.95/$8.95) lacks anchovy, but green beans ($4) are terrific, perfectly al dente. Grilled pork chops with peppers ($15.95) also come with oven-roasted spuds in a "combination" meal with pasta ($16.95), as do hearty veal Parmigiana ($16.95) and luxurious chicken cacciatore ($16.95).

If you must have your sticky fix, go for the ice cream, preferably three scoops of vanilla, chocolate, and espresso fudge ($3.95). Avoid the tiramisu or cheesecake like the plague (and also the wine). The Buca di Beppo chain has spread rampantly up and down the California coast; this is the first and the best.

Buon Gusto Ristorante

The little town of South San Francisco lies just north of San Francisco airport, off Highway 101, which makes it appealing for someone staying at a nearby hotel, or with time to wait for a plane. You don't always want to hang around the airport, and sometimes you crave a cordial atmosphere for a real meal when traveling, and that's where Ristorante Buon Gusto comes in handy. It's also heavily favored for the weekends

Cost $12–35

Address 224 Grand Ave, South San Francisco
℡ 650/742-9776
Open Mon–Sat 11am–11pm
Transportation Caltrain, SamTrans
Accepts All major credit cards except Diners

by locals, especially for big convivial gatherings in one of its two party rooms. The decor is reassuringly East Coast and old-fashioned, with little pictures, soft lighting, small tables, and candles with soft green accents. No need to fly a green, white, and red flag in here; Buon Gusto epitomizes Italian the moment you walk in.

Starters begin with that old favorite of prosciutto e melone ($8.50) and there can be no finer antipasto. From a list of several, the mixed green salad ($7.50) is interesting for its combination of watercress, ricciolina, and radicchio. The pasta is what locals come for, however, and they're right. Carmelo Iacolino and Vincenzo Vecchiola have been running this place for decades, and they do pasta better than any chain. Of the many house specialties, a solidly homemade cannelloni ($12.95) can be recommended, as can pasta alla carbonara ($12.95), along with a great gnocchi al pesto ($12.25). Tagliarini Carmelo ($11.75) of thin noodles in a mellow sauce is another local favorite. Veal marsala ($16.75) is one of a host of veal dishes, in the usual varieties, although a veal piccata ($16.75) is interestingly different for its lemon–caper tang.

Perhaps the most nostalgic moment at Buon Gusto comes with dessert. Not many places do a spumoni ice cream ($4.25) or, come to that, a fluffy zabaglione flavored with Grand Marnier ($5.75). Service is unfailingly friendly and attentive in the old-fashioned way. Shops like Galli's Sanitary Bakery and JoAnn's Cafe line the main street of South San Francisco, signs that a healthy Italian community has long thrived here; may it always.

Cafe Figaro

The suburban town of Burlingame, just south of San Francisco Airport off Highway 101, has two main drags a half-mile apart, both sporting many eating choices, among which Cafe Figaro is one of the nicest. The restaurant has a narrow, low-ceilinged room with an exceptionally convivial atmosphere buzzing around the small booths. It has a firm following among locals as well as businesspeople headed home from meetings or toward the airport. Puccini wafts softly across the room, and service could not be friendlier or more prompt.

Cost $15–40

Address 1318 Broadway, Burlingame
℗ 650/344-8277
Open Tues–Sun 11am–10pm
Transportation Highway 101, Caltrain, SamTrans
Accepts MasterCard, Visa

The meal starts with a little dish of pesto and olive oil and thick slices of sourdough to play with while you wait. Indeed, the menu warns you that there may be a wait ("the essence of culinary art is time," it adds) and craves your indulgence. But in fact there's little to complain of in that line. An insalata mista ($4.50) comes very swiftly, in a choice of several dressings, while insalata Caprese ($6.95) offers really fresh mozzarella balls as well as tomato and basil leaves, tossed in a tarter-than-usual vinaigrette. As well as the usual bruschetta ($4.50) and calamari fritti ($8.75), antipasti choices include a fine carpaccio di manzo ($7.95) of beef fillet slices marinated in olive oil and lemon, and topped with capers and big flakes of Parmesan. The seafood risotto ($17.75) is creamily suffused with fish broth, and its prawns and saffron come in a little marinara; they take it off the flame at just the right moment here, and there's no heaviness or stodge. Pollo ai carciofi ($14.95) is chicken breast lightly simmered in Marsala wine sauce with artichoke hearts, and a total success. They often serve tortes as well as the usual gelati and tiramisu, and raspberry torte ($4.50) comes on a delicious almond crust.

The house Chianti can be had by the half-bottle ($14). Cafe Figaro is somewhat cheaper than many longer-running Italian places in the vicinity, and while it is a fairly simple neighborhood trattoria, its prices belie the high quality of the food. All in all, it's a sweet little place, set back from the hurly-burly of Burlingame Avenue.

Fiddler's Green

Missing your fish and chips and need a touch of home? British and Irish immigrants to the Bay Area often find their way to this rollicking Millbrae pub for Oliver McIlhone's bar menu and the monkish Book of Kells illuminations in the decor. As one regular puts it, "No danger of raw octopus in here!" Happily, instead there's a distinct danger of good grilled fish specials and a better class of fish and chips. Fiddler's (as locals call it) also serves a better shepherd's pie, an old-fashioned Ulster fry, and an honest "Murphyburger," while its Thursday roast lamb and spuds sells out fast to the local office workers. By night, the office and airport employees clear out, and another clientele of locals, Irish emigrants, and fun-seekers arrive to play pool or the eclectic jukebox.

Cost $8–25

Address 333 El Camino Real, Millbrae
☎ 650/697-3419
Open Mon–Sat
10am–9.30pm, Sun
10am–5pm
Transportation BART
Millbrae, Caltrain, SamTrans
Accepts MasterCard, Visa

That shepherd's pie ($7.95) is rich in juicy gravy, with diced carrots, sliced red onions, and well-seasoned chopped beef, topped with a nicely gilded crust of creamy mashed potatoes. It's probably the bestseller, along with the beer-battered fresh pieces of rock cod with excellent chips ($9.50). The Ulster fry ($9.50), with everything from sausages and streaky back bacon to grilled tomatoes will bring tears of nostalgia to your eyes, along with a leap of cholesterol to your bloodstream. Their best-selling sandwich is the Spicy Irish ($7.50), a doorstopper with a hefty portion of corned beef spilling its boundaries and a layer of Jack cheese melting on top. The pesto chicken sanger ($7.95) is another favorite. Specials like blackened catfish and occasional traditional favorites like corned beef and cabbage or steak and kidney pie are written above the bar.

Oliver is a Derryman and he and wife Rose came here twenty years ago from New York, becoming fixtures of the Bay Area's very large Irish community. For fish and chips, only The Liberties in the Mission, O'Reilly's, or the Field in North Beach, Edinburgh Castle in the Tenderloin, or Berkeley's Beckett's are rivals. And it must be added that his place is a strong contender for best pint of draft Guinness ($3.50) in the area.

Flea Street Cafe

Pulgas is the Spanish for "fleas"; hence the name of this longstanding favorite among vegetarians in affluent Menlo Park's Alameda de las Pulgas. Chef-owner Jesse Cool's Menlo Park place is part local California bistro and part personal statement. A little Victorian private home with a suite of interlocking rooms tricked out with dried and fresh flowers, bits of lace and swagging, antique tableware, interesting period furnishings, and the odd little curiosity or trinket, it gives you plenty to look at. But there's nothing antique about the cuisine on offer. Cool is an organic produce activist, so though Flea Street Cafe is not strictly vegetarian (it does fish), it has a definite emphasis on fresh organic fare.

Cost $15–50	

Address 3607 Alameda de las Pulgas at Avy, Menlo Park
☎ 650/854-1226
Open Tues–Sun 5.30–9.30pm, Sun 9am–2pm
Transportation Highway 82, Caltrain, SamTrans
Accepts All major credit cards

Flea Street also bakes its own bread, and brings a basket to you as soon as you arrive, with rolls and fluffy biscuits, or an array of sliced sourdough, ciabatta, and rosemary focaccia, plus a dish of mixed olives, green or black or wrinkly, on the side. Exuberant salads are a big selling point here, with lots of jeweled and color-laden arrangements; a mixed salad ($7.95) retains the distinct charms of frisée, escarole, pissenlit, and arugula, with diced golden beets, Maytag blue cheese, candied walnuts, and apple, in a sharp vinaigrette. A large potato blini ($8.95) with pink slivers of lox comes with a topping of fennel, capers, and crème fraîche, a very generous and handsome serving. Fish of the day (around $16.50) might be grilled salmon resplendent on a little bed of greens. A little motte of mashed potato sits in the middle of the farmer's pie ($14), a virtual terrine of mushrooms, chard, potatoes, and beets.

People drive here from San Jose for the desserts alone. The particular favorite among most regulars is the chocolate truffle ($9), an excruciating death by chocolate fit for a concubine in a harem or a Valentine's Night supper; it arrives with a couple of raspberries and a glass of Bonny Doon's sweet dessert wine as part of the deal. If some of the inventions here are wilder than others, more or less everything works, and all are interesting.

Fook Yuen

Even more than a trip to Chinatown, or to Koi Palace up the road, arriving at Fook Yuen feels a little bit as though you've just walked in straight off a plane to Hong Kong. That's hardly surprising, because this huge dim sum palace is a destination favorite for the San Jose emigrant community, who come here in droves at weekends. Indeed, Fook Yuen is an outpost of a Hong Kong chain with branches all over the Pacific. It's barn-like and not particularly atmospheric, and its huge volume is a two-edged sword. On the one hand there's huge variety in the very fresh fare, but service can be brusque and impersonal, and its enduring popularity makes it something of a mob scene.

Cost $15–40
Address 195 El Camino Real, Millbrae
☎ 650/692-8600
Open Mon–Thurs 11am–2.30pm & 5.30–9.30pm, Fri & Sat 11am–2.30pm & 5.30–10pm, Sun 11am–2.30pm & 5.30–9.30pm
Transportation Highway 280, BART Millbrae, SFO shuttle
Accepts MasterCard, Visa

Fook Yuen offers excellent seafood, delectable roast duck, and a splendid array of dim sum, as well as some excellent barbecued pork dishes and special dinner menus that include a full menu of fish. A dynamite Dungeness crab (around $30) is fried with a chile paste that's a special house recipe. Other good choices are grilled garlic shrimp ($12), calamari in spicy sauce ($15), and a special catfish plate (around $20). It's not stylish in presentation. They serve the dim sum off trays rather than trolleys, but those little steamed mouthfuls of explosive tastiness certainly come quickly, and they're fresh and reasonably priced, from $3.20 to $7.50, according to item. The tray-bearers deliver ha gao, or fat prawns; chun guen, or crispy-fried spring rolls of spiced pork or chicken; cha xiu bao, or squashy barbecued pork buns; xiu mai, or steamed dumplings; xi jap fung zao, or chicken feet; and sticky rice in lotus leaves—not forgetting the custard tarts.

Proximity to SFO also makes this an ideal pre-flight spot, especially for Cantonese emigrants heading home from Gold Mountain. If you have a big hungry family, a gorgeous, crackling-topped plate of Peking duck ($25) with those spongy pancakes and sweet plum sauce makes a very good party.

Koi Palace

Lots of people shop on Serramonte Boulevard's main drag without realizing Koi Palace exists, hidden behind the Bank of America. It's always filled to the brim with exuberant Chinese reunions, but if you're not Chinese, you probably haven't heard of Koi. Not until you stumble into Willie Ng's large, busy seafood house will you finally appreciate the size of this place and its formality. There are doormen, carpets, and an imposing porch outside and, inside, the most enor-

Cost $15–35

Address 365 Gellert
Boulevard off Serramonte
Plaza, Daly City
℗ 650/992-9000
Open Mon–Fri 11am–2.30pm
& 5–9.30pm, Sat 5–10pm,
Sun 10am–3pm & 5–9.30pm
Transportation BART Colma
Accepts All major credit cards
except Diners

mous, 1,500-gallon saltwater fish tank filled with striped sea bass, geoduck clams, shrimp, lobsters from both coasts and oceans, and crabs from the Bay and from Thailand. There's also a koi pond and a two-chambered hall of large, round cherry-wood tables with flowered veneers.

Everything is so impressive that even if there wasn't a mile-long list of dim sum, and they didn't achieve unusually high standards of presentation and variety, you'd be struck dumb. Sew mai ($5) and har gao ($3) dumplings are delectable: three little fists of ground pork with ginger, wrapped in fried wonton pastry, or three plump shrimps with spinach, garlic, and basil, rolled in papery-thin wontons. There are fresh crab claws ($5) and Dungeness crab puffs ($5). Chun guen ($3.75) are vegetarian spring rolls stuffed with tiny sprouts and mushrooms, and cheung fen (from $3.75) are rice noodle rolls with sprouts and thread noodles. Crispy rice flour balls and noh mei gei ($5.50), or sticky rice dumplings in lotus leaves, are also delicious. Sweet daan tad ($2.80) also pass by your table. At dinner, a special Mongolian clay pot menu ($19.50 per head, for a minimum of two diners) kicks in, offering lobster, goose gut, geoduck, clams, and sea bass.

Pretty, black I-Xing teapots are filled with scented teas such as monkey-picked oolong, jasmine-scented poochong, and chrysanthemum, placed over glowing candles to keep them warm. Elaborate Emperor's Teas are also available, including specialties you won't get elsewhere. Wines are not all plonk de plonk by any means—glasses start at $4.50 and range up to a bottle of Lafite Rothschild for $900!

Nawab Indian Restaurant

Over the last few years, a flurry of Indian restaurants have opened around the South Bay, all of them raising the local spice level several notches and encouraging locals to bandy about terms like korma, vindaloo, or sag gosht. So when Onkar (known to regulars as Omi) and his son Danny opened up the Nawab in downtown San Mateo, this community was ready. The neighborhood corner restaurant is high-ceilinged and dim, and surprisingly it's never full, despite seductive aromas wafting from a bargain lunch buffet.

Cost $12–30

Address 5 South Ellsworth Ave, San Mateo
℡ 650/401-8424
Open Daily 11am–10pm
Transportation Caltrain, SamTrans
Accepts All major credit cards except Diners

Several unusual items adorn their menu, from tandoori fish to taro root marinated in ginger and garlic. But why would you mix a banana sliced in a very tangy-spiced sauce with a potato salad, as in their aloo kela chat ($4.50)? The textural dissonance is distracting, though bananas or potatoes on their own are tasty enough. But when chicken vindaloo ($11.50) arrives, zipped up in a fiery, sharp and sour garam masala, and spiked with lots of dry-roasted chile and turmeric, you may think longingly of that banana-potato salad and wish it was still there to cool the heat. However, you can always fall back on a cucumber and yogurt raita ($2.50) to douse your fainting tastebuds. You'll be less challenged by a Punjabi korma ($12.95) of lamb slowly braised in a thick comforter of yogurt and cream, with a mellow yellow spice paste, and almonds voluptuously coating the sweet chunks of meat. It certainly needs no banana, though the occasional piece of potato is welcome. Nawab serves a few fish dishes and also has a couple on its clay oven menu. Saffron-flavored jumbo prawns ($15.50) are marinated in spice, while fish tikka kebab ($15.50) is sea bass in a spice marinade.

Nawab's charming Punjabi, Nepalese, Fijian, and Mexican waiters deserve a mention, as they could give many city staff a lesson in the art of waiting tables. It's an extra sensitivity that anticipates more than just when you'd like another Chardonnay, and they have it.

Viognier

A great swoosh of flowery scents and the overwhelming aroma of chocolate and pastries enfolds you the moment you enter Draeger's Market. All the recherché olive oils, conserves, and tins of goose fat on earth can be found here, fetchingly displayed. Take the elevator upstairs, however, and you're into another world. In Viognier's reassuringly expansive dining room, a guitarist tickles away in the background while a wood-fired oven in the center offers pizzettas for hungry eyes, as well as a warm glow. Well-chosen gouaches caress pastel walls over comfy banquettes, the wide bar is well stocked and well patronized, and a rotisserie stands at the ready in the open kitchen.

Superchef Gary Danko has been replaced by Scott Giambastiani, but his stamp is still on the menu, with a long list of dazzling starters that could be main courses. Everything seems to come in threes, including the velvety three-onion soup with slivers of duckling and smoked Swiss cheese ($10), and a foie gras sampler ($18) of mousseline over brioche, winter vegetable and foie gras soup, and foie gras over sweet potato cake with cherry gastrique. Chilled seafood platters ($30) of oysters, clams, mussels, and prawns, with mignonette sauce and horseradish cream, come straight upstairs from the market. At lunchtime, pizzettas ($12), hefty sandwiches and massive hamburgers (from $11) are nibbled by well-heeled and knowledgeable diners, who often split the huge portions (an extra $2.50). Bar food is served between 2.30pm and 5.30pm, but after that the menu heads deep into serious foodie territory. It would be no surprise to find a Miyagi oyster in chilled tomato as an appetizer to your appetizer, before a dish like a smoky rotisserie half-chicken with wild mushroom risotto ($17) arrives.

Regulars drool over chef Giambastiani's three-course lunchtime tasting menu ($29). It may start with three-mushroom soup, with truffled aioli, roast hazelnuts, and porcini chunks; then move on to pappardelle noodles with bass, rock shrimp, oyster, Maine lobster, and roast squashes in grainy Dijon sauce; and end with a veritable rainbow of tropical fruits.

Cost $20–150

Address Draeger's Market Place, 222 East Fourth Ave, San Mateo
℡ 650/685-3727
Open Mon–Sat 11.30am–2.30pm & 5.30–10pm, Sun 11.30am–2.30pm & 5.30–9pm
Transportation Caltrain, SamTrans
Accepts All major credit cards except AmEx

Zibibbo

South Bay fans of Jody Denton's stylish and inventive Cal-Med cuisine will be pleased to find this outpost of the whirling kitchen dervish's culinary empire, even if there are a few doubters. Superchef Denton and his partner, Marc Valiani, seem to be opening places at a furious pace, but this chic restaurant has some distinctive advantages. Cass Calder Smith's design is one, even if the poor acoustics are the trade-off. There's a pretty entrance garden with a couple of olive trees and a little fountain, and the first room is painted lapis-lazuli blue and a torridly sunny yellow. It's a bit of a zoo, but the more laid-back room beyond is entirely pleasant, with a view of the big open kitchen, multicolored tiling and a busy yet calm buzz.

Cost $15–40
Address 430 Kipling St at University Ave, Palo Alto
☏ 650/328-6722
Open Mon–Thurs 11.30am–10pm, Fri 11.30am–11pm, Sat 11am–11pm, Sun 11am–9.30pm
Transportation Caltrain, SamTrans
Accepts MasterCard, Visa

The food still looks very like LuLu's in San Francisco, the Denton and Valiani flagship, though the menu here is designed to please a Peninsula set with casual snacking rather than real dining in mind. The main novelty is the seasonal regional Mediterranean menu of five to eight small plates (priced from $12 to $20 apiece). Italian plates feature antipasti like grilled sausage and insalata Caprese, while the Greek options include classic dolmas, or grape leaves, with minced stuffing, or else grilled octopus. Spanish tapas show off home-cured morcilla and other housemade charcuterie dishes, along with papas bravas and other tapas staples. Denton juggles these small plates with some of his notable old standards, including his much-copied roast mussels in garlic and wine ($8.95). If you're ravenous, order the grandes assiettes, which bring proper portions of dishes such as rotisserie chicken with rosemary ($12.50), grilled quail ($13.50), whole sand dabs ($14.95), ricotta-stuffed tortellini ($12.50), and a terrific grilled steak ($16.50) with smoky salsa and sautéed potatoes, that is enough to share.

The mile-long list of French, Italian, and Californian wines start in the teens and are fairly priced throughout. It's one of the reasons for coming here, especially if you have a bunch of folks in tow and want to split a few great bottles over appetizers. But pick the back room if you want to talk.

Index

Index of restaurants by name

A–Z note: The Eagle Cafe
appears under E not T, La
Méditerranée under M not
L, and Il Fornaio under F
not I. But Cafe Bastille is a
C, Restaurant Lulu an R
and Gary Danko to a G.

**21st Amendment
Brewery** 235

563 2nd St at Brannan
☏ 415/369-0900

**2223 Restaurant & Bar
311**

2223 Market St at Noe
☏ 415/431-0692

231 Ellsworth 399

231 South Ellsworth Ave
at 3rd, San Mateo
☏ 650/347-7231

42 Degrees 257

499 Illinois St
☏ 415/777-5558

**A. Sabella's
Restaurant** 97

3rd floor, 2766 Taylor St
☏ 415/771-6775

**Absinthe Brasserie
and Bar** 201

398 Hayes St at Gough
☏ 415/551-1590

**Ace Wasabi's Rock
and Roll Sushi** 131

339 Steiner St at
Chestnut
☏ 415/567-4903

**Alamo Square
Seafood Grill** 155

803 Fillmore St at Fulton
☏ 415/440-2828

**Albona Ristorante
Istriano** 73

545 Francisco St
☏ 415/441-1040

Alfred's Steak House 57

659 Merchant St
☏ 415/781-7058

Alice's Restaurant 312

1599 Sanchez St near
29th
☏ 415/282-8999

**Allegro Ristorante
Italiano** 113

1701 Jones St at
Broadway
☏ 415/928-4002

Ana Mandara 98

891 Beach St at Polk
☏ 415/771-6800

Ananda-Fuara 202

1298 Market St at 9th
☏ 415/621-1994

**Anchor Oyster Bar and
Seafood Market** 313

579 Castro St at 18th
☏ 415/431-3990

Andalu 277

3198 16th St at Guerrero
☏ 415/621-2211

Angkor Borei 258

3471 Mission St between
30th and Cortland
☏ 415/550-8417

**Angkor Wat Cambodian
Restaurant** 173

4217 Geary Boulevard at
6th
☏ 415/221-7887

Anjou 5

44 Campton Place
☏ 415/392-5373

Antica Trattoria 114

2400 Polk St at Union
☏ 415/928-5797

Aperto 259

1434 18th St at
Connecticut
☏ 415/252-1625

Aqua 6

252 California St at
Battery
℡ 415/956-9662

Asena Restaurant 359

2508 Santa Clara Ave at
Broadway, Alameda
℡ 510/521-4100

AsiaSF 236

201 9th St at Howard
℡ 415/281-3818

Avenue 9 337

1243 9th Ave at Irving I
℡ 415/664-6999

Axum Cafe 221

698 Haight St at Pierce
℡ 415/252-7912

Azie 237

826 Folsom St at 5th
℡ 415/538-0918

B44 Catalan Bistro 7

44 Belden Place
℡ 415/986-6287

Bacar 238

448 Brannan St at 3rd
℡ 415/904-4100

**Bacco Ristorante
Italiano** 314

737 Diamond St at 24th
℡ 415/282-4969

Baker Street Bistro 132

2953 Baker St at
Greenwich
℡ 415/931-1475

Balboa Cafe 133

3199 Fillmore St at
Greenwich
℡ 415/921-3944

Banzai Garlic Cafe 360

2319 Central Ave,
Alameda
℡ 510/864-7222

Basil Thai 239

1175 Folsom St at 8th
℡ 415/552-8999

**Bay Wolf
Restaurant** 361

3853 Piedmont Ave at Rio
Vista, Oakland
℡ 510/655-6004

Benihana 156

Kinetsu Building, 1737
Post St at Fillmore
℡ 415/563-4844

Betelnut Pejiu Wu 134

2030 Union St at
Buchanan
℡ 415/929-8855

Bissap Baobob 278

2323 Mission St between
19th and 20th
℡ 415/826-9287

Bistro Aix 135

3340 Steiner St at
Chestnut
℡ 415/202-0100

Bistro Clovis 203

1596 Market St at
Franklin
℡ 415/864-0231

Bistro e Europe 260

4901 Mission St near
Geneva Ave
℡ 415/469-5637

Bistro Elan 400

448 California Ave at El
Camino Real, Palo Alto
℡ 650/327-0284

Bix 8

56 Gold St at Sansome
℡ 415/433-6300

Bizou 239

598 4th St at Brannan
℡ 415/543-2222

Black Cat and Blue Bar 74

501 Broadway at Kearny
☏ 415/981-2233

Blue Plate 261

3218 Mission St at 29th
☏ 415/282-6777

Bocce Cafe 75

478 Green St
☏ 415/981-2044

Bodeguita del Medio 401

463 California Ave, Palo Alto
☏ 650/326-7762

Il Borgo 204

500 Fell St at Laguna
☏ 415/255-9108

Boulevard 241

1 Mission St at Steuart
☏ 415/543-6084

Brandy Ho's 58

217 Columbus Ave
☏ 415/788-7527

The Brazen Head Restaurant 136

3166 Buchanan St at Greenwich
☏ 415/921-7600

Brother's Korean Restaurant 174

4128 Geary Boulevard between 5th and 6th
☏ 415/387-7991

Brother-in-Law's BBQ 157

705 Divisadero St at Grove
☏ 415/931-7427

Bubba's Diner 383

566 San Anselmo Ave at Tunstead Ave, San Anselmo
☏ 415/459-6862

Buca di Beppo 402

643 Emerson Ave at Forest, Palo Alto
☏ 650/329-0665

Buca Giovanni 76

800 Greenwich St at Mason
☏ 415/776-7766

Buckeye Roadhouse 384

15 Shoreline Highway, Mill Valley
☏ 415/331-2600

Buena Vista Cafe 99

2765 Hyde St at Beach
☏ 415/474-5044

Buon Gusto Ristorante 403

224 Grand Ave, South San Francisco
☏ 650/742-9776

Butterfly Restaurant & Jazz Bar 279

1710 Mission St at Duboce
☏ 415/864-8999

Cafe Bastille 9

22 Belden Place
☏ 415/986-5673

Cafe Claude 10

7 Claude Lane at Bush
☏ 415/392-3505

Cafe Ethiopia 280

878 Valencia St
☏ 415/285-2728

Cafe Figaro 404

1318 Broadway, Burlingame
☏ 650/344-8277

Cafe For All Seasons 338

150 West Portal Ave at 14th
☏ 415/665-0900

Cafe Jacqueline 77

1454 Grant Ave at Green
☏ 415/981-5565

Cafe Kati 158

1963 Sutter St at Fillmore
☏ 415/775-7313

Cafe Mozart 12

708 Bush St at Powell
☏ 415/391-8480

Cafe de Paris l'Entrecote 137

2032 Union St
☏ 415/931-5006

Cafe Pescatore 100

Tuscan Inn, 2455 Mason
St at North Point
☏ 415/561-1111

Cafe Prague 78

584 Pacific Ave at
Columbus
☏ 415/433-3811

Cafe de la Presse 11

352 Grant Ave at Bush
☏ 415/249-0900

Cafe Riggio 175

4112 Geary Boulevard at
5th Ave
☏ 415/221-2114

Cafe Tiramisu 13

28 Belden Place
☏ 415/421-7044

Caffè delle Stelle 205

395 Hayes St at Gough
☏ 415/252-1110

Caffè Macaroni 14

59 Columbus Ave at
Jackson
☏ 415/956-9737

Caffè Proust 159

1801 McAllister St at
Baker
☏ 415/345-9560

Calzone 79

430 Columbus Ave at
Vallejo
☏ 415/397-3600

**Las Camelias Cocina
Mexicana** 385

912 Lincoln Ave between
3rd and 4th, San Rafael
☏ 415/453-5850

Campton Place 15

Campton Place Hotel, 340
Stockton St at Union
Square
☏ 415/955-5555

Il Cantuccio 281

3228 16th St between
Dolores and Guerrero
☏ 415/861-3899

Capp's Corner 80

1600 Powell St at Green
☏ 415/989-2589

Carta 206

1760 Market St at Gough
☏ 415/863-3516

Cha Cha Cha 222

1801 Haight St at Shrader
☏ 415/386-7670

Chapeau! 176

1408 Clement St at 15th
☏ 415/750-9787

Charanga 282

2351 Mission St between
19th and 20th
☏ 415/282-1813

Charlie's 138

1838 Union St at Laguna
☏ 415/474-3773

Cheers Cafe 177

127 Clement St
☏ 415/387-6966

Chenery Park 262

683 Chenery St at
Diamond
☏ 415/337-8537

Le Cheval 362

1007 Clay St at 10th,
Oakland
☏ 510/763-8495

Chez Nous   160

1911 Fillmore St at Bush
☎ 415/441-8044

Chez Panisse Cafe   363

1517 Shattuck Ave,
Berkeley
☎ 510/548-5525

Chloe's Cafe   315

1399 Church St at 26th
☎ 415/648-4116

Chow   316

215 Church St at Market
☎ 415/552-2469

Citizen Cake   207

399 Grove St at Gough
☎ 415/861-2228

Citron   364

5484 College Ave at
Lawton and Taft,
Rockridge
☎ 510/653-5484

Clémentine   178

126 Clement St between
2nd & 3rd
☎ 415/387-0408

The Cliff House   179

1090 Point Lobos Ave
☎ 415/386-3330

Cobalt Tavern   81

1707 Powell St at Union
☎ 415/982-8123

Le Colonial   43

20 Cosmo Place
☎ 415/931-3600

Coriya Hot Pot City   180

852 Clement St at 10th
☎ 415/387-7888

Cosmopolitan Cafe   242

Rincon Center, 121 Spear
St between Howard and
Mission
☎ 415/543-4001

**Cozmo's Corner
Grill**   139

2001 Chestnut St at
Fillmore
☎ 415/351-0175

**Crab House
at Pier 39**   101

Pier 39, Fisherman's
Wharf
☎ 415/434-2722

Crêpes on Cole   223

100 Carl St at Cole
☎ 415/664-1800

Crustacean   115

1475 Polk St at California
☎ 415/776-2722

Curbside Too   140

2769 Lombard St at Lyon
☎ 415/921-4442

**Delancey Street
Restaurant**   243

600 Embarcadero at
Brannan
☎ 415/512-5179

Delfina   283

3621 18th St at Guerrero
☎ 415/552-4055

Destino   208

1815 Market St at
Valencia
☎ 415/552-4451

Dipsea Cafe   386

200 Shoreline Highway,
Mill Valley
☎ 415/381-0298

**Dottie's True
Blue Cafe**   44

522 Jones St
☎ 415/885-2767

Dusit Thai   263

3221 Mission St at
Valencia
☎ 415/826-4639

**E&O Trading
Company**   16

314 Sutter St at Grant
☎ 415/693-0303

The Eagle Cafe 102

Pier 39, 2nd floor,
Fisherman's Wharf
☏ 415/433-3689

East Coast West Delicatessen 116

1725 Polk St at Clay
☏ 415/563-3542

Eastside West 141

3154 Fillmore St at
Greenwich
☏ 415/885-4000

Ebisu 339

1283 9th Ave at Irving
☏ 415/566-1770

Eliza's 264

1457 18th St at
Connecticut
☏ 415/648-9999

Ella's 142

500 Presidio Ave at
California
☏ 415/441-5669

Emmy's Spaghetti Shack 265

18 Virginia Ave at Mission
☏ 415/206-2086

Empress of China 59

838 Grant Ave
☏ 415/434-1345

Enrico's Sidewalk Cafe 82

504 Broadway at
Columbus
☏ 415/982-6223

Eos Restaurant & Wine Bar 224

901 Cole St at Carl
☏ 415/566-3063

Eric's Restaurant 317

1500 Church St at 27th
☏ 415/282-0919

Esperpento Tapas Restaurant 284

3295 22nd St at Valencia
☏ 415/282-8867

Farallon 17

450 Post St at Powell
☏ 415/956-6969

Fattoush 318

1361 Church St at 25th
☏ 415/641-0678

Fiddler's Green 405

333 El Camino Real,
Millbrae
☏ 650/697-3419

Firefly 319

4288 24th St at Douglass
☏ 415/821-7652

Firewood Cafe 320

4248 18th St at Diamond
☏ 415/252-0999

First Crush 18

101 Cyril Magnin St at
Ellis
☏ 415/982-7874

Flea Street Cafe 406

3607 Alameda de las
Pulgas at Avy, Menlo Park
☏ 650/854-1226

Florio 161

1915 Fillmore St at Bush
☏ 415/775-4300

The Fly Trap Restaurant 244

606 Folsom St at 2nd
☏ 415/243-0580

Fog City Diner 103

1300 Battery St
☏ 415/982-2000

The Food Center 19

Kearney St at Bush
☏ No phone

Fook Yuen 407

195 El Camino Real,
Millbrae
☏ 650/692-8600

Forbes Island 104

Pier 39 at Fisherman's Wharf
☏ 415/951-4900

Foreign Cinema 285

2534 Mission St
☏ 415/648-7600

Il Fornaio 105

1265 Battery St at Levi Strauss Plaza
☏ 415/986-0100

Frascati 117

1901 Hyde St at Green
☏ 415/928-1406

I Fratelli 118

1896 Hyde St at Green
☏ 415/474-8240

Fresca 340

24 West Portal Ave at Ulloa
☏ 415/759-8087

Fringale 245

570 4th St at Brannan
☏ 415/543-0573

Fuji 341

301 West Portal Ave at 14th
☏ 415/564-6360

La Furia Chalaca 365

310 Broadway at Jack London Square, Oakland
☏ 510/451-4206

Galette 162

2043 Fillmore St at California
☏ 415/928-1300

Gary Danko 106

800 North Point St at Hyde
☏ 415/749-2060

Globe 20

290 Pacific Ave at Battery
☏ 415/391-4132

Golden Era Vegetarian Restaurant 45

572 O'Farrell St at Jones
☏ 415/673-3136

Gordon Biersch 246

2 Harrison St at Embarcadero
☏ 415/243-8246

Grand Cafe 46

Hotel Monaco, 501 Geary St at Taylor
☏ 415/292-0101

Grand Palace 60

950 Grant Ave at Pacific
☏ 415/982-3705

Grandeho Kameyko 225

943 Cole St at Carl
☏ 415/673-6828

Great Eastern Restaurant 61

649 Jackson St
☏ 415/986-2500

Greens 143

Fort Mason Building A
☏ 415/771-6222

Grubstake 119

1525 Pine St at Polk
☏ 415/673-8268

Guaymas 387

5 Main Street, Tiburon
☏ 415/435-6300

Hahn's Hibachi 366

63 Jack London Square, Franklin St at Embarcadero, Oakland
☏ 510/628-0717

Hang Ah Tea Room 62

1 Hang Ah St
☏ 415/982-5686

Harbor Village Restaurant 21

2nd floor, 4 Embarcadero Center
☏ 415/781-8833

Index

**Harry Denton's
Starlight Room** 22

Sir Francis Drake Hotel,
432 Powell St
☎ 415/395-8595

Hayes Street Grill 209

320 Hayes St between
Gough and Franklin
☎ 415/863-5545

The Helmand 83

430 Broadway at
Montgomery
☎ 415/362-0641

**Henry Chung's
Hunan** 23

924 Sansome St at
Broadway
☎ 415/546-4999

**Herbivore:
The Earthly Grill** 286

983 Valencia St at 21st
☎ 415/826-5657

Home 321

2100 Market St at Church
☎ 415/503-0333

House of Nanking 63

919 Kearny St at
Columbus
☎ 415/421-1429

House on Ninth 342

1269 9th Ave at Irving
☎ 415/682-3898

**Hung Yen
Restaurant** 287

3100 18th St at Harrison
☎ 415/621-8531

India Clay Oven 181

2435 Clement St
☎ 415/751-0505

Inn Kensington 367

293 Arlington Ave at
Amherst, Kensington
☎ 510/527-5919

**Izzy's Steaks
& Chop House** 144

3345 Steiner St at
Chestnut
☎ 415/563-0487

**Jackson Fillmore
Trattoria** 145

2506 Fillmore St at
Jackson
☎ 415/346-5288

**Jakarta Indonesian
Cuisine** 182

615 Balboa St at 7th
☎ 415/387-5225

Jardinière 210

300 Grove St at Franklin
☎ 415/861-5555

Jasmine Tea House 266

3243 Mission St at
Valencia
☎ 415/826-6288

Jeanne d'Arc 24

Cornell Hotel, 715 Bush St
☎ 415/421-3154

Jeanty at Jack's 25

Address 615 Sacramento
St between Montgomery
and Kearny
☎ 415/693-0941

Jesso's Seafood 368

2817 Telegraph Ave at
29th, Berkeley
☎ 510/451-1561

Just For You 267

732 22nd Street at 3rd
☎ 415/647-3033

Kabuto Sushi 183

5116 Geary Boulevard
between 15th & 16th
☎ 415/752-5652

Kate's Kitchen 226

471 Haight St at Fillmore
☎ 415/626-3984

**Katia's: A Russian
Tea Room** 184

600 5th Ave at Balboa
☎ 415/668-9292

Khan Toke 185

5937 Geary Boulevard between 23rd & 24th
℡ 415/668-6654

King of Thai Noodle House 186

639 Clement St at 7th
℡ 415/752-5198

Koi Palace 408

365 Gellert Boulevard off Serramonte Plaza, Daly City
℡ 650/992-9000

Kokkari Estiatorio 26

200 Jackson St at Front
℡ 415/981-0983

Le Krewe 288

995 Valencia St at 21st
℡ 415/643-0995

Kuleto's 27

221 Powell St
℡ 415/397-7720

Lalime's 369

1329 Gilman St between Peralta and Neilson, Berkeley
℡ 510/527-9838

LaMooné 322

4072 18th St at Castro
℡ 415/355-1999

Lark Creek Inn 388

234 Magnolia Ave at Madrone, Larkspur
℡ 415/924-7766

Laurel's Restaurant 211

205 Oak St at Gough
℡ 415/934-1575

Lefty O'Doul's 28

333 Geary St at Union Square
℡ 415/982-8900

Leticia's 323

2247 Market St at Sanchez
℡ 415/521-0442

Lhasa Moon 146

2420 Lombard St at Scott
℡ 415/674-9898

The Liberties 289

998 Guerrero St at 22nd
℡ 415/282-6789

Liberty Cafe and Bakery 268

401 Cortland Ave at Wool
℡ 415/695-8777

Liverpool Lil's 147

2942 Lyon St at Lombard
℡ 415/921-6664

Lorca Spanish Bar & Restaurant 290

3200 24th St at South Van Ness
℡ 415/550 7510

Lotus 343

1395 Noriega St at 21st
℡ 415/661-0303

Lovejoy's Tea Room 324

1351 Church St at Clipper
℡ 415/648-5895

Lucky Creation 64

854 Washington St at Grant Ave
℡ 415/989-0818

Luna Park 291

694 Valencia St at 17th
℡ 415/553-8584

MacArthur Park 29

607 Front St
℡ 415/398-5700

McCormick & Kuleto's 107

Ghirardelli Square, 900 North Point St
℡ 415/929-1730

Magnolia Pub and Brewery 227

1398 Haight St at Masonic
℡ 415/864-7468

INDEX OF RESTAURANTS BY NAME

Mangia Mangia 370

755 San Pablo Ave near Washington, Albany
☎ 510/526-9700

Mario's Bohemian Cigar Store 84

566 Columbus Ave at Union
☎ 415/362-0536

Marnee Thai 344

2225 Irving St at 23rd
☎ 415/665-9500

Ma Tante Sumi 325

243 18th St
☎ 415/626-7864

Max's Opera Cafe 212

601 Van Ness Ave at Golden Gate Ave
☎ 415/771-7300

Maya 247

303 2nd St at Folsom
☎ 415/543-2928

Mecca 326

2029 Market St at Dolores
☎ 415/621-7000

La Méditerranée 163

2210 Fillmore St at Sacramento
☎ 415/921-2956

La Méditerranée 327

288 Noe St at Market
☎ 415/431-7210

Memphis Minnie's Smokehouse Bar-B-Que 228

576 Haight St at Fillmore
☎ 415/647-7427

Mezes 148

2373 Chestnut St at Divisadero
☎ 415/409-7111

Mi Lindo Peru! 269

3226 Mission St at Valencia
☎ 415/642-4897

Mifune 164

2F Kintetsu Mall, 1737 Post St at Webster
☎ 415/922-0337

Millennium 213

Abigail Hotel, 246 McAllister St at Larkin
☎ 415/487-9800

Miss Millie's 328

4123 24th St at Castro
☎ 415/285-5598

Modern Thai 120

1247 Polk St at Bush
☎ 415/922-8424

Moki's Sushi & Pacific Grill 270

830 Cortland at Folsom
☎ 415/970-9336

Mom Is Cooking 271

1166 Geneva Ave at Naples
☎ 415/586-7000

MoMo's 248

760 2nd St at Willie Mays Plaza
☎ 415/227-8660

Moose's 85

1652 Stockton St at Washington Square
☎ 415/989-7800

Moylan's of Novato 389

15 Rowland Way, Novato
☎ 415/898-4677

Naan 'n' Curry 47

478 O'Farrell St
☎ 415/775-1349

Nawab Indian Restaurant 409

5 South Ellsworth Ave, San Mateo
☎ 650/401-8424

New Asia 65

772 Pacific Ave at Grant
☎ 415/391-6666

Nizza La Bella 371

825–27 San Pablo Ave at Solano, Albany
☎ 510/526-2552

Noi 329

4109 24th St between Castro and Diamond
☎ 415/642-4664

El Nuevo Frutilandia 292

3077 24th St between Folsom and Treat
☎ 415/648-2958

O Chame Restaurant Tea Room 372

1830 4th St, Berkeley
☎ 510/841-8783

Okina Sushi 187

776 Arguello Boulevard at Cabrillo
☎ 415/387-8882

Old Krakow Polish Art Restaurant 345

385 West Portal Ave at 15th
☎ 415/564-4848

Oliveto Cafe 373

5655 College Ave at Shafter, Rockridge
☎ 510/547-5356

Ondine 390

558 Bridgeway at Princess Ave, Sausalito
☎ 415/331-1133

Oriental Restaurant 374

1782 Shattuck Ave at Francisco, Berkeley
☎ 510/644-1005

Original Old Clam House 272

299 Bayshore Boulevard at Oakdale
☎ 415/826-4880

L'Osteria del Forno 86

519 Columbus Ave
☎ 415/982-1124

Pacific Cafe 188

7000 Geary Boulevard at 34th
☎ 415/387-7091

Pakwan 293

3180 16th St at Guerrero
☎ 415/255-2440

Pancho Villa Taqueria 294

3071 16th St at Barlett
☎ 415/864-8840

Park Chow 346

1240 9th Ave at Lincoln
☎ 415/665-9912

Pastis 108

1015 Battery St at Greenwich
☎ 415/391-2555

Peña PachaMama 87

1630 Powell St
☎ 415/646-0018

Perlot 165

Hotel Majestic, 1500 Sutter St at Gough
☎ 415/441-1100

Perry's Sports Bar 149

1944 Union St at Laguna
☎ 415/922-9022

Pesce 121

2227 Polk St at Vallejo
☎ 415/928-8025

Le Petit Robert 122

2300 Polk St at Green
☎ 415/922-8100

Pier 23 Cafe 109

Embarcadero at Greenwich
☎ 415/362-5125

Pizza Inferno 166

1800 Fillmore St at Sutter
☎ 415/775-1800

PJ's Oyster Bed 347

737 Irving St at 9th
☎ 415/566-7775

Index

Plouf 30

40 Belden Place
☎ 415/986-6491

PlumpJack Cafe 150

3127 Fillmore St at Filbert
☎ 415/563-4755

Point Reyes Station House Cafe 391

Main St, Point Reyes
☎ 415/663-1515

Il Pollaio 88

555 Columbus Ave at Union
☎ 415/362-7727

The Pork Store Cafe 229

1451 Haight St at Ashbury
☎ 415/864-6981

Postrio 31

Prescott Hotel, 545 Post St
☎ 415/776-7825

PPQ Vietnamese Cuisine 348

1816 Irving St at 19th
☎ 415/661-8869

Puerto Alegre Restaurant 295

546 Valencia St at 16th
☎ 415/255-8201

Purple Plum 375

4228 Park Boulevard, Oakland
☎ 510/336-0990

R&G Lounge 66

631 Kearny St at Sacramento
☎ 415/982-7877

Ramblas 296

557 Valencia St at 16th
☎ 415/565-0207

Rancho Nicasio 392

1 Old Rancheria Rd, Town Square, Nicasio
☎ 415/662-2219

Rasselas Jazz Club 167

2801 California St at Divisadero
☎ 415/567-5010

Red Herring Restaurant and Bait Bar 249

155 Steuart St at Mission
☎ 415/495-6500

Redwood Park Upstairs 32

600 Montgomery St at Clay
☎ 415/283-1000

Restaurant Doña Tomás 376

5004 Telegraph Ave, Oakland
☎ 510/450-0522

Restaurant LuLu 250

816 Folsom St at 4th
☎ 415/495-5775

The Rice Table 393

1617 4th St at G St, San Rafael
☎ 415/456-1808

Rick's 349

1940 Taraval St at 30th
☎ 415/731-8900

Ristorante Marcello 350

2100 Taraval St at 31st
☎ 415/665-1430

Ristorante Mereb 297

598 Guerrero St at 18th
☎ 415/863-3031

Rivoli Restaurant 377

1539 Solano Ave at Peralta, Albany
☎ 510/526-2542

Rock Soup 273

3299 Mission St at 29th
☎ 415/641-7687

Roosevelt Tamale Parlor 298

2817 24th St at Bryant
℡ 415/550-9213

Rose Pistola 89

532 Columbus Ave at Vallejo
℡ 415/399-0499

Rose's Cafe 151

2298 Union St at Steiner
℡ 415/775-2200

Ross Valley Brewing Company 394

765A Center Boulevard, Fairfax
℡ 415/485-1005

Rue Lepic 33

900 Pine St at Mason
℡ 415/474-6070

Saigon Saigon 299

1132 Valencia St at 23rd
℡ 415/206-9635

Saigon Sandwiches 48

560 Larkin St at Eddy
℡ 415/474-5698

Sam Wo 67

815 Washington St at Grant
℡ 415/982-0596

Sam's Grill and Seafood Restaurant 34

374 Bush St at Belden Place
℡ 415/421-0594

Sanraku 251

1st floor, Metreon Building, 101 4th St at Mission
℡ 415/369-6166

Sanraku Four Seasons 35

704 Sutter St at Mason
℡ 415/771-0803

Sapporo-Ya 168

2F Kunokuniya Building, 1581 Webster St
℡ 415/563-7400

Savor 330

3913 24th St at Sanchez
℡ 415/282-0344

Scala's Bistro 36

Sir Francis Drake Hotel, 432 Powell St
℡ 415/395-8555

Schroeder's 37

240 Front St
℡ 415/421-4778

Scoma's 110

Pier 47, Fisherman's Wharf
℡ 415/771-4383

Seafood Peddler 395

100 Yacht Club Drive, near San Franciso Boulevard, San Rafael
℡ 415/460-6669

Shalimar 49

532 Jones St at Geary
℡ 415/928-0333

Singapore Malaysian Restaurant 189

836 Clement St at 11th
℡ 415/750-9518

Sociale 152

3665 Sacramento St at Spruce
℡ 415/921-3200

Le Soleil 190

133 Clement St at 3rd
℡ 415/668-4848

Soups 50

784 O'Farrell Street at Hyde
℡ 415/775-6406

Spiazzo Caffè 351

33 West Portal Ave near Ulloa
℡ 415/664-9511

Stelline 214

429 Gough St at Hayes
☎ 415/626-4292

The Stinking Rose 90

325 Columbus Ave at
Broadway
☎ 415/781-7673

Straits Cafe 191

3300 Geary Boulevard at
Stanyan
☎ 415/668-1783

Suppenküche 215

601 Hayes St at Laguna
☎ 415/252-9289

Sushi Boom 192

3420 Geary Boulevard at
Stanyan
☎ 415/876-2666

Swan Oyster Depot 123

1517 Polk St at California
☎ 415/679-1101

Tadich Grill 38

240 California St at
Battery
☎ 415/391-1849

Taiwan Restaurant 193

445 Clement St at 6th
☎ 415/387-1789

**Takara Sushi and
Seafood** 169

Japan Center, Miyako
Mall, 22 Peace Plaza
#202, Post St at Webster
☎ 415/921-2000

Terra Brazilis 216

602 Hayes St at Laguna
☎ 415/241-1900

Thai House Express 51

901 Larkin St at Geary
☎ 415/441-2238

Thanh Long 352

4101 Judah St at 46th
☎ 415/665-1146

**Thep Phanom
Thai Cuisine** 230

400 Waller St at Fillmore
☎ 415/431-2526

**ThirstyBear Brewing
Company** 252

661 Howard St at 3rd
☎ 415/974-0905

Ti Couz 300

3108 16th St at Valencia
☎ 415/252-7373

Timo's 301

842 Valencia St at 19th
☎ 415/647-0558

Tita's Hale 'Aina 331

3870 17th St between
Sanchez and Noe
☎ 415/626-2477

Tokyo Go Go 302

3174 16th St at Guerrero
☎ 415/864-2288

**Tommaso's
Ristorante Italiano** 91

1042 Kearny St
☎ 415/398-9696

**Tommy Toy's
Cuisine Chinoise** 68

655 Montgomery St at
Clay
☎ 415/397-4888

Ton Kiang 194

3148 Geary Boulevard
☎ 415/752-4440

**Town's End Restaurant
and Bakery** 253

2 Townsend St
☎ 415/512-0749

Traktir 195

4036 Balboa at 42nd
☎ 415/386-9800

Trattoria Contadina 92

1800 Mason St at Union
☎ 415/982-5728

La Traviata 303

2854 Mission St at 25th
☎ 415/282-0500

Truly Mediterranean 304

3109 16th St at Valencia
☎ 415/252-7482

Tú Lan 52

8 6th St at Market
☎ 415/626-0927

Vanida 353

3050 Taraval at 41st
☎ 415/564-6766

La Vie 196

5380 Geary Boulevard at
22nd
☎ 415/668-8080

Vietnam II Restaurant 53

701 Larkin St at Ellis
☎ 415/885-1274

Vik's Chaat Corner 378

726 Allston Way, West
Berkeley
☎ 510/664-4412

Viognier 410

Draeger's Market Place,
222 East Fourth Ave, San
Mateo
☎ 650/685-3727

Walzwerk 305

381 South Van Ness Ave
at 14th
☎ 415/551-7181

Waterfront Restaurant 39

Pier 7, Embarcadero at
Broadway
☎ 415/391-2696

Watergate 306

1152 Valencia St
☎ 415/648-6000

Woodward's Garden 307

1700 Mission St at 14th
☎ 415/621-7122

Yabbies Coastal Kitchen 124

2237 Polk St at Vallejo
☎ 415/474-4088

Yank Sing 254

Rincon Center Atrium,
101 Spear St at Mission
☎ 415/957-9300

Yankee Pier 396

286 Magnolia Ave,
Larkspur
☎ 415/924-7676

Yokoso Nippon Sushi 332

314 Church St near
Market
☎ No phone

Yoshi's at Jack London Square 379

510 Embarcadero West,
Oakland
☎ 510/238-9200

Yoshi-san's Monkichi 197

200 23rd Ave at California
☎ 415/876-1834

Yuet Lee 69

1300 Stockton Street at
Broadway
☎ 415/982-6020

Yum-Yum Fish 354

2181 Irving Ave at 23rd
☎ 415/566-6433

Zante's Pizza and Indian Cuisine 274

3489 Mission St at
Cortland
☎ 415/821-3949

Zao Noodle Bar 170

2406 California St at
Fillmore
☎ 415/345-8088

Zarzuela 125

2000 Hyde St at Union
℡ 415/346-0800

Zax 93

2330 Taylor St at
Columbus
℡ 415/563-6366

Zibibbo 411

430 Kipling St at
University Ave, Palo Alto
℡ 650/328-6722

Le Zinc 333

4063 24th St between
Castro and Noe
℡ 415/647-9400

Zuni Cafe 217

1658 Market St at Gough
℡ 415/552-2522

Index of restaurants by cuisine

Categories below are pretty self-explanatory, but note that we've given separate listings for "American," "Californian," and "Cal-Med" cuisine—though of course the boundaries overlap. Note also that the category "Indian" includes Bangladeshi, Indian and Pakistani restaurants.

Afghan

The Helmand   83
North Beach

American

See also Bar Menu, Californian, Cal-Med, Creole/Cajun, Gourmet Bar Menu & New York Deli.

A. Sabella's Restaurant   97
Fisherman's Wharf & the Waterfront

Alfred's Steak House   57
Chinatown

Avenue 9   337
The Sunset & West Portal

Balboa Cafe   133
The Marina, Cow Hollow & Pacific Heights

Blue Plate   261
Potrero Hill & Bernal Heights

The Brazen Head Restaurant   136
The Marina, Cow Hollow & Pacific Heights

Brother-in-Law's BBQ   157
Japantown, Fillmore & the Western Addition

Bubba's Diner   383
North Bay & Marin—San Anselmo

Buckeye Roadhouse   384
North Bay & Marin—Mill Valley

Buena Vista Cafe   99
Fisherman's Wharf & the Waterfront

Chenery Park   262
Potrero Hill & Bernal Heights

Chloe's Cafe   315
The Castro & Noe Valley

The Cliff House   179
The Richmond

Dipsea Cafe   386
North Bay & Marin—Mill Valley

Dottie's True Blue Cafe   44
The Tenderloin

The Eagle Cafe   102
Fisherman's Wharf & the Waterfront

Ella's   142
The Marina, Cow Hollow & Pacific Heights

Greens   143
The Marina, Cow Hollow & Pacific Heights

Grubstake   119
Nob Hill & Russian Hill

Hayes Street Grill   209
The Civic Center & Hayes Valley

Home   321
The Castro & Noe Valley

Izzy's Steaks & Chop House   144
The Marina, Cow Hollow & Pacific Heights

Just For You   267
Potrero Hill & Bernal Heights

Kate's Kitchen   226
The Haight Ashbury District & Cole Valley

Lark Creek Inn   388
North Bay & Marin—Larkspur

Liberty Cafe and Bakery   268
Potrero Hill & Bernal Heights

Luna Park 291
The Mission

MacArthur Park 29
Union Square & the
Financial District

**McCormick
& Kuleto's** 107
Fisherman's Wharf & the
Waterfront

**Memphis Minnie's
Smokehouse
Bar-B-Que** 228
The Haight Ashbury District
& Cole Valley

Miss Millie's 328
The Castro & Noe Valley

MoMo's 248
SoMa & South Beach

Moose's 85
North Beach

Perry's Sports Bar 149
The Marina, Cow Hollow &
Pacific Heights

**Point Reyes Station
House Cafe** 391
North Bay & Marin—Point
Reyes

**The Pork Store
Cafe** 229
The Haight Ashbury District
& Cole Valley

Rancho Nicasio 392
North Bay & Marin—
Nicasio

Rick's 349
The Sunset & West Portal

Rock Soup 273
Potrero Hill & Bernal
Heights

**Town's End Restaurant
and Bakery** 253
SoMa & South Beach

Yankee Pier 396
North Bay & Marin—
Larkspur

Bar menu

*See also Gourmet Bar
Menu.*

**21st Amendment
Brewery** 235
SoMa & South Beach

Gordon Biersch 246
SoMa & South Beach

Lefty O'Doul's 28
Union Square & the
Financial District

**Magnolia Pub and
Brewery** 227
The Haight Ashbury District
& Cole Valley

**Moylan's of
Novato** 389
North Bay & Marin—
Novato

**Ross Valley Brewing
Company** 394
North Bay & Marin—
Fairfax

Brazilian

Terra Brazilis 216
The Civic Center & Hayes
Valley

British

Liverpool Lil's 147
The Marina, Cow Hollow &
Pacific Heights

**Lovejoy's
Tea Room** 324
The Castro & Noe Valley

Californian

*See also American &
Cal-Med.*

**2223 Restaurant
& Bar** 311
The Castro & Noe Valley

Bacar 238
SoMa & South Beach

Banzai Garlic Cafe 360
East Bay—Alameda

Bix 8
Union Square & the
Financial District

Boulevard 241
SoMa & South Beach

Chez Panisse Cafe 363
East Bay—Berkeley

**Cosmopolitan
Cafe** 242
SoMa & South Beach

Delancey Street Restaurant 243
SoMa & South Beach

Firefly 319
The Castro & Noe Valley

The Fly Trap Restaurant 244
SoMa & South Beach

Fog City Diner 103
Fisherman's Wharf & the Waterfront

Jardinière 210
The Civic Center & Hayes Valley

Ma Tante Sumi 325
The Castro & Noe Valley

Perlot 165
Japantown, Fillmore & the Western Addition

Purple Plum 375
East Bay—Oakland

Rivoli Restaurant 377
East Bay—Albany

Cal-Med

See also Californian.

231 Ellsworth 399
South Bay & Peninsula—San Mateo

42 Degrees 257
Potrero Hill & Bernal Heights

Aperto 259
Potrero Hill & Bernal Heights

Asena Restaurant 359
East Bay—Alameda

Bay Wolf Restaurant 361
East Bay—Oakland

Bistro Aix 135
The Marina, Cow Hollow & Pacific Heights

Bistro Elan 400
South Bay & the Peninsula—Palo Alto

Bizou 240
SoMa & South Beach

Cafe For All Seasons 338
The Sunset & West Portal

Cheers Cafe 177
The Richmond

Chez Nous 160
Japantown, Fillmore & the Western Addition

Chow 316
The Castro & Noe Valley

Citizen Cake 207
The Civic Center & Hayes Valley

Cobalt Tavern 81
North Beach

Cozmo's Corner Grill 139
The Marina, Cow Hollow & Pacific Heights

Enrico's Sidewalk Cafe 82
North Beach

Flea Street Cafe 406
South Bay & the Peninsula—Menlo Park

Foreign Cinema 285
The Mission

Frascati 117
Nob Hill & Russian Hill

Fringale 245
SoMa & South Beach

Globe 20
Union Square & the Financial District

Grand Cafe 46
The Tenderloin

Inn Kensington 367
East Bay—Kensington

Mario's Bohemian Cigar Store 84
North Beach

Nizza La Bella 371
East Bay—Albany

Ondine 390
North Bay & Marin—Sausalito

Park Chow 346
The Sunset & West Portal

PlumpJack Cafe 150
The Marina, Cow Hollow & Pacific Heights

Postrio 31
Union Square & the Financial District

Redwood Park Upstairs 32
Union Square & the Financial District

Restaurant LuLu 250
SoMa & South Beach

Savor 330
The Castro & Noe Valley

Scala's Bistro 36
Union Square & the
Financial District

Viognier 410
South Bay & the
Peninsula—San Mateo

**Woodward's
Garden** 307
The Mission

Zax 93
North Beach

Zibibbo 411
South Bay & the
Peninsula—Palo Alto

Zuni Cafe 217
The Civic Center & Hayes
Valley

Cambodian

Angkor Borei 258
Potrero Hill & Bernal
Heights

**Angkor Wat
Cambodian
Restaurant** 173
The Richmond

Caribbean

Cha Cha Cha 222
The Haight Ashbury District
& Cole Valley

Charanga 282
The Mission

**El Nuevo
Frutilandia** 292
The Mission

Chinese/
Taiwanese

Alice's Restaurant 312
The Castro & Noe Valley

Brandy Ho's 58
Chinatown

Coriya Hot Pot City 180
The Richmond

Eliza's 264
Potrero Hill & Bernal
Heights

Empress of China 59
Chinatown

Eric's Restaurant 317
The Castro & Noe Valley

Fook Yuen 407
dim sum specialist
South Bay & the
Peninsula—Millbrae

Grand Palace 60
dim sum specialist
Chinatown

**Great Eastern
Restaurant** 61
Chinatown

Hang Ah Tea Room 62
dim sum specialist
Chinatown

**Harbor Village
Restaurant** 21
dim sum specialist
Union Square & the
Financial District

**Henry Chung's
Hunan** 23
Union Square & the
Financial District

House of Nanking 63
Chinatown

Jasmine Tea House266
dim sum specialist
Potrero Hill & Bernal
Heights

Koi Palace 408
dim sum specialist
South Bay & the
Peninsula—Daly City

Lucky Creation 64
dim sum specialist
Chinatown

New Asia 65
dim sum specialist
Chinatown

R&G Lounge 66
Chinatown

Sam Wo 67
Chinatown

Taiwan Restaurant 193
The Richmond

**Tommy Toy's Cuisine
Chinoise** 68
Chinatown

Ton Kiang 194
dim sum specialist
The Richmond

Yank Sing 254
dim sum specialist
SoMa & South Beach

Yuet Lee 69
Chinatown

Creole/Cajun

Chenery Park 262
Potrero Hill & Bernal
Heights

Le Krewe 288
The Mission

PJ's Oyster Bed 347
The Sunset & West Portal

Crêpes

Crêpes on Cole 223
The Haight Ashbury District
& Cole Valley

Galette 162
Japantown, Fillmore & the
Western Addition

Ti Couz 300
The Mission

Cuban

**Bodeguita del
Medio** 401
South Bay & the
Peninsula—Palo Alto

**Laurel's
Restaurant** 211
The Civic Center & Hayes
Valley

Czech

Cafe Prague 78
North Beach

Ethiopian/
Eritrean

Axum Cafe 221
The Haight Ashbury District
& Cole Valley

Cafe Ethiopia 280
The Mission

**Rasselas Jazz
Club** 167
Japantown, Fillmore & the
Western Addition

Ristorante Mereb 297
The Mission

French

**Absinthe Brasserie
and Bar** 201
The Civic Center & Hayes
Valley

**Alamo Square Seafood
Grill**
Japantown, Fillmore & the
Western Addition

Ana Mandara 98
Fisherman's Wharf & the
Waterfront

Anjou 5
Union Square & the
Financial District

Baker Street Bistro 132
The Marina, Cow Hollow &
Pacific Heights

Bistro Clovis 203
The Civic Center & Hayes
Valley

**Black Cat and
Blue Bar** 74
North Beach

Cafe Bastille 9
Union Square & the
Financial District

Cafe Claude 10
Union Square & the
Financial District

Cafe Jacqueline 77
North Beach

Cafe Mozart 12
Union Square & the
Financial District

**Cafe de Paris
l'Entrecote** 137
The Marina, Cow Hollow &
Pacific Heights

Cafe de la Presse 11
Union Square & the
Financial District

Chapeau! 176
The Richmond

Citron 364
East Bay—Rockridge

Clémentine 178
The Richmond

Le Colonial 43
The Tenderloin

Curbside Too 140
The Marina, Cow Hollow &
Pacific Heights

Florio 161
Japantown, Fillmore & the
Western Addition

Forbes Island 104
Fisherman's Wharf &
Waterfront

Galette 162
Japantown, Fillmore & the
Western Addition

Gary Danko 106
Fisherman's Wharf &
Waterfront

Jeanne d'Arc 24
Union Square & the
Financial District

Jeanty at Jack's 25
Union Square & the
Financial District

Pastis 108
Fisherman's Wharf &
Waterfront

Le Petit Robert 122
Nob Hill & Russian Hill

Rue Lepic 33
Union Square & the
Financial District

Le Zinc 333
The Castro & Noe Valley

Fusion

See also International &
Pan-Asian.

Azie 237
SoMa & South Beach

**Butterfly Restaurant
& Jazz Bar** 279
The Mission

Cafe Kati 158
Japantown, Fillmore & the
Western Addition

**Eos Restaurant
& Wine Bar** 224
The Haight Ashbury District
& Cole Valley

House on Ninth 342
The Sunset & West Portal

LaMooné 322
The Castro & Noe Valley

Lotus 343
The Sunset & West Portal

Tokyo Go Go 302
The Mission

Watergate 306
The Mission

German

Schroeder's 37
Union Square & the
Financial District

Suppenküche 215
The Civic Center & Hayes
Valley

Walzwerk 305
The Mission

Gourmet bar menu

See also Bar Menu.

Campton Place 15
Union Square & the
Financial District

First Crush 18
Union Square & the
Financial District

**Harry Denton's
Starlight Room** 22
Union Square & the
Financial District

Mecca 326
The Castro & Noe Valley

Greek

Kokkari Estiatorio 26
Union Square & the
Financial District

Mezes 148
The Marina, Cow Hollow &
Pacific Heights

Hawaiian

Tita's Hale 'Aina 331
The Castro & Noe Valley

Hungarian

Bistro e Europe 260
Potrero Hill & Bernal
Heights

Indian

India Clay Oven 181
The Richmond

Naan 'n' Curry 47
The Tenderloin

**Nawab Indian
Restaurant** 409
South Bay & the
Peninsula—San Mateo

Pakwan 293
The Mission

Shalimar 49
The Tenderloin

Vik's Chaat Corner 378
East Bay—Berkeley

**Zante's Pizza and
Indian Cuisine** 274
Potrero Hill & Bernal
Heights

Indonesian

**Jakarta Indonesian
Cuisine** 182
The Richmond

The Rice Table 393
North Bay & Marin—San
Rafael

International

See also Fusion.

Andalu 277
The Mission

Carta 206
The Civic Center & Hayes
Valley

The Food Center 19
Union Square & the
Financial District

Lalime's 369
East Bay—Berkeley

Irish

Fiddler's Green 405
South Bay & the
Peninsula—Millbrae

The Liberties 289
The Mission

Italian/pizza

**Albona Ristorante
Istriano** 73
North Beach

**Allegro Ristorante
Italiano** 113
Nob Hill & Russian Hill

Antica Trattoria 114
Nob Hill & Russian Hill

**Bacco Ristorante
Italiano** 314
The Castro & Noe Valley

Bocce Cafe 75
North Beach

Il Borgo 204
The Civic Center & Hayes
Valley

Buca di Beppo 402
South Bay & the
Peninsula—Palo Alto

Buca Giovanni 76
North Beach

**Buon Gusto
Ristorante** 403
South Bay & the
Peninsula—South San
Francisco

Cafe Figaro 404
South Bay & the
Peninsula—Burlingame

Cafe Pescatore 100
Fisherman's Wharf & the
Waterfront

Cafe Riggio 175
The Richmond

Cafe Tiramisu 13
Union Square & the
Financial District

Caffè delle Stelle 205
The Civic Center & Hayes
Valley

Caffè Macaroni 14
Union Square & the
Financial District

Caffè Proust 159
Japantown, Fillmore & the
Western Addition

Calzone 79
North Beach

Il Cantuccio 281
The Mission

Capp's Corner 80
North Beach

Delfina 283
The Mission

Emmy's Spaghetti Shack 265
Potrero Hill & Bernal Heights

Firewood Café 320
The Castro & Noe Valley

Il Fornaio 105
Fisherman's Wharf & the Waterfront

I Fratelli 118
Nob Hill & Russian Hill

Jackson Fillmore Trattoria 145
The Marina, Cow Hollow & Pacific Heights

Kuleto's 27
Union Square & the Financial District

Mangia Mangia 370
East Bay—Albany

Noi 329
The Castro & Noe Valley

Oliveto Cafe 373
East Bay—Rockridge

L'Osteria del Forno 86
North Beach

Pizza Inferno 166
Japantown, Fillmore & the Western Addition

Il Pollaio 88
North Beach

Ristorante Marcello 350
The Sunset & West Portal

Rose Pistola 89
North Beach

Rose's Cafe 151
The Marina, Cow Hollow & Pacific Heights

Sociale 152
The Marina, Cow Hollow & Pacific Heights

Spiazzo Caffè 351
The Sunset & West Portal

Stelline 214
The Civic Center & Hayes Valley

The Stinking Rose 90
North Beach

Tommaso's Ristorante Italiano 91
North Beach

Trattoria Contadina 92
North Beach

La Traviata 303
The Mission

Zante's Pizza and Indian Cuisine 274
Potrero Hill & Bernal Heights

Japanese/ sushi

Ace Wasabi's Rock and Roll Sushi 131
sushi specialist
The Marina, Cow Hollow & Pacific Heights

Benihana 156
Japantown, Fillmore & the Western Addition

Charlie's 138
The Marina, Cow Hollow & Pacific Heights

Ebisu 339
sushi specialist
The Sunset & West Portal

Fuji 341
sushi specialist
The Sunset & West Portal

Grandeho Kameyko 225
sushi specialist
The Haight Ashbury District & Cole Valley

Kabuto Sushi 183
sushi specialist
The Richmond

Mifune 164
Japantown, Fillmore & the Western Addition

Moki's Sushi & Pacific Grill 270
sushi specialist
Potrero Hill & Bernal Heights

O Chame Restaurant Tea Room 372
East Bay—Berkeley

Okina Sushi 187
sushi specialist
The Richmond

Sanraku 251
SoMa & South Beach

Sanraku Four Seasons 35
Union Square & the Financial District

Sapporo-Ya 168
Japantown, Fillmore & the Western Addition

Sushi Boom 192
sushi specialist
The Richmond

Takara Sushi and Seafood 169
sushi specialist
Japantown, Fillmore & the Western Addition

Tokyo Go Go 302
sushi specialist
The Mission

Yokoso Nippon Sushi 332
sushi specialist
The Castro & Noe Valley

Yoshi's at Jack London Square 379
sushi specialist
East Bay—Oakland

Yoshi-san's Monkichi 197
sushi specialist
The Richmond

Yum-Yum Fish 354
sushi specialist
The Sunset & West Portal

Korean

Brother's Korean Restaurant 174
The Richmond

Hahn's Hibachi 366
East Bay—Oakland

Mexican

Las Camelias Cocina Mexicana 385
North Bay & Marin—San Rafael

Guaymas 387
North Bay & Marin—Tiburon

Just For You 267
Potrero Hill & Bernal Heights

Leticia's 323
The Castro & Noe Valley

Maya 247
SoMa & South Beach

Mom Is Cooking 271
Potrero Hill & Bernal Heights

Pancho Villa Taqueria 294
The Mission

Puerto Alegre Restaurant 295
The Mission

Restaurant Doña Tomás 376
East Bay—Oakland

Roosevelt Tamale Parlor 298
The Mission

Middle Eastern

Fattoush 318
The Castro & Noe Valley

La Méditerranée 163
Japantown, Fillmore & the Western Addition

Truly Mediterranean 304
The Mission

New York deli

East Coast West Delicatessen 116
Nob Hill & Russian Hill

Max's Opera Cafe 212
The Civic Center & Hayes Valley

Pan-Asian

See also Fusion & International.

AsiaSF 236
SoMa & South Beach

Betelnut Pejiu Wu 134
The Marina, Cow Hollow & Pacific Heights

Index

E&O Trading Company 16
Union Square & the Financial District

Moki's Sushi & Pacific Grill 270
Potrero Hill & Bernal Heights

Zao Noodle Bar 170
Japantown, Fillmore & the Western Addition

Peruvian/Andean

Destino 208
The Civic Center & Hayes Valley

Fresca 340
The Sunset & West Portal

La Furia Chalaca 365
East Bay—Oakland

Mi Lindo Peru! 269
Potrero Hill & Bernal Heights

Peña PachaMama 87
North Beach

Polish

Old Krakow Polish Art Restaurant 345
The Sunset & West Portal

Russian

Katia's: A Russian Tea Room 184
The Richmond

Traktir 195
The Richmond

Seafood

See also Japanese/Sushi.

A. Sabella's Restaurant 97
Fisherman's Wharf & the Waterfront

Alamo Square Seafood Grill 155
Japantown, Fillmore & the Western Addition

Anchor Oyster Bar and Seafood Market 313
The Castro & Noe Valley

Aqua 6
Union Square & the Financial District

Black Cat and Blue Bar 74
North Beach

Crab House at Pier 39 101
Fisherman's Wharf & the Waterfront

Crustacean 115
Nob Hill & Russian Hill

The Eagle Cafe 102
Fisherman's Wharf & the Waterfront

Eastside West 141
The Marina, Cow Hollow & Pacific Heights

Farallon 17
Union Square & the Financial District

Jesso's Seafood 368
East Bay—Berkeley

McCormick & Kuleto's 107
Fisherman's Wharf & the Waterfront

La Méditerranée 327
The Castro & Noe Valley

Original Old Clam House 272
Potrero Hill & Bernal Heights

Pacific Cafe 188
The Richmond

Pesce 121
Nob Hill & Russian Hill

Pier 23 Cafe 109
Fisherman's Wharf & the Waterfront

Plouf 30
Union Square & the Financial District

Red Herring Restaurant and Bait Bar 249
SoMa & South Beach

Sam's Grill and Seafood Restaurant 34
Union Square & the Financial District

Scoma's 110
Fisherman's Wharf & the Waterfront

Seafood Peddler 395
North Bay & Marin—San Rafael

Swan Oyster Depot 123
Nob Hill & Russian Hill

Tadich Grill 38
Union Square & the Financial District

Waterfront Restaurant 39
Union Square & the Financial District

Yabbies Coastal Kitchen 124
Nob Hill & Russian Hill

Yum-Yum Fish 354
The Sunset & West Portal

Senegalese

Bissap Baobob 278
The Mission

Singaporean

Singapore Malaysian Restaurant 189
The Richmond

Straits Cafe 191
The Richmond

Soup

Soups 50
The Tenderloin

Spanish/Tapas

B44 Catalan Bistro 7
Union Square & the Financial District

Esperpento Tapas Restaurant 284
The Mission

Lorca Spanish Bar & Restaurant 290
The Mission

Ramblas 296
The Mission

ThirstyBear Brewing Company 252
SoMa & South Beach

Timo's 301
The Mission

Zarzuela 125
Nob Hill & Russian Hill

Thai

Basil Thai 239
SoMa & South Beach

Dusit Thai 263
Potrero Hill & Bernal Heights

Khan Toke 185
The Richmond

King of Thai Noodle House 186
The Richmond

Marnee Thai 344
The Sunset & West Portal

Modern Thai 120
Nob Hill & Russian Hill

Thai House Express 51
The Tenderloin

Thep Phanom Thai Cuisine 230
The Haight Ashbury District & Cole Valley

Vanida 353
The Sunset & West Portal

Tibetan

Lhasa Moon 146
The Marina, Cow Hollow & Pacific Heights

Vegetarian

Ananda-Fuara 202
The Civic Center & Hayes Valley

Golden Era Vegetarian Restaurant 45
The Tenderloin

Herbivore: The Earthly Grill 286
vegan specialist
The Mission

Lucky Creation 64
Chinatown

Index

Millennium 213
The Civic Center & Hayes Valley

Yoshi-san's Monkichi 197
The Richmond

Vietnamese

Ana Mandara 98
Fisherman's Wharf & the Waterfront

Le Cheval 362
East Bay—Oakland

Le Colonial 43
The Tenderloin

Golden Era Vegetarian Restaurant 45
The Tenderloin

Hung Yen Restaurant 287
The Mission

Oriental Restaurant 374
East Bay—Berkeley

PPQ Vietnamese Cuisine 348
The Sunset & West Portal

Saigon Saigon 299
The Mission

Saigon Sandwiches 48
The Tenderloin

Le Soleil 190
The Richmond

Thanh Long 352
The Sunset & West Portal

Tú Lan 52
The Tenderloin

La Vie 196
The Richmond

Vietnam II Restaurant 53
The Tenderloin

around the world

Alaska ★ Algarve ★ Amsterdam ★ Andalucía ★ Antigua & Barbuda ★ Argentina ★ Auckland Restaurants ★ Australia ★ Austria ★ Bahamas ★ Bali & Lombok ★ Bangkok ★ Barbados ★ Barcelona ★ Beijing ★ Belgium & Luxembourg ★ Belize ★ Berlin ★ Big Island of Hawaii ★ Bolivia ★ Boston ★ Brazil ★ Britain ★ Brittany & Normandy ★ Bruges & Ghent ★ Brussels ★ Budapest ★ Bulgaria ★ California ★ Cambodia ★ Canada ★ Cape Town ★ The Caribbean ★ Central America ★ Chile ★ China ★ Copenhagen ★ Corsica ★ Costa Brava ★ Costa Rica ★ Crete ★ Croatia ★ Cuba ★ Cyprus ★ Czech & Slovak Republics ★ Devon & Cornwall ★ Dodecanese & East Aegean ★ Dominican Republic ★ The Dordogne & the Lot ★ Dublin ★ Ecuador ★ Edinburgh ★ Egypt ★ England ★ Europe ★ First-time Asia ★ First-time Europe ★ Florence ★ Florida ★ France ★ French Hotels & Restaurants ★ Gay & Lesbian Australia ★ Germany ★ Goa ★ Greece ★ Greek Islands ★ Guatemala ★ Hawaii ★ Holland ★ Hong Kong & Macau ★ Honolulu ★ Hungary ★ Ibiza & Formentera ★ Iceland ★ India ★ Indonesia ★ Ionian Islands ★ Ireland ★ Israel & the Palestinian Territories ★ Italy ★ Jamaica ★ Japan ★ Jerusalem ★ Jordan ★ Kenya ★ The Lake District ★ Languedoc & Roussillon ★ Laos ★ Las Vegas ★ Lisbon ★ London ★

in twenty years

London Mini Guide ★ London Restaurants ★ Los Angeles ★ Madeira ★ Madrid ★ Malaysia, Singapore & Brunei ★ Mallorca ★ Malta & Gozo ★ Maui ★ Maya World ★ Melbourne ★ Menorca ★ Mexico ★ Miami & the Florida Keys ★ Montréal ★ Morocco ★ Moscow ★ Nepal ★ New England ★ New Orleans ★ New York City ★ New York Mini Guide ★ New York Restaurants ★ New Zealand ★ Norway ★ Pacific Northwest ★ Paris ★ Paris Mini Guide ★ Peru ★ Poland ★ Portugal ★ Prague ★ Provence & the Côte d'Azur ★ Pyrenees ★ The Rocky Mountains ★ Romania ★ Rome ★ San Francisco ★ San Francisco Restaurants ★ Sardinia ★ Scandinavia ★ Scotland ★ Scottish Highlands & Islands ★ Seattle ★ Sicily ★ Singapore ★ South Africa, Lesotho & Swaziland ★ South India ★ Southeast Asia ★ Southwest USA ★ Spain ★ St Lucia ★ St Petersburg ★ Sweden ★ Switzerland ★ Sydney ★ Syria ★ Tanzania ★ Tenerife and La Gomera ★ Thailand ★ Thailand's Beaches & Islands ★ Tokyo ★ Toronto ★ Travel Health ★ Trinidad & Tobago ★ Tunisia ★ Turkey ★ Tuscany & Umbria ★ USA ★ Vancouver ★ Venice & the Veneto ★ Vienna ★ Vietnam ★ Wales ★ Washington DC ★ West Africa ★ Women Travel ★ Yosemite ★ Zanzibar ★ Zimbabwe

also look out for our maps, phrasebooks, music guides and reference books

ROUGH GUIDES TWENTY YEARS